SCHOOL LEADERSHIP THROUGH ACTION RESEARCH

Joyce P. Logan, Ed.D.

*Associate Professor Emerita, Educational Leadership Studies,
College of Education, University of Kentucky*

PEARSON

Boston   Columbus   Indianapolis   New York   San Francisco   Upper Saddle River
Amsterdam   Cape Town   Dubai   London   Madrid   Milan   Munich   Paris   Montreal   Toronto
Delhi   Mexico City   São Paulo   Sydney   Hong Kong   Seoul   Singapore   Taipei   Tokyo

Vice President and Editorial Director: Jeffery W. Johnston
Senior Acquisitions Editor: Meredith Fossel
Editorial Assistant: Krista Slavicek
Vice President, Director of Marketing: Margaret Waples
Senior Marketing Manager: Darcy Betts
Senior Managing Editor: Pamela D. Bennett
Senior Art Director: Diane Lorenzo
Cover Designer: Jennifer Hart
Cover Photo: Shutterstock
Full-Service Project Management: Penny Walker, Aptara®, Inc.
Composition: Aptara®, Inc.
Printer/Binder: Edwards Brothers Malloy
Cover Printer: Edwards Brothers Malloy
Text Font: Garamond

Credits and acknowledgments for material borrowed from other sources and reproduced, with permission, in this text appear on the appropriate page within the text.

Every effort has been made to provide accurate and current Internet information in this text. However, the Internet and information posted on it are constantly changing, so it is inevitable that some of the Internet addresses listed in this text will change.

Microsoft, Windows, Word, Excel, and PowerPoint are either registered trademarks of Microsoft Corporation in the U.S.A and/or other countries. This book is not sponsored by or endorsed by or affiliated with the Microsoft Corporation.

Library of Congress Cataloging-in-Publication Data

Logan, Joyce.
  School leadership through action research / Joyce Logan, Ed.D, Emerita Associate Professor of Educational Leadership Studies at the College of Education, University of Kentucky. — First edition.
    p. cm.
  Includes index.
  ISBN 978-0-13-248601-9
  1. Action research in education.   2. Educational leadership.   I. Title.
  LB1028.24.L65 2014
  370.72—dc23

                                                                    2013004527

10 9 8 7 6 5 4 3 2 1

ISBN 10:   0-13-248601-6
ISBN 13: 978-0-13-248601-9

ABOUT THE AUTHOR

Joyce P. Logan, Ed.D., is an emerita associate professor of Educational Leadership Studies, the College of Education, University of Kentucky (UK). Dr. Logan's primary responsibilities in this department included courses in leadership for school problem solving (action research) and leadership for human resources in schools. Other courses taught covered computer applications in educational administration, leadership for program improvement, and doctoral courses for leadership in educational organizations. She coordinated principal preparation portfolio reviews for the department and served on master's and doctoral committees, chairing or cochairing 15 committees for doctoral graduates. At UK, she also taught in the Vocational Education Department and the Curriculum and Instruction Departments, prior to joining the Department of Educational Leadership Studies.

Dr. Logan has extensive experience as an educator. She was a high school teacher, state department of education regional coordinator for high schools and community colleges in 10 counties of Kentucky, principal of a 2-year health occupations postsecondary school, and Division Director in the Kentucky Department of Education. She also served as office head for technical schools for the Kentucky Cabinet for Workforce Development before becoming a university teacher educator.

School evaluation and accreditation have been Dr. Logan's major areas of expertise. She has served as chair and as an evaluation team member on numerous accreditation teams in career and technical programs, military training sites, and high schools and elementary schools throughout Kentucky, the United States, and Canada. Over a 10-year span, she served as a field coordinator for the American Council of Education for review of courses taught at military bases. She also reviewed high school and postsecondary school courses for The Distance Education and Training Council and chaired evaluation teams for the Southern Association of Colleges and Schools (SACS). She served as a member and chair of the Commission on Occupational Education when SACS began accrediting career and technical schools and also served two terms as a member of the SACS Board of Trustees. As part of her responsibilities at UK, she served for 2 years as Kentucky State Director of the SACS Commission on Secondary and Middle Schools.

Dr. Logan has published peer-reviewed articles on school leadership and career and technical education in national and international journals. She has served as editor, contributing author, and coauthor for books published by South-Western Publishing Company and Cengage. She has made presentations at state, national, and international (London and Israel) conferences. She administered funded grants while serving as principal of the 2-year postsecondary health technology school and as a regional coordinator for the Kentucky Department of Education. She has been the principal investigator or coinvestigator for funded grants totaling over $300,000 while serving as a university faculty member. Through grants, she has planned and conducted professional-development activities for high school teachers and administrators, principals of technical schools, and adult education curriculum development for Kentucky and West Virginia.

Dr. Logan earned her doctorate degree in administrative leadership from Vanderbilt University. She completed a master of arts degree in secondary education and a bachelor of science degree in business education at Murray State University.

PREFACE

Education research is of little value if it does not find a practical use in school improvement. This purpose is a major goal of this text. I believe that action research can help bring regular use of professional literature and education research into classrooms to guide improvement planning and professional practice for student learning. If this action research resource helps educators bridge the gap between educational research and its application in schools and classrooms, I will consider it to be successful.

Sometimes, our ideas about learning get so wrapped up in educational jargon that we don't recognize how simple those ideas really are and how they recycle themselves. I wrote this entire text and have taught these concepts for almost 10 years, but this morning when I awoke at 4 a.m. and my thinking drifted to finalizing this preface, the pieces came together in a way that I had not previously realized. I began to understand better how useful learning action research can be at all levels of learning, particularly in this technological age when we are almost buried under information. It is an easily understood, systematic step-by-step process that focuses learning.

The steps of action research, often referred to as an *action research cycle*, have been around for years. In this information-rich society, however, action research provides a systematic approach that can help focus learning and motivate administrators, teachers, and students (or individuals in any field of work or area of interest) to take control of their own learning and help them to become life-long learners. In education, we have used such terms as *project learning*, *problem-based learning*, *constructivist learning*, *higher-level learning*, and *cultures of inquiry*.

Action research brings focus and offers a simple, systematic approach that helps direct inquiry, learning projects, and individual construction of learning. Before individuals construct their own learning, they need to know how to approach a problem and identify a learning task. This understanding simplifies the meaning of research and makes it practical. Teachers are adept at translating concepts that they understand well into understandable language for their students.

Research is a pattern of thinking that has been described in so many different ways that it appears complicated. Broken down into five steps (or seven, depending on how you state them), action research becomes a way of thinking that has many applications—particularly, in education—and can help demystify research and make it become a part of daily living. The action research steps simply identify clearly what you want to learn by stating research questions, studying current knowledge related to those questions, and gathering and analyzing additional information and data to understand and reach conclusions that respond to the research questions and identify necessary actions for improvement.

Understanding data requires categorizing the data and knowledge in different ways, thinking about it both individually and/or with others to get multiple perspectives, and taking action or making decisions. This repeats by evaluating the effectiveness of that action or decision and by asking, "What else do I need to know?"

The mystery of research for most people who are not statisticians stems from not having knowledge about, interest in, or experience with applying and understanding statistical formulas. I put myself in that category because I am not a statistician. However, action research and qualitative research do not require the use of sophisticated statistics. Familiar mathematics calculations can be sufficient for numeric data analysis with action research. Visual displays of data that aid interpretations replace advanced statistical procedures. Those data compared and contrasted with perceptual information from multiple data sources provide methodology for such research.

Traditional quantitative research, qualitative research, and action research follow the same basic scientific process steps, and all make contributions to knowledge. Action research focuses on research needed by practitioners in a specific setting. School districts may choose to implement action research for multiple schools in the district and provide shared professional-development days for participating principals and their leadership teams. Or, the impetus for learning and implementation may come from within a school or schools in a district. The electronic copies of sample plans and agendas for three days of professional development available on the resource CD that accompanies this text can be easily modified to meet the need in a particular district or school.

Traditional quantitative research and qualitative research by university researchers differ in purpose by focusing on knowledge applicable in numerous contexts, although colleges of education now also work with school districts in many areas to use action research specific to a school need. In addition, some university principal and superintendent preparation programs, as well as teacher-leader preparation and doctoral research for an Ed.D., now incorporate action research.

Administrators, teachers, and others share leadership roles and responsibilities for student learning. Best practice supported by research comes from collaboration to ensure high levels of learning (Lewis & Imler, 2009). By applying each step of action research within your school or district, in collaboration with a leadership team and other collaborative structures involving school personnel and other members of the school community, educators join forces in "working on the work" (Schlechty, 2002) of school improvement.

How to Use This Text and CD Resources

Materials in this text focus on the work of school leadership to advance student achievement by integrating research into school practice as a part of school improvement. Educators in schools and district offices can use action research, both individually and collaboratively, to systematically bring research into ongoing school practice as they seek effective ways to improve teaching and learning and to remove barriers to learning. Effectively addressing increasing demands on schools to meet diverse needs of each student will require educator growth and expertise in a wide array of teaching and learning areas. Action research parallels a problem-solving process and applies research and collected in-school data—from both achievement scores and school processes—to analyze and determine action for improvements in problems and practices that affect teaching and learning.

School practitioners and other educators who learn and apply the action research process gain familiarity with research and understand its practical use in schools. Participating in a professional-growth process, they are able to become educator-researchers, as well as to incorporate focused studies of research literature, as individuals or members of a learning community. The content and examples in this text and its supplementary CD will guide you step by step through professional-development experiences that apply action research and data-informed decision making to your school and classroom settings. Student achievement is the central purpose of schools. Therefore, school improvement centers on student learning. School improvement planning addresses problem solving that directly or indirectly affects student learning.

School leaders are daily problem solvers. Problems range from low to high importance for individuals or groups of individuals and the school as a whole. The focus of 21st century schools is student learning and development (CCSSO, 2008). All decisions within a school must consider the following question: How does this situation affect students and student learning? The professional-development and leadership resource materials provided in this text relate to data-based decision making, standards for school leaders, and the effects of teachers and school leadership on student achievement. Research references appear at the conclusion of each chapter.

Examples from school settings throughout the action research steps come from my 50 years of experience as a school teacher, school principal, state department of education regional program coordinator and division director, and university educator and researcher. The many former students I have instructed in my university course on problem solving and action research for principal preparation have enabled me to provide 14 different action research reports that illustrate the action research process as completed in actual school settings. These former students were teachers or administrators when they completed the research. Evaluations of my course indicated appreciation for the usefulness of action research in schools. These individuals gave written permission to use their work for examples and to modify it as needed to protect confidential individual school data, as well as school identities by the use of fictitious school names. Each example of a former student's research provides the name of the educator and the current position held.

Examples of action research reports for studies completed in elementary, middle-level, and secondary schools are grouped in a special section at the end of Part 4. These reports and six other examples are accessible on the CD also. Graduate student educators in my action research and problem-solving course found examples of complete reports helpful for reference as they performed the research steps.

I understand the importance of education, the ever-present pressures for improving student learning, and the daily time crunch that educators face. I have kept these pressures in mind while developing the materials for this text. As a teacher, I found that students learn best when they are clear about what they need to learn, and examples help convey this, as well as provide patterns for the task at hand. You will find a wealth of examples as you work through each Part in this text and review the contents on the CD. There are more ways than one to do things; these examples are not meant to be rigidly followed, but are rather to show you systematic ways for conducting action research.

The first six chapters define action research and guide you in systematically conducting research, as well as recording and verifying your work for each step. Chapters are grouped in four parts with two chapters each. Chapter content teaches a specific format for each research step and the final report of your research. The format style used follows the most recent edition (6th ed.) of the *Publication Manual of the American Psychological Association*. This format guide, commonly referred to as APA style, is widely used for school leadership publications and dissertations. There are other style manuals for writing and formatting reports. Selecting and following a specific style manual for consistent placement and format of headings, tables, figures, reference citations, and a reference list or bibliography contributes to the professional appearance of a report.

Chapters 3, 4, and 5 describe a variety of data-collection and interpretation methodology for planning and conducting research for a problem of practice. Chapter content describes what each step may involve and how to do it systematically and carefully to achieve the most accurate results and best recommendations for change.

The chapters and the CD resource supplement provide numerous electronic resources to help make research and professional best practices readily available for busy educators. Sample planning and research planning guides are on the resource CD, as well as electronic blank forms that you may use or adapt. Alternatively, you may design your own version. These CD guides and forms provide multiple worksheets for planning data collection, categorizing information, and verifying data through cross checks and data triangulation (verification) from multiple sources. Use these forms, as appropriate, to make your initial work easier as you learn to be an action researcher.

Chapter materials refer to CD supplementary materials at the point a table or figure directly pertains to chapter content. The CD makes available in electronic form all tables and figures referred to or included in each chapter. Tables and figures are numbered sequentially including the chapter number and sequence number. For example, Table 5.4 identifies Chapter 5 and the fourth table referred to or included in that chapter; Figure 3.2 identifies the second figure shown in or referred to in Chapter 3. Tables or figures referred to as located on the CD, but not inserted as part of a chapter, are labeled as (CD only) on the CD Table of Contents.

The CD items save you time by giving URLs for literature sources that can be opened from the electronic copy without keying in URLs. In Chapter 2, for example, tables that are both in the chapter and on the CD list literature sources with a URL. Having all tables and figures included on the CD, along with other supplementary materials, gives you an electronic copy to use with your research performance tasks. Both the text and the CD include a Table of Contents for all materials provided on the CD.

As you gain experience with school action research, you will select, improve upon, and add to the many ways that data can be analyzed, verified, and understood. Don't be overwhelmed by the volume of process information presented. You will become familiar with a variety of techniques and select only those needed for your particular research. You can refer back to these chapters and CD as a resource text for other research projects or even to write questions that focus work for learning communities or action planning for problems of practice.

Reflection, both individually and with others, is a key component addressed by this text for your work during the research and after completion. Suggested questions help guide your thinking. Most individual reflection may come by making quiet time during other activities—on the road if you are a runner, driving to and from work, or other early-morning or late-night times when you have some quiet time by yourself. When you have a family, reflective quiet time can be hard to come by, and educators with families may need to find ways to schedule short periods for individual and collaborative reflection during the school day—maybe at lunch or during in-service work days.

As a principal, my best reflective time was early-morning runs before I left for school and during my drives to and from my home in the western region of Kentucky to Nashville, Tennessee, to attend weekend graduate classes. Professional conferences can provide quality reflection time, both on an individual basis and with colleagues. During reflective times, think about what you have learned, how you want to use it, and how the process needs "tweaking" to make it more workable, accurate, complete, or helpful, as well as what else you need to learn.

In summary, I am excited about this text. I enjoyed writing it and learned by doing so. I appreciate the thorough and helpful educators who reviewed the early draft. Their comments were on target and especially helpful in refining and completing this action research resource. It is the resource that I could not find when I taught this content in a principal preparation program. I have covered the information that I found to be important for my students to complete research, and that I believe is important for not just principals, but for all school practitioners who wish to make practical use of research for school improvement.

REFERENCES

Council of Chief State School Officers (CCSSO). (2008). *Educational Leadership Policy Standards ISLLC 2008,* as adopted by the National Policy Board for Educational Administration. Washington, DC: Author. Official copies of these standards may be downloaded from the Council's website at http://www.ccsso.org/publications.

Lewis, S., & Imler, S. (2009, August). Leadership through collaborative strategic planning: One school's journey (empirical research). *Academic Leadership: The On-line Journal,* 1–4.

Schlechty, P. C. (2002). *Working on the work: An action plan for teachers, principals, and superintendents.* San Francisco: Jossey-Bass.

ACKNOWLEDGMENTS

The author extends a special thanks to the former graduate students in the Department of Educational Leadership Studies at the University of Kentucky, College of Education, who granted permission for their action research work to be used as examples for this text. These "real school" uses of action research make a major contribution as illustrations of research application by school practitioner-researchers. A note below each example adapted from action research completed by these graduate students names the educator(s) whose work is represented.

Reviewers for this action research text provided numerous perceptive, useful suggestions that made major contributions for improving its content and organization. The author appreciates the time and expertise that the following educators gave in the reviews for finalizing this text: M. Sabriya Dempsey, the School District of Philadelphia; Stephen F. Midlock, University of St. Francis; Emily Pettersen, Rockwood School District; Jason P. Sherlock, West Chester Area School District; Beth Madison, Robert Gray Middle School; and Joy Rose, Westerville City Schools.

BRIEF CONTENTS

PART 1 Using Action Research to Improve Student Achievement   1

Chapter 1   Action Research in School Settings   3
Chapter 2   A Knowledge Base for Action Research   15

PART 2 Identifying and Collecting Research Data   31

Chapter 3   Data-Informed Decision Making   33
Chapter 4   Data Organization, Summarization, and Analysis   52

PART 3 Summarizing Qualitative Data and Completing an Action Research Report and Presentation   67

Chapter 5   Analysis and Interpretation of Qualitative Data   69
Chapter 6   Recommendations, Reports, and Reflections   86

PART 4 Bridging Research with Practice   101

Chapter 7   Action Research as Part of Professional Practice   103
Chapter 8   Research, Reflection, and Professional Growth   119

Example Action Research Reports   135

Glossary of Research-Related Terms   211

Index   216

CONTENTS

Part 1   Using Action Research to Improve Student Achievement   1

Purpose and Outcomes for Part 1   2

In-School Performance Activities   2

Chapter 1   Action Research in School Settings   3

Problem Solving and Action Research   4

The Problem-Solving Process   4

Action Research   5

WHAT IT IS   6

WHAT IT IS NOT   6

School Problems of Practice for Action Research   6

Problem Identification   7

Researchable Problems   8

Problem Statement   8

Leadership for Action Research   12

Key Questions for Review   13   •   Performance Checklist for Step 1
Research Activities   13   •   References   14

Chapter 2   A Knowledge Base for Action Research   15

Action Research Literature Review   15

Selecting Sources   17

Recording and Identifying Resources   22

Literature Review Development   23

Organizing Topics   24

Using Headings and Subheadings   24

Formatting and Referencing   25

Collaborating, Writing, and Editing   27

Other Knowledge Sources   27

Key Questions for Review   28   •   Performance Checklist for Step 2a
Research Activities   28   •   References   29

Part 2   Identifying and Collecting Research Data   31

Purpose and Outcomes for Part 2   31

In-School Performance Activities   31

Chapter 3   Data-Informed Decision Making   33

Data Identification and Selection   33

School Data Sources   34

Research Data Types   34

STUDENT LEARNING DATA   35

SCHOOL PROCESSES DATA   36

DEMOGRAPHIC DATA   36

PERCEPTUAL DATA   37

RECORD AND REPORT DATA   37

Review of Information Needs, Data Types, and Data Sources 37

Involvement of Research Participants 38

Data Collection Methods, Instruments, and Protocol 40

Data Collection Instruments and Research Populations 41

  Research Population 42

  Surveys and Questionnaires 44

  Observations 44

  Interviews and Focus Groups 46

    Key Questions for Review 50 • *Performance Checklist for Steps 2b and 2c Research Activities* 50 • *References* 51

Chapter 4 **Data Organization, Summarization, and Analysis** 52

Field Tests of Primary Data-Collection Instruments and Protocol 52

Methods of Verifying Research Integrity 53

Analysis of Records, Reports, and Other Documentation 53

Organization of Quantitative Data for Interpretation 56

  Descriptive Statistics 56

  Data Storage and Summaries 57

  Quantitative Tables and Graphs 61

    PREPARING AND FORMATTING TABLES 62

    PREPARING AND FORMATTING FIGURES 63

    Key Questions for Review 66 • *Performance Checklist for Step 3a Research Activities* 66 • *References* 66

Part 3 **Summarizing Qualitative Data and Completing an Action Research Report and Presentation** 67

Purpose and Outcomes for Part 3 67

In-School Performance Activities 68

Chapter 5 **Analysis and Interpretation of Qualitative Data** 69

Document Coding and Analysis 70

  Concept Maps, Diagrams, and Word Tables 72

  Data Triangulation 72

Data Analysis and Results 74

Research Methodology 78

Research Conclusions 79

    Key Questions for Review 84 • *Performance Checklist for Completing Steps 3a, 3b, 3c, and Step 4a Research Activities* 84 • *References* 85

Chapter 6 **Recommendations, Reports, and Reflections** 86

Reflection for Research Recommendations 86

Research Recommendations 87

The Action Research Report 90

  Components of the Action Research Report 90

  An Action Research Report Rubric 93

Reflection on Action Research 93

Presentations of Action Research 93

  Presentation Audiences 93

Visual Presentations   97

    Key Questions for Review   99   •   Performance Checklist for Step 3c and Step 4a Research Activities   99   •   References   100

Part 4   Bridging Research with Practice   101

Purpose and Outcomes for Part 4   101

In-School Performance Activities   102

Chapter 7   Action Research as Part of Professional Practice   103

Research Contributions to School Practice   104

Research for School Improvement   105

Action Research and Change in Practice   106

Action Research and Comprehensive Planning   107

Action Research and School-Improvement Planning   108

   Similar Processes and Components   108

   Component Action Plans and Action Research   108

Integration of Research, Planning, and Assessment   110

The Journey as a Destination   111

    Key Questions for Review   116   •   Performance Checklist for Reflection and Action Planning   117   •   References   117

Chapter 8   Research, Reflection, and Professional Growth   119

Reflective Practitioner   119

A Reflective Learner   121

Standards as an Assessment Guide for Professional Development   121

   Where Are We Going?   122

   Who Will Lead?   123

   What About Professional Growth?   124

    ISLLC 2008 STANDARDS   125

    INTASC MODEL CORE TEACHING STANDARDS   129

    Key Questions for Review   132   •   Performance Checklist for Self-Evaluation for Professional Growth   132   •   References   133

EXAMPLE ACTION RESEARCH REPORTS   135

School Improvement Analysis: Writing Achievement of Hispanic Students   136

An Analysis of Content Reading Instruction at Roger Vale Elementary   146

Improving the Reading Skills of Struggling Reading Students at Melody Lane Elementary School   159

The Sophomore Coaching Initiative   172

An Analysis of Mathematics Performance of Jewell High School Students   182

Postsecondary Reading Remediation for High School Graduates   190

A Comparative Review of High School Schedules   197

Middle School Improvement Analysis: Practical Living/Career Studies Test Scores   204

GLOSSARY OF RESEARCH-RELATED TERMS   211

INDEX   216

TABLE OF CONTENTS
FOR CD SUPPLEMENT

The electronic resources on the accompanying CD will help you as you work through in-school research performance activities at the end of content for each chapter. Also, the first resource group on this list will help in planning district professional development for principals and research leadership teams. If a school leader and/or research leadership team is working through the materials without district workshops, reviewing the professional development handouts and activities in this section can help you think through how to plan and begin action research.

Example Agendas and Handouts for Action Research District Professional Development Workshops (only on the CD)

CD 1.a   Introduction to Implementing Action Research as Professional Development

CD 1.b   Overview of Action Research Schedule for the School Year

CD 1.c   Three Professional-Development Workshop Agendas

CD 1.d   Planning Worksheet for Beginning Collaborative Research Tasks

CD 1.e   Ice Breakers Examples and Small Interactive Group Assignments

CD 1.f   Planning Worksheet for Completing Collaborative Research Tasks

CD 1.g   Action Research Reflection Guide

CD 1.h   School Leader Professional-Development Self-Check for *Educational Policy Standards: ISLLC 2008, Council of Chief State School Officers*

CD 1.i   Self-Check for Teacher Professional Development and Improvement Plan for Teacher Leadership Based on Council of Chief State School Officers InTASC *Model Core Teaching Standards: A Resource for State Dialogue*

CD 1.j   Action Research for School Improvement and Student Achievement

CD 1.k   Logan's Top Ten Checklist for Teamwork

These example reports were completed by teachers who were preparing for school administration and principals who were working toward an advanced certification level for their position. The research completed took place in their schools and involved collaboration with colleagues with whom they worked. The first eight examples are printed in a section of the text following Part 4 and also in a file on the CD. The last six reports are not printed in the text but can be found on the CD. Examples from some of these reports are illustrated in the chapters with the source noted.

Example Action Research Reports (Text)

Example 1   School Improvement Analysis: Writing Achievement of Hispanic Students (Ele.) by Sherri D. Turner Wadsworth

Example 2   An Analysis of Content Reading Instruction at Roger Vale Elementary (Ele.) by Michelle C. Ligon and Melissa Rash

Example 3   Improving the Reading Skills of Struggling Reading Students at Melody Lane Elementary School (Ele.) by Kari Kirchner

Example 4   The Sophomore Coaching Initiative (HS) by Bryan Jacobs and Richard Royster

Example 5   An Analysis of Mathematics Performance of Jewell High School Students (HS) by Kim Zeidler-Watters

Example 6   Postsecondary Reading Remediation for High School Graduates (HS) by Janet Sivis O'Connell

Example 7   A Comparative Review of High School Schedules (HS) by Joe K. Matthews

Example 8   Middle School Improvement Analysis: Practical Living/Career Studies Test Scores (MS) by Laura Arnold

Example Action Research Reports (CD only)

Example 9   (CD only) Closing the Tenth Grade Reading Achievement Gap (HS) by Ryan Ray

Example 10   (CD only) An Effective Communication Network for the Response to Intervention Implementation (Ele.) by Dawn Floyd

Example 11   (CD only) School Improvement Analysis: Mathematics Achievement (Ele.) by Amanda Boyd Collier

Example 12   (CD only) Analysis of Gifted and Talented Enrichment Programs (Ele.) by Angela Taylor

Example 13   (CD only) Participatory Action Research Assessment of Saturday Academy (Ele.) by Angela Taylor

Example 14   (CD only) Using a Positive Approach to Student Success (PASS) for Students with Disruptive Behaviors (Ele.) by Angela Taylor

End-of-Chapter Chapter Performance Checklists

Chapter 1   Performance Checklist for Step 1 Research Activities

Chapter 2   Performance Checklist for Step 2a Research Activities

Chapter 3   Performance Checklist for Steps 2b and 2c Research Activities

Chapter 4   Performance Checklist for Step 3a Research Activities

Chapter 5   Performance Checklist for Steps 3a, 3b, 3c, and Step 4a Research Activities

Chapter 6   Performance Checklist for Step 3c and Step 4a Research Activities

Chapter 7   Performance Checklist for Reflection and Action Planning

Chapter 8   Performance Checklist for Self-Evaluation for Professional Growth

The resources on the CD for each chapter list all tables sequentially and figures sequentially in the order included or referenced in the chapter. Tables are numbered sequentially but separate from Figures. Those only on the CD have "CD" as part of the listed title; those without "CD" in the title are on the CD but also are an illustration in the chapter.

Text example materials and other resource materials in electronic format on the CD were developed and may be opened and saved using word processing, spreadsheet, and presentation software from Microsoft® © Corporation, OneMicrosoft Way, Redmond, Washington 989052-6399 U.S.A.

Chapter 1 Resources

Table 1.1   Comparison of Problem Solving and Action Research

Table 1.2   Definitions and Major Characteristics of Action Research

Table 1.3   Examples of Research Problems and Guiding Questions

Figure 1.1   An Example Problem Statement and Research Questions

Figure 1.2   (CD only) An Example Problem Statement Illustrating Double-Spaced Format

Figure 1.3   (CD only) An Example Problem Statement and Research Questions

Figure 1.4   (CD only) General Protocol for Collaborative Teamwork

Figure 1.5   (CD only) Tally Worksheet for Nominal Group Technique

Chapter 2 Resources

Table 2.1   (CD only) URL Locations for Information on Google Docs and Wikispaces

Table 2.2   Examples of Professional Organizations with Student Achievement Resources

Table 2.3   Examples of Government Educational Resources for Improving Student Achievement

Table 2.4   Examples of Education Journal Resources for Improving Student Achievement

Table 2.5   Additional Web Literature Review Resources

Figure 2.1   (CD only) Selected Library Subscription Databases

Figure 2.2   (CD only) Example Literature Resources (Books)

Figure 2.3   (CD only) Worksheet For Literature Review Resources

Figure 2.4   (CD only) Preparing the References List Using Copy and Paste and the Sort Function

Figure 2.5   (CD only) Additional Information for APA Style and Use of DOIs

Figure 2.6   Example Format and Topical Plan for a Literature Review

Figure 2.7   (CD only) In-Text Citation Examples of Sources for APA-Formatted Reports

Figure 2.8   (CD only) Example of Data Additions to Introductory Problem Statement

Chapter 3 Resources

Table 3.1   Planning Chart: Research Questions, Information Needs, and Multiple Data Types and Sources

Table 3.2   (CD only) Planning Chart: Research Questions, Information Needs, and Multiple Data Types and Sources (Blank Form)

Table 3.3   (CD only) Example of Completed Planning Chart From Table 3.2 That Consolidates Sources and Information Needs and Data-Collection Method and Population or Sample Size

Table 3.4   Example 5-Minute Walk-Through Checklist and Walk-Through URLs

Figure 3.1   (CD only) Ethical Responsibilities for Practitioner-Researchers in Schools

Figure 3.2   (CD only) Example Ethics Statements for Data Collection

Figure 3.3   (CD only) Sample Parent Letter for Research of a Sensitive Nature, with Attached Survey and Approval Form

Figure 3.4   Example Survey Instrument with Multiple Types of Questions

Figure 3.5   (CD only) Procedural Guide for Questionnaires and Survey Planning

Figure 3.6   Example of a Classroom Observation of Instruction Chart for Primary and Intermediate classrooms

Figure 3.7   (CD only) Sample Procedural Guide for Observations

Figure 3.8   (CD only) Sample Planning Guide for Classroom Observations

Figure 3.9   (CD only) Sample Visual for Faculty Discussion of Classroom Walk-Through Results

Figure 3.10   Example Protocol and Questions for Conducting Interviews for Research (Career Pathways)

Figure 3.11   (CD only) Sample Procedures for Planning Interview Data Collection

Chapter 4 Resources

Table 4.1   Research Techniques for Data Integrity and Trustworthiness

Table 4.2   Fifth Grade Mathematics Achievement Worksheet for Cross Checking and Triangulating Data Findings

Table 4.3   (CD only) Data Collection Cross-Check Blank Form for Data Triangulation (See Table 4.4 CD for a completed example)

Table 4.4   (CD only) Example of a Completed Data Cross-Check for Triangulation (Based on Table 3.1)

Table 4.5   Sample Student Rating Results From the Figure 4.1 Spreadsheet Summarized (Career and Technical Ed.)

Table 4.6   Status of Faculty Teaching Experience for Grades 1-6 Teachers at Calvert Elementary (N=24)

Table 4.7   Third Grade Reading Attitude Survey Scale (N=21)

Table 4.8   Description of Purposes for Different Graph Types

Figure 4.1   Example Spreadsheet for Storing and Summarizing Survey Data Using Formulas

Figure 4.2   (CD only) Brief Directions for Copying and Pasting

Figure 4.3   (CD only) Directions for Developing Graphs (Charts) Using Spreadsheet Software

Figure 4.4   Sample Observation Chart and a Manual Tally of Results

Figure 4.5   Sample Data From a Student Survey

Figure 4.6   (CD only) Directions for Formatting Tables (Including Examples of APA Style Tables)

Figure 4.7   (CD only) Directions for Formatting Figures (Including Examples of APA Style Figures)

Figure 4.8   Single Bar Graph (HS Tech Prep)

Figure 4.9   Example of an Ineffective Multiple Bar Graph

Figure 4.10   A Single-Bar Column Graph for One Category (Learning Activities) in Whata Elementary School

Figure 4.11   Example Format for a Multiple-Bar Column Graph

Figure 4.12   Example Format For a Pie Chart

Chapter 5 Resources

Table 5.1   Example Code Sheet for Identifying Major Themes From Interview Transcript Data (HS Career Pathways)

Table 5.2   (CD only) Blank Copy of Table 5.1 for Reducing Qualitative Data From Multiple Data Collection Instruments

Figure 5.1   (CD only) Suggestions for Coding Primary Data for Spreadsheet Entry and Summarizing Data

Figure 5.2   (CD only) Sample Contact Summary Form

Figure 5.3   A Concept Map of Qualitative Interpretive Themes

Figure 5.4   Data Analysis Section for an Action Research Report

Figure 5.5   Example Methodology and Research Procedures Section of an Action Research Report

Figure 5.6   Example Methodology Section of an Action Research Report

Figure 5.7   Example of the "So What?" Method (Writing Center UNC-Chapel Hill, n.d.) for Developing Action Research Conclusions

Figure 5.8   Example Conclusions Section of an Action Research Report

Chapter 6 Resources

Figure 6.1   (CD only) Suggestions for Building Research and Reflection Into Ongoing School Practice and Improvement

Figure 6.2   Example 1 of the Recommendations Section for an Action Research Report

Figure 6.3   Example 2 of the Recommendations Section for an Action Research Report

Figure 6.4   Example of Components for an Action Research Report

Figure 6.5   Self-Check Rubric for an Action Research Report

Figure 6.6   Format Example for Final Action Research Report

Figure 6.7   Sample Cover Sheet for an Action Research Report

Figure 6.8   Sample Reflection Guide After Completing the Action Research Process

Figure 6.9   Example Visual Presentation of an Action Research Report

Chapter 7 Resources

Figure 7.1   Composite of Components From Beginning Sections of 18 School-Improvement Plans

Figure 7.2   Composite of Action Plan Components From 18 School-Improvement Plans

Figure 7.3   Sample Action Plan Component of the School-Improvement Plan

Figure 7.4   A Suggested Three-Phase Transition that Advances the Knowledge and Practice of Action Research within a School or School District

Figure 7.5   Gantt Chart Two-Year Cycle for Comprehensive School-Improvement Planning and Action Research Activities

Chapter 8 Resources

Table 8.1   (CD only) Resources Referred to in Chapter 8 and How to Access These Documents

Table 8.2   Council of Chief State School Officers Educational Leadership Policy Standards (ISLLC 2008) Compared With Sample School Leadership Tasks

Table 8.3   (CD only) School Leader Professional Development Self-Assessment based on the ISLLC (2008) Council of Chief State School Officers (CCSSO) Standards for School Leaders

Table 8.4   (CD only) Council of Chief State School Officers InTASC Model Core Teaching Standards with an Abbreviated Format of Performances, Essential Knowledge, and Critical Dispositions

Table 8.5   Self-Assessment for School Leader and Teacher Professional Development Based on Council of Chief State School Officers (CCSSO) InTASC Model Core Teaching Standards: A Resource for State Dialogue

Figure 8.1   (CD only) Portfolio Entry Reflection Sheet

Figure 8.2   (CD only) Instructions for Completion of the Portfolio Reflection Cover Sheet

Figure 8.3   (CD only) Exemplar portfolio reflective cover sheet (2006 version)

PART ONE

Using Action Research to Improve Student Achievement

Each of the four parts of this text provides information, examples, and practical activities that school leaders can use to guide action research in their schools. As an educational leader, you can improve your skills for problem solving and data-driven decision making by applying action research to improve school outcomes. An educator who reviewed the first draft of this text noted a current preference for the term *data-informed decision making* rather than the commonly used *data-driven* descriptor. For action research, in particular, *data-informed* is a better term because it connotes information. Data consist of numbers, perceptions, and facts, but too often, the term brings only quantitative numbers to mind. This quantitative association is especially prevalent because of the evaluative emphasis on test scores. All types of relevant data make up the information analyzed and interpreted through action research to determine the best way to improve problems of practice. As you study Part 2, you will find descriptions of qualitative as well as quantitative data that are useful for researching problems of practice.

Studying the content and completing the activities in each of the four parts in this text will help you to use a problem-solving process for decision making and conducting action research to improve student achievement. Action research conducted in your school adds to the educator-researcher's understanding of school issues and problems and how to address complex problems through collecting and analyzing information and data in order to implement positive change. In addition, you as the practitioner-researcher will enhance your professional growth and expertise. Not only will you learn how to use a research process for school improvement, either individually or collaboratively, but also you will have developed shortcuts and a reference guide for gathering and reviewing research literature to enhance classroom teaching and student learning.

As you learn to conduct action research, you will complete each step of the action research for your school or classroom. Chapters are grouped into four parts. The beginning of each part lists related performance activities that guide completion of your school research steps.

After studying Part 1, you will be able to state questions that focus on what you want to know and to use these questions to locate professional literature that applies in the school or classroom and adds to your professional expertise. Part 2 guides you through collection and analysis of data. Part 3 shows how to describe the research methods followed to study the research questions and how to synthesize the research outcomes as conclusions. It also provides recommendations for action, as well as allows you to reflect on your work and to combine your work into an action research report. Part 4 suggests ways to integrate action research activities with school improvement planning. It also guides individual educators in assessment of their professional planning for leadership career goals and building the expertise to meet emerging teaching and learning needs.

All tables and figures shown in each chapter or on the CD as resources for the chapter are numbered sequentially with the chapter number and table or figure number (for example, Table 1.1, Table 1.2 or Figure 1.1, Figure 1.2). The CD supplement provides an electronic copy for your convenience of all tables and figures shown in the chapter, as well as some worksheets and related resources that appear on the CD only. For a complete list of all tables, figures, and other examples provided as resources, review the CD Table of Contents. Most of the CD-only resources are numbered as tables or figures in the order referred to in the chapter text. Exceptions to this numbering include suggested professional-development material, example action research reports, and the performance checklists for each chapter. Each of these categories has its own numbering sequence.

Purpose and Outcomes for Part 1

Part 1 familiarizes you with action research as a learning and problem-solving process that focuses school improvement on student achievement. This content guides you through the completion of Step 1 and Step 2a for a research problem identified for your school or classroom. See all action research steps in Table 1.1, Chapter 1, page 4. You will be identifying a research school or classroom problem and reviewing relevant literature resources to learn more about the problem.

In-School Performance Activities

Chapter 1

1. Identify a researchable problem in your school that relates to student achievement.
2. Identify research teams and/or other collaborative processes for researching the problem.
3. Draft a statement of the problem, the primary research question, and three to five specific questions to guide data needs for analyzing the problem.

Chapter 2

1. Draft a literature review that briefly summarizes current knowledge relevant to the problem, including author citations and a reference list of sources.
2. Reflect on what you learned from the literature, and review your problem statement and research questions for additions or changes.

CHAPTER 1

Action Research in School Settings

The action research steps covered in this text provide a practical decision-making process that principals, other educational leaders, and teachers can use as a tool for continuous research-based improvement of student learning. Action research is practical research by practitioners within a work setting and addresses ongoing situations and problems of practice too complex for short-term solutions. According to Reitzug (2002), educational leaders should be prepared to initiate and facilitate inquiry as an ongoing school improvement initiative.

As a long-term educator who worked as a teacher at the high school and university levels, as well as a school principal and regional and state administrator for the Kentucky Department of Education and Office of Adult and Technical Education, I know that improving student learning is a complex problem. Student achievement requires effective teachers, effective instruction, and educational leadership focused on continuous improvement that addresses student needs and creates a positive learning environment for students, faculty, and staff.

School improvement initiatives of the 1980s and 1990s referred to changes in education as *school reform*. That term implies a systemic change at a particular time, but 21st century educators recognize that school improvement requires ongoing collaboration and change. Streifer, (2002, p. 75) sees change as "a process or a journey" rather than a destination. School professionals constantly seek better ways to improve learning outcomes for all students. Effective administrators, teachers, and staff collaborate and seek knowledge that helps improve their professional performance.

Adults who view themselves as continuous learners and who share responsibility for ongoing improvement and effective decision making are less likely to experience burnout (Karasak & Theorell, 1990; Maslach & Jackson, 1981; Stoner & Wankel, 1986). A spirit of inquiry (problem solving and applied research) maintained by adults and students in a school keeps the target on learning. "Students develop and learn in environments where adults do the same" (Lambert, 2003, p. 54). "Action research teams capture the essence of inquiry by endeavoring to learn more about compelling questions of practice, leading to new actions" (Lambert, 2003, p. 14).

School leaders work with the faculty, staff, and others in the school community to keep the focus on student learning. There is not any one process or innovation that will bring high achievement for all students in all school settings; however, research studies since 2000 have provided strong evidence that the greatest influence the school has on student learning comes from effective teachers (Nye, Konstantopoulos, & Hedges, 2004; Rivkin, Hanushek, & Kain, 2005; Sanders, 2000; Wright, Horn, & Sanders, 1997) and effective principals (Knapp, Copeland, & Talbert, 2003; Leithwood, Seashore-Louis, Anderson, & Wahlstrom, 2004). Teaching effectiveness grows in an atmosphere of continuous learning. Ongoing inquiry built into professional development through action research and communities of learning can help foster professional growth and expertise in areas that affect student learning.

Inquiry through action research follows a process that informs and guides change for improvement of student learning. An elementary school principal, when asked by me for permission to use a completed action research report as an example in this text, sent two reports of action research completed in her school after she became a principal.

Most of the numerous examples in this text and those on the CD supplement come directly from action research completed in elementary, middle, and high schools and cite these educator-researchers' names and titles. Fictitious school names have been assigned and minor data and other changes made to protect the confidentiality of data gathered and reports written for internal school improvement.

PROBLEM SOLVING AND ACTION RESEARCH

As daily problem solvers, educators use a systematic process for making important decisions. Problems range from low to high importance. Their degree of importance and complexity determines the detail and time required to make a decision. At the simplest level, problems are solved through a mental, almost automatic, process—one that takes place without the educator focusing on each step of the process. Complex problems are difficult to completely solve, but certainly can be improved by increasing and applying knowledge gained through gathering data and information about related issues.

In schools, problem solving is a process for continuous improvement. Educators make decisions and focus intentions on positive change for each problem of practice that occurs. Their goal is to create the best learning environment and the best result for all stakeholders. Decision making requires the best information available, including knowledge about the issues and stakeholder perceptions. The term *stakeholders*, as used here, refers to all persons directly affected by a problem.

The Problem-Solving Process

The problem-solving process has five basic steps: (a) identify the problem, (b) collect and analyze data, (c) consider improvement actions, (d) select and implement the best action, and (e) evaluate the results. Consider your thoughts and actions when you address a problem. Are they similar to steps in this process? If so, you already practice a process similar to action research. Furthermore, these steps resemble procedures for development of a school action plan for improvement. Table 1.1 compares problem-solving steps with the action research process. Note their similarities and differences. Sequential steps are much the same. However, action research requires additional time and study for researching professional information sources, gathering data, analyzing results, documenting research, and recommending actions for improvement in a school setting.

Table 1.1
Comparison of Problem Solving and Action Research

Problem-Solving Process	Action Research Steps

1. Identify the problem.	1. Identify the problem.
	  a. Develop a problem statement.
	  b. State a primary question.
	  c. State three to five guiding questions.

2. Collect and analyze data.	2. Collect and analyze data.
	  a. Review relevant professional literature.
	  b. Determine additional data needs.
	  c. Identify method of data collection and analysis.

3. Consider solutions.	3. Consider solutions.
	  a. Collect, summarize, and analyze data.
	  b. Develop data analysis, and describe research procedures.
	  c. Develop conclusions, and recommend action for positive change.

4. Implement the solution.	4. Implement the solution.
	  a. Prepare an action research report.
	  b. Develop a research-based action plan.
	  c. Implement the action plan.

5. Evaluate results.	5. Evaluate results.

Action Research

Study the action research steps shown in Table 1.1. If you wish to print a copy of this table for a handy reference as you complete your research, you will also find it on the CD Table of Contents under Chapter 1. You will complete all of these steps for a researchable problem of practice in your school as you finish the in-school performance activities at the end of each chapter. This step-by-step learning approach completes a draft for each research step and provides a performance checklist for each performance activity. When you complete all steps, the drafts that you have completed for each step will be assembled, refined, and edited to produce a complete action research report. Because school personnel have busy schedules, and because school size and number of faculty and support staff vary, these factors must be considered when planning collaborative action research. Establish a reasonable time span for completion of research, and organize time for collaborative involvement. Schedule your implementation of action research for the best fit with your school operations and cycle for school improvement plans. Develop a plan for recognition of professional growth and development for personnel who participate in school and classroom action research. Also, work with the school district office to identify and recognize the value of action research for school improvement plans.

Action research authors have used a variety of definitions to describe action research. Table 1.2 shows four of these descriptions and also lists major characteristics of each definition. Note the similarities of purpose and characteristics among these definitions.

Table 1.2
Definitions and Major Characteristics of Action Research

Sources	Definitions	Characteristics
Corey (1962)	Action research is a process by which practitioners attempt to study their problems scientifically in order to guide, correct, and evaluate their decisions and actions (p. 6).	Follows specific steps in a process Provides a guide to correct and evaluate actions/decisions
Hopkins (2002)	Action research is a substantive act with a research procedure; it is action disciplined by inquiry, a personal attempt at understanding while the researcher is engaged in a process of improvement and reform (p. 42).	Uses a research procedure Bases actions on disciplined inquiry Attempts to understand and improve
Stringer (2007)	Action research is a systematic approach to investigation that enables people to find effective solutions to problems confronted in everyday life (p. 1).	Investigates problems systematically Finds solutions Confronts everyday problems
Mills (2011)	Action research is any systematic inquiry conducted by teacher-researchers, principals, school counselors, or other stakeholders in the teaching/learning environment to gather information about how their particular schools operate, how they teach, and how well their students learn. This information is gathered with the goals of gaining insight, developing reflective practice, effecting positive changes in the school environment (and on educational practice in general), and improving student outcomes and the lives of those involved (p. 5).	Uses systematic inquiry Gathers information about their work and work environment to understand, reflect, and improve outcomes

Note. **See Chapter 1 References at the end of the chapter for these resources.**

WHAT IT IS.   If you combine the common characteristics from these four definitions, you know that action research for schools is a *systematic research process* that seeks understanding of a school problem of practice in a particular site in order to guide decisions for improvement. The fact that it is a systematic process implies that the researcher follows specific research steps to learn about a clearly defined issue or problem as a basis for improvement decisions. Action research is *applied research* aimed toward improvement of practice in a work setting.

WHAT IT IS NOT.   Action research is not theoretical research. Although the research steps are similar, they differ in purpose and practice. Theoretical research generally starts with hypothesis statements to be proved or disproved—that is, answered "yes" or "no." Action research asks broader questions which seek possible positive actions that can be taken in your school. The intent of action research is primarily to reach a better understanding of a problem and to identify potential positive actions for improvement. The research findings in action research are applicable specifically to the study site and cannot be assumed to be transferable to similar sites, whereas theoretical research aims for a sufficient number of carefully controlled studies to give evidence of the same result in similar sites. Theoretical research improves validity by the controlled use of inferential statistics and data gathered from numerous sites. Detailed descriptions of relevant literature and methodology in theoretical research reports enable replication of the same study in other sites and increase study credibility.

Action research usually takes place in a specific site or in a limited number of similar sites and aims for improvement at that site or sites. The action research report requires less detail about the site and methodology than a theoretical research report intended for a broader audience. Schools may share action research with others, but its purpose is for internal use for improvement of student achievement. Multiple schools (in particular, small schools or schools with minimal staffing within a district) or personnel from different schools with mutual interest in a problem of practice may collaborate and share expertise to study a problem. Achieving the same results in other schools or even following the same procedures in exactly the same way is not expected. Reviewing action research from other schools related to a problem that you are studying, however, can help inform the problem and provide ideas for stating your research problem, gathering and analyzing data, and identifying possible solutions.

You will note that the action research report examples in this text follow a pattern similar to that of formal research in advanced studies for school leadership. However, there are differences. Advanced study research requires more detailed explanations for a wider audience than are required for internal action research for ongoing development.

Action research is not an activity to be carried out if you have predetermined what the results should be. You may have a prior opinion about the result, but you must be open to different research findings. Looking only for prior knowledge specific to changes that are already determined is not valid research. This approach brings bias to a study because, intentional or not, it is likely that, if the decision has already been made on changes to propose, the search for information is limited to supporting evidence rather than broadened to seeking knowledge to identify the best action for improvement. Not all studies on a topic show the same result. If you narrow the search to positive results for a school practice, the readers may assume that this practice is great. But being open to disconfirming as well as to confirming results could lead to a different conclusion. A valid research study follows and describes procedures for guarding against bias. The procedures for improving validity of results will be described in Part 2.

SCHOOL PROBLEMS OF PRACTICE FOR ACTION RESEARCH

Student achievement includes scoring well on academic tests but also includes positive growth and development for all students. Action research to improve student achievement is an appropriate improvement tool for addressing issues directly related to teaching and learning at particular grade levels—for example, low reading scores by fifth-grade students or a high number of first-grade students held back for a second year. Action research may also address a schoolwide problem such as high dropout rates for a high school or a high number of students with repeated disciplinary actions. Action research that addresses failure to meet academic goals in a particular subject area helps guide decisions for improving student achievement.

Although school leaders examine school data yearly in a planning process that resembles data analysis in action research, research questions and the knowledge base from literature is often missing from that process. Furthermore, in-school data collection of related data, such as perceptual data about the issue, may not be systematically gathered and analyzed. Through action research, educators can take what leaders currently do to determine data-informed needs and select the most pressing need to study by the action research process. Action research can guide decisions about ongoing issues that negatively affect the learning environment, either directly or indirectly, such as improving teaching effectiveness, parental support, counseling services, classroom facilities, school morale, or parental and community involvement.

Problem Identification

A problem is something that (a) deviates from a standard or expectation, (b) has an unknown cause, and (c) causes concern. A problem selected for action research should have these three characteristics. Also, the problem should be recurring over time or be of significant magnitude or complexity to require intensive study of the problem itself, of its causes, and of potential actions for positive change. Does the issue represent a negative trend with an unknown cause? Does the status of the issue cause concern? Does it fail to meet expectations for faculty, student, administrative, or school performance? Is the answer to the problem unknown? Can you briefly name the problem? Is the problem one for which the school can be a part of effecting positive change?

If the best solution for the issue is already known and needs only to be located and reviewed, this is not an action research problem. It does not require data collection and analysis; it requires only locating and reviewing information—much like locating a telephone number or address. The issue stems from a clearly identified question but is a short-term simple problem with an available answer. Some problems may be complex but, because of the nature of the problem, must have a decision within a short time. Therefore, these issues require problem-solving steps but not action research. Action research addresses complex problems that have developed over time and require time to determine the best actions to implement for positive change.

On the other hand, the problem should be narrowed to a topic for which research can be completed in a reasonable time span in order to avoid personnel changes or loss of interest if the research is not completed in a timely fashion. A broad topic may need to be divided into major subtopics to be covered sequentially as two or more research studies. The extent of the problem and information needs will determine the best time span, but a completion date and progress dates should be projected when the study begins and should be reasonable. A complicated, collaborative study extended over two or more school terms may create difficulty for collaboration and completion because of personnel and condition changes.

The examples that follow illustrate school problems with varying degrees of complexity. Some require a short-term decision reached through a problem-solving process; others are appropriate for action research. Consider these situations, and decide which are appropriate for action research.

1. Bus #15 usually arrives at school 25 minutes before the first bell. However, one day last week, it did not arrive until 15 minutes before the bell because the bus driver overslept.
2. Eighth-grade male students consistently score higher than female students on mathematics achievement tests. The achievement gap is a concern because a high percentage of these female students do not meet state mathematics proficiency standards.
3. The dropout rate for the school has increased over the past 3 years.
4. One or more students in fifth grade come to class each day without completing the assigned homework.
5. A fight on the bus between two students took place on Friday of this week. One of the students was involved in a similar altercation last year.

Situation 1 is of concern and does not meet expectations. However, according to the facts that we know, this has occurred only once and the cause is known. The bus arrived in time for students to be in class on time. Although the arrival time may have caused some inconvenience, the problem is not a researchable problem unless it continues as a behavior trend over time. This is not a problem for action research and requires only minimal application of the problem-solving process.

Situation 2 meets all definitions for a problem and is a researchable problem. An expectation exists to close the learning gap between low- and high-achieving students and for all students to reach proficiency, so this issue represents a cause for concern and is happening consistently over time. We may speculate about reasons for test score differences, but without further information, we cannot know the cause(s) or ways to best address the problem.

Situation 3 is a researchable problem. The dropout rate trend is of concern because expectations are to reduce dropouts, and dropouts have increased over time. The cause is unknown, and the problem is complex. This problem could be divided into more than one study to examine in-school practices that address community and home involvement.

Situation 4 may or may not be a researchable problem, depending on the span of time over which this has occurred and its effect on learning. It is a problem for the teacher and the students but may be resolved with short-term solutions such as individual teacher–student conferences and/or teacher–parent or teacher–guardian conferences. If the problem persists, the teacher may do an action research study to learn more about best practices for homework. The teacher also may record data for homework assignments that are similar in type and length to those most often not completed, trying different assignment processes to increase student interest and successful completion, giving time in class for assistance in beginning homework, and analyzing results.

Situation 5 will follow a problem-solving process but will not require action research. It will require action sooner than would be possible with action research. If disruptions on buses become a major concern over time, action research into the larger issue could address causes and possible resolutions.

Researchable Problems

The first step of action research identifies the problem. This sounds simple, but clearly stating the questions to guide your research can be the most difficult part. A complex situation occurs or has occurred over a period that deviates from expectations, has an unknown answer, and is of concern. Our first effort at naming the problem may be to name the topic of concern. Further thought and discussion result in framing this topic as a primary question for investigation to find the best action for change. Next, we develop three to five guiding questions aimed at collecting relevant data to inform the primary question and help formulate positive actions for improvement.

Study Table 1.3 to see how problem topics develop into a primary question. The guiding questions result from brainstorming to explore information topics that may help answer the primary research question. Guiding questions generally relate to what can be learned about causes, best practices, and successful improvement strategies related to the problem. In addition, currently available school data and additional data collection may help us to understand the problem. School practices and school policies that influence the problem may be another area of study. Shulman (1997, p. 4) emphasizes the importance of carefully framing a research question and says that a major accomplishment of research is that it helps you "to become wiser or more discerning about a particular problem or issue."

Note that questions in Table 1.3 begin with Why, How, What, When, Which, or Where to elicit information that helps explain the problem, its causes, and potential ways to address it. Check to see that questions cannot be answered with "yes" or "no." You are not trying to prove an absolute answer; rather, you are learning about a problem to determine the best action for improvement.

Problem Statement

As part of action research problem identification, draft a paragraph or more that explains why this issue is a problem and the importance of improving it. The problem statement

Table 1.3
Examples of Research Problems and Guiding Questions

Problem	Research Question	Guiding Questions
Disciplinary Actions (Elementary School)	How can we reduce the number of disciplinary infractions that result in office referrals and loss of instructional time?	1. Why are students being sent to the office? 2. What are the demographics of students being referred to the office? 3. What practices have proved most effective in reducing disciplinary infractions?
Fifth-Grade Math Scores (Elementary School)	How can student learning in fifth-grade mathematics be improved to reduce achievement gaps among subgroups of students?	1. Which subgroups of students score consistently below their peers on mathematics core content tests? 2. What mathematics skills cause the greatest difficulty for our students? 3. What do research-based practices reveal about effective mathematics programs?
Student Achievement in Practical Living/Career Exploratory Courses (Middle School)	What improvements can be made in Practical Living/Career Exploratory courses that lead to gains in learning and student achievement?	1. What value perceptions do staff and students place on these courses? 2. What instructional and classroom management strategies are currently implemented in these courses? 3. How do these courses contribute to student development and student success? 4. What does previous research say about best practices for instructional strategies, classroom management, and the value of elective courses for middle school students?
Decline in Math Scores (High School)	How can stagnation and decline in mathematics scores be reversed to reflect the overall progress shown by the school's academic index?	1. What trends are evident, and which subgroups of students have declining or stagnant scores? 2. What effect, if any, does the type of entry-level mathematics course have on student performance? 3. What mathematics content strands cause the greatest difficulty for student performance? 4. What variations have occurred in student performance levels from Grade 8 to Grade 11?
Sophomore Coaching Initiative (High School)	How effective is the Sophomore Coaching Initiative in closing the achievement gap in reading and mathematics test scores?	1. What do current data show as achievement gaps in reading and mathematics at the sophomore level for all disaggregated subgroups? 2. What changes, if any, do data show for the achievement gaps in reading and mathematics at the beginning and ending of the semester after implementation of sophomore coaching? 3. What teaching strategies have been most effective for reducing achievement gaps in reading and mathematics?
Truancy and Its Effects (Elementary School)	How can truancy and its effects on academic achievement be reduced for elementary students?	1. How is truancy defined? 2. Why are students truant? 3. What relationships are apparent between truancy and student learning as measured by standardized tests? 4. What existing programs have been successful in preventing truancy?

continued

Table 1.3
(Continued)

Problem	Research Question	Guiding Questions
Mathematics Knowledge and Skills Below Standard (Elementary School)	How can mathematics achievement in the school be improved to a level equal to or above district and state averages?	1. Which groups of students are performing well below their peers on the mathematics state core content tests? 2. What are the characteristics of students performing at novice and apprentice levels? 3. How are students performing on mathematics subdomain areas (i.e., number sense/ computation, geometry/measurement, algebraic ideas, and probability/statistics)? 4. What mathematics instructional strategies have been shown by research to be effective, and what strategies are used in our school? 5. How does the mathematics curriculum align with mathematics state core content and the program as taught in our school?
Decline in Reading Test Scores (Elementary School)	Why are fourth- and fifth-grade students with disabilities achieving at lower levels than their peers, as evidenced by their scores on reading state core content tests?	1. What can the special education student achievement teams do to improve the students' reading levels? 2. What remediation reading programs are currently used in our school to improve learning? 3. What remediation programs are effectively used at other elementary schools in the state? 4. What barriers to learning persist in our special education program? 5. What professional development is provided on research-based special education reading strategies and reading curricula?
Lack of Sustained Reading Improvement Over Time (Elementary School)	How can third-grade reading scores be improved to show a steady upward trend over at least 3 years?	1. What reading elements present the greatest difficulty for reading comprehension? 2. What reading comprehension problems are evidenced by responses to questions about reading passages? 3. What instructional strategies have been found to be effective in improving reading achievement for elementary school students?

Note. **Problems and questions adapted from action research by Kim Haury, Elementary School Teacher; Jennifer Hutchison, Curriculum Coach; Kristina Kinney, Middle School Teacher; Kim Zeidler-Watters, Director, P–12 Mathematics Science Outreach; Bryne Jacobs and Richard Royster, High School Associate Principals; Peggy Henderson, Elementary School Principal, and Diane Wiles, State Project Administrator; Amanda Boyd Collier, Elementary School Teacher; Sara Saylor, Elementary School Assistant Principal/Curriculum Resource Administrator; and Christine M. Rickert, Elementary School Lead Teacher. Examples from research team reports show the report authors' names together joined by "and." The second and third examples in this table are from two-member teams. All examples are used with permission.**

for action research becomes the introduction for the final research report. Keep in mind the report recipients and research participants. These individuals are your audience for the research report. Tell them what they need to know to understand why the research was done and its importance to student achievement. When these two points are clear, you have drafted the problem statement. For an internal school or school district audience, the only school background for this report will be that which relates directly to these two points: What evidence or events have shown this issue to be a problem, and how is overcoming it important to accomplishing the primary mission of the school—student learning?

The written draft for your research report will be completed as you work through each chapter. At the end of this chapter, you will be ready to complete the first of five action research steps, which is to identify the issue in writing by drafting the following: an appropriate problem, the problem statement, the primary research question, and guiding questions.

Figure 1.1 illustrates one way to draft the first section of your action research report. Writing a report as you complete research steps not only makes developing the research report at the completion of research a process of editing and refining, but also documents the process during the research to keep all participants fully informed and on the same page.

Action Research to Improve Mathematics Achievement of Fifth-Grade Students

This action research examined the large mathematics achievement gap between fifth-grade students at Atlantis Elementary School and their age peers for the total school district on the state core content test. Test results for the mathematics test show a 25- to 39-point discrepancy compared with fifth-grade students districtwide and 16 to 29 points below the state average for fifth-grade students. This trend occurred over the past 5 academic years, as evidenced by state performance reports. The gap in student achievement is of great concern and must be addressed. The purpose of this action research project was to analyze the mathematics performance of fifth-grade students at Atlantis Elementary School as a basis for improving student achievement.

The primary research question for this study was stated as follows: How can student learning in mathematics be improved for fifth-grade students at Atlantis Elementary School, as evidenced by reducing the achievement gap on the core content tests between these students and their peers in the district and state?

The following subquestions guided inquiry and data collection for this study:

1. What are mathematics performance differences for fifth-grade subgroups of students at Atlantis Elementary?
2. What research-based instructional practices have been effective for elementary mathematics students?
3. What mathematics skills cause the most difficulty for students?
4. How do assessment practices and instruction for fifth-grade students align with core content tests? How does classroom practice performing problems compare with the same kind of problems that give students the greatest difficulty on core content tests?

Figure 1.1. **An example problem statement and research questions. Adapted from action research completed by Jennifer Hutchison, Curriculum Coach. Used with permission.**

Figure 1.1 uses a direct, brief opening problem statement supported by specific evidence confirming the need for the research and its importance. This is followed by a paragraph with the primary research question that includes the means for determining acceptable results. A specific goal establishing a timeline or stating the percentage targeted for reducing the gap can be added in development of the action plan from this research.

Two other examples of action research questions (Figures 1.2 and 1.3) are in Chapter 1 Resources on the CD. Figures 1.2 and 1.3 are similar to Figure 1.1. Figure 1.2 differs by explaining the need for research in the first paragraph, and its importance as linked to student achievement in the second paragraph. This second paragraph includes the primary research question and a numbered list of guiding questions. Figure 1.3 uses less-specific data but includes more background of the problem in order to establish the need for the research and its importance. Another difference in this example from the first two is incorporation of the primary research question and guiding questions within the last paragraph. Note that with this format, each question is identified by lowercase letters in parentheses rather than by placement in a numbered vertical list.

All three figures use a form consistent with the *Publication Manual of the American Psychological Association (APA)*, 6th edition. This style manual, recently revised in 2010, is often used to format formal papers and dissertations in graduate work as well as journal articles in the field of educational leadership. The style exception is that most of the action research report examples in this text are single-spaced, with extra spacing between paragraphs. Style manuals are aimed primarily at preparing consistent formatting for publication, and the double spacing is for the publisher's edits; the final printed copy is usually single-spaced. School action reports may follow either single- or double–spacing format, according to the researchers' preference.

The style used by a school may differ from the examples here, but these examples provide a guide consistent with APA that is easy to follow for formatting a research report. You may deviate from this format as seems appropriate for your school. However, maintaining consistent formatting for section subheads, references (both for in-text reference citations and the reference list), and tables and figures results in a research report that presents a professional appearance and contributes to the trustworthiness of your research process and results.

The three examples (Figures 1.1, 1.2, and 1.3) for the first report section of action research, with their similarities and differences, illustrate that as long as the most important content is included, there is not a lock-step pattern to follow when writing sections of a report. Notice that the introduction of the problem is written with past-tense verbs. Although you draft this introduction before beginning the research, it will not be distributed in final form until all research steps are completed and refined as a final action research report. The variety of reports illustrated in this text provide content and format ideas for developing each section of an action research report for school improvement.

LEADERSHIP FOR ACTION RESEARCH

Before the organization and beginning of research in a school, planning should involve the principal and superintendent or another designated individual from the board office. Some school districts have a department for research and evaluation that reviews all school research. Check with your district office to learn the requirements for research approval before beginning the research process.

When you use action research as a collaborative inquiry and learning process within the school, bring together a research leadership team that can be involved in framing the problem statement, primary research problem, and guiding questions. Help the team members understand that action research follows a systematic process to gain understanding about a problem or issue and to analyze changes that can result in improvement. Each team member should have a copy of this text and share discussions and work for each chapter.

To involve as many interested people as possible within your school, you may want to add other faculty and staff for specific steps of the research process. If the size of the school permits, the leadership team could have oversight over the whole study. Then, each leadership team member could also represent that team by serving on a literature review team, a research methodology team, a data collection and analysis team, or a conclusions and recommendations team. The leadership team might have five to seven people. Two to three other interested faculty or staff members, in addition to the leadership team member, could be appointed for each of the preceding task teams.

Team members should be interested in and somewhat knowledgeable about the research problem but do not need to have prior experience with research. The data analysis for action research generally involves only descriptive statistics such as summaries, means, and standard deviations. Content in this text prepares you for displaying and interpreting descriptive quantitative data and provides methods for collecting and analyzing qualitative data. Moreover, action research can be conducted by an individual or a team of individuals who are affected by the problem and interested in learning more about it to improve outcomes. Results will be shared with others in the school community after research completion.

In a small school, a schoolwide research project might have only a leadership team consisting of 5 to 10 people who work through all research steps. Staff with technology expertise can guide communication with school community members, and 1 or 2 administrative staff and/or faculty with computer skills can handle report preparation and data formatting for necessary tables and figures. Schools with only 10 to 15 total professional staff might want to partner with a similar school to study a common problem. However, administrators and individual teachers, subject-area teachers, or grade-level teachers may want to complete research to meet specific learning-improvement needs. Some of these special research groups or teachers may partner with peers in similar schools in their district.

The structures mentioned here and throughout this text are simply ideas to get you thinking about different ways to organize and encourage action research in your particular school to add to professional expertise for teaching and learning and to improve problems of practice. Learning Forward, an international nonprofit association of learning educators, has a web homepage that offers learning opportunities, publications, and standards for professional learning (Learning Forward, n.d.). The standards outline characteristics of learning communities, leadership, and resources intended to lead to effective teaching and improved student learning (Learning Forward, 2012).

Schools that have already organized communities of learning or improvement teams can familiarize these groups with action research and make this a tool in their improvement repertoire. CD Resources Figures 1.4 and 1.5 give a handy suggested protocol for organization of research teams and a process for consensus.

Key Questions for Review

1. How is action research similar to, and how is it different from, the problem-solving process?
2. What is the purpose of action research in schools, and what are three characteristics that describe the process of this type of research?
3. How does theoretical research differ from action research?

4. What are five characteristics of an action research problem?
5. What are three topics of researchable problems that could benefit student achievement in your school, and what collaborative structure can be organized to best address such studies?

Note. **Performance Checklist will also appear on CD.**

Performance Checklist for Step 1 Research Activities

You are now ready to complete Steps 1a, 1b, and 1c of action research in your school. Table 1.1 in this chapter, and also on the CD under Chapter 1 Resources, lists all of the action research steps. A checklist of suggested actions for effective completion follows each activity.

Identify and describe a school-improvement problem focused on student achievement.

A. Draft a problem statement.

Performance Check:

1. Check with the school district office for approval of and special requirements for research.
2. Individuals or partners for a common research topic would follow the same steps described here except for organizing structured teams.
3. With a research team collaborating for action research, an organizational team meeting may suffice for drafting the primary research question and three to five guiding questions. These questions may be revised at several points during research, particularly after completion and reflection on professional literature. Steps suggested here should be adapted to fit your situation, and you may rely more heavily on technology than on meetings for collaboration and communication.
4. For schoolwide collaborative research, elect a research leadership team of individuals who have interest in and knowledge of the research topic. Each member should have a copy of this resource and should read the preface and first chapter. A date, time, and place should be communicated for a meeting. Prior to a school meeting, the purpose and intent of initiating action research in the school should be communicated.
5. At the meeting, a protocol for meetings may be handed out, similar to the one in the Chapter 1 Resources on the CD (Figures 1.4 and 1.5) accompanying this text. In addition, review Tables 1.1 and 1.3. As a group, review the

action research steps in Table 1.1 and example topics in Table 1.3 (may be printed from the CD). Then compile a list of complex school issues (5 to 10) that affect student learning and cause concern because of failure to meet expectations or other reasons and also that have continued to be of concern over time (at least 2 or 3 years). Review the list, and briefly discuss why each item is important and how it affects learning. Have each person write and submit a first and second choice of issues. Tabulate the top three. Discuss the top three, and come to a consensus for the topic of the research. Discuss the topic, considering why the problem is of concern, the period that it has been of concern, whether the cause or solution is known or unknown, how it fails to meet expectations, and why it needs attention.

6. Review copies of Figures 1.1, 1.2, and 1.3 printed from the CD. With group input, draft a problem statement for your research issue, or ask a team member to do this. Review the statement to see whether it clearly states why the topic is a researchable problem and its importance to student achievement. Decide how this will be communicated during development and how each member should communicate ideas for changes or additions. The selected communication medium should be one that is familiar to team members. Technology communication, from e-mail to collaborative computer software, may facilitate the process. Designate a specific individual to assume responsibility to receive changes, review the changes with the leadership team chair, and finalize changes, incorporating suggestions.

7. When all changes are made, send the revised copy to leadership team members and place a copy of the first draft, the revised copy, and a copy of each message received with changes in a research file (electronic or paper). This file should include work on all research steps and help bring research sections together for the final action research report.

B. Draft the primary research question and guiding questions.

Performance Check:

1. Review the primary questions shown in Table 1.3. (Note that the wording requires answers that explore the issue by acquiring relevant knowledge and data to understand this problem and develop improvement actions.) Questions for your school research may be completed either in the organizational meeting or through later communication with members.

2. Draft a primary research question. Ask if it can be answered "yes" or "no." If it can be answered "yes" or "no," then reword it to begin with a word such as *Why*, *What*, *Which*, *Where*, or *How*. The primary research question should state generally the desired outcome. Restate the topic of your research as a question that asks what you want to occur as a result of the study.

3. When drafting guiding questions, avoid wording them for "yes" or "no" responses. Reflect on the information needed to study the primary research question. Word guiding questions in such a way as to identify what you need to learn from the literature, from current school data, and from the perceptions of the school community participants who are directly affected by the problem. The number of guiding questions should keep the scope of the research narrowed to a manageable part of a big problem. Aim for positive change. File a copy of the primary question and guiding questions in the research file. Leadership team members should revisit, reflect, and refine the questions as needed, during your work for Chapter 2 and again in Chapter 3.

References

American Psychological Association (APA). (2010). *Publication manual of the American Psychological Association.* Washington, DC: Author.

Corey, S. M. (1962). *Action research to improve school practices.* New York: Bureau of Publications, Teachers College, Columbia University.

Hopkins, D. (2002). *A teacher's guide to action research* (3rd ed.). Buckingham: Open University Press.

Karasak, K., & Theorell, T. (1990). *Healthy work.* New York: Basic Books.

Knapp, M. S., Copeland, M. A., & Talbert, J. E. (2003, February). *Leading for learning: Reflective tools for school leaders.* Seattle, WA: University of Washington, Center for the Study of Teaching and Policy.

Lambert, L. (2003). *Leadership capacity for lasting school improvement.* Alexandria, VA: Association for Supervision and Curriculum Development.

Learning Forward. (2012). *Standards for professional learning.* Retrieved from website home page http://www.learningforward.org/

Leithwood, K., Seashore-Louis, K., Anderson, S., & Wahlstrom, K. (2004). *How leadership influences student learning.* New York: The Wallace Foundation. Retrieved from http://www.wallacefoundation.org/pages/executive-summary-how-leadership-influences-student-learning.aspx

Maslach, C., & Jackson, S. E. (1981). *MBI: Maslach burnout inventory.* Palo Alto, CA: Consulting Psychologists Press.

Mills, G. E. (2011). *Action research: A guide for the teacher researcher* (4th ed.). Upper Saddle River, NJ: Merrill/Prentice Hall.

Nye, B., Konstantopoulos, S., & Hedges, L. V. (2004, Fall). How large are teacher effects? *Educational Evaluation and Policy Analysis, 26*(3), 237–257.

Reitzug, U. C. (2002). Professional development. In A. Molnar (Ed.), *School reform proposals: The research evidence* (pp. 235–258). Greenwich, CT: Information Age Publishing. (A volume in the *Research in Educational Productivity Series,* H. J. Walberg, Series Editor).

Rivkin, S. G., Hanushek, E. A., & Kain, J. F. (2005, March). Teachers, schools, and academic achievement. *Econometrica, 73*(2), 417–458.

Sanders, W. I. (2000). Value-added assessment from student achievement data: Opportunities and hurdles. *Journal of Personnel Evaluation in Education, 14*(4), 329–339.

Shulman, L. S. (1997). Disciplines of inquiry in education: A new overview. In R. M. Jaeger (Ed.), *Complementary methods for research in education* (2nd ed.) (pp. 3–29). Washington, DC: American Educational Research Association.

Stoner, J. A., & Wankel, C. (1986). *Management* (3rd ed.). Englewood Cliffs, NJ: Prentice Hall.

Streifer, P. A. (2002). *Using data to make better educational decisions.* Lanham, MD: Scarecrow Publishing.

Stringer, E. T. (2007). *Action research* (3rd ed.). Thousand Oaks, CA: Sage.

Wright, S. P., Horn, S. P., & Sanders, W. L. (1997). Teacher and classroom context effects on student achievement: Implications for teacher evaluation. *Journal of Personnel Evaluation in Education, 11*, 57–67.

CHAPTER 2

A Knowledge Base for Action Research

After drafting a research topic, problem statement, and research questions, the next step in action research is to collect and analyze currently available literature and school data that increase understanding of the problem. This chapter guides your review of published relevant professional knowledge. The end result of this research step will be completion of an action research literature review, refinement of the research questions, and an inventory of available school data to strengthen the problem statement.

Although action research for school improvement is primarily a process that aids professionals in improving practice and achieving higher student outcomes within a school, each chapter includes formatting examples consistent with the most recent edition of the style manual followed in most education publications, the *Publication of the American Psychological Association* (6th ed.). Using these examples and example action research reports at the end of Part 4, as well as those on the CD, as a guide for formatting each part of the report will help you to produce a professional report for distribution throughout your school community.

Information from the literature review may raise additional questions that result in revisions or additions for the research questions. You may also find this information helpful in identifying national, state, or specific school data that should be added to your problem statement to support the importance of this research problem to students in your school. These benefits of the literature review are in addition to the knowledge gained that helps guide data collection and interpretation. Also, school personnel involved in literature research build professional knowledge and expertise for working with student learning.

ACTION RESEARCH LITERATURE REVIEW

Reading and taking notes from academic and professional knowledge resources begins your search for causes and potential solutions of the identified problem. In your search for information, you should examine topics and subtopics that will help answer your primary research question and one or more guiding questions. Therefore, at least one guiding question should relate to the information that can come from professional journal articles, books, or other professional materials about best practices for your problem topic. For example, in the first three problems shown in Table 1.3 (pp. 9–10) in Chapter 1, the following guiding questions relate to current knowledge about the problems:

Problem 1, Question 3:   What practices have proved most effective in reducing disciplinary infractions?

Problem 2, Question 3:   What do research-based practices reveal about effective mathematics programs?

Problem 3, Question 4:   What does previous research say about best practices for instructional strategies, classroom management, and the value of elective courses for middle school students?

Action research focuses on information and data to help answer a specific school problem of practice. In other words, you are not trying to learn everything written about the topic but are looking for potential causes, contributors, and school practices in seeking ways to overcome a particular problem and contribute to student achievement. The literature review also helps identify currently available data, as well as new data and information, to collect and analyze in your research. In addition, knowledge from the literature will be helpful at the last step of your research when you formulate recommendations and propose changes for school improvement.

With guiding questions narrowing the literature review to specific topics, this step of action research is not as lengthy and detailed as academic theoretical research or dissertation preparation, and may primarily comprise best practices from published reviews of research, professional journal articles, or research publications from professional organizations. Select only literature that has potential for answering your questions about the problem. About 10 to 15 resources may be sufficient for this purpose.

Before the literature review begins, a research leadership team with five to seven members, along with other appropriate faculty or staff directly involved in the research process, should meet and list potential topics or subtopics of interest that address each guiding question and that have the potential for achieving positive outcomes in addressing the problem expressed by the primary research question. This does not preclude adding other subtopics or redrafting the research questions if the literature search indicates different relevant topics or shows a lack of information about topics on the initial list of topics.

The literature review is a valuable step in beginning action research and takes concentrated time to locate resources that can best inform and guide your collection and analysis of data. Therefore, making this a collaborative effort shortens the time for completing it and also involves faculty and staff in an inquiry learning experience for professional growth and development. As Madeline Hunter (1990) wrote at the beginning of major reform in education, the same principles that apply to student learning apply to ongoing professional development of adults. Educators must "continue to think, using research-based principles, emerging data, and intuition" (Hunter, 1990, p. xii).

When you organize teams for carrying out research, invite participation by individuals who have high knowledge of the problem and its related areas for study. Research has found that individuals with a high prior knowledge of problem areas to be addressed will be able to use strategies that complete the tasks more effectively than individuals with low knowledge of the problem area (Alexander & Judy, 1988). High-knowledge team members can help structure thinking, provide context, and focus on the goal for joint problem solving (Hmelo, Nagarajan, & Day, 2000). Persons with limited problem-domain knowledge are less systematic in planning and interpretation.

Technology speeds the literature search process. However, educators generally work under a time crunch; still, the literature review time can be shortened if it is divided among members of your leadership team, or at least two or three interested faculty or staff members, who locate and read the literature and take notes for use in drafting the literature review. Individuals agreeing to do the searches, record the notes, and assist with literature review completion become a literature review team. They will work both independently and collaboratively, frequently communicating electronically and/or face-to-face during the literature search process to compare notes and share ideas for locating information on additional research subtopics. They also can revise the problem statement and research questions if needed.

Teams, in consultation with their principal, superintendent, and technology resource personnel in their school and school board office, should determine the best and most feasible communication media for different steps of the study, depending on technology expertise and sources available. Electronic media for communicating and sharing information within teams and among teams may extend from e-mail to smart phones, Google docs, Google drive, and/or Wikispaces. For example, Google docs and Google drive enable collaboration by allowing selected others to share your files and to access from any location the files that you saved to your Google account from any location. You can create and save documents, spreadsheets, and presentations while controlling security settings that keep the documents private; share them with coworkers and others; or make them accessible to anyone who finds the URL for the site. For further information on Google docs or Wikispaces, see Table 2.1, which presents URLs that will access the Web home pages that provide links to specific features. This table is located on the CD under Chapter 2 Resources.

Guidelines for electronic collaborative communication should be developed cooperatively by the superintendent's designee in the school board office and school personnel, including the principal and designated research team leaders. Consideration should be given to choices for types of digital communication for specific tasks at different stages of the research, as well as to the type of access granted to protect confidentiality of information where required. Technology security for collaborative use may require limited access during the development of initial drafts to team members collaborating on a specific task, but later may grant wider access to others to review final drafts. Security issues become increasingly important when sharing raw data electronically and while protecting the confidentiality and privacy of individual responses. Security issues are of little concern in collecting and sharing the literature review drafts, but have greater importance during the sharing of potential findings, conclusions, and recommendations prior to summarizing and finalizing these report sections.

Wikis and blogs that enable public access and comments should use software settings appropriate for use by selected individuals to ensure different levels of access for different purposes and tasks. In forming research groups, the types of communication and the security levels should be cleared with the school and school board office through the discussion and development of guidelines regarding both the type of technology for collaboration on research tasks and levels of access control to maintain for each research step.

A communication system for sharing literature resources and reviewing summaries among team members throughout the literature review search and development process should enable team members not only to avoid duplication of effort but also to identify apparent additional resources that they may need to locate in order to respond fully to the research questions. Near the end of the literature review, each team member should reflect on the sufficiency of the information gathered from literature in order to answer the research questions and to suggest multiple subtopics and sources of information that should be gathered within their school.

Performance tasks for this chapter ask for reflection on knowledge of the problem gained through the literature review and urge researcher-practitioners to reflect on new knowledge that helps answer research questions, revisiting and modifying or adding to questions as needed. On the basis of reflection and new knowledge gained from the literature, decide whether additional guiding questions, rewording, or additions to subtopics show a need for further research. Make sure that indicated changes or additions to research questions or the problem statement cover additional topics or subtopics about which information has been gained from the literature.

Vescio, Ross, and Adams (2006), in a review of research on professional learning communities, propose that recent expectations of professional development as learning applied to practice can be advanced through collaborative inquiry of teachers exploring new ideas, current practice, and strategies for school and classroom practices that promote student learning. Such inquiry brings together previous researchers' knowledge with classroom teacher expertise in a particular school setting to improve teaching and learning practices. Five studies on professional learning communities showed that student achievement improved over time when there was "collaboration around a clear and persistent focus on data about student learning" (Vescio et al., p. 21).

As instructional leaders, principals play a critical role in getting teachers and staff involved in continuous improvement. Learning to collaborate in applying action research is one means of doing this. Action research is conducted in a series of easy-to-learn steps that aid in problem solving.

Selecting Sources

Identifying and selecting literature sources may be completed mostly through computer data searches. If a university or college is nearby and you are unfamiliar with computer searches, this can be a good place to begin.

The school library or nearby university or college library and librarians can also be of help in locating or loaning important resources that are not accessible full text online or openly available online. Library subscriptions for online databases are licensed for noncommercial, educational, and research use of a university or college for its students and employees and others who are physically present at the library facilities. Therefore, public school personnel may do online research in subscription databases at these libraries. University libraries provide for the public computer searches of many resources from computers in off-campus locations, but resources in a number of databases that are useful within specific fields such as education have restrictions that limit off-site access to only those persons enrolled in or employed by the university. However, these databases may be accessed by the public via computer access in the library on campus, with the librarian's assistance.

Library websites list accessible databases for locating materials by keywords, title, author, publication type, date, or a combination of these. Using a combination of specific terms helps limit the number of resources returned as results for an online search. If the terms are too broad, you waste valuable time selecting relevant resources from a lengthy list of numerous publications. If search terms are too specific, you may not find enough resources. Experiment by searching a number of different keywords relevant to your topic to find the best resources. For a problem related to teaching students whose native language is not English, you might try "English as a second language," "English language learners" or an advanced search with "teaching" and "ESL" or "ELL."

Universities and colleges subscribe to online databases, including the most useful ones for education research, such as EBSCOhost, Dissertations and Theses, and JSTOR. Major universities also catalog free publications from the U.S. Department of Education. See Figure 2.1 on the Chapter Resources CD for a list of selected library databases.

EBSCOhost includes a variety of databases. The most relevant databases for education in EBSCOhost may be found in Academic Search Premier (a wide variety of publications for education and social sciences), ERIC (Education Resource Information Center, a major source for education resources including over 1,300,000 records and more than 23,000 full-text documents), Psychological and Behavioral Sciences Collection (topics in emotional and behavioral characteristics, psychiatry and psychology, mental processes, and observational and experimental methods), PsycINFO (abstracts of scholarly journal articles, book chapters, books, and dissertations, as well as the largest collection of peer-reviewed literature in behavioral science and mental health), Sociological Collection (areas of sociology, social behavior, human tendencies, interaction, relationships, culture, and social structure), and Teacher Reference Center (indexing and abstracts for 280 popular teacher and administrator journals and magazines). Dissertation and theses abstracts may be useful for locating current research on a topic.

JSTOR is an online database of scholarly journals, with 112 titles under Education in full text. You may browse contents of specific journals or use "Search keywords" to locate particular topics. Figure 2.1 in Chapter 2 CD Resources lists selected library databases.

Resources selected for a literature review should be from recognized authors or scholars with educational background or experience related to your research topic. Review available author and publisher information. There are many commercial databases online that charge a fee to access a resource, but my experience with these sources has not been productive when I have been searching for specific topics from recognized education publications or authors. Articles in peer-reviewed journals and publications have been reviewed by education personnel related to the topic before publication. Peer-reviewed journals and publications by education organizations or education-related state or federal government divisions are always appropriate sources. Table 2.2 and Table 2.3 list selected examples of sources from professional organizations, government sources, and other resource centers. A copy of these tables may be accessed on the CD under Chapter 2 Resources to save your time when searching for their publications.

You can search a large number of education topics on the Internet by entering the URL of a professional education association or organization—including those for subject content areas such as reading, mathematics, science, and others, or school administration and school levels. The URLs listed in Table 2.2 provide resource publications on a wide

Table 2.2
Examples of Professional Organizations with Student Achievement Resources

Access the electronic copy on the CD. Hold the cursor over the URL, hold down the CTRL key, and click to open. URLs change frequently. If the web page doesn't come up, enter the association name in a search engine such as Yahoo or Google to find the new location.

Abbreviation and URL		Name of Organization
AASA	http://www.aasa.org	American Association of School Administrators
AERA	http://www.aera.net	American Educational Research Association
ACTE	http://www.acteonline.org	Association for Career and Technical Education
ACEI	http://acei.org	Association for Childhood Education International
AMLE	http://amle.org/	Association for Middle Level Education
ASCD	http://www.ascd.org	Association for Supervision and Curriculum Development
CCSSO	http://ccsso.org	The Council of Chief State School Officers
SERGE	http://serge.ccsso.org/ organizations.html	Special Education Resources for General Educators
IRA	http://www.reading.org	International Reading Association
NAEYC	http://www.naeyc.org	National Association for the Education of Young Children
NAESP	http://www.naesp.org	National Association of Elementary School Principals
NASET	http://www.naset.org	National Association of Special Education Teachers
ISER	http://www.iser.com	Internet Special Education Resources
NASSP	http://www.nassp.org	National Association of Secondary School Principals
NCSS	http://www.socialstudies.org	National Council for the Social Studies
NCTE	http://www.ncte.org	National Council of Teachers of English
NCTM	http://www.nctm.org	National Council of Teachers of Mathematics
NMLTA	http://www.nmlsta.org/	National Middle Level Science Teachers Association
NSTA	http://www.nsta.org	National Science Teachers Association
UCEA	http://www.ucea.org	University Council for Educational Administration

variety of education topics. From the organization's home page, select tabs at the top or sidebars at the left that use terms such as Resources, Research, or Publications. Members of these organizations may have access to journal articles from these sites. However, many online publications are free to the public for full text in pdf or html format that allows you to view, save, and print the documents.

Explore a website to gain familiarity with the location of relevant resource material. For example, the Council for Chief State School Officers (CCSSO), a site that I frequently used for university courses, recently revised its home page. When I first searched the new site, I could find only abstracts because I failed to notice the designation *pdf* beside a title—above the abstract and between the author name and publication date. Clicking on the title revealed the complete research article in pdf format.

Table 2.3 shows sites for education research resources; several of these are linked with the U.S. Department of Education. Some centers are linked to major universities.

Table 2.4 provides a selected list of education journals, most of which are peer reviewed. Publication of a peer-reviewed article includes reviews and recommendations from three recognized colleagues in the field of study. Pay particular notice to the note under Table 2.4; it gives you a URL that takes you to an extensive list of online open-access journals in education. All of the resources and URLs shown in Tables 2.2, 2.3, and 2.4 also are embedded in the Chapter 2 Resources on the supplementary CD packaged with this text. Using the CD saves time in exploring these sites because you can click on the embedded URL for the site on the CD rather than keying it in.

Leads to other resources for a topic can be found by mining the reference list at the end of articles that you select. In addition, specific articles often can be found by entering the

Table 2.3
Examples of Government Educational Resources for Improving Student Achievement

Access the electronic copy on the CD. Hold the cursor over the URL, hold down the CTRL key, and click to open. URLs change frequently. If the web page doesn't come up, enter the agency or center name in a search engine such as Yahoo or Google to find the new location.

Abbreviation and URL		Agency or Center
ERIC	http://www.eric.ed.gov	Education Resources Information Center
ED.gov	http://www.ed.gov	U.S. Department of Education
ies	http://www.ies.ed.gov	Institute of Education Sciences
NCES	http://www.nces.ed.gov	National Center for Education Statistics
NEPC	http://nepc.colorado.edu	National Education Policy Center

What Works Clearinghouse
http://ies.ed.gov/ncee/wwc/reports/
http://ies.ed.gov/ncee/wwc/

Federal and Regional Resource Centers:

RRCP	http://www.rrcprogram.org/	Regional Resource Center Program

Regional Resource Center Programs:
MPRRC Mountain Plains Regional Resource Center (UT)
MSRRC Mid-South Regional Resource Center (KY)
NCRRC North Central Regional Resource Center (MN)
NERRC Northeast Regional Resource Center (VT)
SERRC Southeast Regional Resource Center (AL)
WRRC Western Regional Resource Center (OR)

Other Resource Centers:

The Access Center: Improving Outcomes for All Students K–8	http://www.k8accesscenter.org
Center for Early Literacy Learning	http://www.nectac.org
Center for Implementing Technology in Education	http://www.citeducation.org
Center on Positive Behavioral Interventions and Supports	http://www.pbis.org
The Early Childhood Outcomes Center	http://projects.fpg.unc.edu/~eco/index.cfm
National Center for Research on Rural Education	http://rrcprogram.org/wrrc
National Center on Educational Outcomes	http://www.nceo.info
National Center on Student Progress Monitoring	http://www.studentprogress.org
National Institute for Urban School Improvement	http://www.urbanschools.org

title, date, and author in the Search block of a research engine such as Yahoo. Further resources might come from an abstract, blog, or podcast linked to education-organization online sites. If you record information only from an abstract rather than from the full article or report, show this in the list of references by adding the word *[Abstract]* in brackets after the title. It is preferable to read the report or article, but abstracts may be included as a source (APA, 2010, p. 202). This same reference format is used for blogs, podcasts, wikis, and other types of electronic sources. Key in the type of resource in brackets after the title. Table 2.5 on the resources CD gives titles and URLs for additional online resources. Figure 2.2 on the CD suggests a few books that may be helpful education resources.

Table 2.4
Examples of Education Journal Resources for Improving Student Achievement

Access the electronic copy on the CD. Place the cursor over the URL, hold down the shift key, and click to open. URLs change frequently. If the web page doesn't come up, enter the name in a search engine such as Yahoo or Google to find the new location.

Journal Title	URL	Sponsor
Education Leaders:		
AASA Journal of Scholarship and Practice	http://www.aasa.org	*AASA*
American Educational Research Journal	http://aerj.aera.net	*AERA*
Education Review	http://edrev.info	*NEPC*
Education Week (Education weekly news)	http://www.edweek.org	
Educational Administration Quarterly	http://eaq.sagepub.com/	*UCEA*
Educational Evaluation and Policy Analysis	http://epa.sagepub.com/	*AERA*
Educational Leadership	http://www.ascd.org	*ASCD*
Educational Researcher	http://edr.sagepub.com/	*AERA*
Journal of Educational and Behavioral Statistics	http://jeb.sagepub.com/	*AERA*
Journal of Cases in Educational Leadership	http://jel.sagepub.com/	*UCEA*
NASSP Bulletin	http://www.principals.org/KnowledgeCenter.aspx	*NASSP*
Phi Delta Kappan	http://www.kappanmagazine.org/	*PDK*
Access My Library: Education	http://www.accessmylibrary.com/subject/education	
Principal	http://www.naesp.org	*NAESP*
Principal Leadership	http://www.principals.org/KnowledgeCenter.aspx	*NASSP*
Principal's Research Review	http://www.principals.org/KnowledgeCenter.aspx	*NASSP*
Review of Educational Research	http://rer.sagepub.com/	*AERA*
Review of Research in Education	http://rre.sagepub.com/	*AERA*
Career/Technical Education:		
Career and Technical Education Research	http://scholar.lib.vt.edu/ejournals/CTER	*CTER*
English/Language Arts:		
Language Arts (Elementary)	http://www.ncte.org/journals	*NCTE*
School Talk (Elementary)	http://www.ncte.org/journals	*NCTE*
English Journal (High School)	http://www.ncte.org/journals	*NCTE*
English Leadership Quarterly (High School)	http://www.ncte.org/journals	*NCTE*
Voices from the Middle	http://www.ncte.org/journals	*NCTE*
Mathematics Education:		
Mathematics Teacher	http://www.nctm.org	*NCTM*
Mathematics Teaching in the Middle School	http://www.nctm.org	*NCTM*
Journal of Research in Mathematics Education	http://www.nctm.org	*NCTM*
Special Education:		
Journal of the American Academy of Special Education Professionals	http://www.naset.org/777.0.html	*NASET*
Science Education:		
Science and Children	http://www.nsta.org	*NSTA*
Science Scope	http://www.nsta.org	*NSTA*
Science Teacher (The)	http://www.nsta.org	*NSTA*

Note. A list of open-access journals in education may also be found online at http://www.ergobservatory.info/ejdirectory.html by the Scholarly Communications Unit of the Center for Educational Research for Global Sustainability at Arizona State University, Tempe, AZ.

Recording and Identifying Resources

Before starting to read the resources, members of the literature review team should agree on a consistent format, as well as on the types of information to be recorded for each review. Time will be saved writing the literature review if all necessary information is consistently formatted, clear, and complete. You may want to use the many reference lists in this text at the end of chapters and the example reports as a pattern to follow for formatting references from similar types of resources.

Figure 2.3 (only on the CD under Chapter 2 Resources) provides an electronic worksheet that each literature review team member may open and save to a storage device (USB, CD, DVD, or other mobile storage device). The worksheet can then be opened and used on the reviewer's computer to record essential reference data for each resource selected for the literature review. The worksheet is divided into separate sections for common types of resources: print or electronic books or monographs, chapters or sections in a book or monograph, online or print periodicals, technical and research reports, symposia or conference reports, dissertations and theses, and audiovisual media such as a motion picture, video, podcast, video blog post, or television-series episode. Each section illustrates from one to three APA-style examples and has blank space below the examples for you to record your literature review references. A vast amount of time will be saved if each team member completes the recording of literature source information while gathering the information rather than later trying to find that source again. Having this worksheet, or the required reference information otherwise completed with all elements in a consistent format at the time that you review each resource, and attaching this information to your notes from that source, will enable you to complete the literature review in less time and with less stress. Believe me (and, sadly, I know from personal experience), going back to find the resources to complete a reference list after completion of the written review gobbles hours of time.

One individual will combine each team member's resource information into one list of references to be placed at the end of the action research report. This person may review Figure 2.4 on the CD with time-saving ideas labeled "Tips for Transferring Resource Data to a Reference List." When the literature-review resources are completed by each reviewer, rekeying each entry on the computer becomes unnecessary.

Team members reviewing resources from online articles you have printed may prefer underlining passages on these pages rather than composing handwritten or computer-generated notes important to the study. Usually, you can select a page that is visible on your screen by selecting "current page" instead of "all" on the print menu. To print a selected series of page numbers, note the beginning page number and ending page number shown at the bottom of your screen, and enter these two numbers (separated with a hyphen) on your print function. After the pages print, add highlighting or clearly mark the relevant sections. Note a few brief sentences or phrases that would be good quotes, and record the source page number. Instead of printing, you may be able to scan pdf formats or use the copy-and-paste option to print selected pages or parts of a page to use as notes as a resource for writing the review if the resource page opens in your word-processing software. In addition to collecting pages electronically saved, marked, or printed for use, add your notes summarizing relevant information in your own words and save this or print it, making sure to note the resource author and abbreviated title in a header or footer on these summary pages. Your document summary of notes and the complete reference information that was keyed in on Figure 2.3 (APA Resource Information) should be put together so that it can be shared with your team members.

Reviewing multiple reference lists at the end of each chapter, as well as action research report examples, may serve to illustrate information and the formatting of reference list data to be included when following APA style. Also, you may refer to Figure 2.5 (located on the CD only) for additional formatting notes on punctuation, spacing, or italics. For further information on APA style, refer to the most recent edition of the *Publication Manual of the American Psychological Association*. For online help, go to http://www.apastyle.org/manual/index.aspx

Your first reading of a selected resource is generally a quick scan of the contents to get a general overview and determine which parts relate to topics for your research questions. Once you decide on the topics of interest for your research, go back and reread all parts that help you understand the purpose of the article and major points of interest for answering research questions or making recommendations relevant to your research problem. Note any specific data that support or raise questions about these conclusions.

Most of your notes will paraphrase information obtained from a source. Because the concepts came from a specific resource, you must cite the author's last name and date at least once in each paragraph that includes any part of this information. Your goal is to make clear the source of this particular content, even in parts of the report that synthesize content into paragraphs describing related topics from all sources. APA style citations include the author's name and date within parentheses in the text. After the author's last name, add the page number if you are quoting specific text. Complete location information for each citation will be compiled alphabetically on a list of references at the end of the research report.

Haller and Kleine (2001) emphasize that practitioners have neither the time nor the need to know everything that has been discovered about a problem. Instead, they need a subset of knowledge that adds to what they already know from their background and experience and that helps them think intelligently about the problem. For a strong literature review, use a variety of sources. Also, read the resource material closely enough to assure that the summary notes that you record accurately reflect the author's meaning. If you find another source contradicting that study, do not ignore it; report that source also, and briefly discuss the differences.

Be selective in choosing notes for the written review. Include only those areas directly or indirectly helpful for understanding and addressing your research problem. The most helpful items will be those that discuss causes of the problem and describe practices for improvement. Items that address instructional practices, student learning barriers, school climate or school procedures, and characteristics of persons most affected by the problem may be helpful. For example, if you are researching a question about improving learning in a particular subject area and find instructional practices that have shown success in this area, you may want to clearly describe what was done in instruction (such as activities involving curriculum, time and methods for teaching the major areas, and evidence of learning) in a paragraph or two in your own words. Use quotes sparingly, and place quote marks around the quoted material. In your notes that include a quote from a source, note the author's last name and the page number beside the quote, or otherwise make this information clear in your notes. Always clearly mark the quote with quotation marks.

For articles that you read online at your computer, you can also open a blank word processing page for your summary notes, along with Figure 2.3 for recording the source information. With the article, Figure 2.3, and your document page for notes all opened, you can switch from one file to another by clicking the file name at the bottom of the screen to access each file as needed while reading the article online and recording source information for the reference list. Keeping multiple documents open at the same time and clicking on the different file names when referring back and forth among the documents saves valuable time.

LITERATURE REVIEW DEVELOPMENT

Results from previous research do not guarantee the same results in another school (Haller & Kleine, 2001). However, this knowledge forms a foundation for further investigation through other qualitative and quantitative research (Johnson, 2008; Ling Pan, 2004; & Mills, 2011). Your literature review builds a foundation for your action research.

Once all notes for a literature review have been completed, these should be organized by topics that can be developed as a synthesized summary of information important to your research questions. This is a time to reflect on what was learned from the literature by thinking about new ideas gained and questions raised that may need additional literature searches. After multiple readers and note-takers have reviewed the literature, now is the time for them to collaborate electronically or personally to reflect, organize the notes, and decide how they will develop, assess, and edit the written review.

Organizing Topics

At this point, you are organizing literature notes in big thought categories. Compare the major topics covered in the research notes with the research questions. This step should help you change or refine wording of the research questions, if needed. You should consider also whether there are important components of the questions that are not answered. Ask whether these missing components are important to the study and whether information about them can be found in publications. If so, search again for topics related to missing components to see whether something helpful can be found.

Next, consider the organization and format of the literature review. The literature review will become one of the major sections for the final report of your action research and, as such, should begin with a first-level heading centered in title format (with bold type and uppercase and lowercase letters) if you are using APA format. The literature section may be titled *Literature Review* or *Review of Literature.*

The introductory paragraph or paragraphs that follow immediately after the literature review first-level heading serve as an overview or introduction to the review. There is no other title or subheading before these opening paragraphs, nor do the words *Overview* or *Introduction* precede these beginning paragraphs. In writing reports, remember that at least one paragraph of content should follow each heading or subheading. Also, divide content under subheadings only if you will have at least two subheadings on the same level.

The introductory content for the literature review may include a statement or two about the type of search that you conducted and the types of resources reviewed. A sentence or paragraph might list the major topics covered in your literature review for this study and may describe why they are important for addressing your research problem. Unless you examined the big picture for this school problem in the opening problem statement that will be the first section of your final action research report, a discussion of the prevalence of the research problem and its effects on student learning statewide or nationally may be added to the paragraphs that begin the literature review.

These suggestions about the content to consider in introducing the literature review may help you choose content for writing introductory paragraphs for the review. However, before writing the introduction to that review, you may find it easier first to write the body of the report that covers information describing what was learned from the literature review about your school problem.

The main body of content for the literature review will describe details of what was learned from the major topics that you researched, and the closing portion should summarize the most important things learned that serve to inform and improve the problem. This organizational pattern for the literature review begins with opening paragraphs that introduce the review, followed by the main body of the literature review discussion about what was learned that informs your research problem. The literature review closes with a summary of major points that are most relevant to your research questions.

Using Headings and Subheadings

Most subheadings within the literature review will be second-level headings. In the main body of the literature review, the content that describes details of information gleaned from the review of literature will fall under major-topic second-level subheadings in bold font, uppercase and lowercase title format, beginning at the left margin. The first paragraph under a secondary subheading begins a double space below the subheading (whether the report as a whole is double-spaced or single-spaced).

Decisions about the organization and content of the main body of the literature review begin by identifying, from your literature review notes, approximately three to five major content topics that have the potential for contributing to understanding and analysis of the research problem. These content topics become second-level subheadings for the body of the literature review. Content under each of the subheadings will be a synthesis of information from all literature reviewed that both relates to the particular subheading topic and has relevance for answering your research questions.

If you subdivide content under second-level subheadings because it is extensive and would be better understood if divided into at least two subheadings, describe this content under two or more third-level subheadings. Third-level subheadings for APA style begin the first word with a capital letter, but other words in this subheadiing are lower-case unless they are proper nouns that should be capitalized. Use bold font, and begin third-level headings at the indented paragraph point rather than at the left margin. A period immediately follows the last word of the third-level subheading, and the first sentence of the paragraph begins one space after the period on the same line with the indented subheading.

The last second-level subheading of the literature review will be called *Summary* or *Conclusions*. Under this subheading, briefly summarize the most important knowledge gained from the literature that helps answer one or more of your research questions.

Action research literature reviews focus on specific information helpful in understanding and addressing a school research problem. Such reviews serve practitioners in a specific work setting by helping them to understand a problem and to develop expertise in applying research to improve practices that help advance the goal of high achievement for each student.

Both theoretical and action research purposes can help guide teaching and learning, as well as student achievement, but action research is briefer and more specific to a work setting than theoretical research is. Therefore, action research is useful for problem solving and improving organizational processes and practices in that setting. Theoretical research usually takes place in university settings and seeks to establish the probability of truths about universal problems, thus expanding the ability to transfer this knowledge to understand similar problems that are studied in similar contexts. Expectations regarding the transfer of theoretical research with similar results in similar contexts come about through replicating the research methodology applied in the same way in numerous similar settings. This replication improves accuracy and predictability for similar results in other similar contexts. Action research does not presuppose the transfer of results to other settings, but supports improvements in a particular setting.

Formatting and Referencing

Formatting for a research report or article as described in APA style uses double-spacing throughout to make the publication easier to read and edit because research papers are often published. Therefore, a research article submitted for publication uses a double-spaced format to make editing and coding for final copy easier to add and then converts to a single-spaced printed publication. Schools seem always to have tight budgets, so single-spacing with double-spacing between paragraphs may be chosen to reduce copying costs. Single-spacing may be appropriate for the final report of your research, which should be widely distributed to faculty and staff and to other appropriate school and community groups. The example action research reports are single-spaced in this text. However, the example reports on the supplementary CD only are double-spaced. Either format may be used as a guide.

APA format for the title of a report or article for publication requires a title that lets the reader know the area of study. The title is not bold-type font but uses regular-type font and title case (with uppercase and lowercase letters) and is horizontally centered at the top of the first page of the report. APA style was followed in Chapter 1 for developing the problem statement and the research questions. The literature review is the first part of the report that has a major-division first-level centered title and is also the section most likely to need second-level and even third-level subheadings. The example action research reports in this text at the end of Part 4 illustrate the use of APA style for headings and subheadings.

Figure 2.6 illustrates the first-level section heading for the literature review, the types of content covered for introductory paragraphs, second-level subheadings, and the types of content covered in paragraphs that follow. Such an outline is a plan for the content of a literature review.

Other formatting guidelines pertain to citations for resources within the manuscript text and an alphabetical reference list that goes at the end of the report, with full information on each resource cited within the report. Most of these citations will be from the literature review section of the document, but some also may be added to support the Conclusions and Recommendations section, which is the last major section of the action

---

A Draft Outline: Postsecondary Reading Remediation of High School Graduates
Literature Review *(first-level heading)*

Introductory paragraphs have no subheading. Paragraph content begins immediately after the centered first-level section heading. For a study of reading remediation, content might cover a lack of reading-improvement focus in high school core courses, the influence of a lack of reading proficiency on student self-esteem and successful achievement, and a need for regular practice of reading strategies to improve secondary students' reading proficiencies.

Reading Improvement Strategies

Second-level subheadings begin at the left margin and precede paragraphs discussing the next content topics in the body of the report. Unless each discussion is lengthy, these topics would not have subheadings. If the content needs to be divided into text with at least two third-level subheads, the subheads would begin at the paragraph point, followed by a period, and the content for each subsection would begin one space after the period, with succeeding lines wrapping back to the left margin.

Word Recognition and Comprehension

Assume that this section has enough detailed content to divide into two third-level subheads. Then the paragraphs under this second-level subheading would give an overview of the content covered. Third-level subheads begin at the paragraph point and end with a period, as illustrated by the two-third level headings that follow.

Word recognition and content comprehension. Paragraphs under this third-level subheading could include content that examines interactive strategies for word recognition, such as using a word wall and the Frayer model.

Another paragraph might discuss phonemic awareness and word decoding, as well as strategies for developing these skills.

Comprehension and fluency. This third-level subheading may present skills that help students understand what they read, such as practice for critical reading, guided practice with oral reading, and feedback to develop fluency.

Reading and Self-Esteem Issues

Paragraphs under this second-level subheading may cover encouragement for reading success and how it may influence self-esteem.

Summary

Closing paragraphs synthesize the literature with the most relevance for your research questions.

Figure 2.6.   **Example format and topical plan for a literature review. Plan the content of your literature review before you begin to write. This outline was adapted from an action research report completed in a high school by Janet Sivis-O'Connell, CEO Coordinator and Social Studies Teacher. Used with permission.**

research report. Figure 2.5 and Figure 2.7 on the CD give additional format information about the use of APA style for the reference list at the end of the action research report and also for in-text citations that refer to resources on the reference list. Examples throughout the text and CD resources illustrate in-text citations, different-level headings, and formatting for references. APA formatting for each section of action research reports and their component sections can be reviewed in the example action research reports, as well as in examples within chapters and CD resources. Your school library may have a copy of the sixth edition of the APA publication manual, which describes these formats in detail. If APA format is required for your report and this manual is not in the school library, you may order a copy at http://www.apa.org/pubs/books/4200066.aspx. Examples in this chapter of the APA style for wording in-text citations and references illustrate the most commonly used types of resource publications.

Giving proper credit to resources for materials used in writing is part of professional ethics and also a legal matter for material under copyright. Each member of the literature review team may need to review rules for citations within the text of a paper, as shown on Figure 2.7 under Chapter 2 Resources on the CD. All persons writing parts of the literature review will want to follow the same style that is established for all citations in the action research report. Because these illustrations are on the CD, they are easy for you to print and refer to while writing notes during the review and later when you are finalizing the literature-review section of your research report. The citations illustrated are consistent with the *Publication Manual of the American Psychological Association* (APA, 2010, 6th edition).

Collaborating, Writing, and Editing

Now you are ready to write a draft of the literature review. Your first decision will be to determine the best way to get a comprehensive draft of the literature review written, reviewed, and edited. One approach would be to have a single author collaborate with the other team members who recorded notes from the resources. Another would be to divide the writing tasks among members of the team, who each agree to write a portion of the review, with one member bringing their work together and making all changes necessary for a clear, coherent, and well-organized literature review draft.

Some teams may choose to meet and jointly write the first draft. However, in my experience of working with evaluation teams, joint writing by a team is a slow, laborious process. I have found that teamwork is more efficient when each person completes a part of the task and others review it for suggested changes. All members can then review a changed draft for final approval. Writing is a complex process, and different writers often have various preferences for wording, organization, and edits. Joint writing in a group setting increases the complexity of an already complex task.

All persons who work on the literature review should have an opportunity to review and make content or editing suggestions. These changes can be brought together by one person into a revised copy. The word-processing software tool for tracking changes by multiple individuals is useful for multiple team members to work on the draft of the initial document to make changes and comments. If the same copy of the document goes to one person for computer edits and comments and then is sent electronically to the next person for additional changes and comments, and so on, until all team members review it, each person's comments will appear identified by different colors and names on the consolidated document. Again, one individual could review all of these and develop a second draft for review. Google docs could also be used for reviewing and changing of the document by selected persons.

Certain collaborative-writing strategies (New Century College, n.d.) can help make group work more effective. First, be sure that everyone understands what is to be done and agrees on the major components of the task. Discuss writing style and documentation, and divide the tasks among group members but emphasize that all members share responsibility for the final product. Double-check information from sources, and be sure to cite correctly all resources used. Integrate all parts into a coherent whole. Galvan (2006) emphasizes the need for drafting, reviewing, and redrafting content. Editing involves checking for clarity, word choice, sentence construction, format details, and writing mechanics. Recognition within the school and district should be given to all who carry out the various research responsibilities.

OTHER KNOWLEDGE SOURCES

In an era of school accountability for high achievement by every child, documentation increases in importance. Accountability calls for evidence of the learning that takes place to meet national and state standards and progress benchmarks. With technology resources, state departments of education have developed and made available large databases of information about each public school (Johnson, 1999). These databases include information about every student in every classroom in a state. This provides almost an overload of quantitative data accessible within a district and school. School-data reporting is a big part of accountability to the public but becomes valuable as a tool for improving learning only when accessed—and appropriately summarized and interpreted—as a basis for school improvement.

Literature research gives a background of information that has been previously studied and documented about education, teaching, and learning. After you complete the literature review for action research, your next action research step will be to look back at the initial problem statement that you drafted as introductory paragraphs at the end of Chapter 1 and identify school data that can be added to strengthen that statement by providing specific evidence of the school status related to the identified problem. This may be trend data. For example, if the problem relates to achievement in a specific area, data for the past three years in relation to expectations show an ongoing problem. If the problem relates to student disciplinary actions, school documentation of the number of actions over a specified period and an approximate calculation of missed hours of instruction would provide evidence of the importance of the problem. Likewise, your literature review may have revealed state or national statistics that can be added to the problem statement or the introductory paragraphs of the literature review to show the extent of the problem in the big picture. Figure 2.8 (located on the CD in Chapter 2 Resources) shows an example of school trend data added as graphs to the beginning of the problem statement and research questions.

Now, reflect on information from your literature review to see whether there were topics of importance to the problem that the initial guiding questions did not cover. These broad areas may need to be added as an additional question or as changes to the research questions. These changes will be important when you make decisions in Chapter 3 about data collection needs, data sources, and research methodology. Your guiding questions should reflect all of the major categories needed to address improvement of the research problem.

Action research is interpretive. It doesn't rely on statistical formulas to answer the research questions. It relies on interpretation that uses the logical thinking of experienced, knowledgeable persons, along with multiple data sources, to make data-based decisions about change. Chapters 3 and 4 in Part 2 will guide identification of additional data needs and data collection.

Key Questions for Review

1. What is the main purpose of reviewing literature and gathering data through action research?
2. How are guiding questions used in your literature search and data collection?
3. What information should the introductory paragraphs of the literature review cover?

4. Where on the page are first- and second-level headings set in APA format, and why is it important to follow a consistent style within the research report for headings, subheadings, and references?
5. What content should be covered in the concluding paragraphs of a literature review?

Note. **Performance Checklist will also appear on CD.**

Performance Checklist for Step 2a Research Activities

You will complete Step 2a of action research, gathering current knowledge that adds to your understanding of the research school problem. A checklist of suggested actions for completion follows each activity.

A. Draft a literature review that briefly summarizes current knowledge relevant to the problem, including resource citations and a list of references.

Performance Check:

1. For a literature-review team, select teachers, administrators, or other staff who have interest, knowledge, and experience with the research problem. I suggest including a representative from the research leadership team to also be a literature-review team member. Have literature-review team members study the material in this chapter before organizing and planning the literature review.
2. Hold an organizational meeting of the literature review team for the purpose of agreeing on the team's tasks and preferred mode of collaboration during reviews, as well

as who will finalize the report and how it will be finalized. On the basis of their current knowledge and experience, the team should also brainstorm a list of potential topics to better understand the problem and that have potential for literature searches.
3. Select literature that provides information from research and best practices and that is related to topics generated from your guiding questions and primary research question. Gather pertinent information, including information required for giving credit to sources with in-text citations and a list of references for each different source listed.

B. Refine the literature review draft for the action research report.

Performance Check:

1. Circulate the literature review draft to the literature review team for electronic review. The draft should be checked for content and organization (accuracy, logic, thought flow, and clarity of meaning), wording

refinement (eliminating unnecessary words or phrases, and increasing active verb use), and formatting consistency (headings, in-text citations, and reference list). This task will be easier if team members divide up the different editing tasks rather than having all members edit everything. It is difficult to edit for everything at the same time.

2. Set a time schedule for completion of all reviews and for the final draft. Each team member's acceptance of responsibility for the final report will improve the process. File a copy of the final literature review in the research file.

C. Review the problem statement and research questions for additions or changes.

Performance Check:

1. Reflect on what was learned, and suggest changes to the problem statement, if necessary, to incorporate information from the literature review or specific school data that conveys the importance of the problem. The review of literature may have revealed the prevalence of the problem nationally. If so, this would be a good addition for the opening statement to show the widespread

extent of the problem before discussing the importance of the problem for student learning in your school.

2. Review available data from your school or state database that relate to the research problem. If there is quantitative data that shows existence of the problem over time or the degree of the problem, consider adding these data, either in descriptive numbers within statements or in a descriptive table to show either trends over multiple years or the severity of the problem. These additions to opening paragraphs of the problem statement or literature review help to make a clear case for the importance of the data to your school.

3. Review the data added to the literature review illustrated in Figure 2.8 on the CD under Chapter 2 Resources as you consider the need for additions to your school's problem statement. If change is needed, make a draft of the revised problem statement and research questions. Circulate the revised draft for review by persons directly involved, as well as by the leadership team. File the initial draft with returned comments until completion of Chapter 3 before you prepare a final draft.

References

Alexander, P. A., & Judy, J. E. (1988). The interaction of domain-specific and strategic knowledge in academic performance. *Review of Educational Research, 58,* 375–404.

American Psychological Association (APA). (2010). *Publication manual of the American Psychological Association.* Washington, DC: Author.

Educational Leadership Policy Standards ISLLC 2008, as adopted by the National Policy Board for Educational Administration. Washington, DC: The Council of Chief State School Officers. Retrieved from http://www.ccsso.org/publications.

Galvan, J. L. (2006). *Writing literature reviews* (3rd ed.). Glendale, CA: Pyrczak Publishing.

Haller, E. J., & Kleine, P. F. (2001). *Using educational research: An administrator's guide.* New York: Longman.

Hmelo, C. E., Nagarajan, A., & Day, R. S. (2000, Fall). Effects of high and low prior knowledge on construction of a joint problem space. The *Journal of Experimental Education, 69*(1), Learning with peers: Multiple perspectives on collaboration, 35–56.

Hunter, M. (1990). Preface: Thoughts on staff development. In B. Joyce (Ed.), *Changing school culture through staff development* (pp. xi–xiv). Yearbook of the Association for Supervision and Curriculum Development. Alexandria, VA: ASCD.

Johnson, A. P. (2008). *A short guide to action research* (3rd ed.). Boston: Pearson.

Johnson, E. (1999, Spring). Reform in teacher education: The response to accountability is collaboration. *Education, 119*(3), 381–388.

Ling Pan, M. (2004). *Qualitative and quantitative approaches: Preparing literature reviews* (2nd ed.). Glendale, CA: Pyrczak Publishing.

Mills, G. E. (2011). *Action research: A guide for the teacher researcher* (4th ed.). Boston: Pearson.

New Century College. (n.d.). Collaborative writing, *Online writing guide for students,* George Mason University, Fairfax, VA. Retrieved by selecting *collaboration* from http://classweb.gmu.edu/nccwg/collab.htm.

State Consortium for Education Leadership. (2008). *Performance expectations and indicators for school leaders: An ISLLC-based guide to implementing leader standards and a companion guide to the Educational Leadership Policy Standards: ISLLC 2008.* Washington, DC: The Council of Chief State School Officers. Retrieved from http://www.ccsso.org/.

Vescio, V., Ross, D., & Adams, A. (2006). *A review of research on professional learning communities: What do we need to know?* Paper presented at the NSRF Research Forum held January.

PART TWO

Identifying and Collecting Research Data

The steps outlined in Part 2 begin after you have identified and described a student-achievement related problem, conducted and drafted a literature review as a knowledge base for studying the problem, and refined the problem statement and research questions. Part 2 takes this research to its most interesting phase: planning and collecting original data from your work setting.

This phase involves more of your school personnel in action research than have been directly involved to this point. Members of your school community—administrators, faculty members, support staff, students, parents, and other community representatives—become expert sources of information for investigating related data, possible causes, and potential remedies. Chapter 3 covers the essentials of sources and types of data, identification of data needs, and primary data-collection instruments. Chapter 4 guides you in collecting data from records and reports, summarizing and analyzing quantitative data, and preparing data tables and figures.

Purpose and Outcomes for Part 2

Part 2 takes you through completion of data identification and data collection for Action Research Step 2b on Table 1.1 and begins interpretation tasks for Research Step 2c.

1. Determine data-collection needs, data sources, and instrumentation types that respond to research questions.
2. Develop data-collection instruments and procedures.
3. Field test data instruments and make final revisions.
4. Complete data collection.
5. Summarize data and prepare data displays in tables and figures.

In-School Performance Activities

Chapter 3

1. Inventory data needs, data sources, and data-collection procedures for each research question, and identify multiple data types and sources for each guiding question.
2. Develop data-collection instruments and procedures for use.

Chapter 4
1. Field test and revise instruments or procedures as indicated.
2. Complete data collection and begin summary of results.
3. Develop tables and figures for visual displays and comparisons.

CHAPTER 3

Data-Informed Decision Making

Streifer (2002, p. 8) defines *data-driven decision making* as "the process of selecting, gathering, and analyzing data to address school improvement for student achievement and acting on those findings." That is what you will be doing in Chapter 3 through Chapter 7: selecting data relevant to the problem, gathering data already available, collecting new data, and analyzing data as a basis for school improvement. Action research applies data-informed decision making to school problems in order to improve student learning.

DATA IDENTIFICATION AND SELECTION

Today's schools have more data than ever before from federal, state, and district databases. Sometimes, the volume and variety become almost overwhelming. In this age of technology and accountability, sources of available school data can be expected to continue increasing, along with ease of data access through mobile and collaborative technology.

Recently, a study by the Center on Education Policy (Dietz, 2010) identified a trend toward more high school testing. This study showed an increase in the number of states that are replacing one comprehensive high school mathematics and English exam with an end-of-course test for each of these subject areas. In addition, more states are using a high school exit exam. Also, the number of states requiring students to take college admission exams or a workplace-readiness test is increasing, as is the number of states requiring some kind of portfolio assessment or senior project.

Conducting action research helps you use data effectively to monitor and improve student achievement and school operational processes that affect learning. Action research systematically follows a process that involves school personnel and others in the school community for periodic selection and review of student achievement problems.

After identification of the priority area of concern and research questions, action researcher-practitioners, working with others in the school community, use the research questions as a guide to collaboratively develop a statement of the problem and how it affects student learning. The research questions and the problem statement focus the selection and collection of data necessary to analyze causes and potential solutions. Using their experiential and educational backgrounds, along with what they have learned from literature describing other researchers' results with problems and settings similar to those of your school, school practitioners and stakeholders select available data relevant to the problem, identify additional data collection needs, and logically analyze the data, applying their knowledge to solve the problem.

Both instructional methods and schoolwide processes and procedures can become barriers to learning for some students. Policies regarding student activities, attendance, disciplinary actions, learning support initiatives, teacher recruitment and hiring practices, and professional development opportunities name a few school operation procedures that affect teaching and learning and, therefore, may be areas for examination if they appear to be barriers to learning.

Accountability for achievement emphasizes state and national testing, as well as comparison with international test results. The U.S. Department of Education has an ED Data Express website (http://www.eddataexpress.ed.gov/index.cfm) that profiles educational data for the 50 states, the District of Columbia, and Puerto Rico. This site lets you view a variety of data elements across all states and the nation and create tables with selected states and data elements. *Education Week* has the Education Counts database, with 250 state-level K–12 indicators, at http://www.edweek.org/rc/2007/06/07/edcounts. html. Or you could use a search engine like Yahoo, Bing, or Google and enter the words *education counts database* to find it if the current online location were to change.

School Data Sources

Over the past decade, state departments of education have begun posting on their websites information that summarizes achievement data by state, district, and school levels. In some cases, state and school subject-area or accountability test data are available on worksheets or graphs.

Districts and individual schools receive their student achievement data in a protected digital format, categorized by subgroups of student characteristics, subject content areas, and even skill areas within subjects. Confidentiality of information linked to student names must be protected but accessible to professional personnel responsible for analyzing data and planning learning improvements for students.

In addition to compiling student achievement test data at the state level, schools have other annual school measures reflected on public school report cards. The information from these measures shows schoolwide data. Also, achievement data such as state tests and other data include the results of the Comprehensive Test of Basic Skills (CTBS), National Assessment of Educational Progress (NAEP), and state accountability measures. School report card items include such data as number of graduates, dropout percentages, attendance rate, retention rate, graduate follow-up data for employment or further education, teachers teaching in their degree major or minor, teacher participation in content-focused professional development, computer resources, school policies, parental involvement, and spending per student.

School districts or schools also maintain records for disciplinary actions such as office referrals and suspensions (in school as well as out of school), grade-level retentions, attendance, and extracurricular activities. Add to these data types further detailed records available within a school on instruction and student achievement scores on formative classroom assessments.

Your next action research step is to identify specific data needs for each research guiding question. Using data for the purpose of making school improvements requires that you focus on data types, data sources, and data-collection procedures that address the school problem and research questions. In the identification of data needs, you may continue to modify or add to the research questions and problem statements. Also, you should search for additional data if, after data collection, the research questions are not sufficiently addressed. The focused purpose of action research—for improvement in a school setting—permits necessary adjustments and changes throughout the process if those adjustments improve accuracy and clarity of research results.

Research Data Types

For research purposes, types of data include *quantitative* numerical measurements and statistics, and *qualitative* perceptual information gained from stakeholders' knowledge and interpretation of an issue or problem. School records and reports, as well as written policies and procedures, are the documentation history of school accomplishments, actions, and events. These historical records include both quantitative numbers and qualitative perceptual or process data.

Traditional academic research uses statistical tests of quantitative data for its findings and conducts statistical tests to interpret data and build confidence in the results. Qualitative research analysis relies primarily on the logical interpretation of spoken and written words by practitioners familiar with the problem and its context, but also on the interpretation of descriptive quantitative data. Action research uses descriptive statistics to summarize and compare numerical data presented in visual displays for the purposes of interpretation.

Using more than one data type and multiple data instruments and sources to answer the research questions adds to qualitative research integrity. The research term for using data from multiple sources to aid data interpretation accuracy is data *triangulation*. This procedure and others that promote integrity and trustworthiness of results are covered in Chapter 4 in the discussion of research methodology.

Bernhardt (2004, p. 21) classifies types of school data into four broad categories: student learning, school processes, demographics, and perceptions. Data types and sources of data do not divide neatly and completely into separate categories. Data types and sources overlap partially when categorized. However, category groupings serve as organizers for different ways of thinking about data division possibilities. In this section, data categories follow Bernhardt's grouping, with the addition of records and reports.

The purpose of detailing examples of available school data, organized by category, is to stimulate your awareness of the varied data choices available to schools for action research. Literature on action research uses the terms *trustworthiness* and *credibility* to describe measures of integrity for qualitative research methods (Kincheloe, 1991; Lincoln & Guba, 1985). As you plan your methodology for data collection, keep in mind the importance of data interpretation from multiple data types, data sources, and data-collection methods that build credibility and trustworthiness of research results and gain buy-in for implementation. In this sense, research is like detective work. You are looking for clues. One source does not usually provide enough evidence for you to reach a conclusion with the reasonable degree of certainty necessary for useful improvement action. Evidence becomes stronger as other sources substantiate it or weaker when other evidence refutes it. Your study seeks the most accurate results to support actions for change.

Examining evidence over time (trend data), using different types of data, and incorporating different data sources for each guiding question allow data comparisons and contrasts of data interpretation from multiple sources for each question. Thus, you can decide whether assertions from the data support valid findings. If you get mixed results, search further, examining other data that relate to the primary question or guiding questions. This will improve the trustworthiness of your data for sound conclusions and useful interpretations. The data-collection process should continue until either your initial data interpretation or an alternative interpretation has reasonable support. The major criteria for judging when you have reached the level of reasonable support are your experience and knowledge of teaching and learning, the multiple influences on learning, and information gained from the literature review for this problem. The more knowledge you have about the problem and the stronger support you find from multiple sources for decisions, based on your research data, the greater likelihood there is that your interpretation and conclusions from the research will result in positive change.

STUDENT LEARNING DATA. School personnel are familiar with student achievement data, particularly as the data relate to test data, levels of proficiency, and state and federal accountability standards. Terms for levels of proficiency vary from state to state and usually range in number from four to six. The following examples typify proficiency levels:

California: Far Below Basic, Below Basic, Proficient, Advanced

Kentucky: Novice, Apprentice, Proficient, Distinguished

Ohio: Limited, Basic, Proficient, Accelerated, Advanced

States measure district and school academic achievement and categorize schools by levels of progress toward meeting state standards. The national No Child Left Behind legislation requires Adequate Yearly Progress (AYP) measures for subgroups of students in basic areas. End-of-course tests, school graduation exit exams, and college entrance and work-skills tests provide other sources of student achievement quantitative data.

Student learning achievement in schools extends beyond test results to include portfolio ratings or descriptors of student performance such as community service, athletics, and school organization leadership. Although service, leadership, and portfolio records may be quantified as descriptive numeric data that can be counted, averaged, and summarized, these types of records also provide qualitative interpretations.

SCHOOL PROCESSES DATA.   *School processes* include such information as procedures, policies, finances, curricula, staffing, instructional practices, school support services, teacher and administrator preparation and proficiency, school environment, school climate, parental and community involvement, and physical facilities. Such items are part of school operations that generate a variety of record and report documents with both qualitative and quantitative data. Examples of process data include financial reports, safety records, faculty and student handbooks, student suspensions or other disciplinary actions, transportation records, and faculty and staff professional development records.

In response to teacher quality federal legislation and state policies, school records and reports, as well as many state websites, show teacher data such as the number of teachers in a school who teach in the area of teacher preparation, who hold advanced educational degrees, and who have National Board Certification. Teacher data may include years of teaching experience and teacher retention or turnover rate for the school.

DEMOGRAPHIC DATA.   *Webster's Ninth New Collegiate Dictionary* (1989, p. 338) defines *demographics* as "the statistical characteristics of human populations (as age and income)." Categorizing people by subpopulations according to characteristics such as ethnicity and participation in special programs or activities implies that individuals within each subgroup have at least some commonality beyond the direct reason for being identified within the particular classification. For example, student grouping by grade level, support services, or special programs have specific criteria that placed students in these subgroups. However, assumptions about the learning needs and best teaching practices being the same or even similar for each person in a subgroup may very well not be accurate. The students may differ in many learning-related needs because of differences in cultural backgrounds, life experiences, educational backgrounds, parental support, or many other areas. With an increasingly diverse population, these differences are becoming greater. Categorization into subgroups represents one way to analyze teaching and learning needs and results. Keep in mind, however, that although individuals within a population subgroup have at least one common characteristic, they also have many differences. Using demographics gives only one lens of data analysis.

Most national and state datasets classify subpopulations on the basis of characteristics such as age, race or ethnicity, gender, and income levels when describing numbers of people within communities, school districts, schools or other organizations. Subgroups of a population are widely used in data analysis and have become so common in accountability for school results that the language of *achievement gaps among groups* may contribute to unintentional stereotyping of subgroups and less attention given to individual learning differences.

In the concluding chapter of this text, you will find increasing attention given over to high achievement for each student in national standards that were collaboratively developed by educational leaders from different states under the leadership of the Council of Chief State School Officers (CCSSO, 2008; CCSSO, 2011). Both the Educational Leadership Policy Standards and Model Core Teaching Standards place more attention on high achievement for each student, rather than for all students from various groups. In a sense, one might say that the results are the same, but focusing on each student's learning needs requires a higher level of understanding and expertise about how to determine and address a broader range of needs than is currently available in many schools. A focus on each child may lead to different ways of scheduling and greater collaboration among faculty than is currently found in schools. This need for specialized expertise in identifying and addressing differentiation in teaching and learning may bring career advancement opportunities for faculty.

School personnel now examine subpopulations of students within a special service or program, gender, grade level, or subject area to look for learning barriers and learning needs. State education data include demographics for states, school districts, and schools divided by the following denominators: gender, ethnicity, grade level, subject area, socioeconomic class, and participation in such special support programs as free or reduced lunch, Title I, English language learners (ELL), or special needs. Student data may be grouped by demographic categories for the purpose of examining achievement levels. State demographic data also group the number of students at different grade levels and show their state-defined student proficiency levels as ranging from basic or novice to advanced proficiency. Other examples of demographic counts of people within a school could be the number of students who are earning advanced college credit or dual credit and the numbers of high school graduates who respectively continued their education, gained employment related to career and technical education, gained other employment, and became unemployed.

Staff data may be subdivided by teachers, administrators, and support staff. Other available numeric data include the numbers and percentages of teaching assignments of teachers who are tenured, teachers in their first 3 years of teaching, and teachers teaching within their education major or minor, as well as the types of degrees, the level of participation in professional development, and teacher retention and turnover rates. There are numerous other ways to examine how many people have at least one similar characteristic and who they are.

PERCEPTUAL DATA.   Beliefs, opinions, perspectives, and generally held views about a problem area make up *perceptual data*. Perceptual data generally come from surveys, interviews, questionnaires, observations, and focus groups that gather data about an issue from the participants' perspectives. Portfolios, journals, field notes, audio recordings, checklists, minutes of meetings, and student work samples are a few sources of perceptual data. Other data sources include participants selected as respondents for data collection because of their particular experience, knowledge, or expertise related to the action research problem. Perceptual data may come from students, parents, teachers, administrators, community representatives, business personnel, or other persons who can contribute to an understanding of the research problem.

RECORD AND REPORT DATA.   Schools and districts maintain a variety of school records and reports in addition to student achievement data. These records and reports serve as another available data type and source for research. Examples include school budgets and expenditures; annual or biannual improvement plans; school board policies, state laws, and administrative regulations for schools; state or district curriculum guides; school faculty and student handbooks; school reports prepared for the state or district; school personnel directories; minutes of advisory meetings or parent–teacher organization meetings; and state, regional, or national accreditation reports. Note that these examples overlap with school processes and perceptual data. However, the source of factual data for records and reports comes directly from the written records, whereas process data not only include factual records and reports resulting from policies and procedures, but also may include opinions (perceptual data) from knowledgeable people about the characteristics and effectiveness of school policies and procedures and how they affect students and student learning.

REVIEW OF INFORMATION NEEDS, DATA TYPES, AND DATA SOURCES

Action research guiding questions focus the collection and interpretation of data that inform research findings. However, these questions may be added to or changed if your literature review and additional data identification suggest information needs not covered by your questions. Cowan (2004, p. 40) notes that action research data are "continually organized and analyzed" and that interpretation requires ongoing analysis and continuing review of areas of focus.

You are now ready to specify the information needs that will sufficiently respond to each question. At this stage of action research, your status as an educator in the school or district context and your professional experiences in education become especially valuable as you make decisions about the types and sources of information that relate to the problem being studied. You are familiar with school processes, procedures, programs, and personnel. You will add to that knowledge during the research study; as an educator-researcher, however, you have a head start because you understand the school context. The starting point for determining data needs is to review your completed literature summary. Major areas from this review may suggest some, but not all, specific topics for data collection in your school that need to be studied for you to address the problem effectively. Other data needs for addressing the research questions may be identified on the basis of the practitioner-researchers' previous education and experiences as educators and their knowledge of the school contexts in which they work.

Make a list of research guiding questions, information needed to answer each question, and multiple data types and sources that may provide that information. Looking at both quantitative and qualitative data from more than one source for each question increases the integrity and trustworthiness of the research results. Mendro (1993) emphasized the importance of examining not only the way in which data will be collected and analyzed but also the need to make related school processes a part of the research. He noted that no matter how carefully you design your questions and control the way data are collected, results cannot be interpreted accurately if the researcher did not identify the major data types and sources that can provide information on problem-related factors influencing success.

If a school researches strengths and weaknesses of a program initiative but examines achievement data without looking at the instructional process and conditions during implementation, the resulting data cannot be accurately interpreted. Maybe every teacher in the program taught essentially the same content, but consistency is also important for the implementation process. (Factors that need to be considered are how the program was implemented, how the content was taught, adherence to the process of implementation of the initiative, and knowledge of the teachers who implemented the program, to name a few). Human complexity in teaching and learning presents too many potential variables to identify all possibilities. However, omitting important procedural and perceptual data can lead to inaccurate interpretation.

Most likely, some information needs will be pertinent to more than one research question. Overlap is good. It lets you know before you select or design data-collection instruments that questions on any survey, interview, observation, or other instrument which goes to the same individuals or groups should cover similar information needs for any or all of the research guiding questions. A list of information needs for each question becomes a working draft for data-collection planning, and an overlap of data from different sources provides stronger data for interpretation and improvement action.

If you formed a research leadership team and literature review team, you may have these two teams collaborate to draft a list of information needs and sources to answer the research questions. Each team could brainstorm and develop a list. Then a representative from each of the two teams could work together to consolidate these two lists into a planning chart of information needs and multiple data types, sources, and methods. Table 3.1 shows an example list. Note that all questions do not include both quantitative and qualitative data, but each question has multiple types and/or multiple sources to increase integrity of data analysis. When you complete this chapter, your first performance task is to prepare a list similar to Table 3.1, in the text and also on the CD supplement with this text. Use the blank electronic copy labeled as Table 3.2 in Chapter 3 Resources on the CD supplement to complete a planning chart for your research data identification and collection. Another form, Table 3.3, found under Chapter 3 Resources on the CD supplement, provides an example of a completed planning chart that you can print and use as a guide when you complete Table 3.2 as part of your end-of-chapter performance.

INVOLVEMENT OF RESEARCH PARTICIPANTS

Cowan (2004) sees the benefits gained by education practitioners as a major purpose of action research. She is a teacher, and her parents are educators. The benefits she lists for educators are that action research enhances practice, supports practitioner professional development, builds collegial networking, and helps practitioners identify problems and systematically seek solutions. It can be used at all levels of education (p. 37). She notes that action research addresses real-world real-time concerns and questions posed by educators. As a consequence, practitioners expand their skill sets and grow in understanding of their profession (Cowan, p. 38).

Involvement of faculty as participants in conducting action research or as sources of information for perceptual data, student learning, school processes, or records and

Table 3.1
Planning Chart: Research Questions, Information Needs, and Multiple Data Types and Sources

Research Question: What should be done to ensure alignment of middle school mathematics curricula with state and national standards, instructional practices, and assessment by the 2014 school year as part of school improvement for student achievement?

Research Guiding Questions	Information Needs	Types of Data	Data Sources
What alignment procedures and benefits are advocated through professional literature, research, and professional development?	Alignment benefits and processes	Qualitative Perceptual	Literature review on alignment and professional development
			Math teachers' opinions about alignment and math areas out of alignment
	Math teachers' knowledge of and alignment with experience	Qualitative Perceptual	Math teachers' attitude toward, and background and experiences with, alignment
		Qualitative Quantitative Records and reports	Professional development records for math
How well do the math curriculum guides at each grade level align with state and national standards?	A matrix of state and national standards skill competencies matched with curriculum guide content areas	Qualitative Records and reports	Curriculum guides State standards National standards
	Omissions and mismatches between standards and curricula at each grade level and importance ratings	Qualitative and Quantitative Perceptual Records and reports	Math teachers' identification and importance rating of omissions and mismatches Standards and guides
What math skill areas give which subgroups of students the most difficulty?	Lowest achieving areas for students at each grade level	Qualitative Perceptual	Teachers' and students' perceptions at each grade level of curriculum content areas that are most difficult for students
	Subgroups of students at each grade level who have scored at the lowest levels for each content area	Quantitative Achievement Demographics	Student performance on unit tests and state proficiency achievement or proficiency tests for mathematics at each grade level by demographic subgroups
How does the allocation of instructional time for content domains taught match curriculum guides and standards?	Close estimates of instructional and student practice time for each content domain	Qualitative Quantitative Records and reports	Curriculum guides, standards, unit and lesson plans for each content area at each grade level
	Matrix of curriculum content taught, instructional time, and student practice time with state content and standards for each grade level	Qualitative Perceptual	Teacher and student opinions of instructional time and student practice time on each content domain and standards
How well do classroom practices and instructional strategies match best practices for content covered by curriculum guides and standards?	Comparison and rating for how well instructional strategies and practices match with curriculum guides and standards	Qualitative Records and reports School processes	Alignment and best instructional strategies and practices literature Unit and lesson plans by grade level
		Qualitative School processes	Instructional observations
		Qualitative Perceptual	Math teachers' and students' opinions and ratings of instruction and student practice for content domains from the curriculum guides and standards by grade level
How well does assessment match curricula, standards, and instruction?	Matrix of curricula, standards, and instructional content with formative and summative assessments	Qualitative Records and reports School processes	Types of assessment for each curriculum content area and standards, including formative and summative teacher-made unit assessments for each grade level
	Comparison of students' lowest scores on grade-level achievement test content areas with classroom teacher unit assessment	Quantitative Student learning	Achievement/proficiency test scores that show content areas with lowest achievement scores Classroom unit test scores for curriculum taught
		Qualitative Perceptual School Processes	Teacher and student opinions and ratings of importance about instruction and alignment adjustments to improve achievement

reports can be valuable for improving instruction and student achievement. As a former teacher, administrator, and university associate professor, I realize that involvement in research activities added to an already busy schedule will not be welcomed by everyone. However, if it is viewed as continuing professional development and ongoing improvement, research can help faculty members practice a process for growth in professional expertise and in their educational practice.

Schools with functioning professional learning communities already practice some parts of action research (reviewing literature and problem solving, in particular). I believe that resources such as professional learning communities and activities such as action research should become choices for teachers and administrators that can be approved as part of the school system and school's professional development plans. Professional learning communities and action research both develop and practice collaborative and problem-solving skills for professional growth as school leaders and for improving practice in their work with students. In-depth activities such as these require extra time and effort beyond traditional work roles.

Giving school personnel opportunities and training for action research and making action research one option in the school and school system professional development plan provides an incentive for voluntary participation. Letting individuals decide whether to participate and giving them recognition and credit for their extra efforts will be more likely to increase the numbers who become involved and committed to making action research a part of their ongoing work roles than would requiring everyone to participate.

Action research and communities of learning provide leadership opportunities. Other extrinsic rewards that encourage individuals to complete such activities could include district and school recognition of professional growth that benefits student learning. Such recognition as a news article on the completion of one's action research, supplemental pay, bonus points as part of faculty evaluation, and administrative creative scheduling and clerical assistance to overcome at least some of the time barriers to participation are some of the ways to increase both participation in action research and the use of research results.

As action research on school problems is carried out, there will be opportunities over time for the involvement of all faculty. In addition to serving on research teams as researcher-practitioners, faculty members will have the opportunity to serve as a source of information for data collection, to collaborate and provide ideas and input for the interpretation of data, to help with data collection and data summaries, to offer their technological expertise for the collaborative communication and preparation of tables and figures that display data, to prepare and distribute the final action research results, and to plan and evaluate the implementation of research-based program and school action plans. They also may serve as colleagues who reflect, listen, and interact with others in data interpretations. Different people will be encouraged to become involved in some activities of research problems. Those who serve on research teams and as research participants investigating a problem should be the ones who are most involved with and most knowledgeable about the problem and the various issues that surround it.

DATA-COLLECTION METHODS, INSTRUMENTS, AND PROTOCOL

After determining information needs, data types, and sources, your next step is to identify data sources that require the collection of new data, development of data-collection instruments, and description of the data-collection procedures or protocol. *Sources* identify what or who can provide the data. The *what* refers to specific *secondary data,* already available, such as achievement data or other records and reports. *Who* refers to specific groups of individuals, knowledgeable and available to provide *primary data* (original data) by completing surveys, participating in interviews, attending focus groups, filling out questionnaires, or participating in other data-collection methods such as classroom observations.

Refer back to Table 3.1 as an example of ways to determine primary data-collection needs. This planning list calls for primary data on mathematics teachers' opinions, attitudes, and importance ratings. All of these data from teachers could be obtained by one middle school mathematics-teacher survey. Middle-level school student perceptions of the most difficult math content, instructional time and practice on content areas, and ratings of instruction and practice may come from a middle-level school student survey or from student focus groups for each grade level. Additional primary data would come from classroom observations at each grade level. Secondary data could be gleaned and organized from records and reports such as curriculum guides, standards, curriculum maps, classroom student records, and teacher professional development records. Data from achievement records and student demographic data, as well as literature on best practices, are also secondary data to be gathered, organized, and formatted.

Much of the student learning and school processes data that you collect for action research may be secondary data from school databases, other records or reports in your school; and data on state, federal, or professional organization websites. For example, if you are studying attendance, discipline, or academic achievement, quantitative data may come from records and reports of the number and characteristics of students who have absences within a certain range, types of infractions, and actions taken. The research could investigate records and reports for data such as the most frequent reasons for absences and the number of excused or unexcused absences for different grade levels.

In addition, a study of discipline might lead you to compare numbers of incidents, consequences for those incidents, characteristics of students who have behavioral incidents within a certain range, and perhaps a tally of absences and in-school and out-of-school suspensions. Also, comparing student academic achievement with the number of disciplinary incidents or unexcused absences could provide insight into a possible relationship between absences and grades. Qualitative perceptual data could be gathered from surveys, interviews, or focus groups of teachers, administrators, and students. Such a study might lead to actions to both reduce absences and provide school and community processes that foster positive community service projects and help make up the learning deficit for classroom work missed.

Gathering school data on student achievement may involve summarizing pertinent data over three years or more to identify trends, comparing multiple data sources, looking for patterns, discussing data with colleagues to gain different perspectives on data interpretation, disaggregating data into tables and figures to compare data for different subpopulations, and searching for sources that refute or support your data interpretations and conclusions.

Much of quantitative and qualitative data can be displayed in tables or graphs organized in a meaningful way for interpretation. Organizing data in different ways can reveal different information. Play with the data, and try different arrangements to see what can be revealed. In addition to guarding confidentiality of data from each research participant, it is important when interpreting data not to overstate meanings. For example, don't use terms such as *prove*, *significantly different*, or even *affect* or *effect*. These terms are used with statistical tests of quantitative data and do not apply in action research or most other qualitative research. The word *prove* would be questionable to use even in traditional research.

Most student achievement-related data for action research will be visually displayed in summary form with tables or graphs. These visual displays also aid data interpretation and readers' understanding of the research report. Use visual data displays, including tables and figures, because they are easier to understand quickly than long paragraphs of text. Tables have rows and columns of numbers and/or words and are particularly useful for comparisons of similarities and differences. Graphs visually show trends over time or provide quick comparisons of values or quantities. The development of tables and graphs is covered in Chapter 4 and Chapter 4 resource material on the CD.

DATA-COLLECTION INSTRUMENTS AND RESEARCH POPULATIONS

Review information needs, data types, and sources to determine the methodology and instruments to use for primary data collection (original data not already available). The same data-collection instrument may include questions and inquiry topics for more than one of the research guiding questions. One instrument may suffice for all data needs from the same source, or it may be used to gather similar information from multiple groups. Your next research activity will be selection and development of the types of instruments for each data source and a procedure (*protocol*) for the use of each instrument type. This section addresses data-collection tasks.

Research Population

Research participants who provide information relative to each research question will be either the research population or a sample that represents that population. *Population* refers to all people in the large group of people to whom the research applies. The population for education research often is too large to feasibly gather information from everyone. Therefore, a smaller subgroup may be used to represent the total population if the subgroup includes the characteristics—similar to those in the total population—that most likely influence perceptions and knowledge related to the particular study. This smaller group representing the population becomes a *sample population* for data collection.

In traditional research, studies pertinent to a large population often use a sample population with a much smaller group of people (Borg & Gall, 1983). Traditional research looks at topics that add to a knowledge base for all similar schools. This generalizability of results to other settings and use of no less than established minimum numbers of responses for accuracy of certain statistical tests help validate findings for traditional studies. Such research also evaluates carefully the size and representativeness of sample populations. Action research focuses on one school and one specific problem. Samples should be representative of the characteristics most important to the problem, but sample size is less important as long as the sample population is representative of the total population.

Data from the total school population related to a problem could be of interest and feasible for data collection for some questions about a particular school level or subject area of teachers or administrative roles. Sample populations, however, would be more feasible for parent, community, or student perspectives in most cases. The method of data collection and the type of data source also affect the feasibility of using a sample population versus a total population.

Surveys are usually the instrument of choice for gathering specific types of data from large samples or total populations. Time requirements for interviews, focus groups, or observations limit the number of participants. The accessibility of participants also plays a part in selection of a sample population.

If parent or community views are sought, researchers may choose a representative sample. However, a study of eighth-grade mathematics achievement could use all eighth-grade mathematics teachers as a feasible population for teacher perceptions. For student perceptions in a middle school with four or five sections of mathematics, you may obtain a sample population of selected students representing all sections by choosing similar aptitudes and interests, achievement highs and lows, or other characteristics relevant to the research questions. Sometimes, class schedules or other factors make the only feasible sample one of convenience (referred to as a *convenience sample population*). This type of sample might include only one or two class sections but be the only feasible sample group.

The population may represent several different categories of people—for example, student grade levels or faculty and administrative positions. In this case, a *stratified random sample* may be selected as a sample population. This sample ensures that all important groups are represented reasonably equally or in proportion to the comparative size of each group category in the total population.

Selecting participants of each group randomly helps ensure that selection bias does not creep in by choosing persons because they agree with the researcher's opinion or by selecting participants who do not represent characteristics of the total group. *Random sample selection* gives everyone in a total group or population the same opportunity to be selected. Random selection of a sample population of a school may be as simple as making a numbered, but not alphabetical, list of names in the total population and putting all numbers, or all names, on pieces of paper, folded to not be visible, in a container; shaking or otherwise mixing the pieces of paper; and drawing as many as you have determined for your sample size. If you draw numbers instead of names, match them to the numbered name list to determine who is in the sample. Keep the list in a locked drawer, and destroy it after completing data collection. You may need to draw additional names if some initial selections do not participate.

Respondents should be able to express their views in confidence without being identified specifically with their responses. Avoid writing names on questionnaires or interview notes. Use a code that represents the characteristics of the population subgroup or the sample population. When participants can be assured of confidentiality of responses, you are more likely to get participation and accurate information than you would otherwise.

You can use colors or numbers to code questionnaires for follow-up purposes. You could assign a number, letter, or color to represent each category in a stratified sample, and another identifying each individual within the sample. The following code might be used if mathematics and reading teachers at the sixth-, seventh-, and eighth-grade levels are receiving the same questionnaire:

Red (R) = mathematics teacher	A = sixth grade
Blue (B) = reading teacher	T = seventh grade
	X = eighth grade

Red1A would be the first mathematics teacher for the sixth grade. (Teacher names on the numbered list would not be in alphabetical order when the names are numbered consecutively.) The second sixth-grade mathematics teacher from the list of selected subjects would be Red2A. The researcher would be the only person with the code list that correlates category designations with a participant name list and would check off the names on the list as completed surveys were returned. The confidential names list would be destroyed as soon as the survey and follow-up were complete.

Confidentiality of individual responses is important, and the code itself should not make the respondent identifiable without the confidential coded list of names. For example, R for red would be assumed logically to identify reading, and M for magenta could identify math or 6, 7, and 8 as middle-school grade levels. If a school has only one sixth-grade reading teacher, anyone working with the data might guess which set of data came from that teacher if his or her identity were coded as R16, the first sixth-grade reading teacher. Therefore, use codes that logically don't match the category with only one person. If there is only one sixth-grade reading teacher (for example), make *middle school* the data summary category for teacher perceptions rather than displaying it by grade level. Prepare and discuss data displays in a way that does not identify individuals. Also, avoid prematurely circulating research data or conclusions before checking for accuracy or refining the information for shared input and discussion.

Following a systematic process increases the accuracy of results because all researchers follow the same defined process for gathering data. This means that your research planning not only develops data-collection instruments but also identifies and follows specific procedures for the selection of participants, the distribution or use of data-collection instruments, how and when follow-up will take place to increase returns, and the time schedule for data collection. Chapter 3 Resources on the CD include forms and examples to help you plan information needs, sources, data-collection instruments, and population or sample size: Table 3.2, Blank Planning Chart for Information Needs, and Table 3.3, Example of a Completed Planning Chart, are guides to completing your research planning chart using Table 3.2 from the CD Chapter 3 Resources.

When planning and collecting data, you should consider the education-researcher's ethical responsibilities to the research participants who supply information and to the school system for following district policies. Three resources on the CD for Chapter 3 will help you consider these ethical responsibilities for data collection and data reporting. Figure 3.1 on the CD suggests that you read the administrative regulations for schools in your state to review the code of ethics for school certified personnel. For example, this code of ethics in Kentucky is found on the Legislative Research Commission website. Also, check with your local board superintendent or the designated division for research in your school board office to familiarize yourself with applicable state and board policies and regulations. Figure 3.2 provides statements about voluntary participation and confidentiality for data-collection processes. Figure 3.3 illustrates an information letter similar to one that should be sent to a parent or guardian when the information collected might be considered sensitive, along with a sample student survey and a parent or guardian approval form for permission for the child to participate in the survey. Both Figure 3.2 and Figure 3.3 are on the CD supplement with this text.

Surveys and Questionnaires

Researchers use surveys to gather standardized information from all subjects in the population or sample population (Borg & Gall, 1983). Surveys and questionnaires require less time to use and, therefore, researchers gathering information from a large group generally use this method for data collection. Survey questionnaires are best suited to questions with short responses but may include a few open-ended-response questions.

The same questionnaires may go to multiple groups in a population. However, there could be different versions of the questionnaire, with certain questions the same and wording on others varying somewhat as appropriate for age or position. Comparisons and contrasts of responses for the same topics can be summarized and analyzed for group response differences and similarities if members of the group respond to the same question.

Questions on a questionnaire should be directly related to research questions, stating each question as briefly as possible, while still being complete, and worded clearly to be understood by the survey population. Group together related items or those that use the same question format. Items that are interesting and clearly relevant to the research increase the response rate (Borg & Gall, 1983). Questions on a survey may pertain to more than one research guiding question and may be dichotomous (*true–false* or *yes–no*), multiple choice, open response, or have a 4- or 5-point rating scale for reaction to opinion statements. Questionnaires often end with at least one and not more than five open-response questions. Too many open-response questions discourage participants from responding to the questionnaire and are difficult for researchers to summarize for interpretation.

Questions may pertain to one point in time or past, present, or future associations. Consider how results will be summarized and analyzed before wording questions. A study of career counseling and senior career plans might have a time-ordered open-response question such as, "At what grade level did you begin to consider your career choice?" (Time is past. Type of question is open-ended or multiple choice.) Another question may be, "What school activity or course was the most help for career planning?" (Time is past. Type of question is open-ended or multiple choice.) Other questions may be, "What career choice have you made as a senior?" (present) and, "Five years from now, in what career do you expect to be employed?" (future). The first three questions could be open-ended or multiple choice, but the last two would be open-ended. (For the open-ended questions, possible responses would be varied, and these should be each individual's specific perception.)

Figure 3.4 illustrates a variety of question types on a survey instrument. This form is also on the CD, which will save you time if the question format fits one that you develop. Note the informed consent form wording above Section 1 (voluntary, confidentiality, and purpose).

Figure 3.5 is an electronic copy of a procedural worksheet and guide for the types of information to be decided for the data-collection procedure for each survey used for data collection. Figure 3.5 can be found on the CD under Chapter 3 Resources.

Observations

Observations of classroom instruction have been a part of teacher evaluation at least since the 1980s, when school effectiveness studies (Scheerens, 2004) and time on task (Brophy, 1988) gained attention as initiatives for school improvement.

Classroom observations usually focus on teaching and learning practices and attributes of learning environments, specific behaviors, or other areas that research suggests have potential importance for addressing the research problem. Observations may take place in multiple classrooms or at repeated intervals in the same classroom or other environmental settings. They should be as unobtrusive as possible in order to not interfere with the normal classroom activities.

When professionals complete action research within their own school, a semistructured form for recording observations should be sufficient. Outside researchers studying a school may need to record notes about the environmental context. However, professionals observing for action research within their own school would more likely develop a list

School Improvement Survey
Improving Student Learning in Fifth-Grade Mathematics
Teacher Questionnaire

Completion of the questionnaire is voluntary, and individual responses will be kept confidential. Results in the report will be summarized with no individuals identified. Your responses will be helpful in planning for improvement in student achievement.

Section 1 Directions: Please circle the rating that represents your opinion for each statement. Rating Scale: 5 = strongly agree, 4 = agree, 3 = undecided, 2 = disagree, 1 = strongly disagree

5 4 3 2 1   1. I have adequate time to teach math.
5 4 3 2 1   2. I have adequate materials to teach math.
5 4 3 2 1   3. I have adequate time to work individually with struggling students.
5 4 3 2 1   4. I have adequate time to review previously introduced topics.
5 4 3 2 1   5. Students have opportunities to take tests similar to state content tests.
5 4 3 2 1   6. I have received adequate professional development for teaching math.
5 4 3 2 1   7. Students try their best in class.
5 4 3 2 1   8. Students complete their math homework.
5 4 3 2 1   9. I use student achievement data to plan instruction.
5 4 3 2 1   10. Students have daily practice with open-response math questions.

Section 2 Directions: Enter the estimated average percentage of the mathematics time block that you spend on the instructional activities that follow. Total percentage should equal 100%.

_____%   1. Review of previous lesson
_____%   2. Introduction of new material
_____%   3. Teacher lecture
_____%   4. Teacher demonstration
_____%   5. Independent work or cooperative work groups
_____%   6. Open-response questions

Section 3 Directions: Please share your opinions and ideas by responding to the following open-ended questions:

1. How do you assess student learning in mathematics?

2. What are strengths of the current mathematics curriculum?

3. What factors contributed to last year's overall gain in fifth-grade mathematics achievement?

4. What areas need improvement in the current mathematics program?

Thank you for completing the survey. Please place the completed form (without your name) in a plain envelope by Friday, January 15, in Mrs. Nelson's school mailbox.

Figure 3.4. Example survey instrument with multiple types of questions. Survey adapted from action research by Jennifer Hutchison, Curriculum Coach. Used with permission.

of items as "look-fors" that relate specifically to the research question. This type of form should be easy to use and briefly describe what is observed. Figure 3.6 that follows is also on the CD as an illustration of one format for recording an observation.

Before researchers observe classrooms, teachers to be observed should be told the purpose and time span for completing observations. Cowan (2004) proposed four steps for conducting observational research:

1. Determine what is to be observed.
2. Before observing, record at the top of the form the date, class observed, and time and length of observation.
3. During observation, identify specific behaviors that match and do not match the items to be observed.
4. Complete the observation record, and analyze the data.

Two additional figures in the Chapter 3 CD Resources provide guidance for determining a procedure for conducting classroom observations. Figure 3.7 is a procedural worksheet and guide for planning observations, and Figure 3.8 illustrates an example observation plan and outline for describing the protocol for conducting classroom observations.

Kentucky and other states frequently use classroom walk-through observation instruments with brief yes–no or multiple choice response items entered and summarized on mobile computer technology. Summaries of all of the walk-throughs in the school during a specific timeframe are used primarily for discussion with the faculty as a status report on how well certain initiatives are being implemented and for collaborative planning for improvements.

These classroom observations are frequent, but brief, and are planned to be in the form of a quick checklist that shows a schoolwide picture over a given span of time. Rather than being an evaluation instrument of a teacher, the results of an individual's observation from this brief visit are shared only with the teacher observed as an opportunity for discussion of the initiatives observed.

This computer format for this type of observation can be special software for handheld computer devices or a spreadsheet list prepared with items on rows in the first column and each visit labeled in a column headed only with the observation date. After the last observation, entry in the next column could have formulas that total the entries by row, thus providing totals of the number of classrooms in which the row item was observed. Table 3.4 shows a typical walk-through list of observation items, and URLs shown at the bottom of the table refer you to websites that give additional information on the use of walk-through observations.

School principal preparation students in my action research class sometimes used this type of walk-through observation as part of their action research projects. The syllabus in another course taught for school principal preparation had educators complete an electronic walk-through project in their schools for reflective practice, following the instruction-focused model for improvement of student learning proposed by Downey, Steffy, English, Frase, and Poston (2004). Table 3.4 gives an example of the walk-through checklist format. The mobile technology (PDAs) included word processing and spreadsheet software and later added software specifically programmed for the user to enter and revise the item list, summarize the data, and graph the data.

Figure 3.9 in Chapter 3 CD Resources is a sample summary of graphs prepared by totaling each walk-through item and constructing graphs with presentation software. This sample is designed for collaborative discussions of graphs that summarize total observation results school wide. The purpose is to involve the faculty in reviewing progress toward implementation of new or ongoing school-wide initiatives. Faculty members break into small groups to reflect and discuss current status as it relates to their goals for the initiatives. As a result, they plan changes for improvements that the data indicate will be required to reach their goals.

Interviews and Focus Groups

Interviews are a common form of data collection in descriptive studies and other types of research (Borg, 1981). An interview "involves direct verbal interaction between

Observation Chart: Primary and Intermediate Mathematics

Observation #: _____   Date _____   Time started _____   Time ended _____

Time allotted for Math today _____   Circle: Primary Intermediate

Topic/Topics being covered in lesson: _____
_____

Teaching Strategies/ Practices Used

	Check when observed ✓	Comments
Assessment		
Curriculum Map followed		
Different intelligences addressed		
Estimation used/Anticipate the answer		
High student participation (at least 90%)		
Higher order questioning		
Students called on equally		
Wait time provided		
Individual practice		
Lecture		
Guided practice		
Manipulatives used by students		
Mathematics discussions		
Positive teacher attitude		
Real-life connections		
Test Scrimmaging		

General Comments:

Observation Checklist: Primary and Intermediate Mathematics

Alignment with State Core Content and District Curriculum Maps

	Check when observed ✓	Comments
Number and Number relations		
Computation/Estimation		
Geometry and Spatial Sense		
Addition		
Subtraction		
Multiplication		
Division		
Decimals		
Algebraic ideas		
Probability/Statistics		

General Comments:

Figure 3.6. Example of a classroom observation of instruction chart for primary and intermediate classrooms. Adapted from action research by Amanda Boyd Collier, Elementary School Teacher. Used with permission.

Table 3.4 *Example 5-Minute Walk-Through Checklist and Walk-Through URLs*		
Date observed	12/15/2012	12/16/2012
Time of observation	10:00-10:05	1:00-1:05
Teacher code	14	28
Student Activities: More than one		
Discussion	✓	
Hands-on project		✓
Listening	✓	
Note taking		
Technology use		✓
Textbook		
Grouping of Students: More than one		
Individual	✓	
Pairs/threes	✓	
Small groups		✓
Whole class		
Differentiation		
Not observed		✓
Observed	✓	
Core Content Objectives Posted: One		
Yes		✓
No	✓	
Teacher Activities Observed: More than one		
At desk	✓	
Circulating		✓
Assisting students		✓
Lecture and Questioning		

Walk-through URLs

http://www.naesp.org/resources/2/Leadership_Compass/2007/LC2007v4n4a2.pdf

http://www.districtadministration.com/article/walk-throughs-school-improvement

http://www.nassp.org/Portals/0/Content/55499.pdf

individuals" (p. 86). Interview questions are open-ended, and interviewers ask for facts related to an issue, solicit opinions about events, or request the respondent's own insights into occurrences (Yin, 1983). The respondent may be asked to suggest sources of corroborating evidence and may help with access to these sources. Also, the interviewer should rely on gathering other evidence to corroborate informant insights and should search for disconfirming as well as confirming evidence.

Another type of interview focuses for a short period, perhaps an hour, on selected information topics (Yin, 1983). The interview questions remain open-ended and conversational. However, the interview usually follows a set pattern to corroborate facts or provide opposing views to statements that the researchers have already found to be relevant on the basis of the literature reviewed, other data collected on a topic, or their experience and knowledge of the research problem.

Interviews usually have a group of structured questions to gain information that centers on topics specifically on the research questions. Interview questions must be worded carefully so that the researcher appears naïve about the topic in order to avoid biased responses due to the wording of questions that leads the respondent to a particular response. For example, which of these two questions will be likely to get an unbiased answer? (a) "Do you think more funding is necessary to improve the program?"; or (b) "What do you see as the most important needed change to improve the program?" The wording of the first question suggests an answer, whereas the second requires thought on the part of the respondent and is more likely to yield the respondent's own perception.

The summary of interviews gives only one type of information and should be triangulated with other data types and sources (Yin, 1983). Data from interviews are verbal reports and can be subject to bias or inaccurate meanings.

Interviews should take place in a private setting without distractions. They may be recorded if the interviewee grants permission to do so. The interviewer should listen carefully and take notes to serve as a backup for equipment failure or sound that cannot be deciphered. Figure 3.10 gives an example of interview protocol and questions for a structured interview. Figure 3.11 in Chapter 3 Resources on the CD is a procedural planning guide for conducting interviews.

Focus groups are similar to interviews, but they are not one-on-one. The researcher brings together from four to a dozen participants in a neutral setting at one time to gain insight into their shared understandings and interactions. Gibbs (1997) offers helpful information about the purpose of focus groups, the moderator's role, and their potential and limitations.

The main purpose of focus groups is for the moderator to gain the respondents' attitudes, feelings, beliefs, experiences, and reactions that are revealed within the group by

Interview Protocol

Participant Selection: A total of 12 seniors will be interviewed who have completed three years or more of the Career Pathways program. The current senior class has 35 students who meet this criterion. Twenty are female and 15 male; therefore, the interview sample will include 57% females—7 females and 5 males. Two numbered lists of names will be prepared, one for the 20 females and one for the 15 males. Names on each list will be in no logical order (not alphabetical or any other sequenced order). A list of numbers (1 to 20) will be printed, cut apart, and placed in a small box or other container. After shuffling the numbers, 7 will be drawn for females. Then, numbers 16 through 20 will be removed from the box, and 5 numbers drawn for males. The 7 numbers for females will be matched to the list of 20 numbered females to select potential interviewees. The 5 numbers for males will be matched to the list of 15 males for selection.

Potential interviewees will be contacted in person and given a sheet that states the purpose of the interview, approximate length, a private location at school, and time for the interview. Also on the sheet will be statements that participation is voluntary, there will be no negative consequences for not participating, and that individual interview responses will be confidential, with no names identifying responses. Two questions will follow: (a) *Will you agree to participate in this interview? Circle Yes or No.* and (b) *Would you be willing to review your interview transcript for correctness? Circle Yes or No.* If any potential participants do not wish to participate, additional names will be drawn following the procedures of the initial drawing.

Before beginning the interview, repeat the purpose and if the participant is willing for the interview to be recorded. Notes will also be taken during the interview. The interviewer should ask questions without indicating approval or disapproval of the response, remaining friendly but neutral at all times. If clarification of a response is needed, a probing statement or question may be expressed, such as, *Tell me more, Will you give an example?* or *Will you explain that further?*

Interview Questions

1. Which of your Career Pathways experiences have been most helpful or least helpful, and why?
2. What could have been added or changed to better prepare you for further education or work?
3. Describe a career shadowing or work experience component that you have had, and evaluate its usefulness for your future.
4. If you were entering high school next year as a freshman, would you enroll again in the Career Pathways Program? Why or why not?
5. What plans do you currently have for further education and work?

Figure 3.10. **Example Protocol and Questions for Interviews of 12th Grade Students for Research on Career Pathways Preparation for Higher Education and Work. This is an example procedure for selecting participants and conducting interviews. It should be in writing and kept in a file for the action research as a guide to be followed in the same way for each participant.**

listening to the everyday language of the group members with each other and by observing group culture (Gibbs, 1997). The focus group reveals several perspectives on the same topic(s) through group discussion with group interaction, as well as individual responses to questions or topics posed by the moderator. Within about the same length of time as one interview, researchers can gain insight from several participants. Gibbs points out the importance of ensuring that all participants have an opportunity to contribute their experience or opinion about the topic being studied.

Researchers cannot assume that focus group participants are expressing their own specific attitudes or beliefs, because the group interaction influences the individual messages. Furthermore, because of the group setting, confidentiality should be requested for everyone's responses but cannot be assured.

The researcher arranges the meeting and usually serves as the moderator but must avoid influencing participants' responses. Questions to guide the discussion should be developed similar to those for an interview. Don't show approval or disapproval. Remain neutral, be a good listener, and be nonjudgmental and adaptable (Gibbs, 1997). Sometimes, the moderator asks probing questions for details or steers the conversation back to the topic. Two moderators might be used, with one taking notes or otherwise recording the session (if recording is agreed to by the participants). At the beginning of the meeting, inform participants of the purpose and general topic. Clarify that each participant's contributions are shared with others in the group as well as with the researcher. Encourage participants to keep what they hear confidential. The researcher should assure participants that their names will not be used with the research data.

Key Questions for Review

1. What are three examples of quantitative and three examples of qualitative data available in your school?
2. What are two examples of each of the following data types that are available in your school: (a) student learning, (b) school processes, (c) demographic data, (d) perceptual data, and (e) records and reports?
3. The term *population* refers to all people to whom the research applies. If research in your school concerns a topic that applies to all personnel in the school, but you decide to use a sample population to interview for perceptual data, what characteristics of the population would you consider important for interview participants to be representative of?
4. Which of these data-collection instruments or methods could be used to most efficiently gather information from all personnel in your school: (a) surveys or questionnaires, (b) interviews, (c) focus groups, (d) observations, or (e) records and reports?
5. What is meant by triangulating research data, and why would this strengthen the accuracy of research results and conclusions?

Note. **Performance Checklist will also appear on CD.**

Performance Checklist for Steps 2b and 2c Research Activities

You are ready to complete Step 2 of action research in your school. You completed Step 2a, the literature review, in Chapter 2. Chapter 3 covers the last two activities, Step 2b and Step 2c.

Inventory information needs, multiple data types and sources, and data-collection methods and procedures (protocol).

A. **Identify information needs and multiple data types and sources.**

   Performance Check:

   1. Review Table 3.1, and open and save the blank copy of Table 3.2 from Chapter 3 CD Resources to your device as a blank form for your research.
   2. Enter your primary research question at the top of the form, and enter guiding questions in each section of the first column.
   3. Collaborate with the research leadership and literature review teams to list information needs for each guiding question, type of data, and source that best address each

question. Use Table 3.3 in Chapter 3 Resources on the CD as an example.

B. **Determine the data-collection methods and population or sample size to address the research questions.**

   Performance Check:

   1. Note that the last column of Table 3.2 is an addition to the columns illustrated in Table 3.1. At this point in your research, not only are you thinking and planning the information needs and types of data that can help answer the research questions, but you are also making decisions about data needs from specific records or reports. For each research question, enter in the fifth column details that select specific records and reports, types of data-collection methods, and characteristics of research populations or sample sizes for each type of method, as well as characteristics for sample populations that are representative of the population. See Table 3.3 on the CD for an example.

2. Now review all methods to determine how many sources are listed for the same method. Consolidate question content on each type of collection method to cover information from all individuals for that source so that no person approached as a source receives more than one survey, observation, or interview.

C. Develop data-collection instruments and procedures.

Performance Check:

1. Review Figures 3.5, 3.7, and 3.11 from Chapter 3 Resources on the CD. Save a copy of each of them to your computer storage device to use for planning your questions and procedures for data collection instruments for your research. Use these forms to plan, save, and print a procedure for each type of research survey, observation, and interview that your data collection plan will require.

2. Develop data instruments necessary to gather original data, such as surveys, observations, interviews, or focus groups. Also make a "look for" list of information needs that will come from records and reports. Chapter 4 picks up with data collection from records and reports.

3. Review your completed Table 3.2 planning chart, and word your required survey questions in a yes–no, multiple choice, fill-in-the-blank, or open-ended format. Include questions that cover all information needed (both factual and opinion) from sources in the survey population or sample population. The needed information should include questions that help answer the research questions for your study.

4. Check to ensure that data collection provides multiple types and/or sources of data for each research guiding question and that confidentiality and voluntary participation are ensured.

References

Bernhardt, V. L. (2004). *Data analysis for continuous school improvement* (2nd ed.). Larchmont, NY: Eye on Education.

Borg, W. R., & Gall, M. D. (1983). *Educational research: An introduction* (4th ed.). New York: Longman.

Borg, W. R. (1981). *Applying educational research: A practical guide for teachers*. New York: Longman.

Brophy, J. E. (1988). Educating teachers about managing classrooms and students. *Teaching and Teacher Education, 4*(1), 1–18.

Council of Chief State School Officers (CCSSO). (2008). *Interstate School Leaders Licensure Consortium (ISLLC) standards for school leaders*. Washington, DC: Author.

Council of Chief State School Officers (CCSSO). (2011, April). *Interstate Teacher Assessment and Support Consortium (InTASC) Model core teaching standards: A resource for state dialogue*. Washington, DC: Author.

Cowan, G. (2004). *Understanding & conducting research in education* (2nd ed.). Dubuque, IA: Kendall/Hunt.

Dietz, S. (2010, December). *State high school tests: Exit exams and other assessments*. Washington, DC: Center on Education Policy. Retrieved from http://www.cep-dc.org

Downey, C. J., Steffy, B. E., English, F. W., Frase, L. E., & Poston, W. K., Jr. (2004). *The three-minute walk-through: Changing supervisory practice one teacher at a time*. Thousand Oaks, CA: Corwin Press.

Gibbs, A. (1997, Winter). Focus groups. *Social research update, 19*. Retrieved from http://sru.soc.surrey.ac.uk/SRU19.html

Kincheloe, J. (1991). *Teachers as researchers: Qualitative inquiry as a path to empowerment*. Philadelphia: Falmer.

Lincoln, Y. S., & Guba, E. G. (1985). *Naturalistic inquiry*. Newberry Park, CA: Sage.

Mendro, R. (1993, April). *The place of process evaluation in action research*. Paper presented at the annual meeting of the American Research Association (AERA), Atlanta, GA.

Scheerens, J. (2004). *Review of school and instructional effectiveness research*. (Background report prepared for the Education for All Global Monitoring Report 2005. *The Quality Imperative*). Retrieved from United Nations Educational, Scientific, and Cultural Organization website: http://unesdoc.unesco.org/images/0014/001466/146695e.pdf

Striefer, P. A. (2002). *Using data to make better educational decisions*. Lanham, MD: Scarecrow Press.

Merriam-Webster. (1989). *Webster's ninth new collegiate dictionary*. (1989). Springfield, MA: Author.

Yin, R. K. (1983). *Case study research: Design and methods*. Thousand Oaks, CA: Sage.

CHAPTER 4

Data Organization, Summarization, and Analysis

At the end of Chapter 3, you designed the instruments and described procedures to collect primary (original) data that address your research questions. Earlier in the chapter, you considered the importance of multiple data sources to meet information needs for each question. In this chapter, you will field test the data-collection instruments and use them to gather data. In addition, you will gather and organize pertinent data from records and reports (secondary data) and explore what the data reveal when you organize it in different ways.

This chapter and the next describe in detail different patterns for organizing and summarizing your data-collection results. The chapter guides you through data collection, organization, and displays for quantitative data. Illustrations and references to further examples and details are available on the CD under Chapter 4 Resources. Your knowledge and experience, as well as research purpose, determine how closely you follow the suggested organization guides and adapt the APA format for your action research. For example, classroom research intended only for a teacher's use, with no report circulated external to the school, would not need as much attention to formatting illustrations and preparing a research report as would a schoolwide research product circulated to the school board and wider school community.

Chapter 4 also covers a variety of accepted techniques for verifying the trustworthiness of data and data interpretation. You should consider these techniques and select at least two or three of those most applicable to your research to incorporate and describe in your research methodology. Chapter 4 covers quantitative descriptive analysis, and Chapter 5 in Module 3 describes qualitative data analysis and links quantitative and qualitative data with literature findings for data interpretation.

FIELD TESTS OF PRIMARY DATA-COLLECTION INSTRUMENTS AND PROTOCOL

After developing each data-collection instrument and describing a process for using it to collect data, ask one or more knowledgeable colleagues to read the directions and suggest any needed changes. The goal is to obtain the most accurate responses from this population. These professionals, serving as context reviewers, should consider the population for which the instrument is designed and review for appropriate content, clarity of meaning, logical organization, and user-friendliness of directions. After making needed changes, try each refined instrument and procedure with an individual who has characteristics similar to those of the targeted research population of responders. You can then refine, change, and finalize the instrument for data collection.

METHODS OF VERIFYING RESEARCH INTEGRITY

Before and after data collection and data interpretation, consider how your research process and data analysis can help ensure accuracy and build trustworthiness of research results. Previous chapters mentioned two ways: triangulation of data (use of multiple data types, sources, and instrumentation) and the reporting not only of confirming data but also of disconfirming evidence that differs from conclusions. Both supporting and opposing data should be presented in research findings.

Table 4.1 summarizes a variety of strategies for ensuring integrity of the data analysis, in addition to triangulation and attention to both confirming and disconfirming data. A number of researchers have proposed ways to address validity and reliability in qualitative and action research (Anderson, Herr, & Nihlen, 1994; Guba, 1981; Kincheloe, 1991; Lincoln & Guba, 1985; Maxwell, 1992; Wolcott, 2001). The strategies listed identify a variety of techniques from previous research.

As part of your description of research methodology and data analysis for Chapter 5, you should describe briefly the strategies used to strengthen validity and reliability. Validity and reliability help ensure credibility and trustworthiness of data interpretation, research findings or results, conclusions from findings, and recommendations from the conclusions.

Validity implies a state of being supported by objective truth and suggests that the research data accurately measures what it proposes to measure. *Reliability* means that repetition of the same measurements would yield the same results. Validity of results from action research supports acceptance by the school community and helps ensure usefulness for continuous improvement.

In qualitative action research, *reliability* takes on a meaning that meshes well with *validity*. Both validity and reliability reflect a search for accuracy and truth. Researchers play a major role in interpretation of data. School research by school practitioners focuses on aspects of the school for internal improvement of student achievement. This is a high-stakes issue for the researchers and one about which they are highly knowledgeable and involved; therefore, it is unlikely that they can be neutral observers. *Reliability* for school action research could be interpreted to mean that *repetition* of this study by neutral observers following the same procedures would result in essentially the same conclusions and recommendations. Although bias can be a factor in all types of research, acknowledging possible bias and taking steps to overcome it strengthens research credibility.

ANALYSIS OF RECORDS, REPORTS, AND OTHER DOCUMENTATION

Borg and Gall (1983) refer to school records, reports, and other documentation as *historical resources*. The researcher first must know what records can be made available for review. A potential list of documents, records, and reports of interest for the research questions should be developed and submitted to the principal, superintendent, or other appropriate authority for approval. This process should be relatively easy for researchers within their own school. They are likely to have knowledge of available records information relevant to the problem.

The best time for examining some of these sources may be after gathering data from primary sources. At that time, questions may arise that can be answered or verified by checking historical records specifically for examples of confirming or disconfirming information about related events or related results. Another strategy might be to use accreditation reports and curriculum documents to support or disconfirm previously identified interpretations or conclusions related to the research questions. Developing and using a form to record data from records and reports will produce results in a format that can be interpreted and compared with other data. Table 4.2 shows one such form. Table 4.3 in Chapter 4 CD Resources provides a blank copy similar to this form in an electronic worksheet format that allows you to adapt column headings to your research. Table 4.4 on the CD shows a completed example of Table 4.3.

Table 4.1
Research Techniques for Data Integrity and Trustworthiness

Technique	Definition	Description for Research
Systematic Procedures	Developing and following an operational plan of research methods and procedures that helps ensure the best possible results without compromising individual confidentiality and voluntary participation.	1. For each type of data collection instrument, develop a protocol for how, when, what, and from whom. Follow the procedures in the same manner with all respondents. 2. Carefully record and frequently review and reflect on research procedures for each research step. 3. Gather additional information or change direction as review indicates.
Bias Control	Taking steps to recognize, record, and review potential personal bias or attempts to prove preconceived opinions about research results that reflect personal opinions of the researcher.	1. State any potential bias that research participants or researchers may have about preconceived research results. Identify steps to eliminate bias. 2. Such steps may include reflecting on potential bias, keeping a journal or research log of bias-related issues. Throughout the study, keep an open mind to different perspectives.
Representative Populations	Ensuring that each data collection method includes the total population of applicable participants or a sample with demographic characteristics similar to the total study population.	1. Review and reflect on characteristics of each study population identified to ensure a close similarity and inclusiveness of sample populations that mirror the total population in ways important to the study. 2. Avoid using only convenient populations for all data collection methods.
Confirming and Disconfirming Data	Including data that refute research findings, along with support data to enhance trustworthiness.	1. Include confirming and disconfirming data in the action research report. 2. Review data sources to ensure that people with perspectives different from those of the majority are represented in any sample population in proportion to those in the total population.
Member Checking	Providing members of a study population with an opportunity to review a draft transcript of their information tests its accuracy.	1. Gather perceptual data from individuals within a school community about drafted interpretations of research findings to test their accuracy. 2. Use study participants' language in stating study findings.
Debriefing	Sharing researchers' interpretations of data with knowledgeable colleagues during the formulation of such interpretations in order to test understanding and accuracy.	1. Guba (1981) says that sharing data findings and initial interpretations with a critical friend or colleague improves accurate interpretation. 2. Researchers test their perspectives with peer professionals.
Prolonged Engagement	Demonstrating rigor in on-site procedures for data gathering by researcher persistence and observation to assure understanding of the data and its context (Lincoln & Guba, 1985).	1. Practitioner-researchers should avoid hasty conclusions and bias in data collection and interpretation. 2. Practitioners generally have prolonged engagement in their setting but need sufficient time to reflect and confer with others to reach the most accurate conclusions and beneficial recommendations.
Participatory Validity	Participation in the research by the stakeholders reduces bias, builds confidence in the process, and enhances potential for positive change (Stringer, 2008).	1. Collaborative research encourages participation and buy-in for results. 2. Stakeholders' involvement gives them an opportunity to help verify accuracy and, also, improves research accuracy when they become involved in data analysis and report development.
Confirmation Validity	Maintaining records of the research process along with making the complete report accessible for review (Stringer, 2008) provides an audit trail for confirmation of trustworthiness.	1. Items that support the depth of the investigation, such as raw data (without names) and artifacts such as researcher reflective field notes or journals, strengthen validity. 2. Document and report data summaries and coded transcripts of qualitative data to demonstrate process validation.

(continued)

Table 4.1
(continued)

Technique	Definition	Description for Research
Pragmatic Validity	Recognizing the usefulness of the research is one of the greatest validations of action research (Stringer, 2008).	1. Participants who see effective actions result from understandings gained through research give the results high credibility. 2. Credibility to the research gains buy-in for improvement actions.
Data Triangulation	Comparing and contrasting multiple data types, sources, and methods to gain accuracy, credibility, and trustworthiness of findings.	1. Researchers cross check interpretations from multiple data types and data sources. 2. Case building involves basing interpretations on documented procedures, causes, and results learned from others along with the researchers' experiences (Miles & Huberman, 1994).

Chapter 5 describes the interpretation of qualitative data from interview transcripts, focus group summaries, and other worksheets which you may use to identify common themes that become evident in more than one of these sources. The chapter goes on to describe grouping some of this information for quantitative tallies in tables or figures that show the extent or numeric variation of common perceptions or actions. Most analyses of responses gathered through data-collection methods such as interviews and focus groups, as well as open-ended survey questions, consist of qualitative words that describe major findings and explain the types of support for the interpretations. Comparisons of qualitative results with data from other sources, such as historical records and reports, student achievement data, or curriculum plans and guides, help integrate quantitative and qualitative data in the conclusions of research findings.

Table 4.2
Fifth Grade Mathematics Achievement Worksheet for Cross Checking and Triangulating Data Findings

Perceptual or Student Learning Data		Records and Reports—Related Content	
Sources, Methods, and Themes	Quotes or Conclusions	Curriculum Map—Suggested Activities	Curriculum and Assessment Guide
Teacher Survey and Student Survey: Use of manipulatives	An instructional practice supported by research and also shown by the student survey as preferred practice but not shown on the teacher survey as used.	Numerous manipulatives are described for suggested activities in the curriculum map. Examples under the Numbers/Computation strand: "Use pattern blocks to add and subtract like pieces" (p. 1). "Group manipulatives in different ways and write equations that demonstrate the properties" (p. 11).	"Students will apply standard units to measure and determine weight, perimeter, area, time, temperature, and angles" (p. 3). "Students will choose and use appropriate tools (protractor, meter stick, ruler) for specific tasks to solve real world and mathematical problems" (p. 4).
Estimation and discussions	An instructional practice supported by research and also shown by the student survey as preferred practice but not shown on the teacher survey as used.	"Make a list of items they can afford using a grocery ad and $20. Calculate the actual cost and find the difference from the estimate and the actual amount" (p. 2).	"Students will use charts and tables to determine time schedules, work with time zones and estimate time" (p. 6). "Students will estimate weight, length, perimeter, area and angles using appropriate units of measurement" (p. 8).

Note. This is page 1 of an example worksheet for cross checking perceptual data with records and reports as sources for similar themes. Use multiple pages of a similar worksheet to compare, contrast, confirm, or disconfirm conclusions and interpretations from multiple types, sources, and methods of data collection.

Table 4.4 on the CD shows one way to analyze and integrate information from multiple study results. The table is based on the research questions shown in Figure 3.1. This example triangulates record and report quantitative and qualitative secondary data (including student achievement data) with quantitative and qualitative summaries from surveys, observations, interviews, or focus groups (primary data). Items also include relevant literature.

Interpreting data comes from grouping in different ways, performing calculations, and matching different types and sources of data that support or refute conclusions. With available data, your task is to make sense of the information as related to the research questions for the problem. This process takes deep reflection and an allocation of time, thought, and collaboration that brings your knowledge and experience as an educator to the interpretative processes of comparing, contrasting, checking for procedural similarities and differences, and determining the pros and cons for each interpretation. The first interpretation may not be the best one, so view the data from different perspectives and experiment with different arrangements of data.

ORGANIZATION OF QUANTITATIVE DATA FOR INTERPRETATION

Test scores and other numerical data make up a large part of student-learning data. Numerical data can be summarized and analyzed quantitatively for action research by the use of descriptive statistics. Also, demographic data, documentation of school processes, and data from records and reports, as well as perceptual data, can be partially summarized quantitatively with descriptive statistics. Educators work with achievement data and, thus, have familiarity with summarizing and analyzing quantitative data.

Descriptive Statistics

Action research generally relies on familiar descriptive statistics that show total, percentage, mean, median, and mode. *Mean* is an average, *median* is the middle score (halfway between the high and low score; or if the total number of scores is an even number, the median is the average of the two middle scores), and *mode* is the score that occurs the most frequently in a distribution of all scores. Tables displaying means usually include a column for the standard deviation (SD), or variance. *Standard deviation* shows the degree of variation of scores that fall above or below the mean; thus, it is a measure of variability from the mean (Cowan, 2004).

Adding a column in a table for the standard deviation in addition to means provides important information about the individual scores averaged for the mean. The chance of measurement error must be taken into account when working with test scores, although this is not as important to action research as to traditional research that requires SD as variability for additional statistical testing. One test score is not an absolute measure of what a student knows. The same test given to students on a different day, at a different time, or in a different testing environment would be unlikely to yield the same exact scores for individuals, because of influences on each student at any one time.

The standard deviation helps interpret the spread of individual scores from the mean by comparison with an expected, or normal, distribution of scores around the mean. The normal bell curve is a standard for the normal distribution of scores around a mean. Usually, the normal distribution of all scores plotted as a linear graph scale, with zero at the center of the scale, results in the approximate shape of a bell curve, with 68 percent of scores falling within one SD below the mean and one SD above the mean. Therefore, most scores are expected to cluster close to the mean. Also, 95 percent of all scores in a normal distribution curve fall between roughly two standard deviations below the mean and two standard deviations above the mean. In the normal curve, most of the data occur at the point of central tendency (Leedy & Ormrod, 2001).

A standard deviation of more than two raises questions for researchers as to why this difference from the expected distribution occurred. The outlier scores may indicate something about the test or testing conditions, measurement error, or other factors that affected certain students at the time of the test. The standard deviation, which identifies scores outside the normal range, either higher or lower, raises question about the data and why the difference occurred.

Although researchers seek facts, truth, and accuracy, they recognize the elusiveness of absolute truth. Thus, they use multiple measures and at least some strategies to strive for data integrity and trustworthiness. These measures and strategies help ensure that our interpretation of results has a reasonable degree of accuracy.

Statistical formulas determine standard deviations, but most researchers use software to calculate statistics. Spreadsheet software adapts well for descriptive quantitative functions. The following formulas or functions entered in a spreadsheet at the end of a row or column of numbers give the mean, total number of scores, and standard deviation:

Count =COUNT(A3:A15) Gives total number of responses from cell A3 through cell A15 in column A.

Mean =AVERAGE(A3:L15) Gives average of row of scores from cell A3 through cell L15.

Standard Deviation =STDEV(A3:L15) Gives SD for scores from cell A3 through cell L15.

Sum =sum(a1:a15) gives the total value in column A, rows 1 through 15.

The colon in the formula separates the location of the first cell (column letter, row number) and the last cell (column letter, row number) that includes numeric data contents to be calculated. Formulas for calculations begin with an equal sign. There are no blank spaces within the formulas; either uppercase or lowercase letters may be used.

Enter a formula in the spreadsheet in the blank cell where you want an answer calculated. After the formula is entered, the blank space to the right of the *fx* at the top of the spreadsheet shows the formula that was entered when the cell with the formula is selected. Corrections may be made by moving your cursor to that location *fx* while the cell is selected. After you have entered a formula, the calculated result appears in the cell when you click your cursor in another cell. Experiment with entering data and formulas for summary in a spreadsheet to gain comfort with this useful process, or bring persons familiar with technology to help record and summarize data collected from primary sources.

Because computer software updates occur frequently, I have found it easier to learn how to enter simple formulas in a spreadsheet for descriptive statistics than to become proficient with each new function menu that software updated revisions bring. Newer software will read older versions of the same software, but the converse is not generally true. That is why the electronic forms on the CD for school use were created in a version of the software compatible with most of the versions schools are likely to use. Updated versions of this software are now available. If you use a newer version that doesn't correctly calculate the results, or that shows an error when you enter the formula entered as shown here, select the data and function (fx) menu and note any differences for stating the formula. Then make that change accordingly.

Be sure that you begin each formula with an equal sign. Thinking about how to state the formula sometimes causes me to enter the formula but forget to begin with an equal sign. However, I found use of spreadsheets and formulas helpful as a principal for multiple tasks related to budgeting and scheduling, as well as for visual displays. As a university researcher, I preferred spreadsheets and formula entry for most qualitative research data storage and manipulation of data. SPSS, a statistical research software package, is more widely used for quantitative theoretical research by university researchers who use its advanced statistical functions.

Data Storage and Summaries

A sample spreadsheet file (Figure 4.1) on the CD in supplemental resources for Chapter 4 illustrates data entry for storing data collected from survey questions with a number response. This figure shows the survey questions on one spreadsheet, and another spreadsheet right behind the survey questions illustrates the numerical entries and formulas for summarizing results of survey responses. To move from one spreadsheet to another, click on the tab at the bottom of the workbook of spreadsheets. Formulas, as shown in the previous section, were entered for summary calculations, including the standard deviation.

Table 4.5 displays a format for descriptive statistics that shows mean and standard deviation, as well as mode and median. Mode and median are not always displayed together with the mean and standard deviation. Table 4.6 uses percentages based on a frequency count (using the count formula for each category column) divided by the total responses.

Table 4.5
Effectiveness Rating of Selected Components of the Secondary School Career and Technical Education Program (CTE) from Survey of CTE Graduates

Component	No.	Mean	Median	Mode	SD
Career planning	66	4.27	4.5	4	1.01
Dual credit	66	4.22	3.5	4	0.93
Secondary and postsecondary partnership	54	4.05	3.5	3	1.01
Cooperative ed./other work experience	66	3.95	3.5	5	0.98
Integration of academic and CTE	54	3.74	4.0	4	1.03
Applied mathematics and science	53	3.62	3.5	4	1.10

Note. **This table illustrates use of quantitative mean, median, mode, and standard deviation sorted in descending order by mean. Survey Rating Scale: Strongly disagree = 1, Disagree = 2, Undecided = 3, Agree = 4, and Strongly agree = 5.**

Most of the student data that you will analyze will come from various school databases. For example, if you are studying attendance, discipline, or academic achievement, various school records or a school database may provide data such as the number and characteristics of students who have excessive absences, the reasons given for the absences, and the number of excused and unexcused absences for different grade levels. If your research addresses discipline problems, you may compare data such as the numbers of incidents, the consequences of those incidents, in-school and out-of-school suspensions, and academic achievement levels, as well as other characteristics of students with disciplinary problems.

Because data are already stored and available in databases, you can record your selected research data in a meaningful way in a spreadsheet format that can be easily organized and summarized for your research questions and saved to your research file. Calculations for summarizing these data may be easily completed with a calculator if the number of items is small or on a spreadsheet file with formulas entered for a relevant summary of extensive quantitative data. From the summary of selected data, you would plan graphs and tables that best display these calculations in a way that helps answer your research questions. Then, you can enter the data totals and item and column titles in a spreadsheet to construct a graph or create a table or graph in word processing software.

Table 4.6
Status of Faculty Teaching Experience for Grades 1–6 Teachers at Calvert Elementary (N = 24)

Years Experience	Frequency (f)	Percentage of Respondents
In Grade Level Currently Teaching		
1–5 years	8	33.33
6–10 years	6	25.00
11–15 years	5	20.83
More than 15 years	5	20.83
Totals	24[1]	99.99[2]
In This Location Other Than This Year		
1–5 years	5	29.41
6–10 years	6	35.29
11–15 years	2	11.76
More than 15 years	4	23.53
Totals	17[1]	99.99[2]

Note. **This table illustrates a three-dimensional table (divided into two categories but with the same column headings). It also demonstrates display of frequencies and percentages.**
[1]Three are first-year teachers, and four are experienced teachers in their first year at this school.
[2]Total percentage is less than 100, due to rounding.

Each spreadsheet file with an embedded graph and each word processing file with a table or graph should be saved with a short descriptive file name so that it can be copied and pasted into the action research report later. It is good practice to note the source of the data underneath the table or graph in the file copy of each display. Saving a source note as part of a table or figure as it is developed and saved will ensure ready access to that information when the report is written and a table or figure is copied and pasted into the report. For a table, you may either add the source as part of a paragraph of text by referring to the display and interpreting its meaning or add a source note directly below the table. Source information added below tables would be preceded by the italicized word *Note* followed by a period. Source data for a figure could be added below the figure as part of the caption following the period after the figure number. See Table 4.7 (p. 62) and Figure 4.4 (p. 60) in this chapter for examples of the placement of notes with tables and figures.

As mentioned earlier, a variety of student-learning and achievement data in a school, district, and state is available through your state department of education. Some states make school data available in spreadsheet format. This gives great flexibility for you to select certain data and copy and paste these data into rows or columns in a spreadsheet file opened on your computer. See Figure 4.2 on the CD in Chapter 4 Resources for help in copying and pasting from one spreadsheet to another.

Figure 4.3 on the Supplemental CD in resources for Chapter 4 provides additional help and formats for entering spreadsheet data and transforming the data into tables or graphs. The beauty of the spreadsheet is its usefulness for calculating summary information by entering formulas below a column or to the right of a row of numbers and for producing graphs or diagrams. You may choose to use spreadsheet and word processing software available on mobile technology such as PDAs (personal digital assistants), tablet computers, or smart phones to make your work easy to take with you when you are on the move. Most school districts for today's schools have technology specialists who work with school personnel to implement and manage technology. Make good use of these resources.

Responses from surveys or observations should be first recorded and tallied quantitatively by question or observation and then grouped by similar content and themes emerging from qualitative analysis. How you record and tally these responses depends largely on the number of responders to the survey and the number and types of questions. If there are no more than 20 or 25 responders and not many questions, you may prefer to use a blank copy of the data survey form and tally the summary manually. Figure 4.4 on the next page in this chapter shows an example manual tally on a blank observation form for 10 completed classroom observations. Such a tally might be completed for observations when the number of observations is small. These manual tallies can summarize data required to prepare a table or figure for the action research report.

Open-response questions from surveys, interview data, focus group data, and records or reports need qualitative analysis before you can determine potential quantitative data to be reported or displayed in tables and graphs. Although a low number of surveys or questionnaires might be tallied by hand onto a blank copy of the form, the use of a spreadsheet will make this task easier when there are a greater number of responses or a variety of question types.

The student survey portion of CD Figure 4.1 gives an example of survey data recorded in a spreadsheet. These question responses required a rating scale and are shown on page 61 as Figure 4.5, which also includes a copy of the worksheet summary. The complete spreadsheet for Figure 4.1, on the CD, includes the teacher survey with summaries of multiple response questions, rating scale questions, and an open-response question. Each survey respondent's identifying code (T1, T2, etc.) and individual responses to each question are entered on the same row. Columns for this spreadsheet have abbreviated titles that correspond to each survey question.

The open-response questions on the survey can be summarized on the spreadsheet or entered in a list in a word processing document. In both cases, reorganize the list first by sorting alphabetically to group similar responses, and then group them under broader themes or categories related to your research problem and research questions. Responses under each category could be counted and displayed in a table or figure. Before using the software Sort function, you could look at the list and develop a code list that assigns a letter of the alphabet to the main categories into which the responses fall. Place the assigned letter at the beginning

Observation Chart: Primary and Intermediate Mathematics   Summary Tally

Observation #: 10 total   Date 2/30/2012   Time started_____   Time ended_____

10 total observations

Time allotted for Math today Averaged 55 min   Circle: 6 Primary 4 Intermediate

Topic/Topics being covered in lesson: __Primary: (3) number recognition, (2) counting, (1) addition; Intermediate: (2) estimation, (2) decimals

Teaching Strategies/Practices Used

	Check when observed ✓	Comments
Assessment	3	P: verbal (3)
Curriculum Map followed		
Different intelligences addressed	2	P: singing jingles; phys. moves
Estimation used/Anticipate the answer	2	I: worksheets & discussion
High student participation (at least 90%)	Yes P: 6; I: 4	
Higher order questioning		
Students called on equally		
Wait time provided	P: 6; I: 3	
Individual practice	P: 2; I: 4	P: verbal; I: worksheets
Lecture		
Guided practice		
Manipulatives used by students	P: 4; I: 0	Flash cards; blocks; sticks
Mathematics discussions	I: 2	
Positive teacher attitude	Yes for all 10	Encouraged students
Real life connections	I: 4	Word problems & examples

Figure 4.4. **Sample Observation Chart. This manual tally was of 10 total classroom observations with checks for the number of times each instructional activity was observed. Because there were only 10 total classrooms observed (6 primary; 4 intermediate), a manual count with a summary of the observer comments was recorded on one blank form of the observation instrument. This summary information would be used to make a table to be added to the research report.**

of the response, leaving one space between the letter and the actual response. Then highlight the list and sort, using the Sort choice under Data on a spreadsheet, or the Sort on the Table menu for word processing, to group responses categorized by similar topic.

Figure 4.1 is fully displayed on the CD in Chapter 4 resources and uses T1, T2, and so on in column one to identify each different teacher respondent to the survey. Each respondent's responses are entered in a row beside the identifying designation. In this example, students responded to selected questions that solicited the same information from students as from teachers but the questions were worded appropriately for the middle school mathematics students. Student responses were added as a continuation of the same spreadsheet, with each student case labeled S1, S2, and so on. For relatively low numbers of responses, the single spreadsheet makes it easy for you to compare student responses with teacher responses because they are on the same sheet. You can hide some columns in order to view only selected parts of the spreadsheet. Formulas entered into the spreadsheet will calculate teacher and student summary statistics. Review the electronic copy of the Figure 4.1 spreadsheet in Chapter 4 CD Resources to study the layout of the spreadsheet, along with the survey questions. When

Student Survey Questions With Rating Scale Response (from CD Figure 4.1)

Student Survey of 12 students who represent Grades 6, 7, and 8

Response Rating Scale: 0, Never; 1, Rarely; 2, Sometimes; 3, Usually; or 4, Always

1. In your mathematics class, how often do you practice activities similar to test content?
2. Do you work on mathematics problems related to real-life problems?
3. Do you have books, computer materials, and other resources for mathematics practice?
4. Do you receive the classroom help that you need in order to learn required content for tests or class projects?
5. How often does your mathematics course have you work with algebraic equations to solve for unknowns?

Portion of Spreadsheet for Student Responses (for a report, round decimals to 2 places.)

Students	Practice	Real life	Resources	Class help	Algebra
S1	2	1	3	2	0
S2	0	2	4	3	1
S3	2	0	2	4	2
S4	1	1	3	1	1
S5	0	2	4	3	0
S6	2	2	1	1	2
S7	1	1	2	2	0
S8	1	1	3	2	1
S9	2	2	3	3	2
S10	2	1	2	3	3
MEAN	1.3	1.3	2.7	2.4	2.4
STDEV	0.823273	0.674949	0.948683	0.966092	1.032796
SUM	13	13	27	24	12

Figure 4.5. Sample Data from a Student Survey. Data come from a portion of Figure 4.1 that shows rating questions from a survey of 12 students and the section of a spreadsheet that records and tallies results. Survey return rate was 10/12 = 5/6, or 83% return.

your cursor selects a cell that has tallied rows or columns, the formula used for the tally in the selected cell will appear at the top of the worksheet in the blank space beside the *fx*.

Quantitative Tables and Graphs

In education, we use numbers daily to interpret total sizes of groups, percentages of a whole, relationships of quantities to one another, levels of achievement, relationships of achievement to a standard, and averages of groups. Displaying these numbers visually helps communicate complex ideas.

In the action research report, tables and figures that display graphs or charts should be included to describe complex data that would require lengthy explanations or that can be easier understood with a visual display. Tables and graphs can be developed to show relationships or frequency counts, percentages, or averages of data categories. They can combine and compare related data from one source or multiple sources. They need to be kept simple to be interpreted quickly and accurately by readers. Furthermore, different arrangements of numbers and different selections of data categories to display in tables or graphs may reveal additional meanings. Play around with the data to plan the most informative visual display. Table 4.7 was adapted from a survey with statements to be rated by selecting *Very much*, *Some*, or *Little*. A total of 21 third-grade students responded.

Table 4.7 illustrates one type of source note, but you could use the name of the record or report or data-collection method and source (for example, include *Note:* 2011 Reading Survey of 21 Third Grade Students). Names can be used in reports only with permission. I recommend not using individual names in most cases. For published reports, written permission should be obtained ethically and legally (if material is copyrighted) for use of any visual displays prepared by another person or organization or published on a website. The source notes that provide names under the examples in this text do so to give credit

Table 4.7
Third Grade Reading Attitude Survey Scale (N = 21)

	Very Much		Some		Little	
	No.	%	No.	%	No.	%
I like to read.	13	62	8	38	0	0
I think reading is fun.	14	67	6	29	1	4
I think reading is hard.	2	10	11	52	8	38
I would like to read better.	16	76	5	24	0	0
I want to learn ways to help me read better.	15	71	4	19	2	10
I understand what I read.	11	52	9	43	1	5

Note. **Adapted from an action research report by Christine H. Rickert, Elementary Lead Teacher. Used with permission.**

to educators whose original work was used; the words *adapted from* denote that changes have been made from the original. The source-note wording was approved on the written permission forms signed by these individuals for use of their work as examples in this text.

Many of the table and figures in the text and on the CD follow the APA style manual, which is used in most advanced work in educational leadership publications. Providing consistent formatting throughout the text helps you learn a widely used style format by simply closely following the usage in the given examples when formatting the research components of your action research report. You may choose to use another style format. That is not a problem; however, format consistency in headings, references, tables, and figures enhances the professional appearance of your final report. Also, sequencing of items in a table or figure should be alphabetical, with low-to-high or high-to-low values, or time sequenced from first to last. In other words, items should be arranged logically for the purpose of the display.

PREPARING AND FORMATTING TABLES.   To analyze data, you will first organize them in a way that reveals trends, patterns, and summaries of relevant findings for the research questions. Before writing a discussion of findings, determine which data can be understood best by visual display in tables or graphs. If a data display needs to show detailed data or includes over three types of data over multiple time sequences, a table is the preferred choice, as a table clearly shows detailed data sequences better than a graph. You will be likely to have several tables and figures in your report. Tables and figures will be copied and incorporated in the section of your action report that describes data analysis and findings.

Tables include rows and columns for data display. They may be two-dimensional, with the first row of the table giving subheads for each column. The first column subhead may be blank, but every other column across the first row will have a subhead that names what is displayed in the column below it. Table 4.5 (p. 58) is a two-dimensional table displaying items and their values. Table 4.6 (p. 58) illustrates a three-dimensional table that divides the data into two vertical subcategories of items (Grade Level and Teaching Location). Subcategory headings for column 1 divide the table into three horizontal sections, each with a subtitle. Multiple sections can be combined in one table if the value subheads for columns remain the same for all table sections.

Plan your tables and figures to visually help the reader interpret categories of information. For example, a table for a 10- or 20-question survey could be summarized first quantitatively as a numeric tally of how many respondents gave each particular response. However, this provides too much specific detail for reader interpretation and would require extensive written text along with the table to interpret these individual responses in terms of the research questions. Group questions together that ask about a similar topic so that you can look at a particular aspect of the problem and compare results with other sources. This becomes easier to do if the survey instrument grouped questions together that pertained to broad categories such as instruction, testing, or teaching strategies.

Table 4.8
Description of Purposes for Different Graph Types

Graph	Purpose
Circle graph or pie chart	Compares values and percentages of parts to the whole
Horizontal bar graph	Compares values of different items for the same time period or of one item over a sequence of time periods
Multiple horizontal bar graph	Groups 2 or 3 multiple item values sequentially for the same time period or multiple values of one item over a limited sequence of time periods
Vertical column graph	Compares values of different items for the same time period or of one item over a sequence of time periods
Multiple vertical column graph	Groups multiple item values sequentially over the same time period or multiple values of one item over a limited sequence of time periods
Line graph	Shows change trends over time for one item
Multiple line graph	Compares change trends of multiple items

However, it should be done for interpretation even if the instrument did not group such questions. The instrument may have grouped types of questions such as yes–no, multiple-choice, ratings, and open-ended questions (also referred to as *open response*). This type of grouping in the instrument makes response simple and may improve return rate. The down side is that respondents may give less thought to each response when they answer groups of dichotomous (yes–no) or multiple-choice questions. These types of questions, with check-off type answers, enable respondents to answer quickly.

Word tables, as well as numeric value tables, become helpful when you are writing explanatory text material. In particular, they help you to compare and contrast ideas and assist you with qualitative interpretations. For example, Table 4.8 illustrates a simple word table to explain purposes of different types of graphs. Note that the format of a word table is the same as for a numeric table.

Tables have a number of components. For further details of formatting table components for APA style, review Figure 4.6 under Chapter 4 CD Resources.

PREPARING AND FORMATTING FIGURES.   Figures may be illustrations, pictures, graphs, or diagrams. Some APA rules for figures are the same as for tables; however, there are differences. Figure 4.7 on the CD under Chapter 4 Resources shows APA formatting details for figures.

Before creating a graph, enter your data in spreadsheet cells that make up rows and columns. A *cell* is the data-entry block at the intersection of a column and row. A *cell address* (name) is its column and row location (B1, C5, D3, etc.). Enter the subheads in column cells across the top row to label data that will be in each column. In each row of the first column, enter item labels that relate to the data. Then, highlight the entire section of the spreadsheet, including row and column labels with data, to be graphed. Go to the menu, and select Insert and Chart. The Wizard will open a menu for selection of features of the graph. The last choice you make from this menu is whether the chart is to be on a new sheet or embedded on the same sheet. If you insert the graph on the same spreadsheet with your data, it is easy to select parts of the graph, make changes, and see those changes made. If the data layout needs to be changed, having the spreadsheet next to its data layout and directly linked to a graph on the same sheet makes it easy for you to see changes that you make in the data on the spreadsheet immediately appear on the graph.

More than three different categories displayed on a graph and its legend make distinguishing assigned colors for each category difficult when the graph is printed in black and white. Most reports will not be color printed because of cost, so you may need to select lighter or darker colors for some of the bars or parts of a circle in order to improve the difference in shading for noncolor prints. Choose one very light, one very dark, and one medium color. However, if you need more than three different types of bars, the

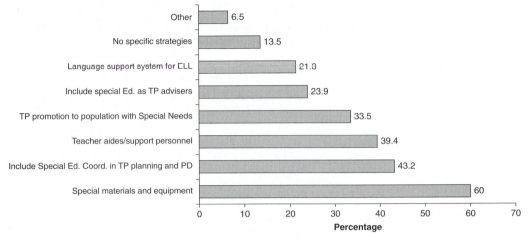

Figure 4.8. **A single bar graph of strategies listed as most effective in promoting the success of Tech Prep enrollees with special needs. Data came from a survey of Kentucky high school Tech Prep secondary and postsecondary partners (372 distributed, with a 42% return. Research participants could mark more than one choice, so percentages total more than 100%. ELL = English Language Learners, Ed. = Education, TP = Tech Prep, and PD = Professional Development.**

graph will appear cluttered; therefore, a table display may be best. You can choose a grayscale color for black-and-white prints, but even having three different columns—and especially, four—makes it hard to distinguish the intensity of the grays.

Compare the single bar graph in Figure 4.8 and the multiple bar graph in Figure 4.9 to see how too many legend categories clutter the display and make it difficult to interpret. The landscape orientation of a bar graph creates narrow horizontal bars when the graph displays seven years for three subjects. This makes each year's value difficult to interpret quickly. A table or a column graph would better serve the purpose for this data than a bar graph. Dimensions for the width of a column graph frames are generally greater than those for the height of column graph frames. Experimenting with different layouts will help you choose the best result.

Save your spreadsheets and graphs with a file name that lets you easily find a particular graph when you are ready to add it to your action research report. If you have trouble developing graphs from your data, a technology-savvy friend or your school or district technology coordinator can help you.

Figure 4.10 illustrates a simple column graph illustrating six teaching activities and the percentage of observations for each activity during the observation period. Figure 4.11 shows a multiple-column graph of three subject areas over a time sequence of seven years.

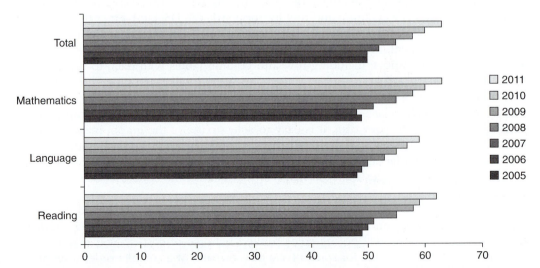

Figure 4.9. **This multiple bar graph shows CTBS scores for three subjects and a total of the three, over seven years for third-grade students in Xcell Primary School. The bar graph format is an illustration of an ineffective cluttered graph. These data should have been displayed in a table or more than one graph.**

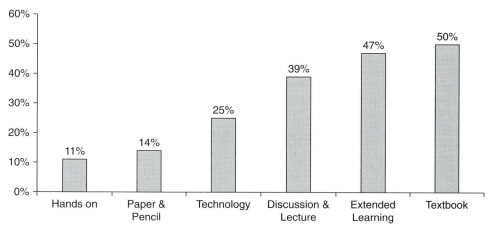

Figure 4.10. A single-bar column graph for one category (learning activities) in Whata Elementary School. Data were recorded on 10-minute walk-through observations of 25 teachers and reflect the learning activities observed during the snapshot observations in each classroom.

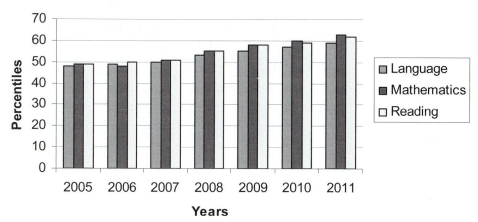

Figure 4.11. Example format for a multiple-bar column graph. This multiple-bar column graph displays the same data shown in Figure 4.9. Because this is a column graph and width is longer than height, there is more space for vertical columns than is true for horizontal bars on a multiple-bar graph.

Information should be logically sequenced on the spreadsheet layout, alphabetically, with high-to-low or low-to-high values, or time sequenced. On a pie graph, such as the one shown in Figure 4.12, sequence items clockwise from the twelve o'clock position from high to low percentage of the whole.

This chapter guided your summary, organization, and visual data displays for quantitative analysis. Chapter 5 will begin with qualitative analysis for data interpretation.

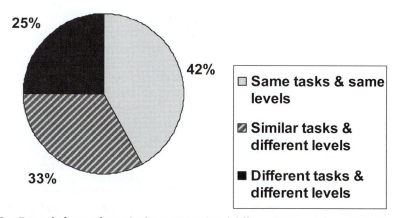

Figure 4.12.   Example format for a pie chart. Instructional differentiation as observed in Whata Elementary School from observation data recorded on 20-minute classroom walk-throughs over a three-month period (March–May 2005). Twenty-five K–5 teachers were observed in a total of 100 observations. This circle graph (pie chart) shows at a glance that the majority of classrooms over this observation period were not differentiating tasks or levels of instruction.

Key Questions for Review

1. Which three of the strategies for data integrity appear to be most useful for your school research?
2. How can tables and figures be useful in explaining research analysis and findings?
3. What data from your research can be displayed in tables or figures?

4. Who with technology expertise in your school or district can be helpful with preparation of tables and figures?
5. How does information from records and reports contribute to interpretive analysis?

Note: **Performance Checklist will also appear on CD.**

Performance Checklist for Step 3a Research Activities

Field test data-collection instruments, summarize quantitative data, prepare quantitative tables and figures, and begin data analysis.

A. Complete field test of each data-collection instrument for primary data: survey, observation, interview, and focus group.

Performance Check:

1. Identify one or more individuals with expertise in the area of study to review each instrument for needed change. Ask them to evaluate whether the wording of the questions on the data-collection instrument will be understood by the individuals in the sample population or the population as a whole. In addition, ask the reviewers to suggest any questions or directions on the instrument which should be reworded to ensure that responses will gather useful information to address the research problem. Have them also review the protocol for administering the instrument on the basis of its purpose and to make suggestions for change that will improve the clarity and appropriateness of the data-collection methodology.
2. Make changes as needed to refine data-collection instruments and procedures, and field test each instrument with someone who has characteristics similar to those of the targeted population. Follow the same protocol that will be used with the population or sample population.
3. Complete data collection, record, and begin quantitative summaries for data interpretation.

B. Analyze quantitative respondent data from your field-tested data-collection instruments.

Performance Check:

1. Involve knowledgeable and interested stakeholders, along with the research leadership team and the literature-review team, in summarizing, interpreting, and analyzing data. They may be involved at any stage of interpretation and analysis if they have studied the chapters in this text through Part 1 and Part 2.
2. Agree on the role that each person will carry out. Have a master list of people, responsibilities, and tasks with completion dates. The list should be developed by the leadership team or a combination of the leadership team and literature-review team. See the supplemental CD resources: Professional Development items CD 1.d and CD 1.f to save electronic planning worksheets for beginning and completing collaborative research tasks.
3. First, record and quantitatively summarize data from each data-collection method. Prepare student-learning data and demographic data, using descriptive statistics and percentages as appropriate for each type of quantitative data. Experiment with how best to display these data for the most accurate explanatory interpretation.
4. Develop tables and figures, along with brief interpretive comments, to include in the action research report.
5. Identify records and reports that may support confirming or disconfirming the initial interpretations of quantitative results.

References

Anderson, G. L., Herr, K., & Nihlen, A. S. (1994). *Studying your own school: An educator's guide to qualitative practitioner research*. Thousand Oaks, CA: Corwin Press.

Borg, W. R., & Gall, M. D. (1983). *Educational research: An introduction* (4th ed.). New York: Longman.

Cowan, G. (2004). *Understanding & conducting research in education: A user-friendly approach* (2nd ed.). Dubuque, IA: Kendall/Hunt.

Guba, E. G. (1981). Criteria for assessing the trustworthiness of naturalistic inquiries. *Educational Communication and Technology, 29*(2), 75–91.

Kincheloe, J. (1991). *Teachers as researchers: Qualitative inquiry as a path to empowerment*. Philadelphia: Falmer.

Leedy, P. D., & Ormrod, J. E. (2001). *Practical research: Planning and design* (7th ed.). Upper Saddle River, NJ: Merrill/Prentice Hall.

Lincoln, Y. S., & Guba, E. G. (1985). *Naturalistic inquiry*. Newberry Park, CA: Sage.

Maxwell, J. A. (1992). Understanding and validity in qualitative research. *Harvard Educational Review, 62*(3), 279–300.

Miles, M. B., & Huberman, A. M. (1994). *Qualitative data analysis: An expanded sourcebook* (2nd ed.). Thousand Oaks, CA: Sage.

Stringer, E. (2008). *Action research in education* (2nd ed.). Boston: Pearson.

Wolcott, H. E. (2001). *Writing up qualitative research* (2nd ed.). Thousand Oaks, CA: Sage.

PART THREE

Summarizing Qualitative Data and Completing an Action Research Report and Presentation

Chapter 5 of Part 3 begins with a discussion of organizing, summarizing, and analyzing qualitative data. Data analysis then brings together quantitative and qualitative data from both primary (original) and secondary data sources, with previously gained knowledge, to synthesize research findings and reach conclusions for school improvement in the problem area studied.

In addition, Chapter 6 shows you how to develop recommendations and combine descriptions of each research step into an action research report. You will also develop a visual presentation that gives a brief overview of the research for sharing within your school, school district, and with others in your school community. As you bring together the results of the research, you and others who helped conduct this study will reflect on what you learned about conducting research and next steps.

Purpose and Outcomes for Part 3

Part 3 completes Steps 3a, b, and c, as well as 4a, of action research. This part guides you through these activities for your research:

1. Analysis and interpretation of qualitative data.
2. Summary of research conclusions.
3. Development of evidence-supported research recommendations.
4. Assembly and refinement of an action research report and visual presentation.
5. Reflection on the research process and next steps for implementation.

In-School Performance Activities

Chapter 5

1. Summarize and interpret qualitative data.
2. Describe the research methodology and procedures followed in conducting the research.
3. Describe research findings from data analysis.
4. Collaborate, review, and reflect to synthesize findings relevant to the research questions, literature review, and data analysis. Develop major conclusions from research findings.

Chapter 6

1. Collaborate and develop data-based recommendations for addressing the research problem.
2. Combine and refine section drafts of the research purpose and questions, literature review, research procedures, data analysis, conclusions, and recommendations into an action research report.
3. Reflect on your research, and develop a presentation slide show and handouts or other type of visual display for communication of research results.
4. Reflect on action research and next steps for implementing results to contribute to improved learning outcomes for all students.

CHAPTER 5

Analysis and Interpretation of Qualitative Data

Analysis of qualitative data from questionnaires, observations, interviews, and focus groups requires recording, organizing, and interpreting documented responses. In particular, interviews and focus groups can yield a large volume of documentation. The number of pages of notes and transcripts depends on the number of questions asked and the number of respondents, as well as the level of detail in the responses to questions. Recognizing the volume of material involved in recording qualitative data underscores the importance of carefully choosing relevant questions and appropriate interview participants who are knowledgeable of the problem issues and representative of stakeholders affected by these issues.

Qualitative data-collection methods seek nonobvious meanings which reveal complexities that address issues important to the research questions. Forget those nice-to-know questions that relate only remotely to the focused research problem. Although some items can be counted with quantitative descriptive analysis, meanings relevant to the research problem must come first and foremost from qualitative, rather than quantitative, analysis. Qualitative study such as action research searches for understanding conditions and perceptions that inform decision making for an identified research problem.

Linn and Erickson (1990) give examples of qualitative research questions that search for depth of meaning about teaching instead of—or to supplement—quantitative research about how student achievement occurs in different classrooms. They refer to qualitative research as an interpretive viewpoint that asks questions about what is taking place and why. In other words, qualitative research gleans meaning from detailed word responses by asking interpretive questions focused on the research problem.

Qualitative analysis for action research depends largely on systematic interpretation of words, sentences, paragraphs, and chunks of text content in order to understand key settings, events, and processes of the major themes and emerging patterns that focus on the research questions (Miles & Huberman, 1994). The scribbled notes and recordings from interviews and focus groups must be processed as draft transcripts before qualitative content analysis can take place.

Transcribing is time consuming and can be done with different levels of detail, sometimes including pauses, word emphasis, *uh's* and *ah's*, mispronunciation, and incomplete sentences. For action research in schools, I suggest that such details be disregarded unless they are important for the research questions. When used for member checking, the transcript should be generally correct technically, as well as marked with the word *DRAFT*. It should be as complete and accurate as possible because the person reviewing it might decide not to let the interview be used if any part is too unsatisfactory.

As an alternative method, member checks of interview transcripts or member checks by a sample of focus group respondents may be delayed until tentative interpretation and summary of meaning from all interviews or focus groups are complete.

Member checks could involve presenting a review copy of a completed summary worksheet, instead of an exact transcript of each interview or focus group discussion, and requesting additions or corrections necessary to accurately include the reviewers' responses. If the transcript is not used for member checks, the typing and technical errors wouldn't have to be corrected as long as the transcript is readable by the researcher(s). This speeds up the transcription process because the draft transcript becomes the working document for the researchers' interpretations and is filed as a working draft for audit review.

To avoid having a respondent in the member-checking process want a complete revision of what was recorded, a note could be attached to the member-check transcript. The note would specify that the purpose of the review is only to correct any errors of fact and to include alternative interpretations not reflected in the transcript or summary of data. Miles and Huberman (1994) advocate using member-check agreements with participants (respondents) in regard to the purpose and responsibility for member checks. In addition, I suggest including a statement of reassurance as an attachment that researchers and the written research report will keep identities of individual responses confidential and that most descriptions will be summary interpretations from the results, as a whole, of each data-collection method.

For a member check of a written summary of interviews—rather than of the draft transcript of an individual's interview—you also could ask a few questions to see how the participant's reactions about their own perspectives and understandings match with the interview summary. Their reactions then become part of confirming or disconfirming evidence and can be reported (without disclosing personal identity) as such, with appropriate changes made in the summary description on the basis of this feedback.

The purpose of qualitative analysis is to understand key settings, events, processes, major themes, and concept patterns that emerge (Miles & Huberman, 1994) as the researchers focus on the research questions, study transcripts and notes, debrief these meanings with colleagues knowledgeable of the research problem, and reflect on these understandings. A number of techniques for qualitative analysis have been identified by researchers. In my professional judgment, processes described in this section provide a usable guide for educational leaders in school settings. The qualitative analysis consists of three concurrent activities: data reduction, data display, and conclusion drawing and verification (Miles & Huberman, 1994, p. 10).

Data reduction takes place even before data collection is informed through decisions about research-question content, instrumentation, and information sources and continues throughout qualitative research (Miles & Huberman, 1994). As data collection proceeds, researchers begin to study their notes and/or transcription of recordings for each interview, focus group, observation, and records and reports. This analytic process to find meaning involves reflecting, selecting, simplifying, abstracting, writing summaries, and preparing word tables or concept maps.

Reflecting, selecting, and simplifying take place throughout planning and collecting, coding, summarizing, debriefing, revising, sharing, concluding, and confirming and disconfirming conclusions and recommendations. Analytic techniques and displays that help reduce the volume of data and guide your search for meaning from written or verbal content include document coding, contact or document summaries, visual displays, and quantitative summaries. Figure 5.1 on the CD under Chapter 5 Resources gives direction for entering survey responses on a spreadsheet for quantitative summaries.

DOCUMENT CODING AND ANALYSIS

Document coding is a process of studying and marking transcripts and researcher notes to identify different themes and patterns that emerge upon reviewing and reflecting on meanings from words, sentences, paragraphs, and chunks of information. The research problem and research questions for the study frame the boundaries for coding.

Although some types of qualitative research do not place predetermined boundaries on information collected or on data interpretation, action research for school improvement is bounded by studying a specific problem or issue related directly or indirectly to student learning within a particular school setting. The context within that setting is studied only as it pertains to the selected problem and what the practitioner-researcher can learn that addresses research questions about that problem.

Action researchers are professional practitioners with knowledge about the context and the problems from previous learning, school experience, and the literature review for this research problem. This knowledge base provides ideas about issues that relate to the problem. The knowledge further informs the researcher of how to read notes and transcripts and look for words, sentences, paragraphs, or chunks of information that reflect beliefs, behaviors, events, and actions from qualitative data collection. Frequently, repeated meanings become themes or patterns from data collected. When reading information from all respondents in interviews, for example, *themes* are categories of meaning that repeat themselves within interviews. *Patterns* reveal how, when, where, and why these themes recur.

After reading and reflecting on the qualitative data, create a start list of codes before you begin to code transcripts and notes. Computer software for qualitative data analysis can facilitate content analysis by connecting relevant data segments to each other but does not replace reflection and analytic thinking. If you wish to research this type of software, you can use a search engine and enter the words "computer software for qualitative data analysis." You also might visit the home web page for one of the widely known qualitative software packages such as http://www.maxqda to learn more about their features.

After your initial formulation of themes and/or patterns from reflection and review of notes and the literature, create a simple coding system to identify and mark the transcript or initial notes. Colored pens may be used to represent each major theme or pattern. Color coding is quicker to use in grouping themes than a code of words or series of letters and numbers. For a printed copy, you can simply have the code sheet and colored pencils nearby as you underline or circle a block of text in the appropriate color. For an electronic word-processing file, use the Find function to locate key theme words, and set a different font color for different themes.

Table 5.1 illustrates a simple code sheet with colors assigned to major themes. Follow each theme or pattern with descriptors to help define indicators or evidences to be marked for that theme. These indicators or evidences could include words with meanings expressive of the themes or brief specific quotes (without identifying a person). A code sheet may also have a blank column to be completed after coding which gives example quotes or comments that support or disconfirm that theme. Table 5.1 shows sample quotes for themes that represent each stratified group included in the interview sample. A blank copy of this code sheet is labeled Table 5.2 in Chapter 5 Resources on the Supplemental CD.

Miles and Huberman (1994) advocate developing an operational definition of codes to help identify word segments fitting the definition. This may help reveal your own biases; awareness of potential bias helps to guard against it. Begin development of a simple coding scheme early, and make coding an ongoing process. All word content doesn't need coding, however. Keep the code list brief, focusing on the major themes important to understanding. Coding need not be exhaustive. Instead, it helps find good exemplars. Don't try to label all content with codes. Identify the major themes and patterns, and create contact summaries for these. Develop codes only for those chunks of information useful in response to the research questions. Remember that action researchers can add to, change, or delete questions as knowledge emerges and the need for change becomes evident to address the research problem.

To help researchers read notes and transcripts for each respondent, you will find it helpful after coding to prepare a summary sheet of one page for each interview, observation, or other contact source. Make sure that information on a contact summary focuses on the main points in that contact, keeping in mind the information needed from this source (Miles & Huberman, 1994, pp. 51–53). Miles and Huberman propose that each contact summary respond to four to five questions that can be completed by brief responses synthesizing the essence of meaning from each contact (interview, observation, or focus group, for example).

I have prepared an electronic blank contact summary form that might be useful in your school research. This form is on the Supplemental CD under Resources for Chapter 5 as Figure 5.2. You can change, add to, or delete questions. I have suggested questions such as the following: Who or what was involved? What were the major themes, patterns, or issues from this contact? Which research question(s) did this content primarily address? Briefly, what was learned relative to the target research question(s)? What questions need follow-up from this source or others? What was the most interesting or important thing learned from this contact? Researcher responses may paraphrase or use short quotes from the draft transcript or notes to express what was learned. A few example quotes (without identifying a specific person) provide support or alternative perspectives for the description of research findings.

Table 5.1
Example Code Sheet for Identifying Major Themes from Responses to Administrative and Faculty Interviews About the High School Career Pathways Program

Color Codes	Major Themes and Definitions	Sample Comments or Quotes for Themes
Blue	Program objectives (goals, objectives, program evaluation measures, and standards)	*Admin.*: "We offer a coherent, articulated rigorous sequence of academic and career-related courses beginning in the 9th grade and leading to an associate or four-year degree and/or a career-related and industry recognized certificate or licensure." *Core faculty*: "All students select course work with the end goal in mind." *Career faculty*: "Pathways include rigorous content that incorporates all required educational and training components necessary for each student's career goal."
Red	Student characteristics (grade levels, group counseling, special education, Title I, after-school program, tutoring, supplementary services, gender, ethnicity, reading and math proficiency levels)	*Admin.*: "All of our students are in career pathways offered at the high school or career academy. We have six career pathways." *Acad. faculty*: "We include students who are in special education with all other students; we have two great resource teachers who work along with teachers to support special populations." *Career faculty*: "We need to make sure that students explore career options and select a pathway consistent with their goal during their freshman year."
Yellow	Program improvement (successes, barriers, problems, achievements, and perceived reasons for achievements and barriers to achievement)	*Admin.*: "With school accountability and focus on working on core content, sufficient time is hard to find for a yearly extended academic/career integration project." *Core faculty*: "We need to improve articulation agreements and dual credit. We need to work closer with colleges and other postsecondary schools our students attend." *Career faculty*: "Our community is not large enough to offer all students work-based learning outside school. We need more in-school ongoing projects like our school bank."

Note. Core faculty members are teachers of English, mathematics, science, and social studies. Career faculty members teach career skill areas.

Concept Maps, Diagrams, and Word Tables

Educators use *concept mapping* to link elements within major concepts. This display tool or other diagrams and word tables help reduce the explanatory comments required in the action research report for reader understanding of complex concepts and relationships. Visual displays are tools that help researchers focus on a clear understanding of themes and patterns relevant to research questions and that help to convey this understanding to others. They can be collaboratively developed or refined. Their use as part of the research final report can quickly identify for report readers an understanding of regularities (patterns) in qualitative data. Concept maps support meaningful learning (Novak, 2008; Novak & Cañas, 2008). Visual displays help to organize and sequence learning tasks and to link new meanings to existing knowledge.

Figure 5.3 illustrates a simple concept diagram. Note that the major items are in circles, squares, or rectangles connected with relationship lines or arrows. They may include short explanatory terms describing the nature of relationships. Concept maps or diagrams take many forms; they can be drawn with word processing drawing tools or spreadsheet chart tools in preparation for copying and pasting as a figure into a report.

Also, word tables can display word relationships that would otherwise take lengthy explanations and can be a useful display tool in the description of findings or literature review. Examples of word tables are Table 4.1, p. 54, and Table 4.8, p. 63, in Chapter 4 and also in Chapter 4 CD Resources.

Data Triangulation

Now that we have covered both quantitative and qualitative data interpretation and analysis of results from different data collection methods and sources, we will look at data triangulation. The triangulation process begins with a comparison and contrast of data from the multiple sources and methods that you have employed. The reliability and validity of

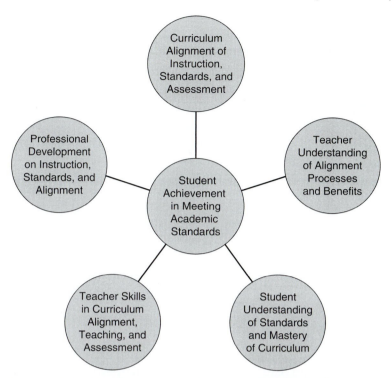

Figure 5.3. A Concept Map of qualitative interpretive themes. This diagram illustrates major themes for curriculum alignment as benefits for student achievement of curricular standards.

conclusions from your data are enhanced through comparison of what you have learned from (a) collecting data from different sources, using the same method; (b) collecting different data from the same sources on the same topic; or (c) collecting similar data by different methods from the same subjects or sources (Cowan, 2004, p. 142).

Chapter 3 covered planning for multiple methods and sources when identifying information needs for your research questions. Looking back at Table 3.1, p. 39, or Table 3.1 under Chapter 3 CD Resources, you will see that to learn about Research Question 1: alignment benefits and procedures, you will compare results from qualitative information in the literature on alignment procedures, benefits, and professional development with results from a particular teacher survey. The survey includes questions of teachers that reveal their knowledge, experiences, and professional development on the meaning, benefits, and process of curriculum alignment, as well as mathematics teachers' attitudes about curriculum alignment. Comparing the survey responses on teachers' professional development (PD) with records of professional development for these teachers gives another cross check. Therefore, this triangulates data on similar topics from three types of data collection (literature, survey, and school records and reports), as well as from three sources (literature, teachers' PD records, and curriculum standards and guides). The teachers' opinion question about the mathematics curriculum component that is most out of alignment reveals something about teachers' knowledge of the curriculum alignment components and could be compared with curriculum guides, standards, and student achievement on content areas.

At this point, data from the literature, as well as survey topics, would be reduced through coding, contact summaries, and displays of tables, figures, and a concept diagram. The next step is to triangulate results by comparing what literature describes from research and best practices about alignment benefits, procedures, and necessary teacher professional development with what teachers know and believe about the importance and benefits of aligning standards, instruction, and assessment for the mathematics curriculum.

In your data analysis for the first research guiding question, you could construct a concept diagram or word table, summarizing major themes from the literature review and curriculum content compared with data related to these themes as reflected by the teacher surveys. A brief narrative would refer to the concept map by figure number and add other essential explanations or examples of similarities and differences. In addition, paragraph text explains themes shown in the concept map or compares them with related data from the literature review and curriculum guides. Interpretations of these data and tentative conclusions could be verified and refined by debriefing with colleagues knowledgeable of the literature and of teacher opinions. Debriefing colleagues can help you examine both confirming and disconfirming evidence. Then, explanatory comments, tables, and figures would be refined and added to the Data Analysis section of the action research report.

DATA ANALYSIS AND RESULTS

Section titles vary among research reports. The data analysis section describes the research findings from summaries, data displays, and interpretation of quantitative and qualitative data. Analysis and interpretation of your data may be titled Data Analysis, Data Interpretation, Research Results, Research Findings, or something similar.

When the full report of your action research comes together, this section will be placed after Research Methodology. However, developing the data analysis section before describing your methodology seems logical for action research even though you will reverse the order when assembling the action research report. The reader will need to read about research methods and procedures before reading the data analysis results, but describing those procedures will be easier for the researcher to do immediately after completing the data analysis. Reversing the order for writing these two sections allows for the flexibility of action researchers as practitioners, with previous knowledge and experience in the research context, to change direction, add or refine questions or procedures, or add data sources as needed during the research.

This chapter content, as well as that of Chapter 3, explains how to analyze and interpret data. Now you are ready to write the Data Analysis Results part of the research final report. After you do the analysis and writing of this section, developing the methodology part of the report should be easy because the methodology describes what you did in collecting and analyzing data for the research problem.

Content in an action research report should present to decision makers, stakeholders, and others clearly described summary knowledge drawn from data analysis and interpretation as related to research questions. Presentation of the data and analysis keeps the focus on the research problem and questions.

Certain data types and sources pertain to particular research guiding questions, and organizing the data presentation by these questions provides one type of structure for this analysis report. If you use such a structure, you can state the question or convert it to an abbreviated subheading at the left margin, that states the essence of the question. For example, the research question "Who are the personnel and how were they involved?" may become a secondary side subheading, "School and District Personnel Involvement." The eight report examples at the end of Part 4 and the six action report examples on the Supplemental CD, although similar in many respects, show different ways of presenting the data analysis section of the report.

Tables and figures display detailed data and simplify complex concept structures. The text comments referring to tables and figures in the analysis section may include reasons that you organized data as you did, the intent and interpretation of visual displays, and a narrative summary interpretation of facts presented. Giving the rationale for your approach to qualitative and quantitative analysis helps the reader understand not only what was done but why it was done. Discuss the findings as they relate to research guiding questions. Provide support for interpretations, and present what you learned from both confirming and disconfirming evidence.

Avoid statements and terms that overstate results, such as *proves*, *significant difference*, *causes*, or *effect*. These have specific meanings in quantitative statistical processes but are not appropriate for qualitative research in general, nor in action research.

A simplified outline for this section of the report could include these items:

I. Brief Introductory Paragraph

II. Data Presentation and Discussion by Guiding Questions

III. Brief Summary Paragraph

Figure 5.4 gives an example of a data analysis section of the action research report. The centered heading for this section could be Data Analysis, Research Findings, or Research Results (or other appropriate heading that you choose).

Research Problem Analysis

This action research analyzed the communication network of a Response to Intervention (RTI) in reading at Merryweather Elementary School, one of three pilot sites in 2010–2011. Literature for new program change emphasizes three important themes as shown in Figure 1.

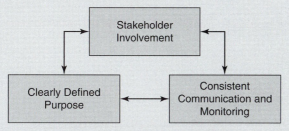

Figure 1.   Important themes for implementation of new programs.

These themes summarize organizational strategies identified in literature as important for new program implementation. Effective change requires demonstrating a high level of commitment to everyone involved and making sure that they understand their roles (Zirkel, 2007). Conveying and understanding the mission and purpose are critical first steps (Putnam, 2000). Early and continuing communication is key to implementing any program (Beagrie, 2005). In addition, a leadership team to regularly review progress, monitor processes, and solve problems is a priority (Putnam, 2008).

School and District Personnel Initial Involvement

Twenty-two Merryweather Elementary School teachers from grades 1 to 5 completed an online survey about the RTI implementation process. Surveys were also completed by five elementary Curriculum Resource Administrators (CRAs), and an interview was completed with the district RTI coordinator. Upon review of these data-collection results, several important factors emerged about the effectiveness of communication for RTI implementation.

Table 1 shows that before the RTI implementation began, 50% of teachers expressed that they had limited knowledge of the RTI program, while 27.3% said that they had no knowledge of the program. No teacher reported that they were well-informed, but 22.7% believed that they had sufficient knowledge to begin the program. The surveys of Curriculum Resource Administrators (CRAs) revealed that three persons (60%) did not feel informed at all about the RTI process, and two CRAs (40%) felt that they had limited knowledge of the RTI process.

Table 1

Teacher RTI Knowledge Prior to Implementation

Knowledge Level	Teachers		CRAs	
	Count	Percent	Count	Percent
Not informed at all	6	27.3	3	60
Some information	11	50.0	2	40
Informed well enough to begin	5	22.7	0	0
Well-informed	0	0.0	0	0
Totals	22	100	5	100

Background information about the RTI was shared with principals, CRAs, and school psychologists in May, three months prior to implementation. In August, the basic format and expectations were shared with all parties. One CRA was able to attend a conference to learn more about RTI during the fall of the pilot year. Two other CRAs attended a similar conference but only after the pilot year had been completed. All five CRAs shared that they did not feel equipped effectively to lead the district initiative in their schools. The basic format was provided, but detailed instructions and guidance were not provided at the onset of implementation.

During the initial stages of RTI implementation, teachers received information in a variety of ways (Figure 2). RTI information was shared most often during staff meetings (87.5%), grade-level meetings (66.7%), Student Achievement Team meetings (SAT) (41.7%), and through emails (45.8%). CRAs received RTI information primarily through CRA bimonthly meetings and RTI quarterly meetings.

Figure 5.4.   Data Analysis section for an action research report. Content in this example analysis was adapted from action research completed by Dawn Floyd, Elementary School Assistant Principal. Used with permission.

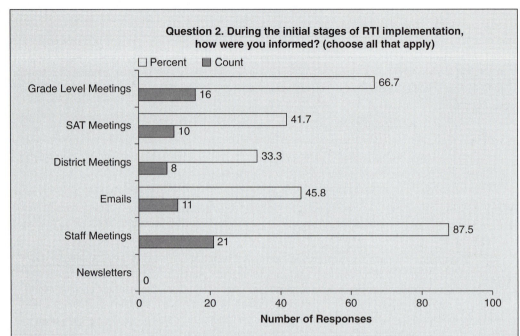

Question 2. During the initial stages of RTI implementation, how were you informed? (choose all that apply)

Figure 2.   Teacher information sources during initial stages of RTI implementation.

Gaps in Initial Communication

The CRAs were surveyed to help identify strengths and needs from a school leadership perspective, as well as to add suggestions for further implementation. The CRAs were responsible for the school-level implementation process. We met monthly with the district coordinators and other pilot schools to discuss issues pertaining to RTI.

The teachers and staff members who were involved with the implementation process during the first-year pilot process were surveyed to identify perceptions of RTI, as well as how the communication process in place at the time supported or hindered the implementation for them and their students. Meeting with teachers after the tabulation of survey results offered more information and suggestions concerning the strengths and needs of the process.

After the research, surveys and interviews were completed and analyzed; the compiled information was shared with the principal and the RTI team for a second time. This allowed all members involved in the implementation to collaborate and examine the results.

Data reflect that teachers and CRAs had a limited level of knowledge and understanding of the RTI program prior to implementation. Administrators had little time to grasp the magnitude of the RTI implementation. The greatest communication gap appears to have existed during early stages of the program implementation. Background knowledge was limited, and school leaders did not feel equipped to effectively lead the initiative.

During initial stages, RTI information was communicated through monthly CRA staff meetings for teachers and district quarterly RTI meetings for CRAs. However, often, the meetings were inefficient, were infrequent, and provided little support. Consequently, CRAs and teachers were unprepared and uncertain. Procedures unfolded as the school year progressed, often resulting in last-minute directions pertaining to data and intervention work.

Post-Implementation Perceptions of Communication

Now that implementation of the process is complete, teachers receive RTI information in various ways (Figure 3). The method of delivery has basically remained the same as it was during the initial stages of implementation but with more assistance from an RTI Student Achievement Coach (SAC). Teachers receive information primarily from SACs, grade level meetings, and staff meetings. Emails and CRAs are also important sources of information.

Figure 5.4.   *(Continued)*

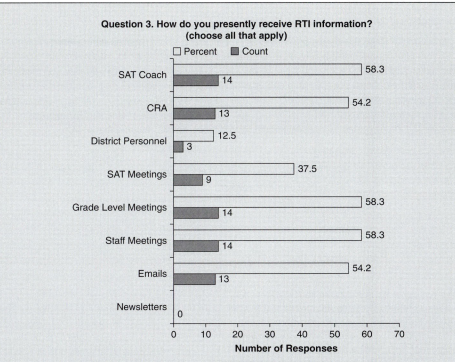

Figure 3. Teacher information sources reported after completion of RTI implementation.

After implementation was complete, the district restructured student achievement teams to include an RTI coach, who would provide teachers with assistance and instruction during grade-level meetings, school RTI/SAT meetings, or one-on-one meetings with the SAC. The additional support allowed the CRAs to better monitor the effectiveness of the program procedures and data. Teacher surveys suggested that these meetings were the most effective source of RTI information (Figure 4). Teacher surveys also indicated that emails appear to be an effective source of communication for teachers. The data suggest that the most effective communication methods are being provided for teachers (Figure 3).

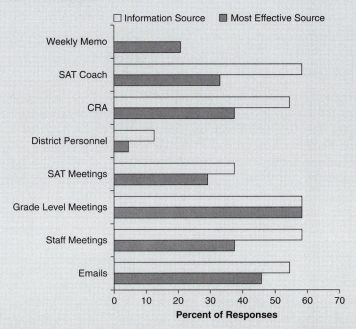

Figure 4. Comparison of actual RTI information sources and those sources considered most effective by teachers.

Figure 5.4. *(Continued)*

CRA Perceptions of Effective Information Sources

According to CRAs, the most effective manner for receiving RTI information during initial implementation was through district monthly CRA meetings and quarterly RTI meetings for administrators. Now that implementation is complete, CRAs continue to gather and share information through monthly CRA meetings and quarterly RTI meetings, but they also gather additional RTI information during monthly Instructional Council (IC) meetings that consist of district elementary principals, CRAs, and SACs. All five CRAs agreed that meetings provide the most beneficial information (Table 2). CRAs also prefer that RTI information be made available through professional development opportunities, emails, and an intranet blog.

Table 2
Most Effective Sources of RTI Information for CRAs (Post-Implementation)

Information Source	Percent of CRAs
Emails	40
Meetings	100
Intranet Blog	40
PD	80

Prior to implementation, the district coordinator spent one year researching and planning for the RTI implementation. She also worked with the district curriculum coordinator to explain the background and procedures of the process. During initial stages of implementation, the most effective means of communicating information was through quarterly RTI meetings with CRAs, principals, and psychologists. After implementation was complete, email and a newly established district RTI blog were the most effective ways to answer and pose questions or concerns. However, the school district coordinator was concerned that email could be ineffective if not checked regularly.

CRA meetings, the Instructional Council meetings, and the RTI meetings continue to be the most effective methods for communicating RTI information for CRAs. The meetings provide a platform for sharing successes and concerns pertaining to program procedures and data in the areas that they are responsible for after implementation. Like teachers, email also continues to be an effective source of communication for CRAs.

District personnel continue to facilitate the monthly district CRA, RTI, and IC meetings when RTI information is discussed or presented. The district coordinator also continues to monitor the district RTI blog. She collects information from meetings and the intranet blog to ensure that all involved are informed.

Figure 5.4. **(Continued)**

RESEARCH METHODOLOGY

At this point, writing the research methodology will be easy if you reflect on what has been done to conduct the research. Think through the steps that you took to this point, and clearly and briefly describe them, with an explanation of why you did what was done. This section is written in past-tense verbs because you are describing what you have completed. It is the section of the action research report that precedes the Data Analysis section in the final report. An outline to guide content for this report section could include these items:

I. Brief Introductory Paragraph

II. Data Collection Sources and Methods

III. Rationale and Selection of Populations, Sample Populations, or Sources for Data Collection

IV. Procedures for Data Collection

V. Procedures or Techniques to Avoid Bias and Support for Integrity of Results

VI. Collaborative Process and Stakeholder Involvement in the Research Process (Avoid using names here; indicate participants by groups or job titles represented.)

VII. Brief Summary Paragraph

In the explanation of data collection, you could include a word table summarizing the types of information and sources you used for each research question, along with your explanatory comments about the methods you used for gathering the information.

Figures 5.5 and 5.6 give examples of methodology sections from two different research reports. Also, see the example action research reports at the end of Part 4 and on the supplementary CD. In Example 12 and Example 14 action research reports on the CD, note how the literature review and methodology sections were incorporated in the data throughout the report rather than isolated into separate sections. This is another way of preparing the final report.

RESEARCH CONCLUSIONS

Interpretation of research results stated as conclusions synthesizes major findings about the research problem and serves as the primary basis for recommendations to address the problem or to evaluate procedures previously implemented to support student learning. Both conclusions and recommendations should be substantiated by data from the study as well as knowledge gained from relevant professional literature. Leedy (1989) describes the summary, or conclusion, section of a research report as a final look backward to interpret briefly and clearly conclusions from the research findings and data analysis that are supported by the data previously presented. These conclusions lead to recommendations for action.

Conclusions come from stepping back from data specifics and determining general patterns, themes, or metaphorical clusters that have meaning for the research problem and student achievement. After reviewing the data analysis for quantitative data aggregation, qualitative patterns and themes, and triangulation of information related to the same question, look for meaning in what the data say about the research questions. Reflect on knowledge gained from literature, experience, and other resources to assist you in reaching conclusions. Does the data analysis logically lead you to conclusions? What you have read and experienced should help you understand factors that may contribute to solving the problem and strategies previously used in other settings and recommended for school improvement.

Recognize preconceived notions about this problem; evidence may substantiate these, but other data may show opposite or different results that disconfirm your first assumptions. Evaluate the strength of evidence, and objectively report conclusions and supporting evidence. To reach reasonably valid conclusions, you must look for both confirming and disconfirming data related to your tentative conclusions after data analysis. The purpose of triangulation is to look at the question from more than one perspective.

Development of conclusions and recommendations should be a collaborative process involving stakeholders and other knowledgeable colleagues and school community representatives. Collaboration during the research process brings together diverse viewpoints and ideas from stakeholders and colleagues who participate in the research and encourages their support for changes proposed and supported by the research.

O'Brien (2001) reminds us that action research participants are co-researchers and practitioners (often referred to as *practitioner-researchers*) and that action research may be referred to appropriately as *action learning*. He cites the *action research* definition of Gilmore, Krantz, and Ramirez (1986), who describe the research process as a dual commitment—to study a system while collaborating with system members in changing it in what is jointly regarded as a desirable direction. Accomplishing this dual goal requires active collaboration and stresses co-learning as primary in the research process. School practitioners wish to improve understanding of their professional practices. Action research in schools is systematic learning that advances knowledge about the research problem to improve school effects on learning.

Conclusions should emphasize what the research results mean. Stating conclusions requires looking again at what the research data reveal and using that information in collaborative dialogue among the leadership team, literature-review team, data collectors, and other professional colleagues and stakeholders to determine answers to such questions as the following: When we study the data and reflect on the literature reviewed,

Methodology

To acquire the data needed to improve student and teacher attitudes and consistent student achievement for exploratory career and technical courses in the middle school, information and data needs were determined for each research guiding question. The primary research question was stated as follows: *How can career and technical exploratory classes be perceived as a valued component of academic student achievement and become a more important contributor of middle school education?* Table 1 displays the decisions for sources of data, types of data, and methods for data collection.

Table 1

Data Collection Needs for Research Questions

Research Guiding Questions	Information Needs and Data Types	Data Sources and Data-Collection Methods
What value do students and staff currently place on these classes?	Qualitative perceptual data about the attitudes and value placed on these classes	Staff survey Student survey
What instructional and classroom strategies are currently implemented?	Qualitative data about classroom strategies currently used	Interviews with each exploratory teacher
Do these classes contribute to student development and success? If so, how?	Qualitative data and quantitative data on how these classes contribute and how they lead to student development	Core content state test data No Child Left Behind data Questions on the previous student survey
How can these classes become more valuable for student success?	Ways in which elective courses such as these can be more valuable	Literature review Questions on the staff and student surveys
What does research literature say about value, instruction, and best practices for elective courses and middle school learning?	Qualitative data on suggestions and best practices for elective courses and middle school learning	Literature review
What improvements in these classes can lead to gains in student learning and achievement?	Qualitative data on how to contribute to gains in student learning and achievement	Literature review Questions on the staff and student surveys

Two separate surveys were developed. One survey was given to the students at the middle school, and a separate survey was created for the staff. The student survey was distributed during homeroom to every student who was present in the building on that particular day. The students used ScanTron sheets to fill in the answers related to the questions asked on their survey. Homeroom teachers collected the completed student surveys and placed them in a designated school mailbox before the end of the school day. All student surveys were conducted and completed anonymously. The completed ScanTron sheets were taken to the board of education office and fed through a ScanTron reader that is capable of analyzing opinion-type questions. Upon completion of running all of the completed ScanTron sheets, the machine printed out data analysis of all of the results for each question. By use of the data received from the analysis, tables and graphs were created to display the targeted data.

The teacher survey instrument, accompanied by a ScanTron answer sheet, was hand delivered to each teacher. Teachers were asked to complete the surveys anonymously within a given amount of time and return them to my school mailbox. An email was sent explaining the importance of the survey and asking for full participation from all teachers. After several days, a reminder email was sent urging teachers to complete and turn in the surveys. After all teacher surveys were collected, the same process used for the student survey was used to analyze the data.

The third data-collection tool used was an interview of the exploratory teachers. The researcher sat down with each of the six teachers and inquired about classroom management strategies and instructional practices currently being implemented in their classrooms. Upon completion of the teacher interviews, the results were analyzed. As a means of comparison of exploratory classes with core classes, an open-ended survey was completed with six core teachers. This open-ended survey contained the exact questions used in the exploratory teacher interviews. Two teachers from each of the middle school teams—sixth grade team, seventh grade team, and eighth grade team—were randomly chosen to participate in the open-ended survey. The survey participants were randomly selected from these teachers, as were participants for the staff survey, to maintain confidentiality. After gathering the data from surveying the six core teachers, a comparison matrix chart showing the results was created.

The surveys and teacher interviews provided us with data and answered several of our subresearch questions: (a) What value do students and staff currently place on the elective exploratory classes? (b) What instructional and classroom management strategies are currently implemented in those classes? To answer the additional subresearch questions, a pool of students was surveyed to acquire data related to improving the value of the classes and also leading to improvements in student learning and achievement. Thirty students were chosen by the

Figure 5.5. **Methodology and Research Procedures. This methodology description was adapted from action research completed by Kristina Marie Kinney, Middle School Teacher. Used with permission.**

principal to participate in the open-ended survey. Those participants consisted of 10 students from sixth grade, 10 students from seventh grade, and 10 students from eighth grade. Of those participants, there were 10 African American students, 10 Caucasian students, 5 special education students, and 5 Hispanic students. A letter of permission was sent to the parents of each chosen participant. Once permission had been given, the surveys began. All of the participants gave their assent to participate in the survey, so the surveys began during homeroom the following day. Ten students completed anonymous open-ended surveys during homeroom for three consecutive days. When the surveys were completed, the data were analyzed. The data collected from the open-ended student surveys helped us find a means for improvement of these classes directed toward improved student learning and achievement and a higher value placed on their contribution to middle school student development.

Figure 5.5. (*Continued*)

Methodology

To carry out this research involved collaboration of the school assistant principal, the school principal, reading specialist, the district's special education director, intermediate special education teachers, and the intermediate classroom teachers (grades 4 and 5). The research examined the possible cause of a widening achievement gap in reading for fourth and fifth grade students at Reddy Elementary. The initial step in this inquiry was to locate and review information from a variety of research-based literature sources pertinent to reading strategies that would provide support for students with disabilities. This information gave an accurate picture of the resources and strategies used in recommendations for special education gap reduction in reading.

The team members represented general education teachers, special education teachers, the special education director, the reading specialist, and the principal. The diverse observations from staff with special education backgrounds versus team members with a variety of regular education experiences helped decrease bias in the analysis of the research results.

Four types of data were gathered and analyzed on fourth and fifth grade students: (a) demographic data comparing the special education and general education student populations; (b) reading student achievement data from KCCT/PAS for the special education and general education student populations; (c) intermediate teacher survey perception data on reading intervention professional-development needs, as well as listing and rating reading remediation programs previously used at this school; and (d) classroom walkthrough observations to record the different types of reading interventions and instructional groupings.

The first part of the study involved identifying and listing the students in two categories: special education students versus general education students. The students were also subgrouped into free and reduced-price lunch, or not. Demographic data came from our school's student data tool provided by the state department of education. Assigning numbers to each student for identification protected confidentiality of the student names. An R next to a number represented a special education student, and an L next to a number represented a student on free or reduced-price lunch.

KCCT and PAS reading scores for the years 2006, 2007, and 2008 came from our school's state performance report. Bar graphs were created to compare and contrast reading scores by subcategory demographics for students with disabilities versus the general education population.

All fourth and fifth grade general education and special education teachers, as well as the reading specialist, were surveyed about their professional-development needs in order to successfully implement a strategic research-based reading intervention program. They were also asked to list and rate remediation reading programs that they had previously used at Reddy Elementary during the past three years. A total of four questions were used on the survey. (See Appendix A for survey questions.) This information was categorized and summarized by types of professional development requested and the listing of successful versus unsuccessful reading interventions used prior to this current year.

Random walkthrough observations in the intermediate grades were used to record the different types of reading interventions and instructional groupings for special education students (see Appendix B).

The research data were shared with the entire research team. We collaboratively developed recommendations for intermediate special education reading program improvement to increase student learning. This information was shared with all stakeholders when the research was completed.

Figure 5.6. **Methodology. This methodology example was adapted from action research completed by Sara G. Saylor, Elementary School Assistant Principal and Curriculum Resource Administrator. Used with permission.**

what conclusions come forth that can help improve the problem studied and support student learning? What did we learn that can guide improvement? What else do we need to learn?

Conclusions *synthesize* rather than *summarize* the knowledge from professional literature and evidence from data analysis. Summarizing helps you to reflect back and cover the main points succinctly, but effective research conclusions result from reflection that searches for meaning and integrates specific data and information into broader, meaningful conclusions of major importance to improving the research problem. This means stepping back from specifics, examining different perspectives, evaluating data that confirm or disconfirm conclusions, and using the tacit knowledge of professional colleagues and knowledgeable stakeholders to interpret concepts about the research problem that have meaning for this school site. *Tacit knowledge* is an inner understanding possessed by individuals that comes from integrating their learning from written and spoken knowledge with their own experiences.

Synthesizing becomes a thinking process that reviews research facts and specifics and uses methods such as clustering, categorization, themes and patterns, comparisons and contrasts, and descriptive metaphors (Miles & Huberman, 1994) to describe what the research means in the broader context of helping this school improve the research problem. Don't just repeat data or literature already stated, but reference support for the conclusions.

As you state conclusions, you are making assumptions based on a better understanding of problem issues in the context of your school. However, avoid the human tendency to believe that building an evidence chain confirms the absolute truth or causality of any elements of the research problem. If a group of students with low achievement also have poor attendance records, don't stop there and assume that improving attendance will raise achievement. Look for other data related to student achievement. What other characteristics describe low-achieving students? What counseling is available? What learning styles do these students have? What knowledge domains give them the most trouble? What instructional strategies help students achieve? You cannot answer all of these questions, but you should look for at least two or three different types or sources of data related to your research question to examine multiple factors that could be present.

You are generating data-based characteristics and related issues that help illuminate the problem and, thus, lead to informed decisions to improve it. Conclusions and recommendations supported by data and previous knowledge from literature, along with interpretations from multiple professional experiences and perspectives, add trustworthiness and validity to results.

As you state action research conclusions, avoid terms such as *proves*, *effect*, and *significant difference*. Also, avoid statements that generalize findings from this particular school context to other settings. These statements have specific meanings in quantitative research; however, we know of instances from the practices of health, medicine, and nutrition in which recommendations that once guided our decisions change later when modified by further research and advanced knowledge in the field. Decision making supported by data and action research is a positive approach that searches for truth but is not infallible.

Don't be fearful of using informed collective expertise to state interpretations of data and reach broad meanings for your school, while referring to data sources leading to these conclusions. Conclusions are interpretive statements as opposed to a restating of the facts, but be wary of terms that imply absolute truth or generalizability to other schools. Action research proposes to achieve improved outcomes by developing growth in understanding among those who study and use data-based evidence in their roles as practitioners for positive change.

Stating conclusions for an action research report is much like writing effective conclusions at the end of a well-written academic paper. The Writing Center website of the University of North Carolina at Chapel Hill ("Conclusions," n.d.) advocates playing the *So What?* game with a colleague or by yourself. Every time you state a conclusion, ask, "So what?" To develop action research conclusions, respond repeatedly to this question until your interpretation reaches a high enough level that it integrates your research findings and literature knowledge into a few broad conclusions that interpret meaning for addressing the problem. Figure 5.7 gives an example of how this might work with a school research problem.

Funneling conclusive statements through the primary research question and stating what was learned about the problem that has meaning to improve the problem or that requires further research is the final step of synthesizing, rather than summarizing, all findings. The data analysis responds to all research guiding questions. Now, sift through that knowledge and data to integrate and interpret varied perspectives useful in improving the problem. State these conclusions clearly and briefly in about two or three paragraphs.

Title of Report: An Effective Communication Network for the Response to Intervention (RTI) Implementation

Primary Research Question: How can a communication system create a more systematic and comparable implementation process within a school?

Using the "So What?" method to develop the first conclusion for this communication system could involve collaborative or self-dialogue that started something like this:

1st Statement

Before the RTI implementation began, 50% of teachers expressed that they had limited knowledge of the RTI program, while 27.3% said that they had no knowledge of the program. (Note: This is just repeating what was already stated in data analysis.)

So What? What does this mean in terms of the problem?

2nd Statement

Teachers had little help because administrators had little time to grasp the magnitude of RTI implementation, and RTI meetings during initial stages were ineffective and irregular.

So What?

3rd statement

A survey of teachers indicated that they often were unprepared during initial RTI implementation because of getting last-minute instructions for their work.

. . . and so on until the reasoning and meaning arrive at major assumptions from the data that will lead to conclusions and recommendations. Here are the final conclusions from this research:

Conclusions

Data reflect that prior to implementation, teachers and CRAs had limited knowledge and understanding of the RTI program, and administrators had little time to grasp the magnitude of the RTI implementation. During initial stages, RTI staff meetings for teachers, monthly CRA meetings, and district quarterly meetings were often inefficient, were infrequent, and provided little support. Consequently, teachers and CRAs were unprepared and uncertain. Procedures unfolded as the year progressed, often resulting in last-minute directions about data and intervention work. Communicating consistently and clearly the goals for the new plan through various means has a positive impact. For program implementation to work well, the staff must view a program as part of their vision for educating children and their roles and responsibilities as professionals (Mellard, 2005).

After addition of an RTI coach to assist teachers during meetings, a teacher survey shows meetings and emails as the most effective means of communication. Also, district personnel facilitated monthly district CRA, RTI, and Instructional Council meetings when RTI information was discussed or presented. After an RTI coach was hired and an RTI blog was added, CRAs were better able to monitor the effectiveness of the program's procedures and data. The district coordinator continues to monitor the district RTI blog. She collects information from meetings and the intranet blog to ensure that all involved are informed. Literature reviewed for the research suggested the importance of an ongoing plan to monitor the implementation process and progress regularly and consistently.

Figure 5.7. **An Example of the "So What?" Method (Writing Center UNC-Chapel Hill, n.d.). This example of the development of action research conclusions was adapted from an action research report by Dawn Floyd, Elementary School Assistant Principal. Used with permission. The supplementary CD includes this complete research report on RTI to improve communication for implementation of instructional innovations. See Example 10 Action Research Report.**

Include only the conclusions most relevant and important to recommendations for addressing the research problem. Conclusions that lead to recommendations form a bridge from the research back to educational practice for improved student learning. Figure 5.8 presents an example of conclusions. Review the conclusions from example action research reports at the end of Part 4 and on the supplementary resources CD.

Conclusions

Data show that most students do not increase their performance level on the state core competency test evaluation from the eighth grade to the eleventh grade. Of the total students tested in the Class of 2003, approximately 60 did not advance performance levels from when they were tested in the eighth grade to when they were tested in eleventh grade. Approximately 43 students went down at least one performance level. It could be inferred that the instruction and assessment at Jewell High School is not helping students to increase their performance level on the state core competency test.

Lack of student success in math could be attributed to one of several factors: "poor instruction, insufficient number of math courses, unintelligible textbooks, or misinformation about math and about who should do well in math" (Crawford, as cited in Furner & Berman, 2003, p. 171).

According to the publication *Improving Student Achievement in Mathematics* (Educational Research Service [ERS], 1999), in order to improve student achievement and understanding, it is important for teachers to be aware of how students construct knowledge and the methods that they use to solve problems. Use of this knowledge should be taken into consideration as teachers plan for and teach mathematics to students. Teaching for meaning and assisting students with construction of meaning have been shown to correlate with a positive effect on student learning, retention of learning, and the ability of students to apply what they have learned in new situations.

According to the mathematics core content test results for the class of 2003, tracking students through this course-taking pattern does not appear to assist students with reaching mathematics proficiency. Oakes (as cited in National Center for Research in Mathematical Sciences Education, 1994) found that students in lower-level courses often do not have the opportunity to encounter the same content as those students in high tracks. Also, because of staff perceptions, students were not receiving the same quality mathematics program. This is supported by the findings of Nathan and Koedinger (2000), who report that the instructional practices that teachers choose to use with students are directly influenced by their beliefs about learning and students' ability.

Teachers at Jewell High School may have to work with the middle school to identify and implement ways to combat student fear of mathematics. In a study conducted by Bower (2001), it was found that around the age of 12, students who fear or feel threatened by mathematics begin to avoid math classes and tend not to do well in the classes that they do take. These students also are the ones who typically score poorly on math achievement tests. This idea is further supported by Kober (1991), who reports that students achieve poorly if they fear mathematics, dislike mathematics, or doubt their mathematics ability.

Figure 5.8. Example Conclusions Section of an Action Research Report. Adapted from an action research report by Kim Zeidler-Watters, Director, P–12 Mathematics/Science Outreach. Used with permission. You will note that in the total report examples at the end of Part 4, these conclusions were integrated with data analysis. They are separated here to identify conclusion statements.

Key Questions for Review

1. What are three ways that data reduction occurs?
2. How can concept mapping and word tables be used in qualitative data analysis?
3. What is the purpose of data triangulation, and how is this done?
4. Who should be involved in your school for collaboration in writing the data analysis, methodology, and conclusions sections of the report?

5. In your own words, compare and contrast the similarities and difference between the terms *summarize* and *synthesize*. Explain what each term means in the context of stating conclusions.

Note. **Performance Checklist will also appear on the CD.**

Performance Checklist for Steps 3a, 3b, 3c, and Step 4a Research Activities

The following checklist for Chapter 5 suggests actions for completion of data interpretation and analysis, research procedures and methodology, and research conclusions:

A. **Analyze qualitative data, and bring together qualitative data analysis with quantitative data analysis.**

   Performance Check:

   1. Analyze and reduce qualitative data through interpretive methods. Develop appropriate data displays, using technology expertise as needed. Involve research team members and other colleagues. Triangulate data from

quantitative data, qualitative data, records and reports, or other sources. Collaborate with knowledgeable, interested stakeholders, including parents and community members, as appropriate to summarize, interpret, and analyze data.

   2. Reach agreement on each person's role, and compile a master list of people, responsibilities, tasks, and projected completion dates. See the CD Supplement professional development workshop Item CD 1.d and Item CD 1.f for electronic planning worksheets.

   3. Complete member checking and debriefing to get answers to questions still unresolved. Look for events,

processes, and perceptions of the major themes or patterns. Complete quantitative checks and tables or figures.

4. Reflect on the data summary. Look back at original notes and transcripts to verify questionable areas. Triangulate data related to each question. Develop narrative with tables, figures, and concept maps of major findings for the data analysis. Include confirming and disconfirming evidence. Collaborate with colleagues to discuss preliminary findings and to get additional input. Make changes or add comments.

B. Summarize data analysis and results, and complete this section for the action research report.

Performance Check:

1. Decide on a title for your description of analysis and results. Write a draft of the findings, organized by research guiding questions or another organization pattern. Use tables and figures and written commentary for each question to describe what was learned.

2. Summarize a written commentary on findings for each question, comparing the findings with literature reviewed. Discuss important findings from this action research, with support for the findings, as well as alternative interpretations and extent of disconfirming evidence.

C. Describe research methodology.

Performance Check:

1. Review methodology examples in this chapter, plus at least one more from a complete action research report from the CD resources or from reports at the end of

Part 4. Give an appropriate title for this section of the report such as Research Methodology, Methodology, or Research Procedures. Note that the title describes the content for this section.

2. Draft an introductory paragraph, and then describe the procedures followed. The first paragraph sometimes includes a restatement of the research problem and explains the role of action research. Draft paragraphs that describe in reasonable detail the research steps involved and how you followed them. Use past-tense verbs in writing this section. Describe procedures followed to increase data integrity, as well as the collaborative process.

D. Develop conclusions that synthesize research findings from your literature review and data analysis.

Performance Check:

1. Collaborate with research team members and other colleagues and stakeholders knowledgeable of the research problem to formulate conclusions. Conclusions should be interpretive of major research findings that are supported by data and best practice from professional knowledge. This section of the report needs broad stakeholder involvement to facilitate understanding and support for effective implementation of needed change.

2. I suggest a research meeting to finalize conclusions. Appoint a recorder and leader. Discuss these to reach a consensus on major conclusions for the report. Send the conclusions to all team members, and file a dated copy in the action research central file.

References

Cowan, G. (2004). *Understanding & conducting research in education* (2nd ed.). Dubuque, IA: Kendall/Hunt.

Gilmore, T., Krantz, J., & Ramirez, R. (1986). Action based modes of inquiry and the host-researcher relationship. *Consultation, 5*(5), 160–176.

Leedy, P. D. (1989). *Practical research: Planning and design* (4th edition). New York: Macmillan.

Linn, R. & Erikson, F. (1990). *Quantitative methods qualitative methods: A project of the American Educational Research Association* (Vol. 2). London, England: MacMillan.

Miles, M. B., & Huberman, A. M. (1994). *Qualitative data analysis* (2nd ed.). Thousand Oaks, CA: Sage.

Novak, J. D. (2008). *Learning, creating, and using knowledge: Concept Maps® as facilitative tools in schools and corporations* [Kindle Edition].

Novak, J. D., & Cañas, A. J. (2008, January). The Theory Underlying Concept Maps and How to Construct and Use Them, Technical Report IHMC CMap Tools 2006-01 Rev. 01-2008, Florida Institute for Human and Machine Cognition. Retrieved from http://cmap.ihmc.us/publications/researchpapers/theoryunderlyingconceptmaps.pdf

O'Brien, R. (2001). An overview of the methodological approach of action research. In R. Richardson (Ed.), *Theory and practice of action research*. João Pessoa, Brazil: Universidade Federal da Paraiba. (English version). Retrieved from http://www.web.ca/~robrien/papers/arfinal.html

CHAPTER 6

Recommendations, Reports, and Reflections

The last part of action research involves developing recommendations for action. Here, all steps and performance components of action research come together in a descriptive report of the completed study. Used collaboratively within a school as a basis for change to improve student achievement, research provides another benefit in that it contributes to faculty and staff knowledge about school problems, learning barriers, and strategies for improvement. Adding to professional practitioner knowledge about teaching and learning in the long term has the greatest potential for improvement of school practice that affects student learning.

In addition to completing the action research report guided by performance checks in this chapter, you will also complete a visual presentation for sharing research results, with both internal and external audiences as deemed appropriate by the school and school system. Both before and after concluding the action research, individual and collaborative reflection takes place. Think of reflection as a continuing part of each research step as you make decisions about stating the research problem and questions, locating literature relevant to areas that sufficiently address the questions, collecting and analyzing multiple data sources, triangulating diverse data types and sources, and describing the research procedures followed. However, because of the interpretive nature of synthesizing research conclusions and the importance of stating recommendations as a platform for positive change, reflection assumes an even greater role before the drafting of recommendations and finalizing of the recommendations and report.

REFLECTION FOR RESEARCH RECOMMENDATIONS

Briefly stop and think about how to define *reflection for determining recommendations* and how to do it. Reviewing dictionary definitions for *reflection* reveals these applicable words: thought, idea, or opinion; a result of meditation; thoughtful and deliberative; careful thought and consideration. Another phrase, *mirror image*, may be useful also, as thoughts bring forth an interpretive image of an event or action of what was, what is, and what should be. Dewey and Schön (as cited in Smith, 2001, 2011) saw reflection as part of learning that adds to practitioners' repertoire of mental images, ideas, and examples to draw upon for future actions. The term *reflective practitioner* had early beginnings in the writings of Schön (1973, 1983, 1987) and has become an emphasis in teacher preparation.

According to Zeichner and Liston (1987), who wrote about teaching reflection to student teachers, an individual's reflective content is colored by preconceived values, knowledge, and experience. Thus, even within the cultural environment of a school, each individual's life and educational experiences are not exactly the same. Therefore, thinking about a common action or experience collaboratively results in a varied array of ideas about what has taken place and what should take place. This is particularly true when each member of a collaborative group has previously reflected individually on the issue for collaboration. Collaborative reflection among research team members and other stakeholders—who are knowledgeable about research results from a study of the problem—brings a wide range of thoughts and ideas to the table for the consideration of conclusions and actions to take for improvement.

Bainer and Cantrell (1991, p. 2) describe practitioner reflectivity as the "ability to assess situations and make thoughtful, rational decisions." Their research on reflection examined the relationship between the nature of preservice teachers' reflective experience and the content of reflection. Bainer and Cantrell's study data showed that most of the preservice practitioners' reflective content fit into four categories: implementation, self, planning, and the reflective experience itself (p. 11).

Bainer and Cantrell's (1991) type of reflection appears appropriate for assessing research results and making thoughtful, rational decisions about positive action for learning-related problems. Reflection about effective recommendations formed from action research conclusions most likely would elicit thoughtful ideas related to planning and implementing change actions (what and how), considering effects on stakeholders (self and others in the school context), and evaluating the action research results that elicited change (quality and improvement areas).

Figure 6.1 on the CD under Resources for Chapter 6 illustrates uses of reflection and collaboration throughout research and problem solving. Reflection comes into play again in Part 4 to support school-improvement action planning and for integration of the process of problem solving and action research as part of the daily work and professional growth of educators.

Although reflection during research or most other times often begins with individual reflection and sense making, collaboration enriches understanding, multiplies possibilities, and achieves insights. Reflections shared by research teams, faculty members, parent groups, site-based councils, and other community representatives provide opportunities for input and subsequent buy-in for school-improvement actions. Collective input for recommendations may take place through communication technology, as well as face-to-face discussions. Reflection can begin with a question as simple as *What have we learned about the problem, and how can we apply what was learned to improve student learning in this school context?*

Most likely, beneficial reflective processes differ somewhat for different individuals. For me, reflection usually begins with consciously thinking about the event, problem, or concern at a quiet time alone, maybe not dwelling on it for long. I have observed that when I think about it again, usually a few days later, my mind seems to have worked on the problem without my conscious awareness of further thought, because this time, conclusions or solutions that were not previously in my awareness come to mind. These thoughts may raise questions in my mind that cause me to research related areas for consideration or form better possibilities for solutions than came to mind upon my initial intentional reflection.

In most cases, sharing ideas with trusted, thoughtful colleagues also brings new conclusions or reasonable solutions. Both individual and collaborative methods result in my most helpful reflection. Sometimes, a group discussion of a topic or problem about which I have previous knowledge but have not consciously reflected upon individually brings a number of new, logical perspectives to mind. Some of these perspectives were mentioned in the group discussion, and some new ideas are generated by what was discussed, along with what was already known. At least, collaboration brings thoughts together from a cadre of knowledgeable people, thereby creating awareness of a number of choices and a chance for input on important decisions.

Recommendations are critical decisions. Implementation takes time and money. This is a particular time to blend practitioner experience, educational knowledge, research findings, and additional research (when needed), before making useful recommendations for action. Effective recommendations bring together best practices from other research and best thoughts from practitioner-researchers' previous knowledge and experiences.

RESEARCH RECOMMENDATIONS

Research recommendations not only take the first step for implementing action to address a research problem but also evaluate current practice related to the problem. Both conclusions and recommendations should be substantiated by research data from the study, as well as knowledge gained from relevant professional literature. As mentioned in Chapter 5, the conclusions and recommendations take a data-informed collective look back for interpretation based on research findings.

Recommendations begin with interpretation that looks ahead at future improvement actions stemming from research conclusions. Recommendations are additions or changes that researchers and colleagues and stakeholders believe to be logically and accurately representative of knowledge about best practice, data relevant to the problem, and support for student learning in the context of this particular school. Also, recommendations may include areas related to this research problem that need further study.

Cowan (2004, p. 217) says that "The making of meaning refers to interpretation of data. It's one thing to have concrete data in front of you. It's quite another to know what the message is. Many factors influence the interpretation of data. Ultimately, though, it is the interpretation, after thorough analysis, that leads you to effective uses of research findings." Conclusions state the message from the research. Recommendations stem from those conclusions, thus bridging research with action planning.

I suggest stating recommendations as a numbered list, perhaps introduced with an introductory statement or two. Insofar as possible and reasonable, state each recommendation clearly and succinctly, recommending improvement actions to be taken in educational practice. Focus all actions on benefits, both direct and indirect, for student learning. For credibility, cite one or more literature sources and/or refer to study data as support for each recommendation. The data reference and research may be inserted in a recommendation, in parentheses, by referring to a figure or table, as (*see Figure 3*) and referring to research, as (*Smythe, 2010*). A brief reference to a conclusion may also provide support, as in a statement directly linking a recommendation to a related conclusion.

Figure 6.2 and Figure 6.3 show examples of action research recommendations. Figure 6.2 presents recommendations that came from conclusions of research on communication

---

Recommendations

Based on the findings of this study and review of professional literature, the following recommendations are made for increasing the effectiveness of communication for the Response to Intervention program:

1. According to Duffy (2008), it is important that stakeholders understand a new initiative, and the purpose of the new initiative should be clearly defined. According to the data, teachers and curriculum resource administrators were not well informed prior to RTI implementation, and it was clearly evident in the communication and procedural development. Elliott (2008) recommended that providing tools to help implement RTI through the most effective means of professional development will enable the district and schools to meet the needs of the students. Initially, this communication should clearly target purpose, goals, and program procedures. The district and school may be providing support systems, but the teachers may be lacking in background knowledge. Providing the tools and techniques prior to and during RTI implementation should improve results. Hall (2008) recommended that reading articles and books and group discussion sessions for sharing ideas for applying these readings in classrooms, in addition to visiting schools that have gone through implementation, would be excellent ways to grow professionally, assist implementation of an intervention, and improve results. Completing a self-assessment pertaining to program knowledge prior to and periodically after implementation could help school leaders and teachers measure how well the program is understood.

2. Putnam (2007) recommended that a well-organized highly-skilled leadership team should meet regularly to review and monitor procedures and processes, as well as setbacks that have been experienced. Meetings for the district have been well planned and held on a regular basis. However, the school RTI Team that consists of a principal, a CRA, a psychologist, an RTI coach, a reading intervention teacher, and two special education teachers has met sporadically. The team should create a schedule of regular meetings, and each meeting should follow a specific format that outlines issues, needs, and successes (McCook, 2006). Wright (2007) suggested that a team drifting away from a problem-solving process could make the team ineffective.

3. Ford (2008) recommends frequent and shared communication through multiple ways. Continue seeking communication methods in addition to the weekly memo and district intranet blog to improve service to CRAs and teachers. Use a quarterly easy-to-answer online survey to monitor understanding of purpose and practices at each stage of RTI, and redirect procedures and practices as needed.

Figure 6.2. An example of recommendations. Adapted from an action research report by Dawn Floyd, Elementary School Assistant Principal. Used with permission.

Recommendations

1. *Review the program strategies used and their effectiveness to teach children how to read.* Reviewing the teaching methods and strategies will allow the Title I teachers and school principal to make appropriate changes to improve instruction and learning. According to Temple (2000), Title I can help to produce positive effects on students' reading ability if the appropriate program is implemented. For example, providing services before and after school allows children to participate in the regular classroom setting without being pulled out for additional services. Summer sessions have also proven to be beneficial for struggling students (Borman, 2003).

2. *Maintain a consistent evaluation process that monitors students throughout the year.* If evaluations are consistent throughout the child's program, rather than once during the school year, Title I teachers can better serve the students' needs and spend less time on their strengths. McDill and Natriello (1998) emphasize the need for an assessment tool that not only holds the students and teacher accountable, but it also provides valuable data to show the progress that each child is making.

3. *Increase Title I staff members to serve more students who qualify for Title I services.* Increasing the number of teaching staff would allow students to work in smaller groups and teachers to collaborate more often with Title I teachers. Additional staff members would help to also serve student populations who are in danger of failing to meet the expectations of NCLB. Providing additional staff members should enable effective Title I programs to be implemented in the school.

4. *Recommendations need to be reviewed and discussed with all stakeholders.* Changes that are made to the Title I program need to be approved by the School Based Decision Making Council for implementation. Changes that take place will need to be followed consistently.

Figure 6.3. A second example of recommendations. Adapted from an action research report by Amanda Ellis, Elementary School Principal. Used with permission.

systems used with Response to Intervention (RTI) innovations. Conclusions pointed to a need to improve communication with teachers and curriculum research assistants, particularly in early stages of implementation, and to the importance of consistent and regular monitoring to ensure understanding of the innovation. The recommendations address these areas and suggest strategies for improving them.

Figure 6.3 illustrates a list of recommendations from a study for improvement in the Title I reading program for the primary (grades 1–3) program. The study results showed a lack of adequate staffing (one certified teacher and three instructional aides) to work on reading with primary grade students. The study described the number of students served and the Title I faculty and staff multiple responsibilities for conducting reading classes and small-group reading sessions, as well as for assisting primary classroom teachers with reading materials. The action research revealed gaps in staffing and instruction that limited effective service for Title I students. Test data evidence of declines in reading and language scores supported recommendations to increase staffing and to improve instruction.

Recommendations are the last section of the action research report, as demonstrated by examples in this text and used with the university problem-solving course that I taught for school leaders. The structure of the report illustrated here is not the only way to organize and format a report from your research, but it has proved to be a simple, workable report structure that easily can be formatted and understood. School personnel enrolled in the university principal-preparation program had the option to make changes in report titles or organization, and you will see differences in the example reports. They all followed APA format because the Educational Leadership Studies Department required this style manual for all student papers, theses, and dissertations. The most recent edition of the *Publication Manual of the American Psychological Association* (currently, 2010) is used for most educational-leadership publications.

Some reports may conclude with additional research studies that emerged during this action research study or may add a brief summary paragraph or two about the research. Because an action research report for schools should be kept to a reasonable and readable length and the total school action research report is usually not more than 14 to 20 pages, a summary at the end of the report is not essential. You probably noticed that in Figure 6.2 a brief statement introduced the recommendations; whereas in Figure 6.3, there was no introduction. Either having an introduction or not having an introduction fits appropriately in the action research report.

THE ACTION RESEARCH REPORT

Examples of stating recommendations and organizing a research report, as illustrated by resources in this text, are appropriate for a formal report of action research presented to decision makers, stakeholders, and other researchers. The format presented is similar to the organization for master's theses or doctorate dissertations. However, even those formal degree reports allow greater flexibility in organization and sections than was once true, and an action research report should be much briefer and less detailed than a thesis or dissertation because of the purpose and needs of its audience.

School personnel and their constituents need and want a clear understanding of (a) why this research was important and what it proposed to do, (b) how the research was carried out and what was learned, and (c) "the bottom line," which answers the following questions: What does this mean? What evidence supports this meaning? What decisions need to be made for action on this problem? The conclusions and recommendations section of the report states the bottom line.

You will find other report formats, section titles, and organizational patterns for action research reports among examples of the action research in this text and in other action research books (e.g., Boog, Preece, Slagter, & Zeelen, 2008; Hendricks, 2009; Johnson, 2008; and Mills, 2011). The example action research report labeled Example 14 on the supplementary CD does not use all of the usual section headings but includes a narrative of what was done, why it was done, and the results of its being done. The subheads used are appropriate for that narrative. The narrative basically includes similar components as outlined in this chapter but presents the report in a different way.

Your knowledge of the audience for your report should help determine the best way to communicate the completed research. However, results should tie conclusions and recommendations to what the study literature and data indicate to be beneficial. These two report elements comprise the data-based evidence and help give validity and trustworthiness to your results.

Components of the Action Research Report

Unique features of this text on action research are not only that it leads you through each part of action research step by step, but it also has you draft a section of your action research report as you complete each research component. This takes place immediately after completing tasks for action research and makes writing a final report much easier than waiting until the research ends to write the complete report. True, when the parts come together to complete the report, you will make changes, additions, deletions, edits, and refinements. But at this point, you already have a draft and examples for each section and can finalize a completed report. If you modify or improve on this structure, you can do this as you refine your component drafts into a unified whole.

Figure 6.4 outlines a complete action research report structure as presented in the previous chapters. You will observe that I have added two sections at the end to the already-presented section titles: Appendices and References. Data and information that make up these two sections have already been prepared.

An appendices section is an optional part of the report. Use it when you want the readers to have data tables or figures that were not presented in the report itself but that contribute to understanding the research. Such items go directly after the end of the report (i.e., after conclusions and recommendations). If only one item goes in the appendix, you can center the heading APPENDIX two lines above the title of the table,

Report Title

The 6th edition of the *Publication Manual of the American Psychological Association*[1] shows the title of manuscripts for publication as regular font (not bold) but in title case. Introductory paragraph(s) under the report title give(s) a brief overview of the importance of the problem to student learning. No title other than the report title precedes this introductory paragraph content. Paragraphs are indented and placed one blank line under all headings and subheadings, except a third-level heading (used if second-level headings that begin at the left margin need to be divided further as third-level headings),

Problem Statement (Subtitles or headings within the report are in bold font.)

Research Questions (primary research question and guiding questions)

Literature Review

Introductory paragraph(s) may give(s) an overview of the major topics and types of literature reviewed, as well as how the literature applies to the research problem.

Major Concept Side Headings (titles descriptive of major areas studied)

If the body of the literature discussion can be organized into at least two subtopics, these subheadings become side headings that are placed flush with the left margin. At least one paragraph under the side heading (second-level heading) would precede each third-level heading. If major first-level centered titles or second-level headings are divided, the division must include two or more subheadings (whether divided into second-level or third-level headings).

Third-level heading. Third-level headings begin at the paragraph indention and are followed by a period. The paragraph content begins on the line with this subheading immediately after the space following the period. Third-level headings use sentence case that begins with a capital letter and uses lowercase letters for words other than proper nouns.

Third-level heading. Before deciding to use third-level headings in a report section, be sure the concept side heading has at least two related paragraphs that break appropriately into content detail and that relate to the side heading major concept under which it is placed.

Second Major Concept Side Heading

Whether or not third-level headings subdivide a concept side heading depends on the length of content details for the content topic and if the content requires dividing into at least two third-level paragraph headings. If not, all paragraphs for a major concept side heading are preceded only by the concept side heading.

Summary (one or two paragraphs synthesizing major areas from the review)

Research Procedures (or Research Methodology)

Introductory paragraph(s) may give an overview of the kinds of information needed and procedures followed to reduce bias in data interpretation and to ensure data integrity and research trustworthiness. Further discussion of content might be divided under subheadings such as those that follow.

Type and Size of Study Population

Data Sources and Instruments

Data Collection Methods

Data Interpretation Procedures

Collaborative Process and Stakeholder Involvement

Summary

Figure 6.4. **An example of components for the final action research report.**

[1] *Publication Manual of the American Psychological Associaton* (6th ed.). (2010). Washington, DC: American Psychological Association.

Data Analysis (or Research Findings)

Introductory paragraph(s) may give an overview of analysis procedures and involvement of stakeholders, along with how individual responsibilities were determined and assigned. The introductory paragraph(s) may be followed by side headings similar to those illustrated below.

Data Presentation and Interpretations

All data summaries and discussions of tables and figures may be discussed in this section and may be organized or divided by topic subheadings related to information needs for each guiding question. As each table or figure is presented, the table or figure number is referred to in the paragraph text prior to inserting it. The figure or table data and meaning pertinent to the research questions should be discussed and briefly interpreted either prior to and/or following insertion of the table or figure in the text.

Data Triangulation and Summary

Content description under that side heading may include how data were cross checked for accuracy and the strength of confirming and disconfirming data for the interpretations that resulted from triangulation.

Conclusions and Recommendations

You may choose to group both conclusions under one centered heading and begin with a lead-in sentence or paragraph and listing of conclusions, followed by a lead-in sentence or paragraph and listing of recommendations.

or

Use two separate sections for conclusions and recommendations similar to the following:

Conclusions

Paragraph(s) synthesizing major interpretations from data and research that lead to the recommendations

Recommendations

List of recommendations supported by data and/or literature best practices

Appendices (if any, attach as separate pages—not at the end but before recommendations)

References (or Bibliography)

Begin at the left margin and use hanging indent, double-space between single-spaced entries, or double-space all entries without extra spacing between each reference. Each citation of references cited in the text must be included in a References list that starts on a new page.

Title a list of resources used with completion of the research, whether or not cited in the text, as a Bibliography. Follow the same format for entries whether the title is References or Bibliography. Start References or a Bibliography on a new page.

Figure 6.4. (*Continued*)

figure, or other information that makes up this supplementary information. If you place two or more items in the appendix, label each one with a capital letter: Appendix A, Appendix B, and so on in the order to be placed in the report. This label should be centered a double space above the title of the appendix. On the section page, key the word *APPENDICES* or *APPENDIXES* centered on the page or centered about two inches from the top of the page. Each appendix item would follow that page.

The last report part that follows the appendix or appendices, if any, or conclusions and recommendations, if there is no appendix, is the References or Bibliography section. You would have already completed your References list when you did the literature review unless the report cites literature additional to the review. If others are mentioned elsewhere in the report, add them to your alphabetical References list.

These references are now moved to the end of the report rather than the end of the literature review.

Double check to ensure that each reference cited in the literature review is entered alphabetically in this list. The cited first words and date should take the reader to the first words of the complete resource entry in the alphabetical list. No source is on a list entitled References unless it has been cited at least once within the report.

If you wish to include sources not cited in the paper but reviewed during the research, add those alphabetically among your cited references, but retitle this list as a Bibliography. Follow the same style manual when formatting all references (whether APA, MLA, or other style guide). Figure 6.4 follows APA style.

An Action Research Report Rubric

The action research report provides a comprehensive communication tool for use with faculty and staff within the school and district and with other stakeholders and school constituents. In addition, its development has provided opportunities for collaboration and support for improvement changes derived from it. Before and after completing your final action research report, referring to the rubric in Figure 6.5 will help you review your work on the report.

Figure 6.6 shows a sample format including placement of the report title and first- and second-level subheadings consistent with APA style, 6th edition. Figure 6.7 illustrates a sample title page for the action research report.

REFLECTION ON ACTION RESEARCH

Before you begin to take action on research recommendations, spend some time on personal reflection on the completed action research that has been described in the action research report. First, think about what worked well, what didn't, and what you would change to improve the process and make it more useful in your school or school district. Then, apply reflection to your work role as an educational leader, and think about how the problem-solving and inquiry processes can promote professional growth for you and others in your school to enhance student learning. Finally, reflect on the research recommendations and on ways to build the bridge from this research to action for improvement. Your reflection will be guided by your own thoughts and questions. Figure 6.8 lists a few examples of potential reflective questions. Again, benefits come from both individual and research-team collaborative reflection.

PRESENTATIONS OF ACTION RESEARCH

The dissemination of action research shares the knowledge gained through your completion of the research steps. The intent of dissemination is to inform and gain support from the practitioners who will become interested stakeholders or implementers of planning and action for improvement. The action research report that you will complete as you go through this chapter will aid your sharing of research results. This section of Chapter 6 guides the development of a visual display for presentations about this research.

Presentation Audiences

The written action research report could be distributed to all faculty and staff within the work setting and to others in the school community who are affected by or interested in the problem studied. Distribution of this report illustrates one way to help all faculty members become familiar with the action research process, as well as to inform them about the research results. Distribution may be via printed or electronic communication of the report. Even with electronic distribution, a number of printed copies should be accessible for further distribution as the need arises.

Self-Check Rubric for an Action Research Report

Review your action research report to determine how well it matches the quality criteria given here and described in Chapters 1–6 of this text. Assign points 1–3 to each numbered criterion, total all points, and divide by 7 to get the average points. If your average is 2.5 to 3, consider that your report meets all seven criteria, with each component representing a high quality of action research and a high quality report of your research. An average of 2 to 2.4 represents work that demonstrates basic action research proficiency, is reported in a manner that professionally represents such work, and meets all seven criteria, but at least two of the seven criteria are met minimally. If the report earns less than an average of 2 points, identify the weakest areas and make improvements for the final report.

The completed action research report demonstrates the following criteria:

Quality Points: 1–3 (3 = highest; 2 = moderate; 1 = needs improvement)

1. _____ The report substantiates that the research problem is a concern and that studying the problem has the potential to benefit student learning. Sufficient data and information should show that the problem has occurred over time, represents a deviation from expectations, has unknown causes, and is complex enough to justify research for improvement. The introduction to the report describes the problem and is followed by a primary research question and a minimum of three sub-area questions that guided the research. The primary research question makes clear what was to be achieved by the study. The guiding questions cannot be answered with a yes or no but lead to understanding problem areas, causes, and strategies for improvement. The description of the problem and the primary research question are stated in terms of student needs. The introductory section is written in the past tense now that the research is completed.

2. _____ Research-based best practices and/or relevant information from journals, governmental publications, books, and/or similar publications from professional educators, qualified authors, and professional organizations are summarized as a literature review and cited appropriately to inform the research questions and to support the interpretation of findings, conclusions, and recommendations.

3. _____ Research procedures and methodology used to collect and interpret data relevant to the research questions are clearly described in sufficient detail so that a reader of the report could understand the steps used to conduct the research, as well as two or three techniques followed to protect the integrity and trustworthiness of data and its interpretation. Examples of such techniques are instrument field test, colleague debriefing, and data triangulation. This section of the report is written in the past tense now that the research is completed.

4. _____ The data analysis (results) section presents data triangulated with multiple types of data and/ or multiple data sources for each research guiding question. Sufficient tables and figures present data in an easily understood format, and text with these data tables and figures interprets the meaning for the school of each data type as related to the research questions. Both confirming and disconfirming data are examined when data are interpreted.

5. _____ Conclusions come from an interpretive, meaningful synthesis of research findings from data results, previous credible research, and professional knowledge. They focus on improving the primary research problem and supporting student learning. The stated conclusions cover major concepts from data analysis that lead to recommendations. Collaborative processes helped form conclusions and recommendations.

6. _____ Report readers can clearly see connections between data results and content in both recommendations and conclusions. Recommendations cover areas for improvement that are supported by data and professional-literature sources.

7. _____ Tables and figures are identified by sequential numbering and referred to in paragraph text before insertion into the report. The format for paragraph spacing and centered and side subheadings is consistent throughout the report. Pages are numbered. The report title appears on the report cover sheet and the top of the first page of the report. The references page is the last page of the report and uses a hanging indent for each entry.

_____ **Total Points divided by 7 =** _____ **Average Quality Score**

Figure 6.5. This rubric can be used to help you rate the quality of your Action Research Report. It provides a rating scale for measuring how well each major section of the report matches the rubric statements. In addition, these ratings are averaged for an overall score.

A Study of Suspensions and Expulsions from 2009–2012

Xxxxxxxxxxxxxxxxxxxxxxxxxxxxxxxxxxxxxxxxxxxxxxxxxxxxxxxxxxxxxxxxxxxxxxxxxxxxxxxx
xxxxxxxxxxxxxxxxxxxxxxxxxxxxxxxxxxxxxxxxxxxxxxxxxxxxxxxxxxxxxxxxxxxxxxxxxxxxxxxx
xxxxxxxxxxxxxxxxxxxxxxxxxxxxxxxxxxxxxxxxxx

Literature Review

Xxxxxxxxxxxxxxxxxxxxxxxxxxxxxxxxxxxxxxxxxxxxxxxxxxxxxxxxxxxxxxxxxxxxxxxxxxxxxxxx
xxxxxxxxxxxxxxxxxxxxxxxxxxxxxxxxxxxxxxxxxxxxxxxxxxxxxxxxxxxxxxxxxxxxxxxxxxxxxxxx

Disciplinary Problems

Xxxxxxxxxxxxxxxxxxxxxxxxxxxxxxxxxxxxxxxxxxxxxxxxxxxxxxxxxxxxxxxxxxxxxxxxxxxxxxxx
xxxxxxxxxxxxxxxxxxxxxxxxxxxxxxxxxxxxxxxxxxxxxxxxxxxxxxxxxxxxxxxxxxxxxxxxxxxxxxxx
xxxxxxxxxxxxxxxxxxxxxxxxxxxxxxxxxxxxxxxxxx

Positive and Negative Actions

Xxxxxxxxxxxxxxxxxxxxxxxxxxxxxxxxxxxxxxxxxxxxxxxxxxxxxxxxxxxxxxxxxxxxxxxxxxxxxxxx
xxxxxxxxxxxxxxxxxxxxxxxxxxxxxxxxxxxxxxxxxxxxxxxxxxxxxxxxxxxxxxxxxxxx

Classroom Climate. Xxxxxxxxxxxxxxxxxxxxxxxxxxxxxxxxxxxxxxxxxxxxxxxxxxxxxxxxx
xxxxxxxxxxxxxxxxxxxxxxxxxxxxxxxxxxxxxxxxxxxxxxxxxxxxxxxxxxxxxxxxxxxxxxxxxxxxxxxx

Home and Community. Xxxxxxxxxxxxxxxxxxxxxxxxxxxxxxxxxxxxxxxxxxxxxxxxxxxxxxxxxx
xxxxxxxxxxxxxxxxxxxxxxxxxxxxxxxxxxxxxxxxxxxxxxxxxxxxxxxxxxxxxxxxxxxxxxxxx

Summary

Xxxxxxxxxxxxxxxxxxxxxxxxxxxxxxxxxxxxxxxxxxxxxxxxxxxxxxxxxxxxxxxxxxxxxxxxxxxxxxxx
xxxxxxxxxxxxxxxxxxxxxxxxxxxxxxxxxxxxxxxxxxxxxxxxxxxxxxxxxxxxxxxx

Research Procedures

Xxxxxxxxxxxxxxxxxxxxxxxxxxxxxxxxxxxxxxxxxxxxxxxxxxxxxxxxxxxxxxxxxxxxxxxxxxxxxxxx
xxxxxxxxxxxxxxxxxxxxxxxxxxxxxxxxxxxxxxxxxxxxxxxxxxxxxxxxxxxxxxxxxxxxx

Causes

Xxxxxxxxxxxxxxxxxxxxxxxxxxxxxxxxxxxxxxxxxxxxxxxxxxxxxxxxxxxxxxxxxxxxxxxxxxxxxxxx
xxxxxxxxxxxxxxxxxxxxxxxxxxxxxxxxxxxxxxxxxxxxxxxxxxxxxxxxxxxxxxxxxxx

Policies

Xxxxxxxxxxxxxxxxxxxxxxxxxxxxxxxxxxxxxxxxxxxxxxxxxxxxxxxxxxxxxxxxxxxxxxxxxxxxxxxx
xxxxxxxxxxxxxxxxxxxxxxxxxxxxxxxxxxxxxxxxxxxxxxxxxxxxxxxxxxxxxxxxxxx

Remedial Actions

Xxxxxxxxxxxxxxxxxxxxxxxxxxxxxxxxxxxxxxxxxxxxxxxxxxxxxxxxxxxxxxxxxxxxxxxxxxxxxxxx
xxxxxxxxxxxxxxxxxxxxxxxxxxxxxxxxxxxxxxxxxxxxxxxxxxxxxxxxxxxxxxxxxxx

Suspensions. Xxxxxxxxxxxxxxxxxxxxxxxxxxxxxxxxxxxxxxxxxxxxxxxxxxxxxxxxxxxxxxx
xxxxxxxxxxxxxxxxxxxxxxxxxxxxxxxxxxxxxxxxxxxxxxxxxxxxxxxxxxxxxxxxxxxxxxxxxxxxxxxx
xxxxxxxxxxxxxxxxxxxxxxxxxxxxxxxxxxxxxx

Expulsions. Xxxxxxxxxxxxxxxxxxxxxxxxxxxxxxxxxxxxxxxxxxxxxxxxxxxxxxxxxxxxxxxx
xxxxxxxxxxxxxxxxxxxxxxxxxxxxxxxxxxxxxxxxxxxxxxxxxxxxxxxxxxxxxxxxxxxxxxxxxxxxxxxx
xxxxxxxxxxxxxxxxxx

Disciplinary Strategies

Xxxxxxxxxxxxxxxxxxxxxxxxxxxxxxxxxxxxxxxxxxxxxxxxxxxxxxxxxxxxxxxxxxxxxxxxxxxxxxxx
xxxxxxxxxxxxxxxxxxxxxxxxxxxxxxxxxxxxxxxxxxxxxxxxxxxxxxxxxxxxxxxxxxx

Conclusions

Xxxxxxxxxxxxxxxxxxxxxxxxxxxxxxxxxxxxxxxxxxxxxxxxxxxxxxxxxxxxxxxxxxxxxxxxxxxxxxxx
xxxxxxxxxxxxxxxxxxxxxxxxxxxxxxxxxxxxxxxxxxxxxxxxxxxxxxxxxxxxxxxxxxx

Recommendations

Xxxxxxxxxxxxxxxxxxxxxxxxxxxxxxxxxxxxxxxxxxxxxxxxxxxxxxxxxxxxxxxxxxxxxxxxxxxxxxxx
xxxxxxxxxxxxxxxxxxxxxxxxxxxxxxxxxxxxxxxxxxxxxxxxxxxxxxxxxxxxxxxxxxx

Figure 6.6. Format example for final action research report. If supplementary tables and figures or other supplementary illustrations are included in the report as Appendices, add them immediately prior to the References section.

References

Xxxxx, X. (xxxx). Xxxxxxxxxxxxxxxxxxxxxxxxxxxxxxxxxxxxxxxxxxxxx. Xxxxxxx: Xxxxxxxx

Xxxxxx, X., & Xxxxxxx, X. X. Xxxxxxxxxxxxxxxxxxxxxx, Xxxxxxxxxxxxxxxxxxxxxxxxxxxxxxxx, x(xx)x, X, xxx-xxx.

Xxxxx, X. (xxxx). Xxxxxxxxxxxxxxxxxxxxxxxxxxxxxxxxxxxxxxxxxxxxx. Xxxxxxx: Xxxxxxxx

Xxxxxx, X., & Xxxxxxx, X. X. Xxxxxxxxxxxxxxxxxxxxxx, Xxxxxxxxxxxxxxxxxxxxxxxxxxxxxxxxxxxx, x(xx)x, X, xxx-xxx.

Xxxxx, X. (xxxx). Xxxxxxxxxxxxxxxxxxxxxxxxxxxxxxxxxxxxxxxxxxxxx. Xxxxxxx: Xxxxxxxx

Xxxxxx, X., & Xxxxxxx, X. X. Xxxxxxxxxxxxxxxxxxxxxx, Xxxxxxxxxxxxxxxxxxxxxx, x(xx)x, X, xxx-xxx.

Xxxxx, X. (xxxx). Xxxxxxxxxxxxxxxxxxxxxxxxxxxxxxxxxxxxxxxxxxxxx. Xxxxxxx: Xxxxxxxx

Xxxxxx, X., & Xxxxxxx, X. X. Xxxxxxxxxxxxxxxxxxxxxx, Xxxxxxxxxxxxxxxxxxxxxx, x(xx)x, X, xxx-xxx.

Xxxxx, X. (xxxx). Xxxxxxxxxxxxxxxxxxxxxxxxxxxxxxxxxxxxxxxxxxxxx. Xxxxxxx: Xxxxxxxx

Xxxxxx, X., & Xxxxxxx, X. X. Xxxxxxxxxxxxxxxxxxxxxx, Xxxxxxxxxxxxxxxxxxxxxx, x(xx)x, X, xxx-xxx.

Xxxxx, X. (xxxx). Xxxxxxxxxxxxxxxxxxxxxxxxxxxxxxxxxxxxxxxxxxxxx. Xxxxxxx: Xxxxxxxx

Xxxxxx, X., & Xxxxxxx, X. X. Xxxxxxxxxxxxxxxxxxxxxx, Xxxxxxxxxxxxxxxxxxxxxx, x(xx)x, X, xxx-xxx.

Figure 6.6. (Continued)

A Study of Suspensions and Expulsions from 2009–2012

Research Leadership Team: Mary Webb, Sam Goodall, Jane Worthy, Jim Mattingly, and Nancy Baumgarten

Child First Academy
Martinville, Wisconsin

March 17, 2012

Note. This research for school improvement was a collaborative effort of faculty and staff at Child First. Credit for this report of action research goes to all individuals who served on research teams, assisted with interpreting or writing parts of the report, participated in any phase of the research, or provided data and expertise.

Figure 6.7. Sample Cover Sheet. Similar information should be displayed on a cover sheet for your action research report, although the arrangement of components may vary. The note is optional.

Action Research Reflection Guide

Think on these questions individually or with a colleague who worked on the action research study completed in your school.

1. Think about the steps in the action research process. Which step(s) did you find to be the most difficult? Why?

2. What did you learn that added to what you already knew about research?

3. How can the results of this research benefit student learning?

4. What did you learn that added to your professional growth?

5. What should be changed to improve the quality or outcomes of the next action research?

6. What learning from this research can be used in your work role? How?

7. What did you learn about collaboration with others in conducting research?

8. What goal(s) would you like to attain through the application of action research?

9. What other knowledge or skills do you need in order to improve results from action research?

Figure 6.8. Sample Reflection Guide. This contains questions to guide reflection about your use of action research, identification of skills learned, professional growth, and goals for future research. Select from this list, or use your own questions that best fit your needs as a practitioner-researcher.

Educators who participated in the research should have a voice in planning for distribution of the action research report and identification of other potential audiences for the written report or oral presentations to appropriate groups. As a school principal, head teacher, or other designated educational leader for the research study, you should confer with the district superintendent for input into planning distribution and delivery of the report beyond the school or district office setting. School board policies often relate to distribution of information from schools and must be followed. In addition to keeping the school and district office on the same page in regard to the value of and results from research, frequent communication with the school system office helps professional personnel at the district level respond to questions that come to them about the research activity or distribution of school materials, as well as helps them to comply with school board policies.

Visual Presentations

Preparation of a visual presentation at the end of the research makes a readily available overview of the research results for school personnel to use with groups interested in learning more about the research or for discussion of the research with school boards, school advisory groups, parent and teacher organizations, or faculty or staff groups. The action research visual presentation may take a form different than visuals prepared with presentation software. Options could extend from something as simple as an outline of major topics on a flip chart to a short video.

Keep in mind the audience and the purpose for such presentations. Also, prepare the visuals to supplement the material rather than to cover the whole presentation. The presentation is not meant to be read to the audience but to reinforce interest and retention as the presenter provides discussion and details about the study. For most audiences, brief points shown on the screen with presentation software provide a readily available information source that can supplement the presenter's dialogue. I limited my students' presentations of their action research to a maximum of 10 slides; most had 10 slides and probably would have had more without this limit. Visuals add to interest and effectiveness but become boring or, at least, lose effectiveness if too many are shown.

Keep the visual items brief and large enough to be easily read by the audience when the presenter calls attention to them as part of the presentation. Figure 6.9

School Improvement Analysis: Student Performance in Mathematics

Hi-Q Elementary: The Facts

- One of six K-5 elementary schools in Fort County
- Highest number of open enrolled students
- 41% of students qualify for free/reduced lunch (District average is 30%)

Student Performance

- Total Accountability Index has improved from 64.4 (2005) to 79.9 (2008)
- Accountability Index exceeds the goal established, and novice reduction requirements have been met
- Total Accountability Index and Total Academic Index are higher than district averages

So, what's the problem?

MATH

The History

	2004	2005	2006	2007	State mean 2008	District mean 2008
CTBS	64	55	57	55	60	60
KCCT	53	53	69	67	66	75

That's a GOOD question!

- How are students performing in mathematic subdomain areas?
- Are certain groups of students' scores significantly different from others?
- What is currently happening in mathematics instruction versus what should be happening?

What's Happening VS. What Should Be Happening?

QUALITY CIRCLE

Plan-Do-Check-Act

Gathering Data

- 2002 CTBS results revealed that in many areas, less than half of all third graders performed at the mastery level
- Third grade students scored substantially lower in math computation than in other areas
- More students scored at the novice level than in any other content area
- Students participating in ESS and students with disabilities' scores were significantly lower than students not identified

VERY INTERESTING . . .

Performances of students with disabilities were NOT significantly different in any other content area.

Just a Few Resulting Recommendations

- Instruction will be problem-based rather than focusing solely on isolated skills.
- Students will have many opportunities to work together to solve problems.
- Whole class discussion will follow group work to emphasize concepts learned.
- Teachers will have the opportunity to visit other classrooms and schools to observe successful research-based mathematics instruction.

Figure 6.9.   An example of a visual handout. This text Figure 6.9 content was adapted from the slide presentation on the CD Figure 6.9 under Chapter 6 Resources. Dr. Carmen Coleman, School System Superintendent, developed the slide presentation from her action research report. Used with permission.

- A mathematics study group will form to meet on a regular basis to share ideas relating to mathematics instruction.
- Assessments will be modeled after those found on state assessments.
- The selection of students for and the structure of the ESS program will be reviewed and revised.
- Specific persons will be assigned to monitor the progress of mathematic improvement initiatives and will report progress monthly to the site-based council.

Figure 6.9. *(Continued)*

shown here—and more effectively as a slide presentation on the CD under Chapter 6 Resources—illustrates an example of a visual action research presentation from a former student who is now a superintendent.

Key Questions for Review

1. Who should be involved in collaborative reflection to provide input for developing recommendations for your research?
2. What evidence-based support should be referenced in the recommendations?
3. What is your definition of a reflective practitioner?
4. What characteristics do you view as most important for the final action research report? For the visual presentation?
5. How does a References list differ from a Bibliography?

Note. **Performance Checklist will also appear on CD.**

Performance Checklist for Step 3c and Step 4a Research Activities

You will complete Step 3c of action research by developing recommendations on the basis of conclusions determined in Chapter 5. For Step 4a, you will prepare and refine an action research report and a visual presentation overview for your action research study.

A. **Develop recommendations from your research that describe what actions should take place for improving student learning. Substantiate recommendations by reference to research findings from your literature review and data analysis.**

Performance Check:

1. Members of the research teams and other colleagues knowledgeable of the research problem, as well as of this study, should formulate recommendations from the conclusions. Recommendations should be supported by data and best practice from professional knowledge. This checklist suggests a possible process. This process will take time—probably 1 to 2 weeks—to come to a decision and develop and refine a list of recommendations. This section of the report, however, will need a high measure of understanding and support to be effectively implemented.

2. Persons involved in developing recommendations should have interest in and knowledge of the action research process and the problem. They should have received a copy of these report sections: (a) research problem statement and research questions, (b) literature review, (c) research methodology, and (d) data analysis and results. Team members should reflect both independently and collectively on recommendations that are based on research conclusions and the literature review. Then, they should engage collaboratively in developing an initial list of recommendations, refining the wording, and assuring that recommendations include support references from research data and literature citations. Send a copy to all team members, and place a dated copy in the action research central file for further review and action planning and implementation.

B. **Use previously drafted report sections to complete a professional action research report that describes the action research problem, related literature, research procedures, data analysis, and recommendations and conclusions.**

Performance Check:

1. All parts of the action research report draft should be brought together by one or two persons and circulated to all team members and knowledgeable stakeholders involved with the research problem. Specify a final date for reviewers to submit written comments and suggestions to a designated leader, who will turn over the copies for compilation and review by the research leadership team.

2. The research leadership team will review Figure 6.5 from the CD and compare the rubrics with the report draft before making changes for the final draft. This group should make decisions about changes for the final action research report, as well as identify an audience and a timeline for report distribution.

C. **Develop a visual display presentation that gives an overview of the research and findings. For a presentation with presentation software, keep the number of visuals to no more than 10 slides.**

Performance Check:

1. Identify persons responsible for development of the visual presentation material and for designing layout. Set a projected completion date. Once it is done, send the presentation electronically to all persons involved with the research. Specify a date for them to return their feedback.

2. According to the feedback, refine the presentation, send out a final copy, and file a copy in the research file.

References

American Psychological Association (APA). (2010). *Publication manual of the American Psychological Association* (6th ed.). Washington, DC: Author.

Bainer, D., & Cantrell, D. (1991, October 16–20). *The relationship between instructional domain and the content of reflection among preservice teachers.* Paper presented at the annual meeting of the Midwestern Educational Association, Chicago, IL.

Boog, B., Preece, J., Slagter, M., & Zeelen, J. (Eds.). (2008). *Towards quality improvement of action research: Developing ethics and standards.* Rotterdam, The Netherlands: Sense Publishers.

Cowan, G. (2004). *Understanding & conducting research in education* (2nd ed.). Dubuque, IA: Kendall/Hunt.

Hendricks, C. (2009). *Improving schools through action research: A comprehensive guide for educators* (2nd ed.). Upper Saddle River, NJ: Pearson Education, Inc.

Johnson, A. P. (2008). *A short guide to action research* (3rd ed.). Boston: Pearson.

Mills, G. E. (2011). *Action research: A guide for the teacher researcher* (4th ed.). Boston: Pearson.

Schön, D. (1973). *Beyond the stable state: Public and private learning in a changing society.* Harmondsworth, United Kingdom: Penguin.

Schön, D. (1983). *The reflective practitioner: How professionals think in action.* London, United Kingdom: Temple Smith.

Schön, D. (1987). *Educating the reflective practitioner.* San Francisco: Jossey-Bass.

Smith, M. K. (2001, 2011). Donald Schön: Learning, reflection, and change. Retrieved from the *Encyclopedia of informal education* website at http://www.infed.org/thinkers/et-schon.htm.

Zeichner, K. M., & Liston, D. P. (1987). Teaching student teachers to reflect. *Harvard Educational Review, 57*(1), 23–48.

PART FOUR

Bridging Research with Practice

Part 4 envisions action research as an ongoing part of school practice and comprehensive school-improvement plans. Collaboration and reflection are features of action research that support both research and school-improvement plans.

Professional-development support for action research in schools stems from the belief that educators who master the process benefit students because the educators continue to use action research as a practical tool for improvement of teaching and learning. Research results—integrated with school practice, planning, and assessment—bring together knowledge gained by practitioner inquiry, data collection, and data analysis blended with relevant knowledge from literature reviews. Collaborative practitioner research shares the tasks and systematically identifies priority needs for school change, with implementation of change integrated as a part of comprehensive school-improvement plans.

Chapter 8 addresses increasing expectations, responsibility, and accountability for schools and educators to collaborate and integrate services with other agencies. The purpose of such collaboration and integration is to provide professional expertise that supports high levels of learning for each and every student. Updated school leadership standards and a proposed model for core teaching standards serve as self-reflection guides for educators who are planning professional growth in order to gain advanced levels of expertise on a career continuum. Professional development requires continuing self-reflection about future roles, responsibilities, and growth activities, plus classroom application of the knowledge gained.

Purpose and Outcomes for Part 4

Part 4 illustrates how action research becomes ongoing practice when integrated with school improvement and instructional planning and assessment. Also, this part completes Steps 4b, 4c, and 5, with recommendations for building action research and reflections into an action-plan component of school-improvement planning and assessment. School leaders engage in these performance activities:

1. Develop an action plan for implementing recommendations from action research.
2. Reflect on and plan for growth activities as part of a professional-improvement plan based on reflection on expectations for leadership and teaching and learning.

In-School Performance Activities

Chapter 7

1. Reflect on how action research can promote professional growth for teachers and school leaders and, also, how you can use action research to support comprehensive planning for school improvement.
2. Develop an action-plan component from your completed action research.

Chapter 8

1. Complete self-assessment guides for school leadership and teacher leadership based on standards developed by the Council of Chief State School Officers (CCSSO) and representatives from member states.
2. From the results of your reflection and self-assessment, write a professional-growth plan for the next two to three years.

CHAPTER 7

Action Research as Part of Professional Practice

Chapter 1 compared action research to a problem-solving process. The major difference in the steps is the extent of detail completed with each step and the inclusion of a literature review that adds new information to the knowledge that practitioner-researchers already have about the problem from previous education and experience. The extent of the problem and the purpose for addressing it play a major role in the amount of detail required for each step.

Chapters 1 through 6 covered an array of details for each action research step and provided multiple possibilities for potential research resources, methods and procedures, data collection and analysis, conclusions and recommendations, and written descriptions of each step. In addition, you have reflected on the completed research, what you learned from it, and how that knowledge can be useful. The many details, examples, and worksheets for each research step provided help intended to save time by showing one or more ways to summarize, plan data collection, analyze and triangulate data, draw conclusions, and state recommendations. As you become an experienced practitioner-researcher, you will think of new and better ways to carry out these tasks and will be able to accomplish more in less time. The first project requires the greatest time and effort because of a high learning curve and a degree of uncertainty about how to proceed. My purpose in providing so much information was to make this text and CD a helpful reference as you gain experience with action research. Working through the standard research process gave you all research steps not just by your studying them but also with a hands-on approach that performed each step for an authentic learning-by-doing experience.

On the basis of my experience as a teacher and administrator, as well as my working with local teachers and administrators in schools for program planning and budgeting, I understood that presenting the detailed material for each step could be overwhelming to many school practitioners who already have complex and time-consuming responsibilities. In spite of this concern, I believe strongly in the benefit of demystifying the research process and integrating it in the work of schools. I feel that there is a need to use current research literature to a greater extent than it is presently used to improve teaching and learning. My work with educators at all levels of education convinced me of the sincerity of the great majority of educators, who care about each student and give unselfishly of their expertise, time, and even money to help students succeed. Educators experience their greatest reward when they see their students succeed.

Today, mobile technology, social networks, blogs, cloud computing, and applications for mobile phones are examples of ever-present and constantly changing means of electronic communication that affect how students and educators communicate. Technology presents exciting learning opportunities. Because of the vast availability of information, however, technology has not decreased, but has expanded, workloads.

Because I understand the pressures of educators to do more in less time, I constructed numerous worksheets and electronic links on the CD as resources for each chapter and for district and school professional-development planning, as an attempt to save your time as you initially work with data analysis and literature search steps of action research. When you have studied Chapters 1 through 6 of this text and completed the performance activities guided by the checklist at the end of each chapter, you have completed an action research study and now need to take the next step. Action research means just that—Action. At the end of Chapter 6, you reflected on your learning experiences up to now with action research in your work setting.

In this chapter, you will explore how your research results connect with school planning and improvement—what implementation changes for improvement should take place, based on your research data and recommendations. The last step is identification of assessment, which will evaluate the appropriateness and success of these changes.

As you study the text in this chapter, think about the school improvement planning that you complete as a part of school and district accountability for the continued improvement of teaching and learning. Consider ways to bridge the gap between research and school practice. How can action research and literature reviews of research and best practice become useful tools for overcoming school problems and building the professional expertise of educators in your school?

RESEARCH CONTRIBUTIONS TO SCHOOL PRACTICE

After reviewing a draft of material for this text, an educator from a school in a northeastern state noted that all schools have the ability to collect and use data to improve instruction and revise curricula. In addition, educational leaders through collaboration empower their faculty to collect and synthesize data in a meaningful process that ultimately will shape and redefine instructional practice. Schools that have organized professional-learning communities and diverse practices for faculty professional development already have initiated a collaborative structure that can readily incorporate action research and reflective processes as part of ongoing professional-development activities. Chapter 8 picks up thoughts about action research and standards for planning professional growth in leading, learning, and teaching responsibilities that meet evolving expectations for schools of the future.

Educators struggle with integrating research knowledge into school practice. Technology makes a wealth of research information on teaching, learning, and leadership readily available from university researchers and peer-reviewed journals. However, building that knowledge base into schools as part of practice has been sporadic at best. Practitioners often see academic research as unrelated to what they do (Ferrance, 2000).

Published research reports can be long and detailed, and educators are always pressed for time. However, they know how to quickly scan material to find information relevant to an issue. Research reports follow a fairly consistent format similar to that covered in the framework of the sample action research reports presented in this text. In both published research reports and action research reports, the beginning gives an overview of the problem and related research, methodology and data analysis come next, and conclusions and recommendations are near the end. Quickly scanning these areas to locate relevant information is not a new experience for educators.

The main difference between traditional academic reports and action research reports is the detailed description in all sections of the traditional report. These reports are written to be read and understood by individuals unfamiliar with the research context, as well as by other researchers who need enough detail to replicate the study for further knowledge about results in different contexts. Action research reports do not require as much detail, because they are developed by and for practitioners who already are familiar with the work setting.

Your becoming a practitioner-researcher has the potential for helping you to do these things: overcome reluctance to use research in school practice or inquiry-based learning in teaching, use research for professional learning, and add to its use as a learning tool for students. In addition, your action research can be applicable to U.S. Federal Government grant requests. Grant applications at times use the term *scientific research*. The term may appear to refer only to theoretical research; however, grant research, as defined by the U.S. Federal Government, fits well with action research. Basic and applied research eligible for federal funding (National Science Foundation, n.d.) is systematic study that gains knowledge or understanding of phenomena and of observable facts, or it is research to gain understanding necessary to determine the means by which a recognized need may be met. Action research clearly meets this definition by following a systematic process and applying multiple measures to control bias and increase research integrity.

Research projects with a narrow focus for a specific purpose do not always need a written report for distribution or a presentation display. A teacher's research focused on a learning problem in the classroom may not need these communication reports. However, a complete file of action research activities should be accessible as an audit trail. A teacher's log of specific activities and results, which includes procedures followed, notes from the literature review, and research results in the classroom, should suffice. To support the credibility of research findings, these records should document methods for avoiding bias and ensuring valid data interpretations.

Previous research clearly identifies the importance of effective teachers for positive school effects on student achievement (Jordan, Mendro, & Weerasinghe, 1997; Sanders & Rivers, 1996; Wright, Horn, & Sanders, 1997). In addition, the school impact of school leadership on student achievement, as shown by research on school effects on learning, is second in effect size only to that of teachers (Leithwood, Seashore-Louis, Anderson, & Wahlstrom, 2004). There is a growing body of literature that suggests that teacher leadership is an important factor for school and district leaders to consider as they seek ways to improve schools (Murphy, 2005). Recognition of the critical nature of teacher and administrator roles for student learning is a strong argument for districts to encourage and require—as well as financially support—professional development for continuous learning that improves role performance in improving instruction and meeting diverse learning needs.

In concluding this chapter, you will consider ways in which the things that you have learned about action research fit with the school-improvement planning and assessment processes: similarities, differences, and contributions. An example of an action-planning component based on research recommendations from action research will help you to visualize how research integrates with planning and evaluating improvements for learning in your work setting. The chapter closes with reflections on a continuum of research, planning, and evaluation, as school practitioners increase their expertise with action research to improve educational practices and positive outcomes for students. An example Gantt chart illustrates how action research on different components of school improvement planning can integrate with developing and scheduling for the accountability comprehensive planning process for school improvement.

RESEARCH FOR SCHOOL IMPROVEMENT

Not all action research books show action research reports including a section that reviews related literature. A literature review is an important action research step, as presented here. Adding published relevant research informs most research problems. Related research might not be available for every school problem, but in today's world of information overload, such unavailability would be rare. This review helps educators bring research knowledge into daily practice in connection with their own practitioner research. Previous peer-reviewed research on school practices is important in helping to state guiding questions, to determine potential causes and concerns for data collection, and to use knowledge about the problem with data and your expertise in order to make decisions. Finding such research is not difficult and far less time consuming than it was prior to the availability of the Internet. Professional-education organizations have publications that synthesize research information in journal articles, reports, or white papers. In addition, the reference list at the end of articles about your research problem may lead you to other resources related to your topic of interest.

Until recent years, published research was difficult for school personnel to locate. Now, technology in homes, schools, and libraries makes research and best-practice information readily accessible to school personnel. A lack of time and the historically isolated nature of classroom teaching, along with a perception that educational research doesn't translate easily to a specific school setting, have been past barriers to using research as a basis for school improvement.

Collaborative school structures for school and data-informed decision making, subject or grade-level teams, and teacher study groups help break down classroom isolation. The school year and instructional time have lengthened, but planning and assessment responsibilities have expanded. The time crunch remains, although school leaders have made progress in scheduling time. Collaborative involvement in research divides the work, and mobile technology makes communication and collaboration possible to complete at a convenient time for participants.

School leaders have begun to find ways to bring teachers together for collaboration on learning and planning. However, leaders should keep in mind that one person cannot dominate the process. Successful collaboration requires clearly identifying tasks to be accomplished, procedures for reaching agreement, and preset times allowed for each person to present and support ideas. Equal respect and equal time for all opinions are essential for effective work. A facilitator should encourage participation by each team member.

Accountability promotes recognition by faculty that "we are in this together" because educators in schools work together to promote effective learning. They are assessed together, and they share consequences of school outcomes and data-informed progress rankings for schools. Over time, all teachers in a school are part of the learning experiences for at least a nucleus of the same students. What takes place in one classroom affects all classrooms at some point. How do these changes affect blending research with practice? School teachers and administrators serve increasingly diverse communities and students and face high expectations and accountability for student achievement—not only overall but for each and every child. Educators are likely to experience a growing need to connect as a community of learners and as continuous learners. Angello (2010) recommends a rethinking of leadership as a collective effort and proposes that a school centered around one leader cannot meet the demands and daily tasks of the complexity and size of today's schools without rethinking and embracing leadership as a collective effort.

Printy (2010) reviewed research studies on school leadership to explain ways that school leadership makes a difference in the quality of instruction. Findings from quantitative studies showed that principals who share in decision making with teacher-leaders in trusting environments and agree on the same targets have great potential for adding to instructional improvement. Also, principals who provide teachers with opportunities to learn new skills in informal interaction and conversation, as well as formal professional development, encourage teacher involvement and learning and create conditions for peer influence and leadership to flourish. With this support, teachers are more likely to undertake new practices for authentic and standards-based instruction.

Review of qualitative studies showed that teacher-leader roles appear to be widely used as a component of instructional improvement (Printy, 2010). For these instructional coaches to be effective, they need principals who have a high level of knowledge about the role of coaches, frequently interact with them, and acknowledge them as experts, thus encouraging teachers to use the coaches. Findings from other studies showed that formal organization of reform activities should align with the informal social organization of the school to enhance trust and increase collective responsibility for learning.

Successful leaders today need to be authentic, be honest about what they can and cannot do well, provide inspiration, and communicate consistent values and accountabilities through distribution of responsibilities and accountabilities (Munby, 2008). They need collaborative skills to lead through influence. A school culture ideal for today's principal to create and lead a learning organization has principals and teachers engaging in continuing dialogue and reflection to bring about improvement (Wise & Jacobo, 2010).

ACTION RESEARCH AND CHANGE IN PRACTICE

Ferrance (2000) lists four types of action research that can take place in a school: (a) individual teacher research in the classroom; (b) collaborative research by two or more educators with a common problem; (c) schoolwide action research on a school issue, problem, or area of collective interest; and (d) district-wide action research on a district issue or on organizational structures. She identifies the benefits of teacher research as improvement of curriculum, instruction, and assessment. Schoolwide research potentially affects school restructuring and change, policy, parent involvement, and program evaluation. Side benefits from collaborative, schoolwide, and district action research may include improved collegiality, collaboration, and communication.

Collaboration, however, does require cooperation and may not work well for everyone. Forcing everyone to participate is not likely to achieve a desired result. Encourage volunteers to become involved, make opportunities available for everyone to learn what action research and collaboration require, and recognize those volunteers who participate fully and show evidence of professional growth through their participation.

Action research helps teachers improve their practice in their own work settings and makes research relevant to student learning in classrooms. Students taught by effective teachers progress academically at greater rates than students in classrooms with poor teachers (Sanders, 2000; Sanders & Horn, 1998; Sanders, Wright, & Ross, 1999; Topping & Sanders, 2000). Furthermore, teacher effects on student learning are additive and cumulative over grade levels (Sanders, 2000, p. 234). Low-achieving students realize the highest gains when placed with effective teachers and can take as long as three years to overcome placement with ineffective teachers (Hanushek, 1992; Stronge & Tucker, 2000; Wright, Horn, & Sanders, 1997). Teaching is a complex endeavor that requires thinking about ends, means, and consequences and putting into action the collective information generated from planning (Beech & Reinhartz, 2000).

Action research is an inquiry tool that follows a systematic process for planning improvements based on the best available knowledge and evidence-supported data applied to school-based problems of learning. Gaining comfort with the use of research and blending the resulting knowledge through reflection on educators' past experiences and learning can be a meaningful part of teacher and administrator professional development and effectiveness. A review of pertinent literature helps frame the problem, determine data needs, interpret data, and recommend change strategies for improvement. Action research results, therefore, base improvement changes on a research repertoire of approaches and strategies.

Teacher action research may take place within classrooms simply on the teacher's initiative. The teacher may learn the process and apply it to questions of learning, curriculum, or assessment for instruction that best promotes achievement for one or more students. Differentiated instruction to meet individual learning needs for a diverse group of students can be improved over time as a teacher builds a repertoire of researched practices for instructional strategies and techniques, as well as updated knowledge in the subject taught. Building literature reviews into a teacher's practice as a part of inquiry for problem solving promotes professional growth through ongoing teacher research or collaborative research.

Although teachers play a leadership role for individual or collaborative research on common classroom issues, support from the principal in the school and from district leadership encourages inquiry as part of school culture when it provides recognition, professional-development credit, substitute teachers or teacher aides, technology, materials, or other resources to assist with the research processes. These types of support activities help generate interest in action research from other teachers. Teacher action research documented as a research portfolio that evidences classroom applications could be a basis for professional-development recognition and/or resource funds. Instructional curricula for higher-order thinking skills include teaching students to practice inquiry and interpret data. A teacher's action research knowledge and experience add to expertise for teaching colleagues and students the inquiry process.

ACTION RESEARCH AND COMPREHENSIVE PLANNING

The previous discussion of the importance of the teachers' and the principal's roles in school improvement emphasized the support characteristics important to improvement of student learning. Leadership sets direction, communicates and supports faculty and staff development, and makes changes to support teaching and learning. School and district office personnel work in a climate of respect for one another and collaborate to make innovations and changes work. In addition, student achievement for all students requires a focus not just on student learning and progress gaps between disaggregated groups but also on identification and support for each student who is not progressing.

ACTION RESEARCH AND SCHOOL-IMPROVEMENT PLANNING

A computer search of school action plans and school-improvement plans showed many common elements of planning across states, districts, and schools. Forms for comprehensive planning differed somewhat in format and terminology, but 18 plans reviewed for this chapter from 10 states were strikingly similar in approach and content. The term *school improvement* was used in most of the titles for the planning process. Several plans incorporated other terms in the title, such as *School Improvement Plan and Resources, School Improvement and Achievement, Differentiated Accountability Program: School Improvement Plan, Strategic and Continuous School Improvement and Achievement Plan,* and *Comprehensive School Improvement Plan.* Other titles were *Integrated Improvement Plan* and *School Action Plan.*

Similar Processes and Components

Basic plan components were similar, although some states added specific programming components and sections to describe such things as parent involvement and use of technology. Other states added data analysis worksheets in the planning directions. Figure 7.1 shows a composite list of the different basic components and terminology found in the district or schoolwide summary portion of a planning document. The order of components varied in a few plans from the order shown in Figure 7.1. For example, assurance statements in some cases were in different parts of the plan. These assurances were, generally, signature verification of statements of compliance with various requirements from the district, state, or federal level.

Component Action Plans and Action Research

Specific component action plans generally followed the overall description and summary of the district or school. Component action plan forms were completed by personnel from core component programs, specialized programs, grant-funded programs with special requirements, and other school initiatives.

Component action plans reviewed from the 10 states varied from plan to plan in format and organization of sections, but most titled these sections with similar terms. Some used a horizontal landscape format, with headings for blocks of space to be completed. Others used a narrative form with a portrait format, or a combination of the two basic formats. Figure 7.2 displays a composite of different terminology and components compiled from the 18 planning forms from the 10 states reviewed for this chapter. No one plan had all of the components listed in Figure 7.2. The outline in Figure 7.2 illustrates, to the extent possible, the different terminology and sections from all 18 plans.

Reviewing these school-improvement plans clearly showed how closely some of the states follow the basic steps of action research as identified in this text, in addition to the action component that implements and evaluates changes or interventions. Some plans even required evidence of support from research for causes or key factors leading to the priority needs and as support for objectives and/or strategies identified for intervention.

In the most current plans (mostly, 2010–2011) reviewed for this chapter, the data analysis product was more than just quantitative academic data. At least two states required multiple data sources to analyze problems and listed—in addition to student learning and local demographic data—school process and program data and perceptual data. A few directions for plans included reflection as a component for determining priority needs and analyzing data. The plans usually specified use of leadership teams and collaborative teams for development. Some plans required descriptions of the process used in plan development and/or in specific plan components.

Stage 1. Orientation and Readiness: Develop cooperation and commitment to support changes from those involved in the improvement process and who understand the district and school vision/mission.

Part I. Plan Components:
Statements and Signatures of Assurances (Cover sheet, letter, or memo)
  Involvement of stakeholders, leadership team, peer review committee, school council
  Required criteria included
    Address all required components
    Reflect sound educational practices
    Have local leadership at all levels for successful implementation
    Have a high probability of improving student and educational performances
    Meet all state and federal criteria
  Student performance measures reviewed for state and ESEA accountability
  Performance indicators
  Measures/matters
  Federal and state expectations
  School results
  Status for meeting expectations/accountability status
  Academic growth gaps
  Postsecondary readiness

Plan Summary or Introduction
  Priorities and evidence
  Process for plan development
  Mission statement and review
  Vision or beliefs
  History of program improvements
    List of components that did not work
    List of components new to this summary
    Review of grant history
  School profile: components, possible indicators, school's information
  General district and school information
  Description of curriculum and assessments
  Attendance data and graduation rate or participation rate

Needs Assessment (Opportunities for Improvement)
  Gather and organize relevant data
    Study internal data to uncover recurring issues, problems, and concerns
    Look for challenges and strengths and most significant gaps and discrepancies
    Collect multiple measures: student learning, local demographic data, school processes/programs data, perception data
    Gather other data leading to strategies and activities in the action plan
    Consider data sources and data analysis
    Review educator qualifications and staff capacity

  Collect survey results—parents/guardians, students, staff, administration
  Analyze data for student learning, demographics, school processes, and perceptual data
  Analyze trends, and identify priority needs (at least three years of data)
  Analyze causes or key factors for discrepancies in the school's capacity to change/control
  Assess curriculum alignment: process, progress (complete, partially, not yet)
  Analyze conclusions for next steps

Reflection on Achievement Results
  Proficiency results
    Achievement at each level (groups and subgroups)
    Increases or decreases
    Causes and contributing factors
    Barriers to increases
    Specific areas of need for nonproficient subgroups
    Strategies to maintain and reach proficiency
    Percentage of students making learning gains
    Formative interim and miniassessments
  Number of teacher and leadership team meetings to review data, problem solve, and redirect instructional focus on student needs

Number of Times for Data Chats Between Teacher and Student and Between Teacher and Administrators
  Ways problem-solving model will support Response to Intervention
  Strengths and weaknesses
  State standards and testing resources—data and instructional implications
    Reading skills
    Writing
    Mathematics
    Science
  Alignment of curriculum, instruction, and assessment
    Discontinue
    Initiate, change, or modify
    Continue
  Priority needs

Data Key Findings or Narrative
  Student learning, demographic, school processes/programs, and perceptions
  Trend analysis and priority needs
  Root cause analysis and verification (evidence) of root cause
  Planning team's assessment of strengths and root causes
  Planning team's assessment of challenges and root causes
  Identify gaps between your current status and where you want to be, and prioritize major gaps

Figure 7.1. Composite of components from beginning sections of 18 School-Improvement Plans. This outline of planning components from the first part of a school-improvement plan incorporates different terms and processes compiled from 18 different school or district improvement-planning documents representing 10 states. In this beginning component of comprehensive planning, school personnel assess current status and complete a needs analysis.

Part 2. Program Action Plan Components:

Components: Core Content Program, Targeted Program, and Intensive Content Program

Component Manager and Goals and Objectives

Research-Based Strategies/Interventions and Diagnostic/Assessment Instrument

Priority Need, Causes and/or Contributing Factors, and Goal for Priority Need

Research-Based Effective Practices, Strategies, Programs, and Interventions

Measurable Objectives

    Conduct assessment measures, monitor success of each objective, provide evidence

    Strategies/activities, action steps for major improvement strategy or intervention

    New strategies or change processes

    Research support for process to facilitate goal

    Continuation strategies

    Expected impact for progress/success for each strategy

    Indicators of success

    Resources needed

    Implementation benchmarks

    Persons responsible and roles

    Time frame, begin and end dates, or completion date

    Evidence of completion

    Cost/Budget or estimated costs and fund source

Formal Reflection on Progress

    Goals and objectives worked on

    Measurable evidence of progress toward goals and objectives

    Next steps and adjustments for continued progress

Part 3. Other Priority School Needs and Plan Components:

Parental Involvement Activity or Parent, Family, and Community Involvement

Goals for parent involvement

Parent activities—assurance of parental involvement in student learning

Provision for the Coordination of Technology

Provision for a Safe and Disciplined Learning Environment

Professional Development Activities, Staff Development, or Professional Learning Cycles

---

Teacher Mentoring; Professional Development Assurance of Expenditure Allocation or Professional Development Activities

    Goals, knowledge level, application level, and impact level

    Strategies and activities, and timeline or start and end date

    Fund source and amount or resources

    Assessment/evaluation

    Timeline

    Person(s) responsible

Student Activities

    Supported by research

    Research-based program implementation for struggling, nonproficient students

    Student activity timeline

    Persons responsible

    Student activities—assurance of incorporation for at-risk students

    Evaluation process

    Program needs

    Individual needs

    Materials for instruction

    Instructional strategies

    Progress monitoring or monitoring the plan implementation

    Indicators of successful implementation

    Parental involvement

    Professional development

Annual Improvement Plan Review, Evaluation, and Revision

    Gather and organize data

    Highly qualified professional staff

    Plan for acquisition and retention

    Strategies to attract highly qualified staff and paraprofessional support staff

    Teacher-mentoring program

    High quality, ongoing professional development

Transition Plan for At-Risk Students

    Strategies for early childhood to elementary programs

    Strategies for elementary to middle school

    Strategies for ELLs from ESOL centers or classes to regular classrooms

    Parent/Family involvement

    Extended learning opportunities

    Coordination of services and funds

Figure 7.2. Composite of Action Plan Components from 18 School-Improvement Plans. This composite outline of component action plans by program or goal, and the other sections of improvement plans that came after them, incorporated terms and processes from 18 school or district improvement plans from a review of planning documents from 10 states. Action plans address core programs and other priority needs.

INTEGRATION OF RESEARCH, PLANNING, AND ASSESSMENT

State departments of education have familiarized schools with most of the action research steps as schools have become responsible for a portion of needs assessment and planning. The recognition of a need for research-supported change, upheld by multiple data sources including academic test data, begins to bring the research and planning process even closer to the action research process. I see this change as a step forward in bringing research on teaching and learning into the classrooms. However, to truly make a difference in results from either planning and assessment or the integration of research with planning, these activities must become an internalized part of ongoing school practice as educators work together for high achievement for all students.

THE JOURNEY AS A DESTINATION

My experiences in accreditation visits over 18 to 20 years has taught me that effective schools are not necessarily the ones that have the most or best plans described on paper. One person can write a great plan and show it to regulatory agencies. However, without involvement and opportunities for input into decision making, school staff may know little about its content, process, or support from data or research and may find it difficult to implement. State departments of education and other regulatory agencies recognize this problem. Plans are mostly consolidated into a comprehensive improvement plan for a school and a district. This allows schools to make the plan a meaningful one—not just a paper form to quickly produce at the last minute and then lay aside.

Wadsworth (2008), a respected Australian author on action research and action learning, as well as a consultant and practice-based theorist, observes that organizations too often suffer from frantically planning and acting without taking time to inquire more deeply into what is being done and why. She notes an apparent compulsion to "repeatedly collect records and data . . . or conduct reviews, consultations, or survey after survey . . . without moving on to reflect what it means or what therefore to do about it." Wadsworth advocates that human service organizations "build in research and evaluation . . . as daily processes of thoughtful observation, reflection, analysis and new practice" (p. 53).

In reviewing plans from 10 states, I learned that all states did not require completion of a needs analysis and plan every year unless the school or program is in a deficiency status. Some states required a complete plan of all schools every two or three years, and some required an annual review or annual update.

The plan is not the destination; it is only the map to take you where you need to go. With school planning, the written plan is important as a road map to get schools to high achievement. Involvement in and input into the planning process produce a plan for action and build understanding of the problems and commitments for improvement by an interdependent, collaborative staff.

Improvement of learning is an ongoing journey of professional growth for teachers and administrators. As they bring increasing expertise to their school work roles, student learning benefits. Administrators and teachers who practice identifying problems, researching information about causes and improvement strategies, and collecting and analyzing multiple sources of school data add expertise in instructional and assessment decision making.

The school-improvement plan describes how to implement and assess recommended changes or innovations from research and data. Times change and students change, so learning for educators and students is a lifelong journey. For school improvement, that journey is continued learning; therefore, the journey is the destination.

How can an educational leader be the catalyst for building a culture of continuous improvement by school personnel and students as learners? I suggest that schools adopting and rewarding action research need to study the following question as an action research problem: How can planning, scheduling, and evaluating action research be integrated as an ongoing component of comprehensive school-improvement planning? After a minimum of one year of action research implementation to develop at least a cadre of school personnel who understand the steps and cycle of both action research and the comprehensive planning cycle, one approach could be to research the following problem: How can action research expertise and practice contribute to the planning and implementation of school improvement in this particular school context? Perceptual and process data gathering and analysis could potentially increase buy-in and improve the integration of research, planning, and implementation.

Now, visualize ways that a school action research report can translate into a component action plan within a school-improvement plan. Information from Example 4 in the action research report section after Part 4 of this text was used to develop Figure 7.3 as an illustration. When you read the action research report and compare it with information and data in the component action plan, you will see that—with the exception of the timeline, reflection, and resources—almost everything in the plan came directly from the research report. I did not add the references list (which could

Action Component__ School ☑ District ❑ New ❑ Revised ☑

District __Example__   School __Xcel High School__   Action Manager __John Well__

Priority Need and Data Source: The priority need addressed in this plan is to reduce the reading and mathematics achievement gaps for sophomore students so that all students gain proficiency or above by the 2014 academic school year. The No Child Left Behind Act of 2001 has an overall goal to close the achievement gap between minority and nonminority students and between economically disadvantaged students and their more advantaged peers. State law KRS 158 also requires closing the achievement gap.

State core content test scores over the past 6 years show a continuing achievement gap between Caucasian students and African American and Hispanic students in both reading and mathematics. At its narrowest, in 2010, the reading achievement gap between African American and Caucasian students showed Caucasians 25% higher. In mathematics, the narrowest gap was 26% in 2009—a dramatic reduction from previous years—and 2010, when the gap remained near 46% higher for Caucasians. The small number of Hispanics distorts average or percentage scores somewhat in comparison to large groups. However, these scores for Hispanics fluctuated from year to year and in 2010 were 20% lower than Caucasians in reading and 27% lower in mathematics. The achievement gap for economic disadvantage in reading shows a difference of 25% and is nearly 40% for mathematics.

The Measures of Academic Progress (MAP) collected at the end of school year 2009–2010 in reading and at the beginning of 2010–2011 for mathematics did not show persistent gaps for disaggregated groups of students. However, in the content-area courses from which these student groups came, students were already separated in the school on the basis of low performance or scheduling preference and thus these scores would not be comparable to schoolwide scores. In reading and mathematics, the MAP data show a difference of about 4 points between the highest and lowest groups.

Clearly, to bring all students to proficiency in reading and mathematics by 2014 is a challenge, with mathematics presenting the greatest challenge. In addition, African American and Hispanic students, as well as students with economic disadvantages, present the greatest need for support for achievement.

Contributing Causes from Research and/or Experience with the Problem: Economics and ethnic origin show a relationship to achievement through these trend results disaggregated from free/reduced lunch data and core content testing. However, the instructional program and support for helping these students are school responsibilities. Research shows that tutorial sessions have produced positive results in raising achievement, particularly with African American and Hispanic students (Denbo, et al., 2002; Gellar, et al., 2006). The sophomore coaching initiative provides scaffolded instructional supports similar to tutorial sessions.

Priority Goal: To bring African American, Hispanic, and low-achieving Caucasian sophomore students who are economically disadvantaged to proficiency or above by 2014.

Objectives and Assessment: Academic achievement data in reading and mathematics over the next 2 years for disaggregated groups of students by race and economic disadvantage will show at least an overall 5% gap reduction and academic progress of at least 5% when compared with 2009 or 2010 core-content and end-of-year measurement of academic progress. Surveys of teachers, coaches, and students will show better-than-average satisfaction with results of the coaching initiative. Minutes of coaching improvement committees will show assessment and monitoring as well as suggestions for improvement and progress status. The professional development evaluation will assess effectiveness of summer seminars and coaching mentors and a report of research motivation strategies by the effective coaches committee who will assess their work.

Action Strategies (Number, and use N for New, C for Change, O for Ongoing):
O1. Sophomore Coaching Initiative. This initiative is a support system for targeted gap groups of sophomore students who are in sophomore English and Practical Statistics courses. These students receive 15–20 minutes of individual or small-group tutoring from a teacher in addition to their other classes with their regular teachers.

C2. Two committees for coaching improvement will be formed and will hold a minimum of one meeting per each grading period to monitor retention data and grades in sophomore English and Practical Statistics and to suggest improvements for instructional content and strategies for the sophomore coaching innovation. Lessons should be rigorous, maximize student engagement, and accommodate discussion and hands-on application of content.

Figure 7.3.   Sample Action Plan Component of the School Improvement Plan. Details for completion of this sample action plan component came from the action research report developed by Bryan Jacobs and Richard Royster, Associate High School Principals. Their action research report is used with permission. The complete report is the HS 4 action research report in the example report section after Part 4 in this text. Only a few items such as cost and dates for implementation were added to their data in construction of this sample action plan. This example demonstrates completion of typical action component items from Figure 7.2.

N3. Professional development for sophomore coaches should include partnership during their initial year with an experienced effective coach as a mentor. PD should also include instruction to familiarize teachers who serve as academic coaches with content and lesson activities and provide information and practice on strategies for interacting with small student-discussion groups. The ultimate program success may depend on these teachers' skills to make connections with the students with whom they work.

N4. A committee of effective sophomore coaches should be formed to research strategies for motivation that can be used to address issues associated with teacher apathy and effective coaching practices.

Research/Best Practices References for Action Strategies: The accountability provisions of No Child Left Behind refer to economic disadvantage and race/ethnicity as underlying causes of current academic inequity. Research and professional literature reveal strategies for reducing and/or eliminating the achievement gap. Literature review shows the following themes: achievement of minority groups related to beliefs and attitudes; cultural responsiveness; community involvement; classroom instruction; access to resources; and beliefs and attitudes of teachers, families, and students. Genuine caring conveys a sense of value and worth to students, which can lead to increased learning (Craig et al., 2002). Parental encouragement of learning and high but reasonable expectations for their children support education and better grades for low-income and minority children (Gardner, 2007). Additional resources have been found to have some effect on achievement of disadvantaged students. There is strong evidence that assignment of minority and disadvantaged students to effective teachers improves their performance (Barton, 2003; Hanushek, 1996).

Start Date and Completion Date: The Coaching Initiative runs concurrent with the academic year. Coaching Improvement committees and mentors will be assigned in May and begin their work in September of the following school year, with completion one week after the academic school year ends. Mentoring sessions, introduction to coaching, and research on coaching strategies will take place in July and August prior to the beginning of a coaching assignment in September.

These sessions will conclude with a seminar on evaluation of evidence for implementation of interactive group strategies on August 23.

The effective sophomore coaches committee will comprise experienced coaches assigned as mentors. Monitoring for effectiveness of the coaching program will begin by the 1st of October and be completed by the end of May. The committee members will conduct action research on the progress of the coaching program during October to May to assess coaching effectiveness in advancing progress for student learning.

Evidence of Progress: The end-of-year measures of academic progress and a survey of students receiving coaching services shall show gain in students' academic progress and reduction of the achievement gap between students in the coaching program compared with all other students enrolled in General Sophomore English and Practical Statistics. Current evaluation showed the gaps to be narrow when the target students were compared with all students in the coaching program, but comparison with all other sophomore students enrolled in general English and Practical Statistics will be the new comparison and should be more meaningful. Qualitative data from students, coaches, and host teachers show better-than-average scores on all items by students with the highest ratings for working in small groups and working with their sophomore coach.

Surveys by teacher coaches showed a below-average score for the coaching lessons for effectively helping students in General English, and an average score for developing meaningful relationships with students. The highest scores by coaches for English students were for student engagement in the coaching sessions and for the increased comfort in asking questions felt by students in small groups. Coaches for the Practical Statistics class had the highest scores for feeling comfortable working with students in a class outside the teacher's content area and students feeling more comfortable when asking questions in small groups. The lowest rating for coaches for Practical Statistics was 3.2, slightly above average, for making students feel valued at the high school.

Date for Formal Reflection on Progress: Weekly, monthly, and annually, informal assessment will be made by host teachers and teacher coaches—formally, each grading period by improvement committees and weekly by the effective coaches committee.

Modifications Needed or Next Steps: Next steps will involve planning and implementation of changes resulting from the improvement committees and implementation of selected teacher and coach motivation strategies based on the effective coaches committee research. In addition, systematic monitoring and revision of this initiative should be ongoing, as indicated by additional research and data, to ensure its success with students as long as the initiative continues.

Resources and Estimated Cost (Professional Development Needs and Other Resources): Personnel and materials cost for the coaching mentors: $4,500 for summer seminars; $1,000 for research supplies and materials, $10,500 personnel cost for June and July.

Figure 7.3. (Continued)

PHASE 1: Orientation to Action Research

- Professional development seminars are held to introduce action research to faculty.
- Faculty volunteers are solicited to conduct individual or partnership action research studies.
- Faculty in practitioner–researcher roles communicate and support each other's research.
- Action research completers report results to all faculty and staff.
- The school and school district office give special recognition to all action research participants.

PHASE 2: Collaborative Action Research for School Problems

- Organize an action research leadership team.
- Conduct a needs analysis and identify a school problem.
- Identify team members to conduct each research step and develop a schedule for the completion of each research step.
- Document and share research results with all faculty and staff.
- Recognize all persons who participated in any phase of the research.
- Develop an action plan for the implementation of research recommendations.

PHASE 3: Integration of Action Research and Comprehensive School Improvement Plans

- Conduct professional development activities to identify how action research should contribute to the school-improvement planning process.
- Organize a research leadership team to complete a needs analysis, determine priorities, and coordinate an action research calendar compatible with the schedule for comprehensive school-improvement planning.
- Organize action research teams for literature reviews, data collection, and data analysis.
- Assign individual responsibilities for specific action plan components for the school-improvement plan.
- Complete all tasks and share results.
- Recognize all research participants and collaborate with appropriate persons to evaluate the integration of action research with comprehensive school-improvement plans.
- Plan the next steps for improving action research and comprehensive school planning to improve student achievement.

Figure 7.4.   A suggested three-phase transition that advances the knowledge and practice of action research within a school or school district: (a) understanding and practicing action research steps by individuals or partnerships that address specific classroom problems, (b) organizing a research leadership team and research task teams to conduct action research on school and classroom problems, and (c) using action research for selected classroom and school problems and also as a part of comprehensive school-improvement plans.

go at the end of the complete school plan for all research cited in the plan), but the priority need, goal, objectives, strategies, and research support came from descriptions in the action research report.

Now let us envision the outcome of integrating the process of action research and improvement planning in a school. Figure 7.4 suggests three phases or stages. The timing and manner of implementation would vary within each school context, but in the suggested approach shown here, all staff members have had an opportunity to learn the action research process by completing their own or a collaborative research project common to their work as they study each chapter. Some staff members will have research experience, but scanning the chapters in this text would help build a common understanding. The persons with research experience might make adjustments in the process but should be aware of all of the research steps.

Everyone may not work on an action research project, and especially not at the same time. Most new teachers need time to gain confidence in teaching and classroom management. But I would encourage all teachers to get involved with a project at some time, either collaboratively with a colleague on a topic of mutual interest, individually to address a classroom learning-related problem, or collectively to address a schoolwide problem.

A major purpose proposed by this text is to make the implementation of action research an ongoing practice within schools to improve student learning by analyzing pertinent data, along with research information and previous knowledge and experience on the part of the faculty, in order to implement improvements. This is also the primary purpose of comprehensive school planning, so ultimately the two processes should complement one another to bring about school improvement. Making the leap to that use of action research at the beginning is a big jump. I propose starting small in the classrooms, where faculty work daily. This text covers collaborative research, particularly for solving schoolwide problems, but suggests that performance activities in organizing and carrying out each step of a research project will differ somewhat, depending on the research to be completed and the research context.

Figure 7.4 illustrates how school personnel may initially learn about action research and how it can add to professional expertise and promote student learning, followed by encouragement and opportunities to engage in action research on a topic specific to faculty needs for their classrooms. Support through the principal and the district office will encourage these efforts. After the first phase develops a cadre of volunteers who have completed and applied action research in their classrooms, the next experience would add opportunities for working collaboratively on priority problems that affect multiple classrooms or school operations. Then, the third phase of action research learning advances and contributes to the integration of action research as an ongoing part of comprehensive school planning.

A within-school sharing session at a midpoint and at the conclusion of faculty research for solving both classroom and schoolwide problems will help faculty members learn from each other's work. Recognition of some kind should be given to all who complete a research project. This may be a certificate, a notice with names and project topics on a bulletin board, or a principal's or superintendent's note or e-mail of thanks commending the researchers for practicing the inquiry process to improve student learning. I have known principals who effectively made a habit of noticing good things that teachers did from time to time and who simply recognized the achievements with a thank-you message. Teachers appreciate that someone cares when they make an extra effort.

Active involvement of the principal in the same activity that others are working on encourages teachers to participate and sets an example for collaborative team work. When a school leader not only shows interest in the work that others are doing but also engages in the project with them, it speaks volumes for the importance of the work and of collaboration.

Phase 2 of an action research project brings teacher collaborative involvement into a schoolwide action research project. Again, make the opportunity for participation available for as many teachers as possible who have an interest in the school problem being researched. Provide recognition for those participants, and share the research results with all staff.

Phase 3 may overlap with one or both of Phase 1 and Phase 2, depending on how often the school develops a school-improvement needs analysis and plan. When an overlap occurs late in Phase 1 or 2, the use of selected action research components in that plan can help the staff to see how research serves to improve both the school and each staff member's expertise. Once Phases 1 and 2 are completed, communication that identifies how accountability planning for school improvement can be enhanced by the action research process may help faculty and staff recognize the roles action research results can play in comprehensive school improvement. Participants also see that their work with research both supports the plan and, on a smaller scale, keeps a focus on improvement as an ongoing process. Having action research as a professional-development component for staff helps provide time and recognition and encourages inquiry as an approach to learning and growth.

Figure 7.5 shows an example schedule for integrating the results of action research with comprehensive school-improvement planning. All research recommendations may not be part of the comprehensive plan. Some could be implemented soon after completion of the plan without being part of comprehensive planning, depending on the type of action recommended. But a number of comprehensive planning components lend themselves to action research that school practitioner–researcher teams could complete as scheduled research activities compatible with the comprehensive school-improvement planning cycle.

Gantt Chart Two-Year Cycle for Comprehensive School-Improvement Planning and Action Research Activities

Activities CP = Comprehensive Plan AR = Action Research	July	Aug	Sept	Oct	Nov	Dec	Jan	Feb	Mar	Apr	May	June
CP Identify process and responsibilities for reviewing plan and current status: vision, mission, and evaluation components; update school and district profile; select priority needs	XX	XX										
CP Update school and district profile; review AR results; select top priorities										XX	XX	XX
CP Reflect on achievement results, and determine priority needs		XX	XX									
AR Research each priority need to determine strengths and weaknesses, issues and concerns; identify research-based strategies and activities for improvement; analyze student learning, school processes, demographics, perceptions, curriculum and instruction, causes, and gaps			XX	XX	XX	XX	XX	XX	XX			
AR Study how to improve faculty collaboration and professional development with a goal to improve student achievement, curriculum alignment, or other areas			XX	XX	XX	XX	XX	XX	XX			
CP Component Plans—Year 2	XX	XX								XX	XX	XX
AR Conduct research for a core content program to determine how to improve results: analyze goals, objectives, success indicators, student support, resources and research-based improvement strategies and activities			XX	XX	XX	XX	XX	XX	XX			
AR Study parent involvement, technology coordination and use, school environment, student activities, professional development, or district priorities			XX	XX	XX	XX	XX	XX	XX			
CP Use key data and literature citations from action research as appropriate for supporting action plans for programs or priority initiatives										XX	XX	XX
CP Develop or review School-Improvement Plan; revise as needed; secure approval of plan and signatures for required assurances										XX	XX	XX

Figure 7.5. **This example incorporates planning components and action plan components selected from Figure 7.1 and Figure 7.2. In addition, it assumes the existence of a leadership planning oversight and decision-making team, set up according to a number of action research projects completed by research teams of three to five faculty/staff members who are stakeholders in the areas to be researched. The items to be studied are those required in the plan.**

Key Questions for Review

1. What do you see as barriers to making research part of an ongoing process of school improvement in your school, and how can you overcome these barriers?

2. Effective teachers and school leadership have been shown to have a positive effect on student learning. When new teachers begin teaching, they need support for professional growth and confidence for instructional effectiveness. What do you believe to be the three most important things that a principal can do to positively affect this growth?

3. How can action research promote teacher professional growth and instructional effectiveness?

4. Compare action research with school improvement planning. How are the two processes similar, and how are they different?

5. How is the planning process or action research both a journey and a destination? Reflect on your perspective of this concept.

Note. **Performance Checklist will also appear on CD.**

Performance Checklist for Reflection and Action Planning

This chapter bridges action research with practice and translates research recommendations into action. Assessment measures should yield evidence of success, need for modifications, or need for change. Steps 4b, 4c, and 5 of action research become a component action plan in the school improvement planning and review process.

A. Reflect on the recommendations from your action research process, and determine which recommendations should become an action component in a school-improvement plan. Draft this plan, using your state format for an action plan component.

Performance Check:

1. Decide whether the development of the action plan based on your action research results requires further collaboration with others to develop and implement or whether the recommendations from your action research results can be translated into action within a short time and who will be responsible for implementing and evaluating the results. If implementation directly affects others, decide who needs input into the plan and ask them to join you in its development or to share with you ideas for implementation, timing, and assessment. If a large number of others should have input, you may choose to develop five or six questions to use as a survey to gather their opinions before developing the plan.

2. Locate the action component plan used for your comprehensive school improvement plan. If you have not previously been involved with completing a school plan, review a copy of the last completed or updated plan. If your completed action research results and recommendations should be built in with the comprehensive school plan, determine who should help with drafting an action component for the next planning process. If you are collaborating with development of the plan, review and discuss the plan jointly and determine who will

write and set a time schedule for the completion of each section for a comprehensive action plan component.

B. Reflect on the recommendations from your action research process. Decide which recommendations can be implemented prior to the next school-improvement plan. Draft a plan that includes the responsibility for how activities will be implemented to carry out the research recommendations. Identify objectives and expected results, how the results of implementation will be assessed, who is responsible for implementation and monitoring, a timeline for implementation and assessment, and specifications for what will serve as evidence of the plan's success.

Performance Check:

1. Decide whether the implementation of the action research results before the next comprehensive school improvement planning process requires collaboration with others or whether it pertains to an action that you will be responsible for implementing. If the implementation of the results directly affects others, decide who needs input into the plan and ask them to join you in developing and implementing the plan or to share with you ideas for its implementation, timing, and assessment.

2. If you are unfamiliar with a school action plan, review a copy of the last completed or updated plan most related to your action research recommendations. Use that as a guide for selecting essential components for planning implementation. If you prefer, use your own format. Draft a plan for implementation, objectives, an assessment process, each person's responsibility for implementation and monitoring, and a timeline for implementation and assessment. Also, identify what will serve as evidence of success. If you are collaborating with others in development of the plan, review and discuss the plan jointly and divide the writing responsibility for each section.

References

Angello, M. (2010). Leading in a new decade. Bright Tree Consulting Group, LLC. Retrieved from http://EzineArticles.com/?expert=Matt_Angello

Beech, D. M., & Reinhartz, J. (2000). *Supervisory leadership: Focus on instruction.* Needham Heights, MA: Allyn & Bacon.

Ferrance, E. (2000). *Action research: Themes in education* (Series Booklet). Providence, RI: Northeast and Islands Regional Educational Laboratory, The Education Alliance, Brown University. Retrieved from http://www.alliance.brown.edu/pubs/themes_ed/act_research.pdf

Hanushek, E. A. (1992). The trade-off between child quantity and quality. *Journal of Political Economy, 100*(1), 84–117.

Jordan, H., Mendro, R., & Weerasinghe, D. (1997, July). *Teacher effects on longitudinal student achievement.* Paper presented at the Sixth Annual Evaluation Institute sponsored by CREATE, Indianapolis, IN.

Leithwood, K., Seashore-Louis, K., Anderson, S., & Wahlstrom, K. (2004). *How leadership influences student learning.* New York: The Wallace Foundation.

Munby, S. (2008, Summer). Building the perfect team: Leadership in the twenty-first century. *Education Review, 21*(1), 31–389.

Murphy, J. (2005). *Connecting teacher leadership and school improvement.* Thousand Oaks, CA: Corwin.

National Science Foundation. (n.d.). Definitions of research and development: An annotated compilation of official sources, U.S. Federal Government (pp. 1–7). Retrieved from NSF website: http://www.nsf.gov/statistics/randdef/fedgov.cfm.

Printy, S. (2010). Principals' influence on instructional quality: Insights from U.S. schools. *School Leadership and Management, 30*(2), 111–126. doi:10.1080/13632431003688005.

Sanders, W. L. (2000). Value-added assessment from student achievement data: Opportunities and hurdles. *Journal of Personnel Evaluation in Education, 14*(4), 329–339.

Sanders, W. L., & Rivers, J. C. (1996). *Cumulative and residual effects of teachers on future student academic achievement* (Research Progress Report). Knoxville, TN: University of Tennessee Value-Added Research and Assessment Center.

Sanders W. L., & Horn, S. P. (1998). Research findings from the Tennessee value-added assessment system (TVAAS) database: Implications for educational evaluation and research. *Journal of Personnel Evaluation in Education, 12*(3), 247–256.

Sanders, W. L., Wright, S. P., & Ross, S. M. (1999). *Value-added achievement results for two cohorts of Roots and Wings schools in Memphis: 1995–1998 outcomes.* Memphis, TN: Center for Research in Educational Policy, The University of Memphis.

Stronge, J. H., & Tucker, P. D. (2000). *Teacher evaluation and student achievement.* Washington, DC: NEA.

Topping, K. J., & Sanders, W. L. (2000). Teacher effectiveness and computer assessment of reading: Relating value added and learning information system data. *School Effectiveness and School Improvement, 11*(3), 305–337.

Wadsworth, Y. (2008). Action research for living human systems. In B. Boog, J. Pree, M. Slagter, & J. Zeelen (Eds.), *Towards quality improvement of action research: Developing ethics and standards* (pp. 83–96). Rotterdam, The Netherlands: Sense Publishers.

Wise, D., & Jacobo, A. (2010, April). Towards a framework for leadership coaching. *School Leadership and Management, 30*(2), 159–169. doi:10.1080/1363241003663206.

Wright, S. P., Horn, S. P., & Sanders, W. L. (1997). Teacher and classroom context effects on student achievement: Implications for teacher evaluation. *Journal of Personnel Evaluation in Education, 11*, 57–67.

CHAPTER 8

Research, Reflection, and Professional Growth

Learning and applying the action research process enhances the professional expertise of educators in locating research relevant to classroom and school procedures that affect learning. The process also helps educators to effectively address school problems. Action research is a basic tool to improve practice, educator professional growth, and student learning.

Using previous research and adding practitioner research to address student needs in a specific context makes sense. Previous educational research demonstrates the importance of excellent teachers and school leaders in improving student learning, and currently, information related to teaching and learning is prevalent and accessible to educators through technology. Practitioners of action research use techniques that guard against personal bias, gather multiple perspectives from multiple sources, and triangulate data to verify results. These techniques and others support the integrity of research results. A collaborative data- and research-based focus on inquiry to address school problems—with education colleagues at the school, district, and university levels—divides the workload and multiplies ideas for gathering and analyzing data.

Action research may be the most efficient and effective way to address professional development for teachers (Johnston, 1999). It helps them become more reflective and analytical in their teaching practice. They learn from action and then reflect on how this learning fits with what is already known to build a schema for improving teaching effectiveness.

REFLECTIVE PRACTITIONER

Reflective practice is associated with successful learning (Borkowski, Carr, Kurtz, & Pressley, 1987; Garner, 1990). The term *reflective practitioner* became a buzz term in university settings a few years ago while I was teaching at the university level. (Or, as this generation of students would say, the term went *viral*). My first awareness of the term *reflective practitioner* was in 2006–2007, when the University of Kentucky College of Education was preparing for accreditation. When we were updating the college mission, preparation of reflective practitioners became part of our mission. Faculty members were asked to include statements about student reflection in all course syllabi descriptions as one evidence of preparing reflective practitioners. I added the terminology and considered ways that it could be used in my courses, but didn't give much reflection at the time to the importance of intentional reflection on new learning for school practitioners.

As a former public school teacher and principal and a highly task-oriented individual who felt an ever-present need for more time, I thought *reflection* to be a fancy term without much substance. Journaling thoughts became one way for teachers and students to reflect. I confess that spending time writing my thoughts never caught on with me, but the reflective process did.

I became interested in the importance of reflection for learning as I read more about its role in learning and then saw it exhibited by educators as they completed principal preparation portfolio reviews. The general definition of *metacognition* as "thinking about thinking" (Livingston, 1997, p. 1) appealed to me. *Metacognitive knowledge* refers to general knowledge about the ways by which individuals learn and process knowledge. Integrating new knowledge into what we already know does require intentional thinking about our learning experiences and what this new knowledge means when reflected upon through the lens of our previous knowledge, experience, and family and community roles. Only then does learning become meaningful to the learner. Reflection becomes a purposeful thought process that makes new knowledge meaningful and useful to the learner and aids knowledge retention.

In the principal preparation program at the University of Kentucky, the faculty initiated the use of a student portfolio as one measure of proficiency for a principal's position. Each student prepared and defended a portfolio at the completion of the first year of eligibility for a principal internship, and at the end of the advanced level for principal certification eligibility. Students selected a work sample from their preparation course projects to place in their portfolio as a demonstration of their credentials for each standard for educational leadership. Our state was an initial adopter of the ISLLC Standards for School Leadership (CCSSO, 1996) as a guide for principal preparation.

Our faculty developed a reflective cover sheet formatted for students to complete and add in front of each portfolio course project. In this cover-sheet form, students explained how the selected course project demonstrated their understanding of each standard. Figure 8.1, Figure 8.2, and Figure 8.3 on the CD under Chapter 8 Resources are copies of this form, directions for its completion, and a completed exemplar to assist with its preparation. The form guided each educator's reflection on how his or her project work demonstrated the identified standard in the portfolio and how what they learned would improve their effectiveness as a principal.

As a member of the portfolio review committees who scored portfolios, I found those completed reflection forms somewhat revealing of students' thoughts about their learning from course work and how they saw the relationship between their learning and the work of a principal. However, the most in-depth thoughts generally gave greater evidence of personal reflection when a faculty review committee met with each student for dialogue on the portfolio and how it related to the work of a principal. These conversations with students centered on their portfolio selections and relevance to the standards for school leaders.

Conferences with the program completers showed strong evidence of the benefits of reflection. Often, they said that work on the portfolio helped them realize how much they had learned. They talked about how reflecting on the standards as they selected their portfolio projects from their course work helped them to recognize how their program prepared them for taking on the responsibilities of a principal. Their feedback also gave the faculty thoughts for identifying strengths and weaknesses of the program.

A department faculty colleague and I completed an action research study that used five years of portfolio quality rating data as a proxy for learners' depth of understanding of each standard. The purpose was to identify areas of strengths and areas that needed more attention in our program. Averaging the portfolio quality ratings for each standard gave an indication of how well students in each group of those who completed the program could relate their school leadership course work to a specific leadership standard that described expectations for performance as a principal. The research was published in the *International Journal of Leadership in Education* (Knoeppel & Logan, 2011).

Tracking the ratings of portfolios submitted midway through the program compared with those at program completion indicated improvement in Standard 2, which described instructional leadership. This pleased us because this standard was a special focus in the program. However, the standard pertaining to legal and ethical standards was of concern and possibly did not receive much program emphasis outside of the school law and human resources courses.

In the portfolio review conferences with students completing the program, I became convinced of the importance of reflection on learning as a thought process. The benefits gained justified the hours we spent reviewing portfolios and serving on review committees. As a result of this work, I also became a more reflective practitioner than before. I don't write about my thoughts, although many people may find doing so helpful. I think about new learning experiences, reflect on what I learned, consider how this learning applies in the context of what I do, and decide how I can use it to improve what I do. The University of Kentucky, College of Education, now uses a defense of an eportfolio for principal preparation for the completion of Level II.

A REFLECTIVE LEARNER

Table 8.1 on the CD in Chapter 8 Resources lists a few references for further exploration of learning reflections, as well as a list of online documents referred to in this chapter. One such article published in *Teachers College Record* (Frederick, 2009) describes a language arts teacher's action research to help ninth-grade students think reflectively about their work. His hope was to help them see that they are learners and that reflecting on what they learn not only reinforces that learning but enables them to apply it to future endeavors. With these students, the teacher identified three subskills for reflection, metacognition, or self-assessment of learning: (a) clearly articulating and naming the skill, (b) pointing to evidence in the students' work that showed specific learning, and (c) setting goals for future learning.

STANDARDS AS AN ASSESSMENT GUIDE
FOR PROFESSIONAL DEVELOPMENT

The standards for school leaders referred to in the earlier section, Reflective Practitioner, were entitled the *Interstate School Leaders Licensure Consortium (ISLLC) Standards for School Leaders* (CCSSO, 1996). The Council of Chief State School Officers (CCSSO) is a nonpartisan, nationwide, nonprofit organization of public officials who head departments of elementary and secondary education in the states, the District of Columbia, the Department of Defense Education Activity, and five U.S. extra-state jurisdictions. CCSSO provides leadership, advocacy, and technical assistance on major educational issues. The council seeks member consensus on major educational issues and expresses its views to civic and professional organizations, federal agencies, the U.S. Congress, and the public.

The *ISLLC 1996 Standards* for School Leaders and their updated version, ISLLC 2008 Educational Leadership Policy Standards, were developed by the Council of Chief State School Officers (CCSSO, 2008) and member states. Copies of these standards, as well as other publications such as forward-thinking white papers on creating a vision for the 21st century, may be downloaded from the council's website at www.ccsso.org.

About now, you may be wondering, "Okay, what does this have to do with action research or with me?" I believe that if you keep reading, you will see the connection and find this chapter helpful for school-improvement research, reflection, and educator professional growth. The whole purpose of this text is school improvement for student learning through weaving research and professional growth for educators into the fabric of K–12, K–14, and K–16+ or K–20 school practice for teaching and learning. Learning the process of action research, using it in schools to learn and plan, and practicing reflection on what has been learned and the action to take for improving practice add to professional expertise for teaching and learning.

The chief state school officers for 44 states and the District of Columbia, working with CCSSO, have committed to developing next-generation systems for education and accountability. They identified four strategic focus areas for transformation of teaching and learning: (a) Next Generation Learning; (b) Standards, Assessment, and Accountability; (c) System of Educator Development; and (d) Comprehensive Data Systems. A number of working papers have been developed and are available from their home page www.ccsso.org by selecting the Resources tab and then Publications. Individuals can key in at least four words of the document title to locate, read online, or print these documents.

In particular, this chapter discusses some of the CCSSO working papers about future directions for schools in this century and identifies knowledge and performance activities that will help guide administrators and teachers in a self-assessment that examines professional growth needs related to leading and teaching in 21st century schools. The self-assessment guides used at the end of this chapter to analyze areas for professional growth are adaptations of two groups of recently updated standards for all educators—the CCSSO *ISLLC 2008 Educational Leadership Policy Standards* (CCSSO, 2008) and *InTASC Model Core Teaching Standards: A Resource for State Dialogue* (CCSSO, 2011). InTASC is CCSSO's Interstate Teacher Assessment and Support Council.

These standards for both teaching and leading are important documents to help all educators envision knowledge and skill expectations during the 21st century and, therefore, are helpful to educators who are thinking and planning for future challenges and expertise required to meet responsibilities to learners. The standards are important to faculty and students in university preparation programs for teaching and school leadership and for teacher and leader practitioners currently working in schools. The standards demonstrate that in this second decade of the 21st century schools have begun work on updating, identifying, envisioning, and advocating school change to meet the educational needs of each learner.

With educational reforms of the 1990s, the schools began changing and have increased district and school-site responsibility for meeting state-approved standards and data-based accountability measures of student achievement. School planning and student support concentrated on demographic groups of students who did not meet proficiency levels. The focus of improvement appeared to be largely on a concern for gaps in student achievement between low- and high-achieving groups and summative achievement tests to measure these gaps.

Two decades of societal, technological, and economic change since those reforms increased accountability demands for schools. The complexity of meeting diverse student needs has also increased but without the structures and support for educators to adequately address those needs. In addition, merely measuring gaps among groups of students insufficiently addresses the need for a rigorous, high quality education for every child. Thus, the CCSSO initiatives underway seem to be bringing together educators from most of the states and many professional education organizations to rethink 21st century student needs for learning and to envision transformed supports and structures to address those needs. The thinking assumes that major direction for shaping this transformation will come from state education officials and schools working together to create and advocate legislation and funding to bring it about.

Where Are We Going?

The state school officials, as members of CCSSO, have identified four focus areas necessary to enable each learner to be ready to enter a career or higher education. A CCSSO publication, *Transforming Education: Delivering on Our Promise to Every Child* (CCSSO, 2009) identifies and explains these four areas for school transformation for the 21st century. Other working papers with related ideas of interest to educators are *Transforming Teaching and Leading: A Vision for a High-Quality Educator Development System* (CCSSO, 2010) and CCSSO's policy statement for *ESEA Reauthorization Principles and Recommendations* (CCSSO, 2010) to support a new vision of teaching and learning. Table 8.1 on the CD in Chapter 8 Resources lists these documents, as well as others mentioned and referenced in this chapter. I encourage you to go to the Council of Chief State School Officers website (www.ccsso.org) and familiarize yourself with at least some of these documents that envision school transformation and review other publications available by clicking on the Resources tab and then clicking Publications.

Will action research and reflection fit with new visions of 21st century schools, educator delivery systems, and professional development needs and opportunities? With so many innovative instructional and delivery systems under discussion and the rapidly increasing diverse society in this country and its schools, research and expertise in inquiry learning and the use of data will be as great as or greater than they are in schools presently for differentiation of learning and tools for lifelong learning. Discussions of the need for expanded sources and types of data already are included in most comprehensive state planning documents that I reviewed. Research was required as evidence in planning improvements. In several of the 18 state planning documents that I reviewed for Chapter 7 data collection included survey and procedural data.

An emerging recognition of the need for multiple types of learning assessment doesn't tell school practitioners anything they don't already know. They recognize that too much emphasis is on summative achievement data. In spite of the necessity for summative test data, the emphasis on this type of testing is unpopular with many educators who know that more attention should be given to substantive formative data at regular learning intervals from each learner. This type of assessment is timely for necessary improvement during the learning process.

Formative data can take many forms that can be documented for research, along with other assessment data. Two school districts in the central Kentucky area have successfully involved each student in setting goals and monitoring progress for their own learning. The first school in this area that initiated this process of self-monitoring of progress by students was a new elementary school. Imagine the student motivation and progress that might result if the practice continued for this group of students as they progressed through middle and high school levels! Such a scenario exemplifies students who assume their share of responsibility for their own learning progress.

Structures and support envisioned for schools will require greater flexibility than is presently true for delivery systems, learning modes, and instructional time and place. Staffing of schools and scheduling of learning may finally break out of the time gridlock of a six-period school day and present flexible staffing and scheduling opportunities for leadership with specialized expertise. Greater use of technology delivery systems and hybrid learning systems allow greater flexibility for time and place of learning. I think this change is likely to be one of the early structural changes because of how rapidly mobile communication and virtual offices became a reality for mobile workers in business. The availability of mobile computer devices will likely expand as an instructional delivery mode beyond their current use as e-textbooks. Young people are constant users of mobile phones for instant and ongoing communication.

Although the thoughts expressed here were stimulated by the working papers from CCSSO, the commentary in this section of the chapter comes from my perspective of some of the changes that may become part of schools and student learning in the next 5 to 10 years to bring greater flexibility in the time and location for teaching and learning. I believe that there are many teaching and learning practices that will stand the test of time, but schools need improvements in structural and delivery systems to support teacher, as well as student, learning. Data systems need further improvement for multiple kinds of accurate school data to support learning and research on learning.

Who Will Lead?

An identified research base from scholars and experts in education administration, in addition to input from organizations and leaders in the field, undergirds ISLLC 2008 Standards for School Leaders. Over the last decade, education administration scholars produced more research than ever about education leadership and its role in raising student achievement (CCSSO, 2008, p. 3). ISLLC 2008 presents a framework and foundation for state policies and expectations of school leaders, as well as for professional-development and evaluation systems that facilitate performance growth.

With diversity in the nation's schools requiring greater leadership responsibility and teaching skill to instruct each student in a rigorous but supportive learning environment, research shows an increase in schools turning to distributive leadership (Camburn, Rowan, & Taylor, 2004; Spillane & Camburn, 2006). Studies of the distribution of responsibilities for leading and managing schools reveal both formally designated leadership positions and teachers and other professional staff involved in leading a variety of activities without formal leadership titles. Distributive leadership that fosters collaborative opportunities has been shown to increase capacity for change and improvement (Harris, 2002, p. 4). The distributive perspective of leadership centers on how leadership can be distributed among formal and informal leaders and includes the activities of individuals within the school who mobilize and guide other teachers in instructional change (Spillane, Halverson, & Diamond, 2003). Spillane, Diamond, and Jita (2003, p. 12) conclude that successful education leaders must be able to engage others in leading in order to provide the teaching and learning specialties required to address each student's learning needs).

No single leadership style can meet the diverse range of challenges faced in difficult circumstances. The distribution of leadership and management responsibilities varies from school to school and also differs depending on the type of activity (Spillane &

Camburn, 2006). Leaders other than the principal are more likely to lead the instruction- and curriculum-related activities that currently are the principal's responsibility.

What About Professional Growth?

Meeting future education challenges will require ongoing self-assessment by educators of their own professional knowledge and skills required to meet the learning needs for each and every child. The staffing of teams of educators for certain areas of instruction or learning problems may become a regular part of practice. This will require more prepara- tion for building relationships for effective collaboration.

The CCSSO (2010) working paper *Transforming Teaching and Leading: A Vision for a High-Quality Educator Development System* names effective educator teams and educators who are culturally proficient, self-aware, and reflective as implications for a changing environment of schools. This vision also includes "ongoing, embedded professional development for teachers and administrators around 21st century content knowledge, skills, and pedagogical strategies" (CCSSO, 2010, p. 4). The Education Workforce White Paper envisions a career continuum with four stages: preparation, novice, professional, and expert. The career continuum concept presented as a work- ing paper is stated as an intention to start a dialogue rather than presenting a strict position on its design.

A career continuum as described by CCSSO has multiple levels. Growth opportuni- ties extend from initial preparation and practice at a novice level to job-embedded growth activities and participation in learning communities at a professional level and then to advanced certification with specialized skills at an expert level. The expectation for highly skilled educators to facilitate learning for each student, with multiple opportunities to meet high learning standards, is for these educators to have learning opportunities and support to become highly effective over the course of a career continuum.

The professional level represents increasing competence and expertise through building on strengths and overcoming challenges, largely through "working with col- leagues to collect and analyze student data and respond to student needs. It is as a mem- ber of this professional learning community that educators at the professional stage, both teachers and administrators alike, strive to collectively achieve broader school and district goals" (CCSSO, 2010, p. 7). The multiple career pathways at the expert level would de- velop specialized skills for leadership opportunities—for example, as mentors, coaches, content specialists, or professional association leadership.

Transforming schools as envisioned in the CCSSO white paper on teaching and leading involves a system of shared responsibilities and rewards. Teaching and leading will be team activities that utilize all available talent and that demand a "coherent and high-quality educator development system" (CCSSO, 2010, p. 7). Achieving this transfor- mation will require different ways of scheduling personnel to support collaboration and teamwork, along with utilizing technological advances that provide multiple ways for student learning. Expectations for administrators and teachers include being continuous learners who are grounded in research evidence on how students learn, personalized learning practices that address each student's unique needs, and use of technology to individualize learning.

This chapter guides you through a self-assessment of your knowledge and skills by use of both the CCSSO ISLLC 2008 Leadership Policy Standards and the InTASC Model of Core Teaching Standards, while you keep in mind some of the school changes and career structure changes being envisioned for 21st century learning. You will use the leadership standards, whether you are currently a teacher or an administrator, because a restructur- ing of work roles brings expectations for more teacher-leader or team-leader roles for different learning needs or other instructional specialties.

The *InTASC Model Core Teaching Standards: A Resource for State Dialogue* (CCSSO, 2011, p. 3) "outline what teachers should know and be able to do to ensure every K–12 student reaches the goal of being ready to enter college or the workforce in today's world." These standards resulted from updating the 1992 CCSSO *InTASC Model Standards for Beginning Teacher Licensing, Assessment and Development: A Resource for State Dialogue* to be consistent with new understandings of learners and learning, with accountability for every student to achieve to high standards, and with broadening the scope for the standards to embrace all teachers.

Because this group of standards represents what all teachers should know and be able to do as a practitioner teacher, it seems perfectly suited to represent the knowledge areas about teaching and learning important for school leaders of instruction. The common core standards are those areas of teaching practice that every teacher in every subject area and at every grade level should be able to know and practice. Therefore, they fit well as part of professional growth self-assessment for instructional leaders, as well as teachers. A leader cannot be a subject specialist in every area of school but can become knowledgeable of common core teaching standards and can assess professional needs on the basis of these teaching standards, as well as the standards for leadership.

An understanding of strengths and growth needs for current and future responsibilities within the next three to five years will help you plan professional-development learning opportunities to attain those skills. Consider the possibility of becoming an expert in a specialty learning interest. The importance of meaningful professional development embedded in the work role and reflected in improvement of learning for students has come to the forefront, and its importance is emphasized in almost all literature about the increasing complexity of schools and the importance of highly skilled educators to improve student learning. Therefore, your performance activities for this chapter include reflection and self-assessment for planning professional growth over the next three to five years.

ISLLC 2008 STANDARDS.   Review and reflection of the earlier version of the leadership ISLLC standards (CCSSO, 1996) was the final performance activity in the action research course that I taught at the University of Kentucky in the principal preparation program. As mentioned earlier, we used it as a critical-thinking reflection tool about what students learned from their action research project, which standard their work demonstrated, and how their research applied to that standard.

I believe that understanding the standards for your educator roles and using them for professional-growth planning are important content in a university problem-solving and/or action research course that prepares school practitioners. I believe that it is equally important for educators already practicing in schools who are learning action research for the same purpose—problem solving and professional growth. However, state agencies determine the standards that are adopted. If your state is not one of the CCSSO member states or did not adopt the ISLLC standards, I suggest that you keep future directions for education systems and student learning in mind as you plan professional growth, but use your state standards in the leader self-assessment performance activities.

Educational leaders at both the district and school levels, as well as classroom teachers not currently teacher-leaders, will want to reflect on these leader standards and the knowledge and skills that they will need to know and be able to do as part of their current role and to progress toward an expert level on a career continuum. The working-paper career continuum focuses on preparing to lead schools for high levels of learning for each and every student.

Table 8.2 shows the CCSSO ISLLC 2008 standards and functions, as adopted by the National Policy Board for Educational Administration, in the first column. Column 2 gives an example of types of tasks that school leaders do that relate to each standard. This form is modified from the publication available at www.ccsso.org in that it has become an assessment tool for growth needs, and I added leadership task examples to get you to relate each standard to tasks in your current or future leader role. The tasks that I listed are intended as thought provokers, not as exemplar models. Use them to help you think of your leadership tasks related to each standard. When identifying tasks, think of those that you do in your current role and also those for planned new career roles. This is the first step in assessing areas of strength and areas for growth and development.

Table 8.2
*A Comparison of ISLLC 2008 Standards for School Leaders
Daily Tasks of School Leaders as a Self-Assessment for Professional Growth Planning*

The standards from the Council of Chief State School Officers (CCSSO) are in the first column. The second column represents selected tasks from the work of principals and other school leaders and did not come from CCSSO. These sample leadership tasks were added to guide reflection on your current role as a school leader. Consider your own daily leadership tasks as related to each ISLLC standard and its functions. Then decide the strengths or areas of growth to include on a professional development plan. Each educator should consider your own daily leadership tasks in your current role and which of your tasks relate to these ISLLC standards and functions in the left column. You should then identify your strengths and address areas to include on a plan for professional growth.

ISLLC Standards and Functions	Sample Leadership Tasks
Standard 1: An education leader promotes the success of every student by facilitating the development, articulation, implementation, and stewardship of a vision of learning that is shared and supported by all stakeholders.	1. Collaborate with stakeholders to identify, collect, and analyze multiple sources of data on the school and its effectiveness for achieving success for every student.
Functions:	2. Organize and meet with representative teams of school stakeholders to collaboratively review and update the shared school vision, mission, and goals.
A. Collaboratively develop and implement a shared vision and mission.	3. Collaboratively identify priority goals for improvement; research, plan, and implement action and assessment for progress monitoring.
B. Collect and use data to identify goals, assess organizational effectiveness, and promote organizational learning.	4. Reflect on and refer frequently to the vision and mission for advancing learning and success for every student as a central part of decision making.
C. Create and implement plans to achieve goals.	
D. Promote continuous and sustainable improvement.	
E. Monitor and evaluate progress, and revise plans.	
Standard 2: An education leader promotes the success of every student by advocating, nurturing, and sustaining a school culture and instructional program conducive to student learning and staff professional growth.	1. Collaboratively develop and apply high-quality teaching standards for recruiting and hiring teachers.
Functions:	2. Work with teacher teams to ensure curricula alignment with state, district, and school standards and assessment.
A. Nurture and sustain a culture of collaboration, trust, learning, and high expectations.	3. Provide frequent assistance, resources, support, and contacts for new teachers on the basis of need and stage of development.
B. Create a comprehensive, rigorous, and coherent curricular program.	4. Collaboratively plan and budget updated classroom technology, induction activities, professional development, and other resource needs for effective instruction.
C. Create a personalized and motivating learning environment for students.	5. Walk through all classrooms regularly, and adjust the frequency, formality, and purpose according to need.
D. Supervise instruction.	6. Collaborate with staff to assess professional-development needs and plan activities to meet those needs.
E. Develop assessment and accountability systems to monitor student progress.	
F. Develop the instructional and leadership capacity of staff.	
G. Maximize time spent on quality instruction.	
H. Promote the use of the most effective and appropriate technologies to support teaching and learning.	
I. Monitor and evaluate the impact of the instructional program.	

(continued)

126

Table 8.2
(continued)

ISLLC Standards and Functions	Sample Leadership Tasks
Standard 3: An education leader promotes the success of every student by ensuring management of the organization, operation, and resources for a safe, efficient, and effective learning environment. Functions: A. Monitor and evaluate the management and operational systems. B. Obtain, allocate, align, and efficiently utilize human, fiscal, and technological resources. C. Promote and protect the welfare and safety of students and staff. D. Develop the capacity for distributed leadership. E. Ensure teacher and organizational time are focused to support quality instruction and student learning.	1. Assign staff responsibilities, monitor, and collaboratively evaluate effectiveness on the basis of evidence identified through assessment standards. 2. Provide opportunities for staff to develop expert skills in content areas or leadership for schoolwide initiatives. 3. Support staff time for learning and data analysis aimed at student learning by providing substitutes, designated PD time, or creative scheduling that protects time for teaching and learning. 4. Appoint and train a school safety team who regularly does safety inspections and reports safety threats; rotate staff-member service on the team so that all will become competent in safety issues. 5. Collaborate with each staff member to provide opportunities and ongoing support for each individual to become an expert teacher or teacher leader.
Standard 4: An education leader promotes the success of every student by collaborating with faculty and community members, responding to diverse community interests and needs, and mobilizing community resources. Functions: A. Collect and analyze data and information pertinent to the educational environment. B. Promote understanding, appreciation, and use of the community's diverse cultural, social, and intellectual resources. C. Build and sustain positive relationships with families and caregivers. D. Build and sustain productive relationships with community partners.	1. Provide opportunities and encourage interested staff to learn and conduct action research for improvements in classroom and school aimed at success for every student. 2. Collaborate with teachers to develop ongoing communication with families and caregivers, sharing good news and soliciting support for their child's progress. 3. Participate and encourage staff participation in community organizations and activities that can support student needs.
Standard 5: An education leader promotes the success of every student by acting with integrity and fairness and in an ethical manner. Functions: A. Ensure a system of accountability for every student's academic and social success. B. Model principles of self-awareness, reflective practice, transparency, and ethical behavior. C. Safeguard the values of democracy, equity, and diversity. D. Consider and evaluate the potential moral and legal consequences of decision making. E. Promote social justice and ensure that individual student needs inform all aspects of schooling.	1. Monitor individual student progress and work with teachers to analyze causes behind low achievement and provide support for students who are not progressing. 2. Show special appreciation to staff who go above expectations to support and inspire student learning. 3. Communicate frequently with all staff as individuals, expressing interest in their activities and well-being and providing support as needed. 4. Consult and follow regulations and statutes when decisions have legal implications. Focus all decisions on effects on every child's progress, respect for all concerned, and equitable treatment appropriate in addressing each student's needs.

(continued)

Table 8.2
(continued)

ISLLC Standards and Functions	Sample Leadership Tasks
Standard 6: An education leader promotes the success of every student by understanding, responding to, and influencing the political, social, economic, legal, and cultural context. Functions: A. Advocate for children, families, and caregivers. B. Act to influence local, district, state, and national decisions affecting student learning. C. Assess, analyze, and anticipate emerging trends and initiatives in order to adapt leadership strategies.	1. Be an active member of professional organizations for school leadership, and contribute to activities that benefit children, families, and caregivers. 2. Share ideas for improving learning environments for children, families, or caregivers, and attend board meetings as appropriate to be an advocate on their behalf. 3. Become acquainted with local state legislators and congressional members, and be an advocate for decisions affecting student learning and those that benefit children and their families or caregivers. 4. Regularly read professional and education news to anticipate changes that may affect school organization, instruction, and students. Reflect on evident trends, and determine what you can do that would help prepare you and your school constituents to adapt to these changes.

Note. The source for the standards and functions in the first column are from the Council of Chief State School Officers (CCSSO). (2008). *Interstate School Leaders Licensure Consortium (ISLLC) Standards for School Leaders.* Washington, DC: Author. Used with permission. The Interstate School Leader Licensure Consortium (ISLLC) Standards were developed by the Council of Chief State School Officers (CCSSO) and member states. Copies may be downloaded from the Council's website at www.ccsso.org

Table 8.3 is on the CD under Resources for Chapter 8 as a self-assessment worksheet, with three blank columns beside each standard for you to record your strengths, growth areas, and types of professional development that you identified from reflection on leadership standards summarized in Table 8.2. The worksheet should address professional growth over the next three to five years. Use your reflection on the ISLLC 2008 standards and functions in the first column as a guide to assess your strengths and areas for growth. The Performance Checklist at the end of this chapter guides the use of this self-assessment worksheet. All of these tables are on the CD under Resources for Chapter 8.

INTASC MODEL CORE TEACHING STANDARDS. The InTASC Model Core Teaching Standards not only incorporate what the beginning teacher needs to know and do but extend to the expert leadership roles for teachers and apply to all teachers, without regard to subject or grade level (CCSSO InTASC, 2011).

The core standards as published by CCSSO state the performances, knowledge, and critical dispositions as complete statements, each beginning with "The teacher." (See www.ccsso.) I have deleted repetition of these words, for brevity, in Table 8.4 and Table 8.5 but have not otherwise changed the content. Table 8.4 located on the CD under Resources for Chapter 8 helps you compare your skills and growth needs with the 10 standards, statements of performances, knowledge, and critical dispositions required to meet these standards. Consider the level of skill that you aspire to reach for each standard over a period from three to five years when identifying growth areas and planning professional development. Assume that within five years, the transformed system of career continuum for educator development will have levels from novice to professional to expert. The novice represents early years in the educator role (maybe one to three). These professionals are increasing competence and strengthening teaching skills. The expert level has multiple career pathways and opportunities for increased responsibilities and recognition—such as engaging in action research, seeking national certification, mentoring novice educators, and coaching educators at the professional stage.

For reflection, regardless of whether you are a state, district, or school leader or a beginning or experienced teacher, you will want to review Table 8.4 on the CD because teaching and learning are central to your responsibilities. Consider how each of these standards applies to you, in regard not only to the expectations and tasks of your current role but also to those of the role you aspire to attain within the next three to five years.

Table 8.4, only on the CD, includes all 10 standards, with performance tasks and essential knowledge and dispositions required to meet each standard. The InTASC standards were developed by the CCSSO and member states. Official copies of these standards may be downloaded from the council's website at http://www.ccsso.org.

Table 8.5, included in this chapter and also on the CD Resources for Chapter 8, is a self-check worksheet with three columns for recording the professional strengths, growth areas, and professional-growth activities planned to meet the Model Core Teaching Standards given in Table 8.4. Table 8.4 may be printed from the CD to use with the performance activities for reflection on the standards. Table 8.5, in this chapter, is an illustration of the form for your self-assessment.

Use the electronic copy of Table 8.5 for the self-check worksheet by locating the table under resources for Chapter 8 on the CD and saving it to a word-processing file on your computer for recording your self-evaluation. If you completed the reflection on professional growth for both sets of standards from printed copies from the CD of Table 8.2 and Table 8.4, lay each copy by your computer to use as reference notes from that review of all standards as you complete the self-checks given in Table 8.3 and Table 8.5.

The performance check at the end of this chapter will guide you through steps for completing the self-assessments for growth activities according to standards and performances described in ISLLC 2008 and the Model Core Teaching Standards. These four tables will be useful for you in your writing of a professional-growth plan for the next three to five years.

Table 8.5

Self-Assessment for School Leader and Teacher Professional Development Based on Council of Chief State School Officers (CCSSO) InTASC Model Core Teaching Standards: A Resource for State Dialogue

Directions: Read the items in the left column and list your strengths for each standard, along with areas of the standard that you would like to improve and the kind of professional development activities that would enable you to reach your improvement goals.

Core Standards	Strengths	Needs	PD Activities
Standard 1: Learner Development The teacher understands how learners grow and develop, recognizing that patterns of learning and development vary individually within and across the cognitive, linguistic, social, emotional, and physical areas, and designs and implements developmentally appropriate and challenging learning experiences.	*Example:* *Understanding cultural roles and cognitive development*	*Example:* *Improve knowledge of social and emotional development and instructional modifications*	*Example:* *In-school PD Study Group to collaborate for research and identify ways to address those needs with instructional modifications*
Standard 2: Learning Differences The teacher uses understanding of individual differences and diverse cultures and communities to ensure inclusive learning environments that enable each learner to meet high standards.	*Strengths:*	*Needs:*	*PD Activities:*
Standard 3: Learning Environments The teacher works with learners to create environments that support individual and collaborative learning, encourage positive social interaction, active engagement in learning, and self-motivation.	*Strengths:*	*Needs:*	*PD Activities:*
Standard 4: Content Knowledge The teacher understands the central concepts, tools of inquiry, and structures of the discipline(s) he or she teaches and creates learning experiences that make these aspects of the discipline accessible and meaningful for learners.	*Strengths:*	*Needs:*	*PD Activities:*
Standard 5: Application of Content The teacher understands how to connect concepts and use differing perspectives to engage learners in critical thinking, creativity, and collaborative problem solving related to authentic local and global issues.	*Strengths:*	*Needs:*	*PD Activities:*
Standard 6: Assessment The teacher understands and uses multiple methods of assessment to engage learners in their own growth, to monitor learner progress, and to guide the teacher's and learner's decision making.	*Strengths:*	*Needs:*	*PD Activities:*

(continued)

Table 8.5
(continued)

Core Standards	Strengths	Needs	PD Activities
Standard 7: Planning for Instruction The teacher plans instruction that supports every learner in meeting rigorous learning goals by drawing upon knowledge of content areas, curriculum, cross-disciplinary skills, and pedagogy, as well as knowledge of learners and the community context.	*Strengths:*	*Needs:*	*PD Activities:*
Standard 8: Instructional Strategies The teacher understands and uses a variety of instructional strategies to encourage learners to develop deep understanding of content areas and their connections, and to build skills to apply knowledge in meaningful ways.	*Strengths:*	*Needs:*	*PD Activities:*
Standard 9: Professional Learning and Ethical Practice The teacher engages in ongoing professional learning and uses evidence to continually evaluate his/her practice, particularly the effects of his or her choices and actions on others (learners, families, other professionals, and the community) and adapts practice to meet the needs of each learner.	*Strengths:*	*Needs:*	*PD Activities:*
Standard 10: Leadership and Collaboration The teacher seeks appropriate leadership roles and opportunities to take responsibility for student learning, to collaborate with learners, families, colleagues, other school professionals, and community members to ensure learner growth, and to advance the profession.	*Strengths:*	*Needs:*	*PD Activities:*

Note. The self-assessment columns 2, 3, and 4 are not part of the CCSSO standards document. These three columns were added for this chapter to be used for performance self-assessment based on CCSSO InTASC standards. The first column lists the standards from the Council of Chief State School Officers (CCSSO). (2011, April). Interstate New Teachers Assessment and Support Consortium (InTASC) *Model Core Teaching Standards*. Washington, DC: Author. Used with permission. The Interstate and New Teacher Assessment and Support Consortium (InTASC) standards were developed by the Council of Chief State School Officers and member states. Copies may be downloaded from the Council's website at www.ccsso.org

Key Questions for Review

1. How do you see action research, school-improvement planning, and distributed leadership providing professional growth for teachers and administrators over the next three to five years?
2. How can technology access and time scheduling be provided in your school to be a support for collaboration and professional growth?
3. Compare your vision of change in responsibilities of schools for student learning accountability over the next three to five

years with the views expressed in this chapter from the CCSSO working papers. How are they alike, and how do they differ?
4. What types of school job-embedded professional-development activities do you foresee as helping novice teachers advance to the professional level on a career continuum, and what support will be needed to encourage this development?
5. Does your school vision relate or refer to professional growth and continued learning in any way? If so, explain how; if not, do you believe that it should?

Note. **Performance Checklist will also appear on CD.**

Performance Checklist for Self-Evaluation for Professional Growth

This chapter focuses on professional growth and development of educational leaders and teachers who are or will become school leaders. Performance activities include (a) reflecting on recently released standards for educational leadership and proposed model core teaching standards; (b) completing self-assessment guides for school leadership and teaching as a basis for professional growth; and (c) using these reflections and worksheets to write a professional-growth plan for the next three to five years.

A. **Reflect on the ISLLC 2008 standards for educational leadership shown in Table 8.2. Use the electronic copy from the CD (Table 8.3) to identify strengths, growth areas, and professional-development activities based on standards for school leaders shown in Table 8.2.**

   Performance Check:

   1. Print a copy of Table 8.2 from Chapter 8 resources on the supplemental CD, and save Table 8.3 to a word-processing file on your computer for completing the self-assessment for professional growth. Use the printed copy of Table 8.2 to review and reflect on leadership standards and functions in Column 1. Pencil in an S by the Table 8.2 functions that describe your strongest knowledge and skill areas and a G by those that you believe to be areas for growth at a professional or expert level of performance. Consider both your current job responsibilities and your career aspirations for the next three to five years.
   2. Referring to your notes on Table 8.2, use the electronic copy of Table 8.3 on your computer to assess strengths, areas for growth, and professional-development activities that address your needs for your current job responsibilities and career aspirations. Also, consider building on strengths and developing new, or improving current, skills and knowledge.

B. **Reflect on the Model Core Teaching Standards shown in Table 8.4. From the CD resources, print a copy of Table 8.4 to make notes for reflection. Save an electronic copy of CD Table 8.5 to your computer, and use it to complete your self-check for professional growth.**

   Performance Check:

   1. Use the printed copy of Table 8.4 to review and reflect on the teaching standards, performances, essential knowledge, and critical dispositions in Columns 1 and 2. As you reflect, think about what you need for your

current job responsibilities and your career aspirations for the next three or five years. Pencil in an S by performance, knowledge, and/or skill areas that describe your strongest abilities and a G by those that you believe to be areas for growth as a professional or expert level of performance for your current responsibilities or those that you aspire to reach for career advancement.
   2. Referring to your notes on Table 8.4, use your word-processing file of Table 8.5 to assess professional-development needs. List strength areas, growth needs, and professional development to meet those needs. Consider building on strengths, as well as growth needs, and developing new or improved skills and knowledge.

C. **Develop a reflective paper as a professional growth plan. File a copy for annual assessment and updating of your professional-growth worksheets and growth plan.**

   Performance Check:

   1. Review your completed Figure 8.3 leadership skills and Figure 8.5 teaching skills self-check worksheets. Then, develop a narrative or outline as a professional growth plan that reflects where you are now in your level of knowledge, skills, and performance in terms of providing instructional leadership or school leadership to your career continuum and to meet the standards at professional or expert level for 21st century learning. Cover specific topics similar to the list that follows, but adjusted to fit your needs. Specific topics will vary by individual choices.

Professional Growth Plan

Current position and years of experience in education

Educational and personal background related to your position

Career goals and projected timeline

Analysis of Leadership

Leadership strengths

Knowledge about teaching and learning

Management of school operations and resources

Problem solving, research, data analysis, and planning

Promotion of success for every child

Advocacy for children, families, and caregivers

Growth Goals and Activities

Leadership

Knowledge about teaching and learning

Problem solving, research, data analysis, planning, and assessment

Collaboration with others for school and instructional improvement

Strategies for success for every child

Professional growth activities and projected timeline

2. File a copy of your self-analysis professional-growth plan. Review it periodically to assess progress or changes and to make any needed updates.

References

Borkowski, J., Carr, M., & Pressley, M. (1987). "Spontaneous" strategy use: Perspectives from metacognitive theory. *Intelligence, 11,* 61–75.

Camburn, E., Rowan, B., & Taylor, J. (2004). Distributed leadership in schools: The case of elementary schools adopting comprehensive school reform models. *Educational Evaluation and Policy Analysis, 25*(4), pp. 347–373.

Council of Chief State School Officers[1] (CCSSO). (1996). *Interstate School Leaders Licensure Consortium (ISLLC) standards for school leaders.* Washington, DC: Author.

Council of Chief State School Officers (CCSSO). (2008). *Interstate School Leaders Licensure Consortium (ISLLC) standards for school leaders.* Washington, DC: Author.

Council of Chief State School Officers (CCSSO). (2009, March). *Transforming education: Delivering on our promise to every child.* (CCSSO Strategic Initiatives Discussion Document). Washington, DC: Author.

Council of Chief State School Officers (CCSSO). (2010). *ESEA reauthorization principles and recommendations* (A Policy Statement of CCSSO). Washington, DC: Author.

Council of Chief State School Officers (CCSSO). (2010). *Transforming teaching and leading: A vision for a high-quality educator development system.* Education Workforce White Paper. Washington, DC: Author.

Council of Chief State School Officers[2] (CCSSO). (2011, April). *Interstate Teacher Assessment and Support Consortium (InTASC) Model core teaching standards: A resource for state dialogue.* Washington, DC: Author.

Frederick, T. (2009). Looking in the mirror: Helping adolescents talk more reflectively during portfolio presentations. *Teachers College Record, 111*(8). Retrieved from http:www.tcrecord.org ID Number: 15501.

Garner, R. (1990). When children and adults do not use learning strategies: Toward a theory of settings. *Review of Educational Research, 60,* 517–529.

Harris, A. (2002, October 9). *Distributed leadership in schools: Leading or misleading?* Presentation at a council meeting of the International Confederation of Principals, Toronto, Canada. Retrieved from ICP Online http://www.icponline.org/index.php?option=com_content'task=view'id=130'Itemid=50.

Johnston, R. C. (1999, May). Texas study links teacher certification, student success. *Education Week, 18,* 19–20.

Knoeppel, R., & Logan, J. P. (2011, July–September). Linking theory with practice: A longitudinal analysis of student portfolios in principal preparation. *International Journal of Leadership in Education, 14*(3), 337–349.

Livingston, J. A. (1997). *Metacognition: An overview.* Retrieved from http://gse.buffalo.edu/fas/shuell/CEP564/Metacog.htm.

Spillane, J. P., & Camburn, E. (2006). *The practice of leading and managing: The distribution of responsibility for leadership and management of the schoolhouse.* Paper presented at the annual meeting of the American Educational Research Association, San Francisco, April 7–11.

Spillane, J., Diamond, J., & Jita, L. (2003). Leading instruction: The distribution of leadership for instruction. *Journal of Curriculum Studies, 35*(5), 533–543.

Spillane, J., Halverson, R., & Diamond, J. (2003). *Distributive leadership: Toward a theory of school leadership practice.* IPR Working Papers. Evanston, IL: Northwestern University Institute for Policy Research.

[1]The Interstate School Leaders Licensure Consortium (ISLLC) Standards were developed by the Council of Chief State School Officers (CCSSO) and member states. Copies may be downloaded from the Council's website at www.ccsso.org.

[2]The Interstate New Teacher Assessment and Support Consortium (InTASC) Standards were developed by the Council of Chief State School Officers (CCSSO) and member states. Copies may be downloaded from the Council's website at www.ccsso.org.

EXAMPLE ACTION RESEARCH REPORTS

Completed in K-12 Schools by School Practitioners

Example 1   Writing Achievement of Hispanic Students (Ele.) by Sherri D. Turner Wadsworth

Example 2   An Analysis of Content Reading Instruction (Ele.) by Michelle C. Ligon and Melissa Rash

Example 3   Improving the Reading Skills of Struggling Reading Students (Ele.) by Kari Kirchner

Example 4   The Sophomore Coaching Initiative (HS) by Bryan Jacobs and Richard Royster

Example 5   An Analysis of Mathematics Performance (HS) by Kim Zeidler-Watters

Example 6   Postsecondary Reading Remediation for High School Graduates (HS) by Janet Sivis O'Connell

Example 7   A Comparative Review of High School Schedules (HS) by Joe K. Matthews

Example 8   Practical Living/Career Studies Test Scores (MS) by Laura Arnold

EXAMPLE 1 OF A COMPLETE ACTION RESEARCH REPORT

School Improvement Analysis: Writing Achievement of Hispanic Students

Rural Valley Elementary School is a new school, only now in its second year of operation, which makes it difficult to compare data over time. The school, located in a rural setting, serves students from surrounding rural farms as well as urban houses and apartments. This creates a very diverse student body composed of Caucasian, African-American, Hispanic, and Asian children. During the past 10 years, our county has experienced an unanticipated influx of immigrant children; as a result, the school now has the highest number of Hispanic students in the district and is said to have the highest percentage of Hispanic students in the state.

Analyzing the performance of Hispanic students and searching for ways to enhance their performance is not only important for promoting their academic achievement but is mandated by the federal education law enacted in 2001 and entitled the No Child Left Behind (NCLB) Act. This law requires all states to report adequate yearly progress in the content areas of reading and mathematics for all groups of students in all schools. Schools use disaggregated student data to determine whether achievement gaps exist between certain groups of students and then develop strategies to improve instruction and eliminate the gaps (Wilhoit, 2003).

Research to describe the problem began by disaggregating writing scores by ethnicity to determine whether or not an achievement gap existed between Hispanic students and their peers. Disaggregated data make it impossible for schools to hide the fact that all of their students are not moving at the same pace toward proficiency. Even schools with high accountability indices found instances in which their high performance was covering up the fact that children of color, students in poverty, students with disabilities, or students for whom English is a second language (ESL), for example, are not learning as well as the schoolwide performance data indicate (Wilhoit, 2003).

Table 1 shows data taken from the state performance report which reveal that writing portfolio scores for Hispanic students are lower than that of any student group.

Table 1
Rural Valley Elementary Writing Portfolio Performance Levels Disaggregated by Ethnicity for Grade 4 Performance Compared with Total School Enrollment Performance

	Percentage of Students at Each Performance Level			
Grade 4	Novice	Apprentice	Proficient	Distinguished
Caucasian	6	69	24	2
Hispanic	20	80	0	0
African American	15	66	19	0
School Performance	9	71	18	2

Table 2 also contains data taken from the state performance report which show that On-Demand Writing scores for Hispanic students are lower than that of any other ethnic group.

Example 1 of a Complete Action Research Report   **137**

Table 2
Rural Valley Elementary Grade 4 On-Demand Writing—Percentage of Students for Each Performance Level Disaggregated by Ethnicity

Grade 4	Percentages by Performance Levels			
	Novice	Apprentice	Proficient	Distinguished
Caucasian	31	59	7	2
Hispanic	67	33	0	0
African-American	45	55	0	0

As shown in Table 1 and Table 2, all Hispanic students scored in the novice and apprentice ranges, with no Hispanic students receiving a score of proficient, which is the state goal for all students. Data from the Comprehensive Test of Basic Skills (CTBS), as seen in Figure 1, also give additional evidence of a gap in achievement between Hispanic students and their peers and show Hispanic students consistently scoring lower than any other group in every subject area, including reading and language, two vital components of successful writing. Therefore, Hispanic students are exiting primary school with their peers but are the least prepared of all students for fourth grade.

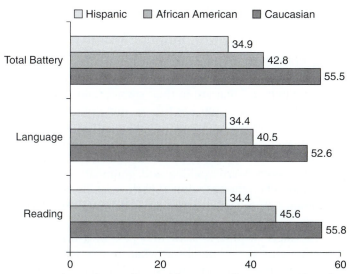

Figure 1. CTBS scores are shown for reading and language, disaggregated by ethnicity.

In the No Child Left Behind Adequate Yearly Progress Report, our school is listed as a school that is meeting its Annual Measurable Objectives (AMO). However, further examination of the percentage of students at or above proficiency reveals that Hispanics, once again, scored lower than all other groups of students in both reading and math, as is shown in Figure 1. Although data were available for only 1 year for our students, available data clearly show that writing performance is a problem for Hispanic students who speak English as a second language.

Research Questions

The confirmed gap in achievement of Hispanic students led to the primary research question for this study: What school processes can be implemented to help Hispanic students meet the student achievement standard for writing by the end of the biennium?

The following guiding questions narrowed the focus of the study to gathering and analyzing information that could guide changes for improvement:

1. Which writing skills are most difficult and present the greatest problem for Hispanic students, and do these skills differ from skills that are shown to be difficult for all other students?

2. What demographic characteristics describe the Hispanic students—specifically, gender, special programs, and economic or achievement data?

3. What current processes are leading Hispanic students toward meeting the standard by the end of the biennium?

4. What writing programs or strategies have demonstrated effectiveness in improving writing proficiency with Hispanic students?

Literature Review

A comprehensive search and review of literature provided information regarding writing modifications for Hispanic students. Overall recommendations at the end of this study include related reference data from the review of literature.

Writing is a continuing process of discovery. Finding the most effective language for communicating one's thoughts and feelings can be challenging, whether one is writing in one's native language or in a second language (Bello, 1997). Good writing instruction prepares students to communicate for a variety of purposes and audiences in a variety of real-world forms (Kentucky Department of Education [KDE], 2003).

Process Writing

Process writing in multicultural, multilingual classrooms is an integrated approach to writing and has many advantages for language learning. Students begin reading with words that they have written and that are in their own speaking vocabularies. They learn reading skills, such as phonics, in a purposeful, meaningful context. Therefore, they are more prepared to comprehend what they read. Students become more independent language learners through writing and become aware of their own writing strategies. They learn to use many resources including peers, teachers, other adults, and reference works. Students who write frequently learn spelling and grammar skills better when they use them in composition than when they are drilled in those skills, without the opportunity to compose (Eastern Stream Center on Resources and Training [ESCORT], 1996).

Best practice produces writing as a natural part of a unit of study; for example, students share their thoughts in writing about what they've learned in science or mathematics, how they feel about a novel, or what stance they take on an issue. It's important for students to write every year, not just in those years during which their portfolios are submitted for scoring (Wilhoit, 2003).

Students need daily experiences with composition. Like learning to speak a first or second language, learning to write is a gradual developmental process. For beginning students, composition may consist of dictating and/or writing in a native language. Students may progress to labeling pictures in English and writing important words such as family names. Gradually, given encouragement and ample opportunity to write, students begin to write longer pieces about topics that are familiar and important to them (ESCORT, 1996).

Teachers and students in our state now have the opportunity to reach beyond the limits of traditional classrooms to build a community of learners through our state computer network. The electronic classroom exchange program was designed to help teachers and students use technology to give students interaction with authentic audiences for their writing exercises. Students can share their work via e-mail, and this gives them the opportunity to create real and meaningful communication (Lindsey, 2003).

Teachers need to provide learners with many opportunities to write about topics that are relevant to their lives, to participate in various writing activities such as the state network, and to feel that their writing has value. By integrating writing with content at every level of instruction, teachers help learners find their own voices in their

Example 1 of a Complete Action Research Report   **139**

new language and develop the ability to communicate effectively in different contexts and with different audiences (Bello, l997).

Instruction in Two Languages

If we are to be successful, we must create school and classroom environments that encourage students to take risks and attempt their first and second languages, and that promote an acceptance of linguistic and cultural backgrounds (Whittaker, Salend, & Gutierrez, 1977).

Special English instruction is an essential component of the ESL student's education (Riddlemoser, 1987). It is possible for the classroom teacher to work productively with ESL students in his or her classroom in order to increase the student's exposure to authentic language during the school day. However, the time spent in the ESL classroom is critical in order to mainstream the ESL population into the regular academic program.

During their 10 years of conducting research on English language programs and school effectiveness, Thomas and Collier (2003) discovered the key to the successful future of U.S. education: meaningful, grade-level, and accelerated instruction in two languages.

There are many things that classroom teachers can do to enhance the time that ESL students spend in the classroom. Riddlemoser (1987) describes eight key components to best meet the ESL student's social and academic needs in the regular classroom:

1. The first and most basic need is to ensure that the ESL student feels comfortable and secure.

2. A "buddy system" is an excellent way to ensure that the ESL student is cared for.

3. Include the ESL student in as many activities, lessons, and assignments as possible, even if only for the socialization aspect.

4. Present a positive approach to the class when dealing with the ESL student.

5. Maintain high expectations for ESL students.

6. Collaborate and establish a close relationship between the ESL student and the ESL teacher.

7. Encourage and expect the student to make use of native language dictionaries, bilingual dictionaries, and picture dictionaries.

8. Individualize, adapt, and modify class work.

Alternative Assessment

Alternative assessment holds great promise for ESL students (Tannenbaum, 1996) and refers to "procedures and techniques which can be used within the context of instruction and can easily be incorporated into the daily activities of the school or classroom" (Hamayan, 1995, p. 213). The following paragraphs give a brief description of some types of alternative assessments that have proven to be effective when working with children with limited English proficiency:

Nonverbal assessment strategies are one form of alternative assessment and allow the student to point or use other gestures rather than speaking or writing. Students can also perform hands-on tasks or give demonstrations to act out concepts or events. Pictures can be used when giving nonverbal responses. The student can make the illustrations, or they may choose to manipulate an existing picture by labeling it.

Another type of alternative assessment is oral performances and presentations. The oral aspect of the task takes the assessment to a higher level and allows the teacher to assess the stages of language development and determine English proficiency. Oral and written products are useful when assessing ESL student's progress and now encourage the use of writing through reading response logs and dialogue journals. Finally, portfolios have become the standard for all students and are used to collect samples of student work over time to track student development.

Action Research Methodology

For this study, I collaborated with the school principal, ESL staff members, and fourth grade teachers to determine reasons that Hispanic students are achieving at lower rates than their peers in writing and to identify ways in which their writing skills can be improved to be equal to or exceed the district average on the CATS test over the next biennium. Three types of data (demographic, achievement, and procedural) were collected for this issue of interest and obtained from the state department of education and the county public school district:

1. The school report card and state performance report provided demographic data describing the Hispanic and general-education student populations.

2. The state performance report and student data tool provided school process data showing special programs and modifications used by Hispanic students.

3. The student data tool, state performance report, and CTBS results provided student achievement data for comparing the academic performance of Hispanic students and their peers. The NCLB reports also provided student-achievement data regarding the school's federal accountability and Adequate Yearly Progress (AYP).

Once all assessment data were disaggregated and examined, the achievement gap was confirmed and showed a need for recommendations to improve the writing performance of Hispanic students. I presented the information to the building principal, who also confirmed the writing scores of Hispanic students to be the area of greatest need.

Difficult Writing Skills

We now needed to determine which writing skills were most difficult and presented the biggest problem for Hispanic students and whether these skills differ from skills that were shown to be difficult for all other students.

Student characteristics. Research has identified a variety of factors that appear related to the achievement gap: students' racial and/or economic background, their parents' education level, their access to high-quality preschool instruction, school funding, peer influences, teacher's expectations, and curricular and instructional quality (Education Commission of the States, 2003; Jaekyung, 2002).

The next step in the research process was to determine characteristics that describe the Hispanic students in our school—specifically, gender, special programs, and other demographic data. A comparison of enrollment data from 2002–2003 with enrollment data of 2003–2004 showed Hispanic and Asian populations increasing in numbers while all other groups decreased.

Review of processes. The confirmed gap in achievement and demographic characteristics of Hispanic students led to questioning school processes already in place that were designed to lead Hispanic students toward meeting the standard by the end of the biennium. I interviewed the principal to determine changes now in place to achieve this goal. A survey of fourth grade teachers gathered information on instructional strategies to help students struggling with writing performance. I developed a survey questionnaire to collect teacher perceptions. A copy of the survey instrument is in the Appendix of this report.

Example 1 of a Complete Action Research Report **141**

Stakeholder Input for Data Analysis

Rural Valley has seen many positive changes in the first semester of the 2003–2004 academic year; however, there is still a great need to determine which writing programs and strategies have demonstrated effectiveness in improving writing proficiency with Hispanic students. During my review of literature, I discovered many such programs but narrowed my results to those which literature suggests have shown the most success consistently over time.

For this analysis, I conferred with the building principal, who shared all data relating to my study and assisted me during the data analysis. ESL and fourth grade teachers offered additional information regarding current instructional practices, which led to my recommendations for implementation. The analysis shared with the principal provided an additional source of data for planning and making curriculum decisions regarding Hispanic students at Rural Valley Elementary.

Data Analysis and Research Findings

Table 3 shows reading and mathematics percentages of fourth grade students who achieved proficiency in 2003, as well as the percentages at the low and high range of proficiency. The Hispanic students' percentage scoring proficient was the lowest of all other groups in these two academic areas, although the Hispanic percentage of those at the high range of proficiency is encouraging when compared with that of all students, collectively.

Table 3
No Child Left Behind (NCLB) Proficiency Achievement: Adequate Yearly Progress Report–2003

	Reading 2003		Math 2003	
Students	**% Proficient (low, high)**		**% Proficient (low, high)**	
All Students	58.62	(44.63, 72.61)	44.33	(31.01, 57.65)
White	70.37	(53.61, 87.13)	62.50	(45.08, 79.92)
African-American	NA		NA	
Hispanic	44.67	(6.98, 86.36)	27.27	(0.00, 54.79)
Asian	NA		NA	

Figure 2 gives a summary of scores from the state testing system writing categories, both portfolio and on-demand. These scores were disaggregated by performance level and ethnicity to show achievement gaps between Hispanic students and their peers.

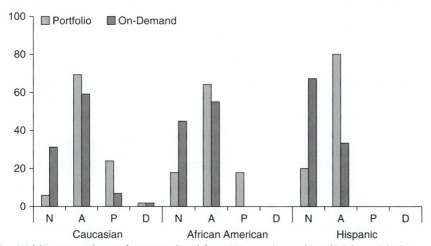

Figure 2. **Writing scores by performance level for 2002 are shown by ethnicity, with the percentages shown for each group as scores categorized as N—novice, A—apprentice, P—proficient, and D—distinguished.**

According to the data in Figure 2, on-demand writing proved to be the most difficult form of writing, not only for Hispanics, but also for all students. Further analysis showed narrating an event for a purpose to be the most difficult area of on-demand writing with 52% of all novice scores falling in this category.

Figure 3 illustrates the increase in Hispanic enrollment from 2002 to 2003 and supports the prediction that the Hispanic population is rapidly growing and the number of Hispanic students attending the school will continue to rise. This new information increased the level of concern for the need to improve the performance of Hispanic students and prompted further demographic investigation. All student groups other than Hispanic and Asian showed decreases.

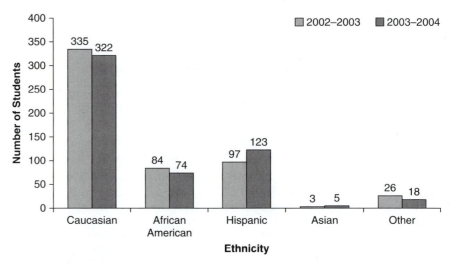

Figure 3. Change in enrollment from 2002–2003 to 2003–2004 school year by ethnicity shows the greatest increase for the Hispanic students at Rural Valley Elementary School.

Table 4 shows the characteristics describing the fourth grade Hispanic population and also lists their participation in any special programs.

Table 4
Demographics of Fourth Grade Hispanic Students

Male	Female	Free Lunch	Migrant	ESL	Gifted/Talented	ESS
55%	45%	100%	13%	50%	6%	81%

The additional demographic data help explain why Hispanic students are performing lower than their peers at Rural Valley. Notice that 100% of Hispanic students receive free lunch, indicating a situation of poverty; 50% receive ESL instruction, suggesting a language barrier to learning; and 19% are from migrant families who move from place to place to harvest seasonal crops.

The struggles faced during the 2002–2003 academic year were addressed; school and district administrators knew that dramatic changes would need to be made if Rural Valley was to become a successful school.

Changes were made for the new 2003–2004 school year. Additional ESL and migrant staff were added to the faculty, taking the total from 1.5 classified positions to 4.5 certified and classified positions.

A brief interview with the principal and fourth grade teachers provided the information that follows on instruction and how it is currently individualized to support struggling writers. A copy of the 4th Grade Teacher Questionnaire that I developed can be found in the Appendix.

Example 1 of a Complete Action Research Report **143**

From the teacher survey and principal interview, I learned that assessments similar to core content tests are now mandatory in all classrooms across all grade levels. These assessments are collected and reviewed by teachers and administrators; the school principal plans to develop a master resource file so that all teachers will have access to these quality assessments.

Scoring of fourth and fifth grade scrimmage tests, including on-demand writing, is now a schoolwide process. As they work together to score the KCCT scrimmage pieces, primary and specialty area teachers are now more involved in the testing process and have a better understanding of what is expected of their students once they reach intermediate grades. The teacher survey responses are not included as part of this report, but a summary of results brought to teachers an awareness of the current writing practices and priorities for struggling ESL students. The purpose was to foster internal classroom improvement by teachers.

Early release days have become another opportunity to address the needs of Hispanic students and have prompted schoolwide professional development of Ruby Payne's Poverty Training. The training has given teachers a wonderful resource, helping them to understand their students on a different level and offering suggestions for ways in which many issues involving poverty can be addressed.

Conclusions and Recommendations

Overall, writing performance for ESL students at Rural Valley Elementary is neither equal to nor at least 90% of the performance scores of their peers, and instructional practices used in the past seem to be unsuccessful in addressing the academic needs of Hispanic students.

Classrooms across the United States have English language learners who are learning to speak, read, and write in their new language (Ducker, 2003). The racial achievement gap is real; educating every child is the greatest moral challenge of our time.

The recommendations that follow for improving the writing instruction and performance of Hispanic students are based on this research, analysis of test data, survey of staff members, and collaboration with administration. These six recommendations should improve writing instruction, resulting in increased performance by Hispanic students.

1. Create a school and classroom environment that promotes an acceptance of linguistic and cultural backgrounds and encourages ESL students to take risks, through the use of a buddy system and cooperative learning (Riddlemoser, 1987).

2. Implement schoolwide professional development that focuses on the writing process and ways to implement writing instruction by using best practice in all grade levels to enhance the writing of all students, including Hispanics.

3. Offer content instruction in two languages, and individualize, adapt, and modify class work for ESL students (Thomas & Collier, 2003).

4. Implement alternative assessment techniques to be incorporated into the daily activities of the classroom (Hamayan, 1995; Tannenbaum, 1996).

5. Provide daily experiences with compositions (ESCORT, 1996) for students in all grade levels, including ample practice and writing narratives.

6. Increase opportunities for frequent narrative writing practice and feedback.

Appendix   4th Grade Teacher Questionnaire

Instructions: *Please take a few moments to fill out the following form. Your responses will be kept confidential and will help us understand how we can individualize instruction and offer additional support to our struggling writers.*

1. How often do you teach writing?

   a. Every day

   b. Every other day

   c. Once a week

   d. Never

2. How often do you assign writing homework?

   a. Every day

   b. Every other day

   c. Once a week

   d. Never

3. How often do your students plan, draft, and revise their writing?

   a. Always

   b. Sometimes

   c. Only if they are asked to do so

   d. Never

4. How often do your students share what they have written with a partner or small group?

   a. Every day

   b. Every other day

   c. Once a week

   d. Never

5. How often do your students use a dictionary or thesaurus when writing?

   a. Every day

   b. Every other day

   c. Once a week

   d. Never

6. How often do your students use technology when writing?

   a. Every day

   b. Every other day

   c. Once a week

   d. Never

7. Which writing skills are most difficult and present the biggest problem for Hispanic students, and do these skills differ from skills that are shown to be difficult for all other students?

8. What writing programs or strategies have demonstrated effectiveness in improving writing proficiency with Hispanic students?

9. What new writing ideas, assignments, or techniques would you like to use in your class?

10. How do you support your struggling writers?

Example 1 of a Complete Action Research Report **145**

References

Bello, T. (1997, June). *Improving ESL learners' writing skills*. Retrieved from ERIC Digest National Center for ESL Literacy Education website: http://www.cal.org/ncle/digests/Writing.htm.

Ducker, M. (2003). What reading teachers should know about ESL learners. *Reading Teacher, 57*(1), 22–29.

Education Commission of the States. *Closing the achievement gap*. Retrieved from website: http://www.ecs.org/html/issue.asp?issueID=194.

Eastern Stream Center on Resources and Training (ESCORT). (1998). *Help! They don't speak English starter kit for primary teachers*. Oneonta, NY: Author.

Hamayan, E. V. (1989, Summer). Teaching writing to potentially English proficient students using whole language approaches. *Program Information Guide Series, 11*. Silver Spring, MD: National Clearinghouse for Bilingual Education.

Jaekyung, L. (2002). Racial and ethnic achievement gap trends: Reversing the progress toward equity? *Educational Researcher 31*(1), 3–12.

Kentucky Department of Education. (2003). English/Language Arts—Writing. (KDE website). Retrieved from http://www.kentuckyschools.net/cgi-bin/MsmGo.exe?grab_id=1521582&EXTRA_ARG=&host_id=1&page_id=464&query=writing&hiword=WRITING.

Lindsey, C. (November, 2003). KY Net provides authentic audience for student writing. *Kentucky Teacher*. Frankfort, KY: Kentucky Department of Education.

Riddlemoser, N. (1987, November), *Working with limited-English proficient students in the regular classroom*. Washington, DC: ERIC Clearinghouse on Languages and Linguistics, Center for Applied Linguistics.

Tannenbaum, J. (1996, May). *Practical ideas on alternative assessment for ESL students*. Washington, DC: ERIC Clearinghouse on Languages and Linguistics, Center for Applied Linguistics. (ERIC Document Reproduction Service No. EDO-FL-96-07).

Thomas, W., & Collier, P. (2003, October). The multiple benefits of dual language. *Educational Leadership, 61*(2), 61–64.

U.S. Department of Education. Reaching out . . . Raising Hispanic achievement. Retrieved from website: http://www.ed.gov/nclb/accountability/achieve/achievement_hisp.htm.

Wilhoit, G. (2003, October). State and federal accountability rests on CATS data. *Kentucky Teacher*. Frankfort, KY: Kentucky Department of Education.

Wilhoit, G. (2003, November). Writing, we don't have it right yet. *Kentucky Teacher*. Frankfort, KY: Kentucky Department of Education.

Whittaker, C. R., Salend, S. J., & Gutierrez, M. B. (1997, March). Voices from the fields: Including migrant farm workers in the curriculum. *The Reading Teacher, 50*(6), 482–493.

Note. **This example report was adapted from action research by Sherri D. Turner-Wadsworth, Title I Coordinator. Used with permission.**

EXAMPLE 2 OF A COMPLETE ACTION RESEARCH REPORT

An Analysis of Content Reading Instruction at Roger Vale Elementary

The report shown here analyzes and addresses the reading scores at Roger Vale Elementary over the last 2 years on the state accountability testing system. During the past 2 years, the reading score has basically flat-lined, decreasing 1.79 points from the 2006–2007 school year to the 2007–2008 school year.

Table 1
Two-Year Comparison of Roger Vale Elementary Content Area Index Trends

Content	2007	2008	Difference
Reading	95.84	94.05	−1.79
Math	92.16	91.56	−.60
Science	98.11	90.94	−7.17
Social Studies	72.09	78.24	+6.15
Arts/Humanities	79.75	82.57	+2.82
PL/VS	89.67	83.29	−6.38
Writing	78.79	86.20	+7.41
Total Academic Index	**89.2**	**88.2**	**−1**

Research Questions

Our primary research question is *How can reading achievement be increased by 5.95 on the state accountability testing system in the content area of reading during the next testing cycle?*

1. Why did reading scores slightly decrease in 2008 at Roger Vale Elementary?

2. What are the most problematic areas in reading for Roger Vale Elementary students?

3. Are there specific student subgroups that represent students who are struggling with reading?

4. When looking across the grade levels, are there specific concepts that students consistently struggle with in reading?

5. What teaching reading strategies can teachers use to help students who are struggling with specific skills?

6. What barriers are interfering with progress in the area of reading?

Rationale for the Study

The rationale for this study was to analyze reading scores of Roger Vale Elementary on the core content tests, as well as to find solutions to increasing reading scores. If every school is mandated to reach 100 in every accountable content score by 2014, scores must begin to increase at a steady level. The stakeholders at Roger Vale Elementary want to reverse the stagnant trend in testing cycles. School stakeholders also must keep in

Example 2 of a Complete Action Research Report   **147**

mind that Senate Bill 168 requires schools to significantly close achievement gaps within schools. Reading is a content area that affects all other content areas. If a child cannot read, then taking tests in other content areas becomes increasingly difficult. Reading is the foundation of learning.

Literature Review: Content Reading

When readers reach a certain point in their academic careers, many teachers assume that all students should be able to read and comprehend content passages. Content teachers, such as social studies and science teachers, shouldn't have to teach reading skills in their classrooms. They are responsible for teaching only their content, right? Well, anyone who believes that isn't going to help a child succeed in school. Reading strategies must be taught in every class by every teacher. It takes a community to educate a child. Reading is the most essential concept that a student will learn in school. If students can't read, then how can they even begin to make connections and learn about information from content-area courses? "The primary purpose for teaching the reading process is to help students acquire content skills and apply them to *real* reading" (Hager & Meeks, 1993, p. 1); therefore, this literature review centers on two questions that have to be answered:

1. Why is content reading difficult for students?

2. What strategies can teachers teach students to help all students comprehend content reading materials?

Administrators must help teachers find answers to these two questions if we are to improve student achievement and help our students to be life-long readers and learners.

Why Do Teachers Care About Content Reading?

Most of the state program of studies, the document that drives the statewide curriculum and assessment, promotes content and informational reading. Teachers often lament not finding a way to help students understand content-area reading in a textbook that is written for proficient readers. One of the most obvious challenges in teaching content-area reading is the increasingly difficult content in texts that students encounter as they progress through the grade levels (Vacca, 1981). This poses a large problem for struggling readers and constantly requires educators to ask how the text can be adapted to meet the needs of struggling readers. If students can't understand the text, then they will struggle with the content. All students are tested on the same content, regardless of reading level. This makes the teacher's job increasingly difficult. There may be days that textbooks are unused because students have difficulty understanding the technical aspects of the content, such as sentence structure, vocabulary, and semantics. Teachers may try "piece-mealing" reading passages of various content together so that students can comprehend the text and understand the content. There is a constant search for content reading strategies that will make a difference in student achievement.

In addition to the immediate concerns of standards-based instruction and performance assessment accountability, the future of our students to become life-long learners and the ability to hold gainful employment will depend on reading and writing in the digital world.

> The U.S. economy today demands a higher level of literacy than ever before. The literacy demands of today's technical society require that students be able to read and write not only in the print world but also in the digital world. (Moss, 2005, p. 46)

The capacity to read expository writing has become a necessary life-long skill. Many students across the nation struggle with content reading every day in their classrooms. Proficient readers breeze through the content with relative ease, but struggling readers often become very frustrated in content courses, thus falling farther behind. These students may find the content interesting but feel defeated when they can't understand the text. There are several reasons that some children struggle with content reading. One of the primary reasons that expository text is more difficult for students to read than literary text is directly related to exposure ("Reading in the Content Areas," 2005). Most primary students are not exposed to a wide variety of expository texts throughout their primary program. Most primary programs focus on literary and narrative texts instead of expository texts. According to Armbruster, Anderson, and Ostertag (1987), the second reason that many students struggle with content reading is a lack of motivation or interest in the topic at hand. The third reason that many students become frustrated with content text is that they do not have enough prior knowledge about the topic to understand what the text is trying to convey.

> In order for information to be understood, a learner needs to be able to connect new information with what is already known. Thus, to be effective, an expository text must strike a balance between what a learner knows and does not know yet. If what a learner knows is not sufficient background for him/her to be able to understand the target ideas in the text, then reading comprehension of the material may be out of reach. (Beck & McKeown, 1991, p. 484)

The fourth reason that content reading is difficult for some students is that they are not familiar with the structure of expository texts (Moss, 2005). This stems from the lack of exposure to expository texts. Expository texts are not predictable and do not have a predictable structure. Students often have difficulty seeing patterns within expository texts. When students begin to understand the structures within expository texts and the purpose of the text, they will begin to increase their comprehension and understanding of the text. All of these issues combined together can make some content classes very daunting for many students (Moustafa, 1999).

Struggling Readers Versus Proficient Readers

Proficient readers have learned strategies along their educational journey that have helped them comprehend a wide variety of texts. When a proficient reader reads a difficult text, he or she "reads, rereads, paraphrases, considers context, infers, questions, reflects, and perhaps consults other materials without conscious decision. The application of reading skills to a difficult text is automatic for a proficient reader" ("Reading in the Content Areas," 2005, p. 1). Unfortunately, a struggling reader does not have this repertoire of reading strategies at his or her disposal. Therefore, reading within a content area can be very difficult for struggling readers. All readers need the necessary tools and strategies to be successful in all content areas ("Reading in the Content Areas").

If children read in a classroom, then the teacher is responsible for teaching them reading strategies needed for them to be successful in that classroom. People used to think that reading teachers taught reading, that math teachers taught math, and that social studies teachers taught social studies. That may be true in theory, but every teacher must reinforce the reading strategies that help make children successful students. Every student should be taught to break down every reading assignment into three parts ("Reading in the Content Area," 2005, p. 2):

1. Students must be taught 'Before-Reading Strategies' before they attempt to read a selection. This step in the reading process activates a student's prior knowledge and establishes the purpose for reading. 'The Before Reading Strategies' include brainstorming, predicting, skimming, assessing prior knowledge, previewing headings, and learning crucial vocabulary.

2. Students must also be taught 'During-Reading Strategies' to use while they are reading. This step in the reading process helps students measure comprehension, clarify any questions, visualize the text and build connections. The strategies in this step include rereading, inferring, questioning, supporting predictions, and summarizing.

Example 2 of a Complete Action Research Report   **149**

3. The final step that students must be taught is what to do 'After Reading' a selection. This step expands prior knowledge, builds connections, and deepens understanding. The strategies in this step include rereading, confirming predictions, summarizing, synthesizing, reflecting, and questioning.

When all teachers begin to teach readers effective reading skills and strategies, students will improve with confidence and increased knowledge.

Sara Thompson, a reading specialist, defines strategies as "any mental operation that an individual uses, either consciously or unconsciously, to help him or her learn" (Thompson, 2000, p. 1). Thompson stresses that if we want students to learn, we must teach them how to do it.

> Reading is not how well you pronounce words as you glide across the page, but rather, how your eyes of understanding are open to the extent that the words are transformed into meaningful thought within your cognitive frame of reference; thereby completing the comprehension process. Reading requires that students make meaning from what they read in text. Regardless of which subject the reading is done in, it will include comprehension, vocabulary, critical reading, textbook skills, library tools, following directions, and study skills. Therefore, if comprehension increases in content areas it will increase overall. (Thompson, p. 1)

Teachers must begin to help students construct meaning from the text. They must also teach students to focus on the big idea when they are reading expository text. Students need to learn how expository texts are organized, which means that students must learn how to read subtitles, pictures, diagrams, labels, indices, and tables of contents. Vocabulary also has to be strengthened if students are to become successful content readers. There are specific strategies that will help students reach proficiency when they are reading expository texts. These strategies help students before they read, while they read, and after they read (Thompson, 2000, p. 1).

Before-reading strategies help students connect their previous knowledge to new information about the same topic. There are many strategies that teachers can teach students to help them before they begin to read a passage. The following strategies will help students before they read (Thompson, 2000):

1. *Brainstorming.* This provides the teacher with information about what students already know about a topic. Graphic organizers can be used to aid in this process.

2. *Survey Technique.* This particular strategy sets the purpose for reading. When students are taught this strategy, they are taught to analyze the text features: the title, subheadings, graphics, introductory paragraphs, and main ideas.

3. *Structured Overview.* With this strategy, students use graphic organizers and visual devices to relate new vocabulary and concepts to known vocabulary and concepts.

4. *Advanced Organizers.* Used to activate a student's prior knowledge, these organizers link new concepts to existing concepts. There are three steps involved in completing an Advanced Organizer:

    a. Identify the main ideas or concepts of the selection to be read.

    b. Establish parallels between the concepts and the child's prior experiences.

    c. Tell children how their prior experience directly relates to the selection that they are going to read. (Thompson, 2000 p. 6).

5. *Graphic Organizer.* The K-W-L chart is a useful tool to use while students read and do research. You can use this chart before, during, and after reading. Students tell what they know, what they want to know, what they will learn, and how they can learn more about a concept.

6. *Predicting.* This strategy helps the reader to set a purpose for reading and to ask questions and monitor himself or herself while reading (Thompson, 2000).

All of these strategies can help students increase content-area reading comprehension.

Vocabulary development is also very important when learning content-area reading. There are many strategies that students can learn to help them learn new vocabulary.

> Vocabulary development has been linked to academic achievement. It is a critical aspect of success in reading. Vocabulary limitations are attributed to the lack of gains in reading. The failure of children to have access to the meanings of words representative of the concepts and content of what they read causes difficulty in children's comprehension of texts, limits their ability to make a connection with their existing background knowledge, and inhibits their capacity to make coherent inferences (Thompson, 2000, p. 8).

There are many strategies that teachers can teach to help students improve their vocabulary. These strategies include the following:

1. *Webbing.* This allows students to graphically connect words that are related.

2. *Vocabulary Self-Collection.* This strategy tells students words that they need to know in order to be successful in class.

3. *Vocabulary Log, or Journal.* With this tool, students keep a record of new words and the definitions that go along with each word. The students can draw pictures or illustrations to help them remember the vocabulary words.

4. *Word Sleuthing.* This teaches students how to investigate the meaning and origin of a word. The students are also taught about categorizing words into a word family.

5. *Flash Card.* This strategy helps students who are visual learners to learn vocabulary words and definitions. Students could also draw a picture next to the definition to help them remember the word (Thompson, 2000).

6. *Word Splash.* This activity prompts students to quickly generate words associated with a topic that they will be reading. It is a strategy that provides a purpose before reading (Sheakoski, 2008).

All of these strategies can help students increase their vocabulary skills in content classes. Students also must learn how and why texts are organized the way they are and what the author's purpose was in a particular selection.

> Text organization includes the physical presentation and structure of text. The physical presentation includes visual textual clues such as headings and subheadings, signal words, and location of main ideas in sentences. Text structure involves the organizational patterns of text written to convey a purpose, i.e., persuade or entertain. Typographical aids are also included in most content area textbooks to assist the reader in determining the organization of the information presented. These include the title, subheads, colored panels, sidebars, bullets, use of color type and words printed in italics or boldface. As readers read, they should interact with these typographical aids (Thompson 2000, p. 10).

There are many strategies that help students understand the organization of a text. These strategies include the following:

1. *Study Guides.* Study guides help students organize the information in a given text and reflect on it.

Example 2 of a Complete Action Research Report **151**

2. ***Pattern Guides and/or Flow Charts.*** These guides help students identify the organizational pattern in a particular text. Is the main idea at the beginning of each paragraph? Do the details follow the topic sentence in each paragraph?

3. ***Summarization.*** This strategy allows the student to think about what was in the text and reflect on it.

4. ***Question Generation.*** This strategy teaches the student to ask questions to aid in comprehension. Teachers usually teach the student to turn the subheadings into questions. This helps the reader focus on the content in the passage (Thompson 2000, p. 10).

5. ***Writing to Learn.*** This strategy teaches the student to summarize the passage.

6. ***Journal Writing.*** Students freely write what they think about a particular passage.

7. ***Graphic Organizers.*** These are great tools to help students take notes about what they read (Thompson 2000, p. 10).

All of these strategies should be taught to all students. These strategies are the necessary tools that students need to learn to be successful while reading in the content areas. If students are given the tools to help them understand and comprehend expository reading, then students will be more successful across the curriculum. These strategies can be expected to positively affect students' grades, test scores, and achievement.

Teachers must continually research the latest strategies that help students become more successful in the classroom. With the pressure of assessment and the No Child Left Behind legislation, teachers must constantly use best practice methods to help students' achievement scores continue to increase. Content reading is a large portion of the core content test in fourth and fifth grades. Students must be able to read and comprehend the material on the test to answer the questions correctly and completely. Fourth and fifth grade teachers spend a vast amount of time teaching students how to be successful expository readers. Students must be familiar with literary, persuasive, informational, and practical types of reading. Primary programs are beginning to include these genres in their programs, which is going to benefit all readers and address a variety of learning styles. We must expose our students to all types of genres to become life-long readers and learners.

Strategies from the literature in this section can be beneficial to assessment level teachers, reading interventionists, and teachers of students with special needs. The strategies learned will be very advantageous to students. The strategies will help the students learn how to ask questions and set a purpose before reading. The strategies will also enable students to learn more vocabulary, which will help them comprehend various texts. When students learn how expository texts are structured, they will begin to comprehend more and more texts. Teaching strategies can benefit all students in the classroom, especially struggling readers.

Methodology and Research Procedures

All stakeholders were involved in data collection to address why content reading is difficult for students and to discuss strategies that teachers can use to help all students comprehend content reading material. We collaborated with teachers, parents, students, the Title I Reading teacher, the Read to Achieve teacher, the principal, the district literacy coordinator, and the project manager for Title I Reading Services. We examined a review of literature to find reasons that students have difficulty reading expository texts, to compare struggling readers and proficient readers comprehending informational texts, to discover why it is important to teach content-area reading, to identify who is responsible for teaching reading, and to select a variety of strategies and skills that would facilitate the instruction of content-area reading.

Data sources included (a) student achievement data from the state core content tests, (b) student achievement data from disaggregated data from the Comprehensive Test of Basic Skills (CTBS), (c) passage comprehension data from Scantron for Reading, (d) GRADE (Grade Level Reading Assessment and Diagnostic Evaluation) genre question data, (e) parent survey data on reading preference of children, (f) student survey data on how students see themselves as learners in content-area reading, and (g) teacher self-assessment survey data.

The core content test and the CTBS disaggregated data revealed the strengths and weakness of students' reading of nonfiction and informational texts. Scantron Reading assessments showed trend data for reading expository writing. GRADE data uncovered the genres that students are able to read and understand (as evidenced by their ability to answer questions in those genres) and the genres that students are not able to read and understand (as evidenced by their inability to answer questions in those genres). Surveys were given to teachers, parents, and students. Teachers clarified what they believe about teaching expository writing and whether or not they observe their students' reading and understanding informational texts in all content areas. Parents were asked if they observed their child's reading informational material and if their children seemed to enjoy reading nonfiction. Students were given surveys so that they could share ways in which they saw themselves as readers of informational materials.

All data collected served as a basis for making recommendations to improve content-area reading instruction. A plan to provide additional professional development on how to implement content-area reading instruction strategies was recommended. Additionally, it was recommended to involve all stakeholders in monitoring the progress of all students who have access to expository writing and monitor the progress of students who comprehend informational reading materials.

Data Collection and Analysis

Figure 1, State Performance Report scores for Roger Vale Elementary over a three-year period, illustrate reading, mathematics, science, and practical living/vocational studies increases and decreases. Social studies, arts and humanities, and writing scores have increased. Roger Vale Elementary has been experiencing inconsistent overall improvement and has not made progress toward proficiency, as evidenced in the 2008 Kentucky Performance Report (KPR).

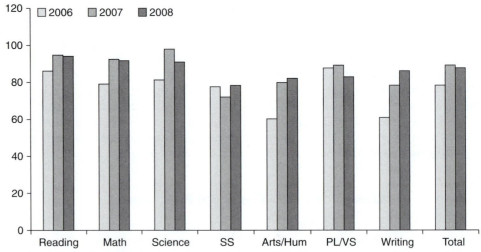

Figure 1. **State Performance Report of scores for Roger Vale Elementary over a 3-year period.**

To be in compliance with the Read to Achieve grant, the GRADE has been administered every fall and spring since 2006. It is used, specific to primary students, as a formative and summative assessment and as a diagnostic assessment tool to inform instruction in reading. Data from the GRADE revealed strengths and weaknesses of students in various subtests and reading skill areas. Although all students in the primary program

Example 2 of a Complete Action Research Report **153**

were administered the GRADE, Figure 2 represents only the percentage results of nonfiction questions correctly answered by students at the end of third grade.

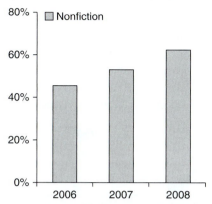

Figure 2. **GRADE percentage of nonfiction questions correctly answered by students at the end of third grade.**

Although the trend seems to indicate improvement in students in the answering of nonfiction comprehension questions, third grade students entering fourth grade have not been able to answer nonfiction comprehension questions with at least 70% accuracy.

Scantron is a technology-based assessment that reveals individual, class, and grade-level reading comprehension performance and trends. It is administered to second through fifth grade students and is used as a district-wide formative assessment to analyze academic improvement toward the core content testing that is given in the spring.

The current trend represented in Figure 3 from data from the Scantron for the fall of 2008 assessments indicates some improvement toward students' answering all comprehension questions correctly. However, no grade level from second to fifth is achieving at least 70% success in answering nonfiction comprehension questions. Also, students seem to be better able to answer fiction comprehension questions than nonfiction questions at all grade levels.

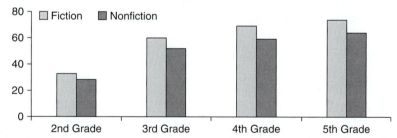

Figure 3. **Scantron Fall of 2008 Assessment of Roger Vale Elementary fiction and nonfiction reading achievement.**

The core content test data are summative assessments that analyze the progress toward proficiency in 2014. Data disaggregated by type of questions in Reading Comprehension analyze Literary, Informational, Persuasive, and Practical/Workplace. Figure 4 represents a 3-year period of the mean score from the state performance report of the Reading Informational Subdomain for Roger Vale Elementary.

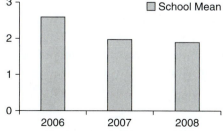

Figure 4. **State Performance Report for Roger Vale Elementary fourth grade reading informational subdomain.**

The school mean comprehension score in the fourth grade indicates a decline since 2006 in Informational Reading. Data disaggregated by students receiving free/reduced lunch and non-free/reduced lunch show the performance in reading. Figure 5 compares students receiving free/reduced lunch and non-free/reduced lunch for 3 years, indicating a gap between the two subgroups.

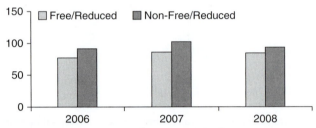

Figure 5. **Index Disaggregated Reading Data for Roger Vale Elementary.**

We surveyed three convenience sample populations throughout the course of the research study. The first sample consisted of 30 fourth grade students (16 males and 14 females) from two fourth grade classes at Roger Vale Elementary. These two fourth grade classes were selected to participate in the study because their students have at least, or more than, 1 year of experience with core content testing. Permission to participate in the survey was obtained from each child's parents.

The second sample consisted of 35 parents of fourth grade students. We sent home a cover letter to each fourth grade child's parents, explaining the purpose of the survey. We attached the parent survey to this letter. We received 35 out of 57 (61.4%) parent surveys back from parents. The third sample consisted of 13 certified teachers (grades K–5) from Roger Vale Elementary. We sent a cover letter with an attached teacher survey to 20 certified teachers, explaining the purpose of this research project. We received 13 out of 20 (65%) teacher surveys back from the certified teachers.

Survey Design

Three separate surveys were developed for this study. Each sample population received a similar survey. Likert scales on the surveys measured perceptions of survey participants. The scale ranged from 1 to 5 and had the following descriptors:

1 = Strongly Disagree

2 = Disagree

3 = Somewhat Agree

4 = Agree

5 = Strongly Agree

Student survey. The student survey consisted of seven statements. The survey included statements that dealt with content reading, reading strategies, graphic organizers, fiction versus nonfiction, and ability to read informational texts. Before the survey was given to the students, instructions were provided on how to answer the survey with the Likert scale. Each statement was read to the students. Sufficient time was provided for students to circle their answer before the next statement was read. This allowed some of our struggling readers to have a clear understanding of each statement.

Example 2 of a Complete Action Research Report   **155**

Parent survey. The parent survey consisted of eight statements. The survey included statements that dealt with the content reading, reading strategies and/or graphic organizers that the child used to help understand information texts, fiction versus nonfiction, and their child's ability to read informational texts.

Teacher survey. The teacher survey consisted of eight statements. The survey included statements that dealt with perceptions about content reading, teaching reading strategies and/or graphic organizers that students used to help them understand informational texts, length of time spent reading fiction compared with time spent reading nonfiction texts, and students' ability to read informational texts.

Data Collection and Analysis

After the return of surveys from parents and teachers, the student survey was administered to both fourth grade classes; the collection of the data generated from the surveys proceeded. For each survey, a chart was generated to record the data for each statement. Each set of surveys was reviewed and tallied for the total of 1s, 2s, 3s, 4s, and 5s marked for each statement. If a statement was left blank, the neutral answer was circled. The total tallies for each cell were calculated and converted to percentages. For example, when statement one was calculated, the researcher divided the number of people who circled "1" by the total number of people in the sample. This gave the percentage of people who circled "strongly disagreed" for their answer to statement one. This calculation was computed with the data gathered for each statement. After collecting and computing all data, data analysis for each survey type was completed.

Data Analysis

Table 2, *Data from Student Survey,* Appendix A, shows that most students somewhat to strongly agree that they like to read nonfiction and that they have been taught before-, during-, and after-reading strategies through the use of information from books and articles. However, 42% of the students strongly disagree, disagree, or somewhat agree they use graphic organizers to help understand information in books and articles.

Table 3, *Data from Parent Survey,* Appendix B, shows that 51% of the parents disagree or somewhat agree that their children use graphic organizers to help understand content-area reading. Of parents surveyed, 48% disagree or somewhat agree that their children read equal amounts of fiction and nonfiction. Also, of parents surveyed, 48% believe that their children will select information books to read for pleasure. Furthermore, 66% of parents surveyed somewhat agree, disagree, or strongly disagree that their children prefer reading informational texts.

Table 4, *Data from Teacher Survey,* Appendix C, indicates that 47% of the teachers neither agree nor disagree that they regularly use graphic organizers to facilitate content-area reading strategies. Of the teachers surveyed, 47% neither agree nor disagree that they fully understand how to teach expository writing, 47% neither agree nor disagree that their students read equal amounts of fiction and nonfiction. Ninety-two percent of the teachers surveyed either disagree or remain neutral in thinking that their students prefer to read informational text. Only 30% of the teachers surveyed believe that their students are able to read expository writing well.

Research Results and Conclusions

Data from the GRADE for 3 years and Scantron Assessments for the fall 2008 suggest that students at Roger Vale Elementary are not able to read and respond to nonfiction comprehension passages (Figure 2 & Figure 3). From the state core content-area index trends, disaggregated reading data for Roger Vale Elementary, and core content tests for reading informational subdomain, Roger Vale Elementary is slightly declining in reading, with an emphasis on the inability of students to read and respond to content area/informational reading.

Student perceptions of content-area reading in their textbooks seem to be positive, but many students indicate that they do not regularly choose information books to read from the library. Parent perceptions show understanding of why informational reading is taught, yet many of these same parents believe that their child does not prefer to read informational texts. Teacher perceptions of teaching expository writing, the use of graphic organizers, and students reading equal amounts of fiction and nonfiction are indeterminate. Teacher perceptions of their students' preferring to read informational texts or able to read expository writing well range from disagree to neutral.

Students seem to like to read science and social studies texts, which indicates that motivation is not an issue. There may be a need for students to gain experience in reading nonfiction text in order to understand and apply the information essential for successful responses to comprehension questions. Reading and writing are reciprocal processes. If the students are not sure how to write expository texts, they may be having trouble reading expository texts for meaning. Teachers do not demonstrate a passion for teaching nonfiction informational text, as evidenced by many neutral responses to the Teacher Survey.

Recommendations

The recommendations that follow are based on the findings of this study and the literature resources that describe how to teach content-area reading or nonfiction strategies and skills, as well as the research on nonfiction comprehension. These recommendations are made to improve overall reading achievement for all students.

Intentional, specific instruction in nonfiction reading materials needs to take place at every grade level—kindergarten to fifth grade (Fried, 2006; Moss, 2005).

1. Provide teacher professional development to improve the teaching of expository writing.

2. Plan teacher professional development so that teachers may learn to use a variety of strategies, techniques, and skills to teach nonfiction or content-area reading.

3. Offer students opportunities to self-select nonfiction reading materials for independent practice in reading informational text.

4. Incorporate more nonfiction in Title I, RTA, and special education to achieve a balanced instructional approach to teaching genres of literature for struggling readers.

5. Use graphic organizers to facilitate written expression and demonstration of comprehension. Reading and writing are reciprocal processes. Help students organize and respond to nonfiction.

6. Provide additional nonfiction resources and materials that support the state *Program of Studies* and the school district *Curriculum Maps* to support the instruction of reading in the content areas.

Example 2 of a Complete Action Research Report   **157**

Appendix A

Table 2
Data from Student Survey

Statement	Strongly Disagree	Disagree	Somewhat Agree	Agree	Strongly Agree
I like to read my science and social studies books.	0%	3%	33%	41%	23%
I can read my science and social studies books well.	0%	0%	3%	21%	76%
I choose information books in the library.	3%	3%	47%	21%	26%
My teacher taught me how to use before-reading strategies with information books and articles.	0%	3%	7%	40%	50%
My teacher taught me how to use during-reading strategies with information books and articles.	0%	3%	10%	47%	40%
My teacher taught me how to use after-reading strategies with information books and articles.	0%	0%	16%	36%	48%
I use graphic organizers to help me understand information in books and articles.	3%	13%	26%	47%	11%

Appendix B

Table 3
Data from Parent Survey

Statement	Strongly Disagree	Disagree	Somewhat Agree	Agree	Strongly Agree
I believe teaching content reading strategies is important.	0%	0%	0%	46%	54%
My child is regularly taught reading strategies and skills in all content areas.	0%	2%	22%	52%	24%
My child regularly uses graphic organizers to help understand content-area reading.	0%	8%	43%	35%	14%
I fully understand why my child should read informational/nonfiction writing.	0%	2%	2%	46%	50%
My child reads equal amounts of fiction and nonfiction.	0%	17%	31%	40%	14%
My child feels comfortable asking questions when he/she is with students working at the same ability level.	0%	3%	39%	42%	13%
My child will select information books to read for fun.	0%	25%	23%	26%	26%
My child prefers to read informational texts.	6%	27%	39%	17%	11%
My child reads information books and articles well.	6%	3%	31%	49%	11%

References

Armbruster, B. B., Anderson, T. H., & Ostertag, J. (1987, Summer). Does text structure/summarization instruction facilitate learning from expository? *Reading Research Quarterly 2*(3), 331–346.

Beck, I., & McKeown, M. G. (1991, October). Research directions. Social studies texts are hard to understand: Mediating some of the difficulties. *Language Arts 68,* 482–490.

Fried, M. D. (2006). Reciprocity: Promoting the flow of knowledge for learning to read and write. *Journal of Reading Recovery 5*(2), 5–14.

Hager, J. M., & Gable, R. A. (1993). Content reading assessment: A rethinking of methodology. *Clearing House, 66*(5), 269–272.

Kentucky Program of Studies. (2006). Frankfort, KY: Kentucky Department of Education. Retrieved from http://www.kde.state.ky.us/oaa/implement/0102/KPR07_181020.pdf.

Literacy Matters. *Reading: Questioning.* Retrieved from http://www.literacymatters.org/content/readandwrite/question.html.

Moss, B. (2005). Making a case and a place for effective content area literacy instruction in the elementary grades. *Reading Teacher 59,* 46–55.

Moustafa, B. (1999). *Content area reading: Summary of reference papers.* California State University, 1–14.

Sheakoski, M. (2008). Word splash vocabulary strategy for primary kids. *Primary School Curriculum.* Retrieved from http://primary-school-lesson-plans.suite101.com/article.cfm/word_splash.

Reading in the content areas: Strategies for success. *Teaching Today* (2005, April). Retrieved from http://www.glencoe.com/sec/teachingtoday/educationupclose.phtml/12.

Thompson, S. (2000). Effective content reading comprehension and retention strategies. *ERIC,* 1–59.

Vacca, R. (1996). *Content Reading strategies.* Retrieved from http://pec.jun.alaska.edu/consortia/Lit/Reading?Contentrdg.html.

Note. **This example report was adapted from action research by Michelle C. Ligon, Reading Recovery and Title I Intervention Teacher, and Melissa Rash, Elementary School Educator. Used with permission.**

EXAMPLE 3 OF A COMPLETE ACTION RESEARCH REPORT

Improving the Reading Skills of Struggling Reading Students at Melody Lane Elementary School

Melody Lane Elementary (MLE) continues to search for ways to help all students reach proficiency in reading skills. In our 11th year as a school, we still see that, although there is not a significant gap between identified groups of students on reading assessments, we still have almost 8% of students at the primary level who do not have formally identified disabilities, but who struggle as readers nonetheless.

Three years ago, Melody Lane received a state-funded Read to Achieve grant that provided the school funding for a reading specialist and materials to begin a research-based reading intervention program for struggling readers in kindergarten through third grades. Although the intervention program helped many struggling students achieve at higher levels, we still have approximately 8% of students at the primary level who score below grade level or are teetering just on grade level, as measured by the Group Reading Assessment and Diagnostic Evaluation (GRADE), the Scholastic Reading Inventory (SRI), and/or the Developmental Reading Assessment (DRA). In examining the scores in the areas of phonological awareness, phonics, comprehension, vocabulary, and fluency, as measured by these instruments, areas where students seem to struggle the most can be identified. Surveys and/or questionnaires completed by classroom teachers, reading tutors, and the reading specialist also provide pertinent information regarding causes for the skill deficits. Gathering and studying possibilities for further intervention and instructional strategies can help the students reach proficiency in reading.

Even with the implementation of a research-based intervention program in grades kindergarten through three, approximately 8% of our primary students are still reading below or barely on grade level.

Statement of the Problem

Reading is a foundational skill that paves the way for content learning in all other subjects. Very few children with serious reading difficulties ever graduate from college. They suffer from a higher incidence than their peers do of social problems such as delinquency and drug abuse. Their job prospects are limited. Beyond the economic and social factors, people who cannot read or cannot read well are unable to experience the joys of learning, the opportunities for self-reflection, or the simple pleasures of being lost in a book (Whitehurst, 2001). As the world becomes more complex, reading is an important skill for children trying to find their place in it (Alexander, 2007). Because reading is a crucial building block in a child's education, it is important to help each child build strong literacy skills so that he or she may use these skills to acquire other knowledge.

Research Questions

In light of the circumstances described, the primary research question is this: What instructional methods can the teachers and staff at Melody Lane Elementary implement that will help these students reach proficiency in reading? More specific questions to be addressed included the following:

1. Are there specific areas of reading in which these students struggle? If so, which ones?

2. Who are the students who are struggling, and how do they learn best?

3. What teaching strategies can be implemented in the problem areas to help these students reach proficiency in reading?

Literature Review

In studying the literature concerning the characteristics of struggling readers, a number of things came to light about diagnosis of their skill deficiencies. For children who struggle with reading, school can be a daily battle. This academic weakness can surface in almost all activities within the classroom (Hettinger & Knapp, 2001). Many struggling readers can decode printed text, but organizational skills and memory for detail are weak. Recalling facts and responding to questions are difficult because the reader cannot easily sort main ideas from supporting details, identify cause-and-effect relationships, and sequence events within a story (Arthaud & Goracke, 2006).

Therefore, helping struggling readers involves taking a careful look at each struggling reader to see what that child does as she reads, juxtapose that information against what a proficient reader does, and make teaching decisions on the basis of that information. Observations and assessment of the student while she is engaged in reading always inform our instruction, and knowledge of the reading process guides the way (Johnson, 2006).

According to our study of the literacy program at MLE, many research-based practices are already in effect. Teachers model lifelong excitement and rewards of reading by reading, themselves, during silent reading time, talking about favorite books, and reading aloud to students. There is a wide variety of engaging materials of varying reading levels available in the classrooms. In the intermediate grades, especially, this is very important for struggling readers, whose interests and comprehension abilities may be several grade levels above their decoding abilities. Many bright struggling readers really enjoy *The Magic School Bus* or *Science I Can Read* series books. These books can help them satisfy their curiosity about the work around them.

At MLE, "round-robin" reading is avoided, as it requires the reader to read text orally for the first time in public. Instead, children do choral reading, prepare and read poetry or parts in plays, or read their own writing in the "author's chair" sessions during Reading/Writing Workshop (Hettinger & Knapp, 2001).

A Language-Saturated Classroom

Struggling readers need to be saturated with language in the classroom. In order to accomplish this, the amount of language a child hears and uses should be increased. Teachers at MLE can play books on tape, conduct read-aloud sessions, and use a variety of oral activities. Each room has a word wall and a classroom library. Core content vocabulary for each subject area is clearly visible and is used in reading and writing activities. MLE lower primary students participate in the Sunshine at Home program, which sends books home with students. The students read the book with their parents, complete a short homework activity, and bring the book back to exchange for another (Crystal & Campbell, n.d.).

The reading intervention program used at MLE provides for systematic phonics instruction, including phonemic awareness activities that require children to focus on and manipulate phonemes in syllables and words. This instruction also contains the teaching of blending sounds and word patterns. Sight word practice is crucial for struggling readers. Students in our reading and intervention programs are given a variety of ways to do this through flash cards, matching games, silly sentences, and computer games.

Effective vocabulary instruction provides both definitional and contextual information about the meaning of new words. It also involves students in the active learning of new words and offers multiple exposures to meaningful information about words and related words.

Example 3 of a Complete Action Research Report **161**

Instructional Consistency and Intentionality

In working with struggling readers, teachers provide feedback and (a) ignore miscues that do not change the text's meaning; (b) include wait time before responding to meaning-change miscues so as to give the reader an opportunity to self-monitor and self-correct performance; and (c) begin with a focus on meaning construction. Repeated readings are also used to build fluency (Wood, 2005).

The program was studied to see whether activities or strategies may be at odds with each other or may be causing students to have difficulty in reading proficiently. During this study, a few possible concerns arose. Struggling readers may have only one-third of the language experience of those students who come from enriched environments. Because of this, the struggling readers lack competence with oral language and many emerging literacy skills; therefore, if lower primary programs focus on letters, sounds, blends, and word-recognition skills, these students have an uphill battle. If they do not develop alphabetic knowledge and word-recognition skills, they will have great difficulty becoming fluent readers, and this lack of fluency will affect their comprehension skills (Brownell & Walther-Thomas, 2000). If the curriculum in the regular classroom employs one set of strategies and the intervention program employs yet another set, this can cause confusion for the struggling reader. We discovered that in some instances at MLE, the teaching of "reading fix-up strategies" was being implemented by the use of language and definitions that differed enough from one teacher to the next that it could be a possible stumbling block for struggling readers.

With all of this in mind, I looked for research-based strategies that can be put in place in all learning venues in the school to bring consistency and intentionality to instruction and thus enhance teaching for learning.

First of all, teachers must actively teach reading comprehension strategies by explicit instruction. They can help students understand the value of learning strategies and how the students can use them to facilitate their reading. Educators can then help students recognize the value of learning strategies, and they can use them to facilitate their reading. Second, educators can describe how to use these strategies and, through "think-alouds," demonstrate these strategies to students. (For example, "As I find a word that I don't recognize, I can 'get my mouth ready' to sound it out—I can look for small words that I recognize in a big word.") Third, teachers can provide ongoing opportunities, with teacher support, to use strategies so that students can become fluent in their use, reminding students to use the strategies—if they fail to employ them independently—as they read. These strategies need to become an ongoing part of classroom instruction and practice. For struggling readers, this is long-term instruction. It is even more important for school faculties to work together to teach and support student use of these strategies by using common language and modeling so that, after several years, students work toward being self-regulated learners (Brownell & Walther-Thomas). The real key to scaffolding is to provide just enough support to help the child, without giving answers.

The secret behind truly powerful teaching and learning lies in developing students' metacognitive abilities—their ability to initiate and complete meaningful self-assessment. Students need many opportunities to practice and receive feedback about their performances (Hobson, 1997). In order to give students frequent feedback, it is important to do the following tasks:

1. Assess often. Revisit targets. Let students see growth in their own understanding.

2. Keep learning targets central to all assessment. Search for evidence of understanding of target content in all aspects of classroom activity.

3. Chart individual student progress toward each of the content targets instead of through undifferentiated scores (such as a percentage or letter grade).

4. Design formal cumulative assessment with attention to the target understanding implicit in each individual question.

5. Use a variety of assessment forms (multiple choice, oral, classroom discussion, journals or other writing, or other student activities).

6. Allow students to rate the certainty of their responses by a scale—for example, 1 (not sure) to 4 (certain)—in order to gauge the depth of their understanding (Watterson, 2007).

Many struggling readers are passive learners. It is important for the teacher to actively model strategies to understand what is being read. After practicing, students should be allowed to engage in discussions about their strategies and set goals for improving their comprehension (Walker, 2005).

Struggling readers who are also English language learners (ELL) typically lack confidence in reading. Thus, it is important for teachers to help these students set goals that are specific and challenging but achievable. It is important for students to see their own progress in the early stages of the intervention. This can be accomplished by students self-recording data on assessments. If students self-record data, both the student and teacher get concrete feedback regarding behavior and help to identify reinforcers for effective reading. (Tam, et al, 2006).

Two strategies that are very helpful to students with organizational deficits are the structured story web and the outline strategy. Story webbing involves the creation of a visual display of interlinked concepts or story elements and involves a process that results in a graphic organizer designed to assist the reader with organizing and remembering important details from the text. In a web-like design, the main idea or topic is located in the center and supporting details are placed as branches extending from the central point. Students are given repeated practice and are gradually asked to complete more and more of the web, independently, as they learn the process. When given extensive opportunities to use these designs throughout the school year, students begin to use them for all types of activities. The result of the use of this strategy has been improved response to comprehension questions, increased amount of detail recall, and more enthusiasm for the reading process (Arthaud & Goracke, 2006).

Johnson (2006) describes a framework for struggling readers that includes four steps: *Here's what*—In this step, the teacher discerns what the child can do, can almost do, or cannot do as a reader. There are a number of strategies employed by competent readers. These skills can be assessed through running records, anecdotal notes, miscue analysis, reading conferences, and checklists. *So what*—Once a child's present level of skill has been diagnosed, decisions can be made for teaching strategies that the child does not know. *Now what*—Teaching the reading strategies through the following process is the next step:

1. Modeling—clearly demonstrating with explicit language.

2. Scaffolding—supporting the child; doing it with him.

3. Prompting—saying something that will remind the child to try the strategy or behavior.

4. Backing off—letting your supports fade away, dismantling your scaffolds, so that the child takes more responsibility for initiating the strategy.

5. Reinforcing—naming the strategy or behavior that the child used, praising it, and showing him how it worked in this instance.

Example 3 of a Complete Action Research Report   **163**

This step involves teaching the student something that they cannot do, scaffolding or prompting for things that they can almost do, and reinforcing the things that they can do. *Then what*—Watch the child to see whether he has taken the strategy on and uses it independently. Has he *learned* it?

Formative Assessment and Stated Learning Objectives

In determining how a student is progressing, formative assessment is any process that helps students to become aware of how they can make progress. Formative assessment helps students to (a) learn more effectively, (b) feel more involved in their educational process and become less alienated from it, (c) promote individual instruction, and (d) produce positive effects, particularly evident with struggling learners.

Formative assessment should meet these criteria:

1. Be clearly understood by the learner

2. Have specific rubrics that are clearly understood by the learner so that the learner knows exactly what she has to do and how to do it to proficiency

3. Inform students where they are in the learning process at the beginning of the task

4. Give students opportunities to set their own goals

5. Provide models of good work for students (Highland Learning and Teaching Toolkit, n.d.)

In order for formative assessment to be most effective, there should be a whole-school approach to it, with colleagues sharing best practice and planning for improvement. Learning intention (target) needs to be in child-friendly language so that the students know exactly what it is that they are going to learn. The learning objective and success criteria (how I show what I know) need to be visually displayed for every lesson. Having students read the objective and success criteria aloud and discuss the meaning will help children of all learning styles to be able to understand what they will learn. There might be an objective posted that describes several lessons, or there may be different goals for different groups—it just needs to be made clear to the students what the objective is. It is also advisable to put up the objective and have the children help design the success criteria—an activity that will show that they have learned what was intended.

Sharing learning intentions benefits students, teachers, and parents. It keeps students more focused. They can recognize their achievement, and the sharing experience changes their emphasis from completion of the task to achievement of the learning intention. As a result of sharing learning intentions, students benefit in several ways:

1. Learn to work for themselves rather than for the teachers

2. Begin to say "What are we going to learn?" instead of "What are we going to do?"

3. Ask for the learning objective to be posted if it is forgotten because they realize that it helps them focus

4. Become more focused, particularly if they are troubled learners

5. See learning as "real life"; and

6. Have ownership of the learning and be more persistent about achieving the goal

Teachers benefit from sharing learning experiences in these ways:

1. Helps to focus learning tasks

2. Sharpens teacher knowledge of core content and program or studies (learning intentions)

3. Raises expectations for students

4. Helps teachers focus on quality rather than "getting it done"

5. Reinforces core content vocabulary (Clarke, 2001)

Parents benefit from shared learning intentions that are communicated by teachers with these things in mind:

1. Using parent-friendly language when sending home learning intentions or posting learning targets in newsletters or on websites

2. Being clear about learning objectives and communicating to parents the depth and breadth of the academic work in which their children are engaged

Parents can focus their help in productive ways if they understand the learning targets. Clear learning objectives help parents understand what grades mean in terms of what their children have and have not learned. Stiggins et al. (2006) encourage parents to talk with their children about strengths and areas for improvement and help them avoid damaging generalizations such as "I'm no good at reading."

Formative assessment allows teachers to collect data on students that will help them adapt instruction in order to meet student needs. For struggling learners, formative assessment helps most of all because it focuses their learning on what they need to know, thereby reducing the range of achievement and enabling them to raise their achievement level overall. Formative assessment helps struggling learners to concentrate on specific problems with their work and gives them a clear understanding of what is wrong and how to put it right (Black & Wiliam, 1998).

The next step is to answer the question *How can their effectiveness be assessed?*

Summary

In summary, the literature on literacy instruction for struggling readers supports specific, intentional instruction for these students that includes a variety of learning experiences—from a print-rich environment to visual, auditory, and hands-on reading activities. Assessment for literacy development should be ongoing and frequent, as well as conducted through a variety of means. Instruction in all five strands of literacy—phonemic awareness, phonics, vocabulary, comprehension, and fluency—is essential. It is also important for the teacher to frequently observe these students when they are reading, engage them in conversation about what they read, and listen to them read aloud in order to measure both fluency and comprehension.

Methodology and Research Procedures

In order to conduct this research, I collaborated with MLE's administrative team, district reading specialists, our school's reading specialist, ELL teachers, and primary teachers to study the data pertaining to reading achievement levels for students scoring

Example 3 of a Complete Action Research Report   **165**

below grade level in kindergarten through grade 3. The group working on this project numbered about 30. Experience in the education profession ranged from 3 to 30 years. With this diverse group of professionals examining data and research, we were able to come up with a comprehensive look at our existing literacy program and its strengths and weaknesses. All members of the group also contributed to the construction of a walk-through instrument and the teacher survey that would be conducted to evaluate the existing program and the implementation of additional research-based strategies to assist struggling readers. A district reading specialist gave valuable feedback about what had been observed around the district regarding struggling readers and consistency of language utilized by all staff in literacy instruction. The group also came to consensus about—and set up the calendar for implementation of—the additional research-based strategies that are to be used during reading instruction in the primary classrooms and resource rooms.

The data that we examined (KCCT Reading scores in Table 1) also included GRADE diagnostic assessments (see Figure 1) for third graders over the past 2 years. We then disaggregated the data according to student demographics to look for any common characteristics among our students who are not reading proficiently.

Table 1
Melody Lane Elementary—CATS Assessments Reading Open-Response Performance Grade 3

Reading Skill Area	Percentages of Students at Performance Level			
	Novice	**Apprentice**	**Proficient**	**Distinguished**
Developing Understanding	5	59	26	10
Interpreting Text	8	52	27	12

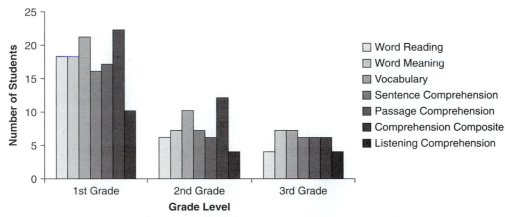

Figure 1. Students scoring below grade level on the GRADE assessment—Fall 2007.

Data review was followed by examining the literature for information about effective strategies for teaching struggling readers in the primary grades and comparing these with our existing literacy program. Our current program was evaluated for successful strategies that are in place and those that may be causing confusion for struggling readers. We then spent time reading about and discussing the research-based intervention strategies that we could add to our program to improve instruction. We also studied and discussed formative evaluation methods that could be put in place to measure student progress and give valuable feedback to teachers, who could in turn modify instruction to meet these students' needs.

I spoke with the district reading specialist, our school's reading specialist, the principal, and teachers about the strategies that we felt would be implemented in addition to our present literacy program in order to help our struggling readers. Once the walk-through instrument and teacher survey instruments were complete, they were utilized over a period of 4 weeks to monitor the use of the chosen research-based strategies that we wanted to implement to enhance instruction for all students, but especially targeting those struggling readers. I conducted the walk-throughs, along with the principal. We collated the data so that we could share it with the staff and get feedback from them about the new strategies and the effects that they had seen in student literacy development.

I met with the principal, reading specialist, and primary teachers during grade level meetings to discuss the information gathered from the walk-throughs and to get their feedback about the effects of the newly implemented strategies on the reading progress of our targeted students.

Problem Analysis

As data were further analyzed, the demographics of the students performing below grade level were examined to see whether patterns existed. As evidenced by Figure 2, there is a higher percentage of boys than girls who scored below grade level. As far as the other categories are concerned, no gaps of 10% or more are apparent. It was because of this lack of gaps that it was decided to examine classroom practice as a relevant factor in student learning in reading.

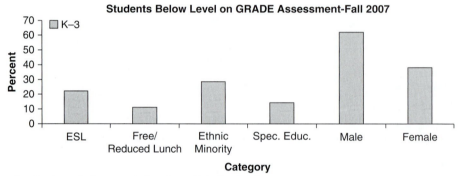

Figure 2. Students below grade level on GRADE—Grades K–3.

Research Results and Conclusions

Data disaggregated by depth of knowledge (Figure 3) show that the majority of instruction (70%) was at the DOK 3 (Applied Learning) level and DOK 2 (Skills, Concepts, and Basic Reasoning) levels. This evidences strong use of strategies by teachers that require higher-level thinking and application of learning by students.

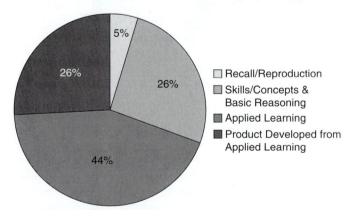

Figure 3. Melody Lane Elementary—Depth of knowledge of learning activities in primary reading classes from walk-through observations (20 teachers, 80 observations).

Almost all student work (98%) in these classrooms (Figure 4) was current, congruent with the Kentucky Program of Studies (POS) and Core Content 4.1, had an appropriate Core Content label displayed by the work, and was of high quality. The classroom environments speak strongly to the importance of learning to read and working at high levels of rigor. This looks to be an area of instructional strength throughout the primary program at MLE.

Example 3 of a Complete Action Research Report   **167**

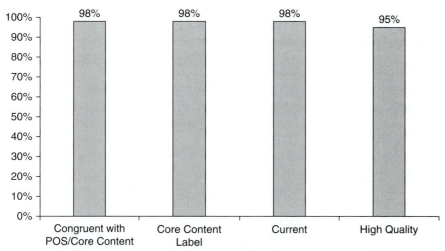

Figure 4. **Melody Lane Elementary—Posted student work in primary reading classrooms from 5-minute walk-through observations, October through mid-November, 20 K–3 teachers, and a total of 80 observations.**

In the area of outcomes presented in the classrooms (Figure 5), the data were more diverse. Almost all teachers had Ice Cream Cone Reading Objectives, Core Content Power Verbs, and Reading Strategy posters on the walls. This is evidence that teachers are planning collaboratively and promoting consistency in instruction across the primary grades to help students learn at high levels and to produce written pieces and products that are pertinent to high achievement and are of superior quality. All of these factors contribute to increased skill acquisition in reading. The majority of classroom teachers posted daily objectives as well. This affords students structure and preparation for the day's learning activities. Observed to a lesser level in classrooms were daily goals shared orally (33%) and in written form (15%).

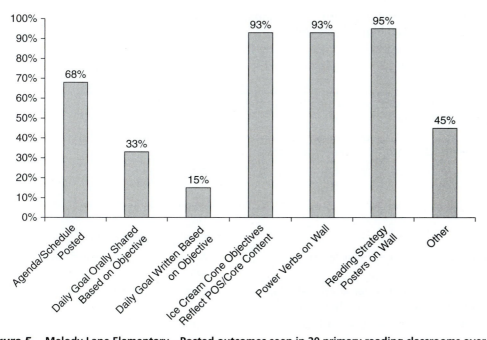

Figure 5. **Melody Lane Elementary—Posted outcomes seen in 20 primary reading classrooms over 80 walk-throughs over 6 weeks.**

Teacher feedback observed (Figure 6) showed that almost every classroom teacher employed clear, positive, and specific feedback to students during the lesson and that half of the teachers also modeled correct responses for students during instruction. Just a few examples of student revisions being required as part of the lesson were recorded.

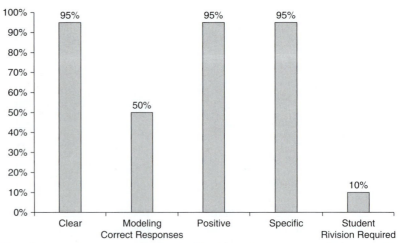

Figure 6.   **Melody Lane Elementary—Teacher feedback in primary reading classrooms observed during walk-throughs (20 teachers, 80 observations).**

On the basis of the literature review completed, a survey of teaching strategies employed in the classroom was conducted. From this survey (Table 2), we found that many of the strategies discussed in the literature review were indeed in use, as well as a wide variety of other successful strategies.

Table 2
Melody Lane Elementary—Reading Instructional Strategies to Assist Struggling Readers in the Primary Grades (Gathered from a Survey Completed by 15 Primary Teachers)

	Strategies specifically discussed in literature are in bold font	
Reading Strand	**Grades K–1**	**Grades 2–3**
Phonemic Awareness	Elkonin boxes to help segment words into sounds—2	**Alliteration poetry**
	Sound and picture boxes (used to identify the sounds that students hear when looking at a picture)	Beginning and ending sounds spelling words—phonemes
	Slide letters down a slide blend. Use a fly swatter to swat individual sounds before blending.	Elkonin boxes
	Tapping sticks	Onset/rhyme word wall activities
Phonics	**Posters we ordered for on-demand writing lessons help children to look for the sound.**	**Word wall wizards**
	Hands-on games (file folder, teacher-made) and centers to help students match and read sounds and words	Analogies—context clues
	Spin three spinners three times and write down if a word is created.	Sort by patterns.
	Ghost writing—hold up picture and write vowel that is in the picture.	Word blending activities
	Caterpillar game	SCRATCH—blend game
	Letter and word match—beginning, middle, end sound	Making words—word sorts; vowels/digraphs/blends
Vocabulary	**Vocabulary word walls—individual word walls for phonics and theme topics (i.e., word families)**	**Word meaning charts**
	Word wall charts and on-the-back activities	Alpha boxes
	Word wall words hanging from ceiling—pull down and let go if you know the word.	**Weekly word wizards**
	New words found in literature are taped to the ceiling.	Sentence completion
	High frequency word study in poems (daily)	**Word of the day—content vocabulary**
	"fancy word" charades	Vocabulary—look up definitions
		Open-response questions

(continued)

Example 3 of a Complete Action Research Report   **169**

Table 2
(Continued)

Reading Strand	Grades K–1	Grades 2–3
Comprehension	Character sketches	Timelines (sequencing)
	Drawing connection activities: text to self	Reading response journals
	Text to world	Story maps and webs
	Ribbons given on book bags for passed reading counts test	Comic strip sequencing
	Sequencing stories through pictures	**Venn diagrams—compare and contrast**
	Gift-wrapping books—peel a small piece of paper at each turn—predicting what the book is about by the cover, a small piece at a time.	**Sequencing activities—making connections sheets**
	Character traits—put on masks, and describe characters by what they look like.	**Open-response questions**
Fluency	**Poetry notebooks**	**Word wizards**
	Tape recording students—read over multiple days to hear progress in fluency and expression.	**Small group prosody evaluation**
	Choral reading—daily poems	**Reading theaters**
	Reading into karaoke machine	**Re-reading a whole group story into a "fluency phone"**
	Role model "robot" reading vs. reading with prosody, "like a flowing river."	**Repeated reading on tape recorder**
	Great Leaps	**Great Leaps fluency program**
		Timed assessments and reading rate accuracy and speed

Recommendations

Based on the findings of this study and the professional literature pertaining to effective literacy instruction, the following recommendations are made to help bring all primary-level students at Melody Lane Elementary to proficiency in reading:

1. Continue implementation of research-based strategies to promote literacy. The learning objective and success criteria (how I show what I know) need to be visually displayed for every lesson. Having students read this display aloud and discussing what it means will help children of all learning styles to be able to understand it. There might be an objective posted that describes several lessons, or there may be different goals for different groups—it just needs to be made clear to the students. It is also advisable to put up the objective and have the children help design the success criteria and/or activity that will show that they have learned. (Clarke, 2001)

2. Assess often. Revisit targets. Let students see growth in their own understanding through continuing the following successful practices (Hobson, 1997):

   a. Keep learning targets central to all assessment. Search for evidence of understanding of target content in all aspects of classroom activity.

   b. Chart individual student progress toward each of the content targets instead of through undifferentiated scores (such as a percentage or letter grade).

   c. Design formal cumulative assessment with attention to the target understanding implicit in each individual question.

   d. Use a variety of assessment forms (multiple choice questions, oral questions, classroom discussion, journaling or other writing, or student activities).

3. Teach the reading strategies through the following processes:

a. Modeling—clearly demonstrating with explicit language

b. Scaffolding—supporting the child, doing it with him

c. Prompting—saying something that will remind the child to try the strategy or behavior

d. Backing off—letting your supports fade away, dismantling your scaffolds, so that the child takes more responsibility for initiating the strategy

e. Reinforcing—naming the strategy or behavior that the child used, praising it, and showing her how it worked in this instance. (Johnson, 2006)

Example 3 of a Complete Action Research Report **171**

References

Arthaud, T. J., & Goracke, T. (2006, March). Implementing a structured story web and outline strategy to assist struggling readers. *The Reading Teacher, 59*(6), 581–586.

Black, P., & Wiliam, D. (October 1998). Inside the black box: Raising standards through classroom assessment. *Phi Delta Kappan*, 80, 139–148.

Brownell, M. T., & Walther-Thomas, C. (November, 2000). An interview with—Dr. Michael Pressley. *Intervention in School and Clinic, 36*(2), 105–108.

Clarke, S. (2005). *Formative assessment in action: Weaving the elements together.* London, UK: Hodder Murray.

Clarke, S. (2001). *Unlocking formative assessment.* London, UK: Hodder and Stoughton.

Highland Learning and Teaching Toolkit. (n.d.) *Formative assessment.* Retrieved September 7, 2007, from http://www.highlandschools-virtualib.org.us/ltt/inclusive-enjoyable/formative.htm

Guskey, T. R. (2003, February). How classroom assessments improve learning. *Educational Leadership, 60*(5), 6–11.

Hettinger, H. R., & Knapp, N. F. (2001, Spring). Lessons from j.p.: Supporting underachieving readers in the elementary classroom. *The Reading Teacher, 55*(1), 26–29.

Hiebert, E. H., Skalitzky, K., & Tesnar, K. A. (1998). *Every child a reader: Companion readings: Selections from the international reading association publication the reading teacher.* Ann Arbor, MI: Center for the Improvement of Early Reading Achievement.

Hobson, E. H. (1997, Novermber–December). Forms and functions of formative assessment. *The Clearing House*, 71, 68–70.

Johnson, P. (2006). *One child at a time: Making the most of your time with struggling readers K–6.* Portland, ME: Stenhouse.

Kelly, C., & Campbell, L. (n.d.). Helping struggling readers. *New Horizons for Learning.* Retrieved September 9, 2007, from http://www.newhorizons.org///teaching/kelly.htm

Stiggins, R. J., Arter, J. A., Chappuis, J., & Chappuis, S. (2006). *Classroom assessment for student learning: Doing it right—Using it well.* Portland, OR: Educational Testing Service.

Tam, K. Y., Heward, W. L., Heng, M. A. (2006). A reading instruction intervention program for English-language learners who are struggling readers. *The Journal of Special Education, 40*(2), 79–93.

Walker, B. J. (2005, April). Thinking aloud: Struggling readers often require more than a model. *The Reading Teacher, 58*(7), 688–692.

Wood, M. (2005). Progress with pleasure: Success with struggling beginning readers. *The New England Reading Association Journal, 41*(2), 30–36.

Note. **Adapted from action research by Kari Kirchner, Elementary School Principal. Used with permission.**

EXAMPLE 4 OF A COMPLETE ACTION RESEARCH REPORT

The Sophomore Coaching Initiative

The instructional leader promotes the success of all students by sustaining a school culture and instructional program conducive to student learning (Council of Chief State School Officers [CCSSO], 1996). Essential to maintaining a culture that supports student learning is the knowledge of the characteristics of a school's student population. Examination of students' needs provides administrators and educators with data by which instructional strategies may be tailored to suit the needs of an individual school. The use of data can have an enormous impact in school reform efforts by helping schools identify how to improve school processes and maximize student learning (Bernhardt, 2004, p. 3).

Data can also be used to identify problems or barriers that may be limiting students' access to the curriculum. Identifying a problem is the first step toward nurturing a school culture that supports the learning of all of its students. Once barriers have been identified, administrators must identify research-based interventions, monitor their subsequent implementation, collect additional data to evaluate the effectiveness of the intervention, and make adjustments as needed along the way. Such actions ensure productivity and foster a school culture that supports the continuous improvement of the learning organization.

This action research project analyzed the achievement gap in math and reading scores for students at Belmont High School (BHS) and the effectiveness of a new initiative known as "Sophomore Coaching." In the previous Comprehensive School Improvement Plan (CSIP), BHS affirmed its intent to identify and implement initiatives aimed at addressing gap-reduction targets, as mandated by state Senate Bill 168 (KRS 158). The Sophomore Coaching initiative was created to support targeted "gap groups" in their transition from the 10th to the 11th grade. During the 2009–2010 school year, all students in General Sophomore English and Practical Statistics classes received 15–20 minutes of individual or small-group tutoring from a teacher, in addition to instruction from their regular classroom teachers. All teachers at BHS gave 15–20 minutes of their planning time each day that the class met to work with each student in these designated classes. To monitor the effectiveness of this program, school leaders intended to use student retention data as a short-term measure of success. School leaders predicted that as retention rates decreased, nonacademic indicators such as attendance, drop-out rates, and successful transitions into adult life would improve as well.

Research Questions

The primary research question was *How effective is the Sophomore Coaching Initiative in closing the achievement gap in reading and math scores at Belmont High School?* Subquestions that helped answer the primary question included these:

1. What are the current data on the achievement gap in reading and math at the sophomore level for all disaggregated groups?

2. Does the achievement gap in reading and math show any improvement over the course of the semester after the implementation of Sophomore Coaching?

3. What teaching strategies seem most effective in improving the achievement gap in reading and math?

Example 4 of a Complete Action Research Report   **173**

Rationale

The rationale for this study is the necessity of closing the achievement gap, as required by KRS 158 and the federal No Child Left Behind (NCLB) Act. Specifically, KRS 158 identifies and describes the importance of diagnosis and intervention in properly addressing student achievement gaps in reading and math. Both of these subjects are regarded as "gateway skills" necessary for achievement in all other academic areas and for transition to the workplace.

Discrepancies in student achievement are not new phenomena, but rather challenges that educators have been dealing with for over a half-century. Fundamental changes in the education of students who have socioeconomic or other disadvantages can be traced back at least as far as World War II, when soldiers returned from duty and took advantage of the G.I. Bill. Most who graduated were the first in their families to do so, raising career and education expectations for themselves and their descendants. This period also marked the beginning of the larger Civil Rights movement, which was instrumental to the changes that occurred later in education. As a result, improved minority access to K–12 education followed. School desegregation, brought about by the Supreme Court's decision in *Brown v. Board of Education* in 1954, allowed some African American students to attend schools with more material resources and more teachers with educational preparation in their teaching field than was available to them previous to this landmark legislation.

Political efforts to avoid racial integration had the effect of improving African American schools as well. In particular, local school districts poured additional resources into African American schools to provide an incentive for African American students to stay in their segregated schools. The federal Title I and Head Start programs also contributed to the rapid increase in school resources targeted toward young minority students, as did later lawsuits that questioned the constitutionality of inequitable state funding systems. In summary, the decades following World War II can be viewed as a period of increasing exposure of minorities to the resources and academic content that had long been available only to whites.

New social pressures began to develop by the late 1970s and early 1980s, however. Average scores on the SAT were on the decline, and there was widespread belief that schools had lowered academic standards and shifted away from rigorous academic content. It turned out that achievement had probably not declined (Carson et al., 1993; Grissmer et al., 1994), but there were legitimate concerns about the direction of the education system arising from the general social tolerance of the 1970s and the associated creation of "cafeteria-style" schools that allowed students to go their own way. These trends were also related to ongoing efforts to increase equity by making schools friendlier to students who might otherwise drop out. Despite slight gains in minority student achievement data, the public perception was that equity was being achieved by watering down standards for all rather than by raising the bar.

The overall goal of the NCLB Act of 2001 is to close, by the end of the 2013–2014 academic year, "the achievement gap between high- and low-performing children, especially the achievement gap between minority and non-minority students, and between disadvantaged children and their more advantaged peers" (NCLB, 2001, Sec. 1001[3]). Under the federal NCLB mandates, adequate yearly progress (AYP) targets must be set for the entire period from 2002 to 2014 in order to ensure that all students and all schools eventually meet the content and performance standards adopted in their respective states.

The accountability provisions in NCLB clearly refer to two demographic variables underlying the current inequity in public education: economic disadvantage and race/ethnicity. It is obvious that the essence of accountability, according to the NCLB, is accountability for subgroups—particularly, subgroups that have been disadvantaged historically by their low income and minority status.

Review of the Literature

The research and professional literature reveal many strategies for reducing and ultimately eliminating the achievement gap. Though there are no definitive solutions to closing the achievement gap, some schools have been successful in addressing this issue. Embedded in the literature are themes that have proven to be successful in maximizing the achievement of minority students and subsequently narrowing achievement gaps. Those themes include changes in beliefs and attitudes, cultural responsiveness, community involvement, effective classroom instruction, access to resources, and teacher quality.

The importance of beliefs and attitudes of teachers, parents, families, and students has been well documented. Genuine caring conveys a sense of value and worth to a student, which can lead to increased learning (Craig et al., 2002). Teacher expectations of themselves and their students also play a large role in how well students perform.

Learning begins with the learners' frame of reference. Teachers provide their instruction from their personal cultural framework, and students learn from within the context of their own experience. Research emphasizes the importance of honoring students and their heritages (Lynch, 2006). Professional development (PD) for teachers needs to include culturally responsive content and skills.

The literature stresses the importance for schools to utilize support from the community at large. The notion of parental involvement extends beyond attendance at school functions or field trips. When parents encourage learning at home, express high but reasonable expectations, and support their children's education, low-income and minority students get better grades and test scores (Gardner, 2007). The community may also have the capacity to support students through extended educational opportunities for lower-achieving students. Close cooperation between schools, parents, and the community is one of the keys to closing the achievement gap.

Effective instructional strategies are essential to addressing achievement gaps in public schools. Schools can provide greater opportunities for students to learn by offering extended academic time (e.g., all-day kindergarten, before- or after-school classes, summer school), using rigorous and challenging courses as the main curriculum, and expanding access in enriched and varied programs. By exposing minority students to a more rigorous and challenging curriculum, some schools have been successful in tackling achievement gaps (Denbo et al., 2002; Gellar et al, 2006). The "new science of learning" emphasizes the importance of learning with understanding. Such instruction has been shown to dramatically improve the performance of traditionally underachieving students.

Various types of studies have been used to evaluate the effects of increased access to educational resources. Grissmer et al. (2000) provide an extensive review of studies that used experimental, nonexperimental, and trend analyses. They concluded that extra resources have probably had very small positive effect on the average, but that "additional resources have been used most effectively for minority and disadvantaged students" (p. 41). Although there remains disagreement about the need for further increases in overall resources, it appears clear that the additional resources provided in earlier decades to students with disadvantages played an important role in reducing the gap.

Although some of the studies suggest that equality in resources has already been achieved, this is easily disproven through a more careful review of other school quality measures—especially those related to teacher quality. There is strong evidence that minority students are assigned to the least effective teachers, as measured by teacher preparation and experience (Barton 2003). In addition, teachers are more prone to turnover in predominantly black schools (Hanushek, 1996). Thus, it is apparent that the improvement, discussed previously, in equity of content quality may not exist in all classrooms and could be masking inequities in what is actually taught in classrooms, due to the differing skills and knowledge levels of teachers. These findings suggest that attract-

Example 4 of a Complete Action Research Report **175**

ing and retaining effective teachers in low performing schools is critical to reducing the achievement gap.

What is clear from the collection of evidence in this section is that the capacity of schools attended by minority students has increased substantially over the past half-century, and that this has contributed to a reduction in the achievement gap. It is also evident that significant gaps remain. The fact that these gaps are less obvious when education spending, class size, and other common factors are measured indicates only that the problem has evolved rather than declined.

Sophomore Coaching and the Literature

Though no similar programs to the Sophomore Coaching initiative could be found in the literature, there does appear to be a research basis for this initiative. The scaffolded instructional supports that students receive during these Sophomore Coaching sessions are similar to tutorial sessions that have produced positive results in other studies, particularly with African American and Hispanic students (Denbo & Beaulieu, 2002; Gellar & Werner, 2006). One noninstructional effect of this initiative is that students will feel a greater sense of value and, subsequently, feel more connected with the school. The implied effect is that students participating in this initiative will feel as though they are a greater part of the BHS community. Research suggests that sense of community can be beneficial in addressing achievement-gap issues (Gardner, 2007).

Methodology and Research Procedures

This section describes the data collected and analyzed to measure the impact of sophomore coaching. Both quantitative and qualitative data were gathered to address the research questions.

Quantitative Data

Before beginning our data collection, we collaborated with the dean of students and the head principal to get input on the best data available. The literature review was completed to determine available related knowledge from research.

We realized early that our research would be preliminary. Data collection would be confounded by the time frame of the research. It was decided that we would examine state Core Content Test (CCT) scores to determine the existence and scope of the student achievement gap in both math and reading overall. Data were gathered from various state performance reports about BHS.

Then, to narrow the scope of our research, we would focus on data from the Measures of Academic Progress (MAP). The MAP is a standardized instrument used to assess student learning and provide a means of frequent monitoring of student progress. We used the MAP data to determine the student achievement gap in both math (a course called Practical Statistics) and reading (from the general-level Sophomore English). This would be our initial measure of the achievement gap within the comparison group.

Because we are measuring the impact of sophomore coaching on the achievement gap, we decided to use two types of data to determine the impact. Survey data would be used to determine teacher impressions of the effectiveness of sophomore coaching and also to determine whether the students themselves believed that sophomore coaching was making a difference in either student achievement or in developing a sense of belonging to the school. Additionally, student grade reports would be gathered as a proxy for student achievement on standardized tests because standardized testing results would not be available. This research actually constitutes the first stage in an overall analysis of the effectiveness of Sophomore Coaching. Data that will be available in the spring semester will be used to further this research study.

Core content test data were collected from the 2005–2010 school years. Achievement data of BHS students during this time show sizable and persistent achievement gaps when comparing race and income (as measured by free/reduced-price lunch status). Tables 1 and 2 show these gaps based on race. At its narrowest, in 2010, white students scored had a gap of +25 points, or 25%, higher on the reading assessment than African American students. In math, the narrowest gap was 24 points (26%) in 2009—a dramatic deviation from other years (including more recent data from 2010) in which the gap remained near 46% (41 points) higher for white students, although the score for white students had declined by 7 points since 2005. The scores of Hispanic students often fluctuated due to the small sample size.

Table 1
Core Content Test Scores in Reading, by Race

Year	2005	2006	2007	2008	2009	2010
Caucasian	90.72	94.85	86.79	95.06	100.81	102.67
African American	62.67	63.22	62.08	64.55	67.51	78.13
Hispanic		80.38	57.44	81.34	67.66	85.57

Table 2
Core Content Test Scores in Mathematics, by Race

Year	2005	2006	2007	2008	2009	2010
Caucasian	96.26	98.1	96.79	89.42	91.54	89.15
African American	41.96	51.12	50.46	46.38	68	48.39
Hispanic			44.4	54.48	54.11	62.1

Tables 3 and 4 show these gaps based on income. Steady, albeit gradual, gains are evident when comparing reading assessment results between high- and low-income groups. By looking at the achievement gaps in both 2009 and 2010, it can be observed that the gap has fallen to about a 25% difference. Examining the math data, one can see that the gap has closed to its lowest level so far but still remains high at nearly 40%.

Table 3
Core Content Test Scores in Reading, by Free/Reduced Lunch Status

Year	2005	2006	2007	2008	2009	2010
Not Approved	91.16	98.69	89.36	95.17	89.36	104.99
Approved	57.66	59.68	56.11	63.67	71.79	79.86

Table 4
Core Content Test Scores in Mathematics, by Free/Reduced Lunch Status

Year	2005	2006	2007	2008	2009	2010
Not Approved	96.56	96.43	98.24	92.62	92.50	91.16
Approved	48.13	51.78	49.63	40.96	50.15	51.79

MAP (Measures of Academic Progress) data were collected from the end of the 2009–2010 school year in reading and the beginning of the 2010–2011 school year in math. The MAP assessment data do not show the persistent gaps found in the KCCT scores. This is, no doubt, due to the fact that content-area classes from which the subject groups came were already separated from the rest of the student body on the basis of low performance or scheduling preference. Both the General Sophomore English class and the Practical Statistics class are the lowest level available for sophomores. This provides a guide for further research. MAP data must be compared across all student levels to determine whether meaningful progress is being made. Table 5 shows the MAP scores in reading, and Table 6 shows the MAP scores in math. An examination of the scores reveals

Example 4 of a Complete Action Research Report **177**

that the gap between the highest performing group and the lowest performing group in reading amounts to only one standard deviation (12.3, to be exact). In math, the story is essentially the same. The difference between the highest and lowest performing group is less than one standard deviation of 11.6.

Table 5
MAP Results in Reading for General Sophomore English

Year	2010
Caucasian	224
African American	216
Hispanic	212
Approved F/R Lunch	215
Not Approved F/R Lunch	223

Table 6
MAP Results in Math for Students in Practical Statistics

Year	2010
Caucasian	227
African American	220
Hispanic	223
Approved F/R Lunch	222
Not Approved F/R Lunch	224

Despite the closeness of the initial data points, preliminary data after sophomore coaching occurred indicate a small measure of success. The data among this group in these classes have closed even more. Of course, data analysis will need to be conducted in the future to see how students from these classes compare with the rest of the student body. Table 7 and Table 8 show the class averages from these same groups as of the end of November. In General Sophomore English, the difference between the group with the highest and lowest class grades amounted to only 4 percentage points. The standard deviation among this group was 12.6 percentage points, indicating a very narrow gap—one that has, in fact, narrowed, if only slightly, from an already slight figure from the MAP data. Similar results are found in the math data. The difference between the highest and lowest groups in terms of class grade is just under 4 percentage points, with a standard deviation of 11.5 percentage points.

Table 7
Student Grade Averages in Reading in General Sophomore English

Year	2010
Caucasian	79.6
African American	76.7
Hispanic	75.9
Approved F/R Lunch	77.4
Not Approved F/R Lunch	79.0

Table 8
Student Grade Averages in Practical Statistics

Year	2010
Caucasian	77.5
African American	73.7
Hispanic	78.0
Approved F/R Lunch	75.2
Not Approved F/R Lunch	76.7

Qualitative Data

In addition to the compiled data discussed previously, we collected the opinions of participants in the Sophomore Coaching initiative. Survey data were collected from students, coaches (teachers doing the coaching), and host teachers (teachers in the content area being coached). Each survey consisted of six statements that respondents were asked to rate as follows: *strongly disagree, disagree, no opinion, agree,* or *strongly disagree.* Ratings were then converted to a numerical scale for the benefit of this report. The lowest rating, *strongly disagree,* corresponds to a score of 1, and the highest rating, *strongly agree,* corresponded to a score of 5. Table 9 shows the survey questions and results from the perspective of the students in general-level Sophomore English. Table 10 shows the survey questions and results from the perspective of students in Practical Statistics.

Table 9
Student Survey Results in General Sophomore English

Survey Questions	Average Score
I enjoy working with my sophomore coach.	4.0
I feel more comfortable contributing to discussions when in my small groups.	3.9
I feel more comfortable asking questions in my small group.	3.9
The activities I do with my coaching mentor help with my understanding of this class.	3.5
Sophomore coaching has helped me feel more confident in this class.	3.4
Sophomore coaching makes me feel valued at school.	3.3

Table 10
Student Survey Results in Practical Statistics

Survey Questions	Average Score
I enjoy working with my sophomore coach.	3.7
I feel more comfortable asking questions in my small group.	3.7
The activities I do with my coaching mentor help with my understanding of this class.	3.6
I feel more comfortable contributing to discussions when in my small group.	3.5
Sophomore coaching has helped me feel more confident in this class.	3.5
Sophomore coaching makes me feel valued at school.	3.4

Several conclusions can be reached from an examination of the data. Students appear to have more positive feelings about coaching in the English class than in the Practical Statistics class. Overall, the feelings are generally positive, but not overwhelmingly so. Also, those questions than deal with learning content (first and fifth) and sense of worth (sixth) have the lowest positive outcome. The greatest benefit, according to these surveys, seems to be that students feel freer to participate.

Tables 11 and 12 show the survey results from the perspective of the coaches in English and Practical Statistics, respectively. Coaches come from the entire staff, with the exception of those teachers in the freshman academy due to the fact they already have additional duties. The surveys show a similar pattern to those of the students. In general,

Example 4 of a Complete Action Research Report **179**

coaches were positive, but least positive on the question involving student achievement (first) and a sense of worth (sixth). Coaches were most positive on questions involving student participation.

Table 11
Coach Survey Results in General Sophomore English

Survey Questions	Average Score
Students are engaged during coaching sessions.	4.1
Students feel more comfortable asking questions when they are in small groups.	4.1
I feel comfortable working with students in a class outside of my content area.	3.3
Sophomore Coaching makes students feel valued at school.	3.3
Sophomore Coaching allows me to develop meaningful relationships with sophomores.	3.0
Sophomore Coaching lessons effectively help students to be successful in this class.	2.9

Table 12
Coach Survey Results in Practical Statistics

Survey Questions	Average Score
I feel comfortable working with students in a class outside my content area.	4.1
Students feel more comfortable asking questions when they are in small groups.	3.9
Sophomore Coaching lessons effectively help students to be successful in this class.	3.7
Sophomore Coaching allows me to develop meaningful relationships with sophomores.	3.7
Students are engaged during coaching sessions.	3.6
Sophomore Coaching makes students feel valued at school.	3.2

Finally, the remaining two tables reveal the attitudes of the host teachers to the Sophomore Coaching initiative. Table 13 and Table 14 detailed opinions of the host teachers in General Sophomore English. Once again, the general pattern holds true and reveals agreement between the three groups surveyed. Although generally positive, host teachers were least likely to have favorable perceptions of either the academic impact or the affective impact of the initiative. Respondents were most positive regarding student participation.

Table 13
Host Teacher Survey Results in General Sophomore English

Survey Questions	Average Score
Coaches are developing meaningful relationships with sophomore students.	4.3
Students are engaged during coaching sessions.	4.2
My coaches are adequately prepared when they come to my class.	4.0
Sophomore Coaching lessons effectively help students to be successful in my class.	3.8
Students are more likely to ask questions when working with their Sophomore Coach.	3.6
Sophomore Coaching makes students feel valued at Belmont High School.	3.6

Table 14	
Host Teacher Survey Results in Practical Statistics	
Survey Questions	**Average Score**
My coaches are adequately prepared when they come to my class.	4.7
Students are more likely to ask questions when working with their Sophomore Coach.	4.3
Coaches are developing meaningful relationships with sophomore students.	4.3
Sophomore Coaching makes students feel valued at school.	3.7
Students are engaged during coaching sessions.	3.3
Sophomore Coaching lessons effectively help students to be successful in my class.	3.3

Recommendations

Based on the quantitative findings of this research study, the results are inconclusive. Although small gains were evident in student assessment data, we feel that results will be more compelling over time. What is apparent, however, is that systematic monitoring and revision of this initiative is essential to the program's overall effectiveness. Subsequently, many of our recommendations focus on strategies for monitoring the success of the initiative. As mentioned in our report, this study provides the groundwork from which future instructional leaders may continue to build.

Qualitative data suggest that structural and motivational changes to the initiative may be beneficial. Therefore, some recommendations center on ways in which Sophomore Coaching may be improved.

1. Student assessment data should continually be used to monitor current achievement gaps and the impact that the Sophomore Coaching initiative has in closing those gaps.

2. Student retention data may be a strong indicator toward the success of this initiative. In theory, fewer students should fail General Sophomore English and Practical Statistics if this program is working. Therefore, close monitoring of these data is essential toward the overall monitoring process.

3. Committees armed with the tasks of improving the instruction curriculum for Sophomore Coaching sessions need to be organized and become active. Lessons should be rigorous and should maximize student engagement. Students reported feeling more comfortable participating in small groups; therefore, lessons should accommodate methods that encourage discussion and hands-on application of the content.

4. Professional development needs to be created to train Sophomore Coaches. PD should focus on familiarizing teachers with the content and lessons, but also should inform teachers of strategies for interacting with students in a small-group basis. It should not be assumed that teachers automatically know how to do this. The ultimate success of the program may hinge on the educators' ability to make a connection with the students with whom they are working.

5. A committee of effective Sophomore Coaches should be created to address issues associated with teacher apathy. Strategies for motivating Sophomore Coaches need to be further explored and implemented according to need.

Example 4 of a Complete Action Research Report **181**

References

Barton, P. (2003). *Parsing the achievement gap.* Princeton, NJ: Educational Testing Service.

Bernhardt, V. L. (2004). *Data analysis for continuous schoolwide improvement.* Larchmont, NY: Eye on Education.

Carson, C., Huelskamp, R., & Woodall, T. (1993). Perspectives on education in America. *The Journal of Educational Research 86,* 259–310.

Craig, J., & Haycock, K. (2002, August). Closing the gap. *School Administrator, 7,* 16–21.

Council of Chief State School Officers. (1996). *Interstate School Leaders Licensure Consortium standards for school leaders.* Washington, DC: Author.

Denbo, S. J., Beaulieu, L. M. (2002). *Improving schools for African American students: A reader for educational leaders.* Springfield, IL: C. C. Thomas.

Gardner, D. (2007, March 1). Confronting the achievement gap. *Phi Delta Kappan, 88*(7), 542. (ERIC Document Reproduction Service No. EJ758188)

Geller, J., & Werner, M. (2006, September 1). *Latino students in our public schools: A closer look.* Mankato, MN: Center for Rural Policy and Development. (ERIC Document Reproduction Service No. ED494114.)

Grissmer, D., Flanagan, A., Kawata, J., & Williamson, S. (2000). *Improving student achievement: What state NAEP test scores tell us.* Santa Monica, CA: The Rand Corporation.

Grissmer, D., Kirby, S., Berends, M., & Williamson, S. (1994). *Student achievement and the changing American family.* Report RB-8009. Santa Monica, CA: The Rand Corporation.

Hanushek, E. (1996). A more complete picture of school resource policies. *Review of Educational Research 66*(3), 397–409.

Lynch, M. (2006). *Closing the racial academic achievement gap.* Chicago: African American Images.

No Child Left Behind Act of 2001. (2002). Public Law 107-110, 115 STAT. 1425.

Senate Bill 168. (2002). Kentucky Revised Statute (KRS) 158.649. Kentucky Legislative Research Commission, Frankfort, KY. Retrieved September 10, 2007, from http://www.lrc.ky.gov/recarch/02RS/SB168.htm.

Note. Adapted from action research by **Bryan Jacobs, High School Associate Principal, and Richard Royster, High School Associate Principal. Used with permission.**

EXAMPLE 5 OF A COMPLETE ACTION RESEARCH REPORT

An Analysis of Mathematics Performance of Jewell High School Students

Student performance in mathematics at Jewell High School has declined or stagnated over time. Even as the academic index of the school increased, the mathematics index declined or remained essentially the same.

According to the state accountability testing system, schools are to show continuing success in all of the academic areas in order to reach proficiency by 2014. Although the high school has continued to show progress overall, as substantiated by their academic index score, the achievement index in mathematics has lagged behind the school's academic index and all other content areas.

The research question for this study is as follows: How can the decline and stagnation of mathematics scores be reversed so that these scores reflect the overall academic index of the school? In order to better understand the underlying causes for the decline and stagnation of the mathematics index, the following subarea questions were formulated: (a) Is the stagnation or decline in student performance on the mathematics component of the state core content test a general trend, or does it occur only in certain subgroups of students? (b) Does the type of entry-level course at the high school relate to student performance? (c) Do the students perceive that they are having difficulty learning mathematics? (d) What strands of mathematics content cause the greatest difficulty for student performance? (e) Have student performance levels increased from the eighth to 11th grade? (f) What strategies have been effective for improving mathematics achievement at the secondary level?

This study was a collaboration of the regional rural systemic initiative, the regional teacher partner (RTP) assigned to facilitate mathematics improvement at Jewell High School, the mathematics faculty, and members of the mathematics leadership team (principal, assistant principal, district instructional supervisor, district assessment coordinator, special education mathematics teacher, parent, two mathematics faculty members, and the regional teacher partner). The purpose of the study was to examine the mathematics performance of the 2003 graduating class over a 4-year period to identify patterns that might explain the lag in mathematics performance over the past 4 years.

Data examined for this study came from the state department of education, student records, and school-administered questionnaires. The types of data collected and analyzed were (a) state accountability testing system core content test, (b) course-taking patterns, and (c) student perceptions. From the information that emerged from the data and the literature review, conclusions and recommendations were developed that address the overarching problem.

Background of the Problem

Jewell High School is located in a rural setting, but with transportation corridors that link it to nearby cities. According to 2000 U.S. Census data, 50% of the workers commute to work, and their average travel time is 28 minutes, which means that these individuals are most likely employed out of county. Menaska County has a large low-income population. The median household income is $23,475. Approximately 45% of the population is employed in occupations such as farming, construction, transportation, and manufacturing. The county has a small professional community that is typical of any county seat. Of those in the population who are 25 years of age and over, 8% have a bachelor's or graduate degree.

Example 5 of a Complete Action Research Report **183**

The district and school have made a concerted effort to raise academic achievement in all content areas. This is evident in their involvement in a variety of initiatives on the state, regional, and federal level that have assisted the school and district with development of an improvement infrastructure—for example, Gear-up, Effective Schools, Southern Regional Education Board (SREB), the National Alliance for Restructuring Education, Appalachian Rural Systemic Initiative (ARSI), Appalachian Math and Science Partnership (AMSP), and Appalachian Collaborative Center for Learning Assessment and Instruction in Mathematics (ACCLAIM). With this infrastructure in place, the school and district are poised to continue to improve academic achievement.

As illustrated in Table 1 and Figure 1, mathematics core content test results are consistently below the overall school academic index.

Table 1
Jewell High School Mathematics and Academic Indices

	1999	2000	2001	2002
Mathematics index	48.6	59.2	59.9	52.2
School total academic index	59.8	62.5	62.4	58.5

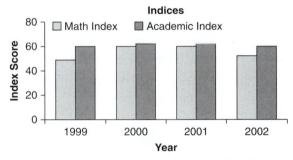

Figure 1. **Mathematics and academic indices for 4 years at Jewell High School.**

If the school is to meet proficiency by 2014, the mathematics scores need to increase significantly. Therefore, the research question for this study is as follows: How can the decline and stagnation of mathematics scores be reversed so that the scores reflect the overall academic index of the school?

Research Procedures and Problem Analysis

The decline and stagnation of scores could be occurring for very different reasons. These reasons were investigated so that recommendations for improvement could be formulated. Six subquestions were developed, as indicated in the introduction, to guide the research.

The steps for data collection and analysis utilized in this study to answer the subquestions included examining the eighth grade core content test scores and the 11th grade core content test scores to identify changes in performance levels. The 11th grade results were analyzed to determine how subgroups performed, which strands were the strongest, and how the math scores compared with the other content areas. A survey was administered to identify student attitudes about mathematics. The student records were examined to document the course-taking patterns of this class through the junior year. The data were examined to identify trends that existed and from those trends to make recommendation to strengthen the mathematics program on the basis of recognized best practices.

Trends and Subgroups

All subgroups are performing at about the same level. Except for the gifted and talented, all other subgroups have a large percentage of students scoring novice, and too small a percentage of students scoring proficient and distinguished. As shown in Table 2 and Figures 2 and 3, all groups need to increase their performance level. Even gifted and talented need to reduce the percent of students scoring novice.

Table 2
Demographic Student Subgroup Performance for 2002 and 2003

Subgroups	2002		2003	
	% Novice	% Proficient/ Distinguished	% Novice	% Proficient/ Distinguished
Female	47	17	24	29
Male	44	24	45	20
Extended school service	35	9	49	0
Gifted and talented	4	65	4	78
Free/reduced lunch (approved)	64	7	37	14
Not free/reduced lunch	30	20	35	32
Career and technical education	49	19	38	24
No disability	42	22	32	26
Disability			76	0

Lack of student success in math could be attributed to one of several factors: "poor instruction, insufficient number of math courses, unintelligible textbooks, or misinformation about math and about who should do well in math" (Crawford, as cited in Furner & Berman, 2003, p. 171).

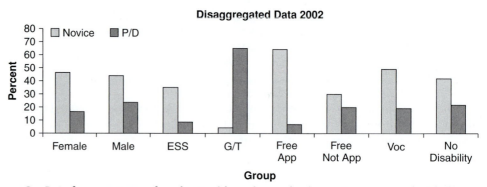

Figure 2. Data for percentage of students with novice academic progress compared with the percentage achieving proficient and distinguished levels, disaggregated by student subgroups.

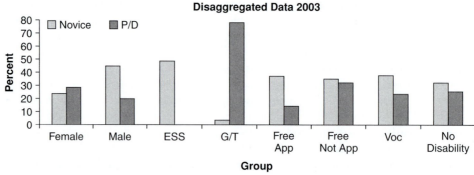

Figure 3. Data for percentage of students with novice academic progress compared with the percentage achieving proficient and distinguished levels, disaggregated by student subgroups.

According to the publication *Improving Student Achievement in Mathematics* (Educational Research Service [ERS], 1999), in order to improve student achievement and understanding, it is important for teachers to be aware of how students construct knowledge and the methods by which they solve problems. Use of this knowledge should be taken into consideration as teachers plan for and teach mathematics to students. Teaching for meaning and assisting students with construction of meaning has been shown to have a positive effect on student learning, student retention, and the ability of students to apply what they have learned in new situations.

Example 5 of a Complete Action Research Report   **185**

Entry-Level Courses

Freshman entering Jewell High School had four mathematics courses in which they could enroll: Basic Math, Integrated I, Algebra I, and Data and Measurement. Enrollment in these courses as a freshman dictated the remainder of their high school mathematics course requirements and often was a predictor of their performance as juniors on the state core content test. Students enrolled in Basic Math were all special education students in a self-contained classroom. Integrated I students were students who were perceived to need remediation. Students taking Algebra I, the majority of freshmen, were considered to be "your average student." Students who were labeled as mathematically talented were enrolled in Data and Measurement. Additionally, these were students who received an Algebra I credit for work done in the eighth grade. However, upon further investigation, it was evident that a formal Algebra I course following the Program of Studies was not taught. Teachers reported that the majority of these students did not have the background necessary to be successful in Algebra II.

It is evident from Table 3 and Figure 4 that most students who began their high school career enrolled in Basic Math or Integrated I scored novice on the mathematics core content test. Students in a portion of the freshman class were deemed so mathematically able that they could skip Algebra I and begin their high school career in Data and Measurement. However, only 56% of these students scored proficient or distinguished, and 4% scored novice, as juniors on the core content test.

Table 3
Performance Level of Class of 2003 Compared with the Freshman Mathematics Course

Course	Basic Math	Integrated I	Algebra 1	Data and Measurement
% P/D	0	3	17	56
% Novice	100	72	41	4

Note. **Only four students from the 2003 junior class took Basic Math as their freshman course.**

According to the mathematics core content test results for the class of 2003, tracking students through this course-taking pattern does not appear to assist students with reaching mathematics proficiency. Oakes (as cited in National Center for Research in Mathematical Sciences Education, 1994) found that students in lower level courses often do not have the opportunity to encounter the same content as students in high tracks. Also, because of staff perceptions, students in lower level courses were not receiving the same quality mathematics program. This is supported by the findings of Nathan and Koedinger (2000), who report that the instructional practices that teachers choose to use with students is directly influenced by the teachers' beliefs about learning and students' ability. Furthermore, teachers generally reported that when planning for instruction, the most important factor they take into consideration is the data they had on their students (Borko & Shavelson, as cited in Nathan & Koedinger, 2000).

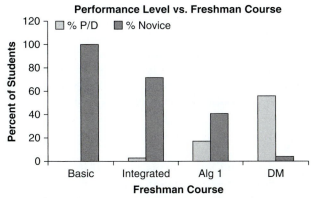

Figure 4. Eleventh grade mathematics progress level on the mathematics core content test is compared with the freshman mathematics course completed. Only four students took Basic Math from the 2003 eleventh grade mathematics students; all of them scored Novice.

Students' Perceptions

As seen in Table 4 and Figure 5, data obtained from a student survey show that students like mathematics the least of any of the academic areas.

Table 4 *How Well Do You Like the Following Courses?*				
Course	Social Studies	Language Arts	Math	Science
Female	1.30	1.02	0.61	0.91
Male	1.11	0.57	0.73	0.92
All	1.20	0.79	0.67	0.92
2 = A Lot				

Note. 0 = Don't like, 1 = Like somewhat, and 2 = Like a lot.

It can be inferred from these data and the lagging mathematics scores that students are presented mathematics instruction that is not reaching a majority of students. This is supported by the core content test results in 2002 and 2003. If we are to improve student performance, then programmatic changes need to be made to improve student perception toward mathematics and students' ability to do mathematics.

One way to change student perception can be through improvement of the methods used in instruction. The methods that teachers choose to use in instruction appear to play a key role in how students feel about mathematics (Jackson & Leffingwell, as cited in Furner & Berman, 2003).

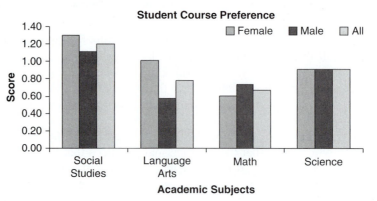

Figure 5.   Student course preferences reported on student survey.

Teachers at Jewell High School may have to work with the middle school to identify and implement ways to combat student fear of mathematics. A study conducted by Bower (2001) found that around the age of 12, students who fear or feel threatened by mathematics begin to avoid math classes and tend not to do well in the classes that they do take. These students also are the ones who typically score poorly on math achievement tests. This idea is further supported by Kober (n.d.), who reports that students achieve poorly if they fear, dislike, or doubt their mathematics ability.

Mathematics Strands

Looking at the core content test data, as reported in Table 5 and Figure 6, we see that there appears to be little difference in performance among the different strands of the mathematics core content. Therefore, the school needs to consider adoption of instruction and assessment strategies that strengthen all subdomain areas of mathematics.

Example 5 of a Complete Action Research Report   **187**

Table 5
Differences in Student Performance in Mathematics Strands of Core Content Tests

	2002 Strands		2003 Strands	
	School	State	School	State
Number/Comp	1.5	1.8	1.6	1.7
Geometry/Measurement	1.4	1.6	1.4	1.5
Probability/Statistics	1.5	1.7	1.6	1.7
Algebraic Ideas	1.5	1.7	1.5	1.6

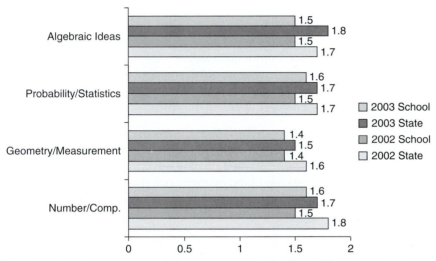

Figure 6.   The mathematics student performance at Jewell High School for 2002 and 2003 on the core content strands is compared with statewide student performance on these mathematics strands.

The data in Figure 7 indicate that most students do not increase their performance level on the state core competency test evaluation from the eighth grade to the 11th grade. Of the total students tested in the class of 2003, approximately 60 did not advance performance levels from the time they were tested in eighth grade to the time they were tested in 11th grade. Approximately 43 students went down at least one performance level. This suggests that the instruction and assessment at Jewell High School is not helping students to increase their performance level on the state core competency test.

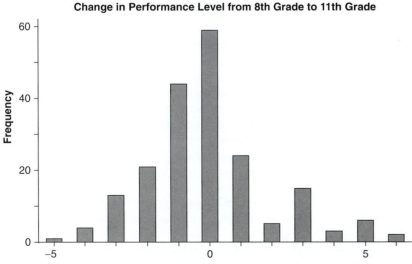

Figure 7.   This scale uses 0 as the center to show frequency of decreases (negative changes to the left of 0 on the linear scale), as well as increases (to the right of 0 on the scale).

Stakeholder Input for the Analysis

As was stated in the introduction, this study was a collaboration among the regional rural systemic initiative, the regional teacher partner assigned to facilitate mathematics improvement at Jewell High School, the mathematics faculty, and members of the mathematics leadership team (principal, assistant principal, district instructional supervisor, district assessment coordinator, special education mathematics teacher, parent, two mathematics faculty, and the regional teacher partner). Once the data were collected and the research for this study completed, the mathematics faculty and the regional teacher partner reviewed the results and made recommendations for improvement to the leadership team. The leadership team then reviewed the data, the research, and the recommendations from the mathematics faculty. They then selected the areas that they felt needed immediate attention and began to identify ways to change policy and implement improved practices.

Recommendations

The recommendations for improving student performance in mathematics come through the leadership team from recommendations made by the mathematics faculty. The recommendations are based on an analysis of state accountability test system data, student surveys, and student records. They are as follows:

1. All incoming freshman will take Algebra I, with the exception of some students with severe mental handicaps. Algebra I credit will no longer be given at the eighth grade. Instead, middle school students will receive a broad, integrated curriculum that focuses equally on strands of the mathematics core content as recommended in the *Principal and Standards for School Mathematics* (NCTM, 2000).

2. A variety of methods of instruction should be examined and incorporated into the mathematics program. As advocated by the NCTM Standards (2000), mathematics instruction should decrease the time spent on paper-and-pencil algorithms without a context, and increase and emphasize the time spent on making meaning and connections among concepts and applying problem-solving strategies to real-world situations. In order for students to be assisted with application of learning and understanding of concepts within a context, an intentional effort should be made to incorporate, on a regular basis, a variety of instructional strategies as part of the instructional program. These include, but are not limited to, problem-solving, real-world application, technology, manipulatives, cooperative group and individual work, differentiated instruction, and whole class discussion.

3. According to the publication *Improving Student Achievement in Mathematics* (Educational Research Service [ERS], 1999), to improve student achievement and understanding, it is important for teachers to be aware of how students construct knowledge and the process and methods by which they solve problems. In order for teachers to understand how students at Jewell High School are constructing knowledge, to recognize the methods and processes that students are using to solve problems, and to identify and provide remediation for recurring errors, a more intentional effort should be made to incorporate formative assessment into the instructional program. Alternative forms of summative assessments need to be utilized to determine student conceptualization of mathematics content and to allow students the opportunity to demonstrate their knowledge. Data gleaned from both formative and summative assessments should be applied by teachers when planning for instruction (Educational Research Service [ERS], 1999).

4. Grossnickle, Perry, & Reckzeh (1990) note the importance of developing the student's ability to relate math to real-life requirements. Developing this ability can result in students' having a more positive attitude about mathematics and, thus, improved learning. A plan for relating math learned in school to students' career aspirations should be designed and implemented as a mechanism to improve student attitudes about mathematics at Jewell High School.

Example 5 of a Complete Action Research Report **189**

References

Bower, B. (2001, June). Math fears subtract from memory, learning. *Science News, 159*(26), 405.

Educational Research Service (ERS). (1999). *Improving student achievement in mathematics* (2nd ed.). [Booklet]. Arlington, VA: Author.

Furner, J. M., & Berman, B. T. (2003, Spring). Math anxiety: Overcoming a major obstacle to the improvement of student math performance. *Childhood Education, 79*(3), 170–175.

Grossnickle, F., Perry, L., & Reckzeh, J. (1990). Discovering meanings in elementary school mathematics (8th ed.). Fort Worth, TX: Holt, Rinehart and Winston.

Kentucky Department of Education (KDE). (2002). *Spring 2002 CATS performance report for Jewell High School.* (KDE website). Retrieved from http://www.kde.state.ky.us.

Kentucky Department of Education (KDE). (2003). *Jewell High School Student Data Tool.* Frankfort, KY: Author.

Kentucky Department of Education (KDE). (2003). *Spring 2003 CATS performance report for Jewell High School.* (KDE website). Retrieved from http://www.kde.state.ky.us.

Kober, N. (n.d.). *EDTALK: What we know about mathematics teaching and learning.* Council for Educational Development Research.

Nathan, M. J., & Koedinger, K. R. (2000, March). Teachers' and researchers' beliefs about the development of algebraic reasoning. *Journal for Research in Mathematics Education, 31*(2), 168–190.

National Center for Research in Mathematical Sciences Education (NCRMSE). (1994, Fall). *Equity and mathematics reform.* Retrieved November 4, 2003, from the National Center for Research in Mathematical Sciences Education website: http://www.wcer.wisc.edu/ncisla/publications/

National Council of Teachers of Mathematics (NCTM). (2000). *Principles and standards for school mathematics.* Reston, VA: Author.

United States Census Bureau Data. (2001). *Census data by county.* Retrieved November 28, 2003 from http://factfinder.census.gov

_____

Note. **This example report was adapted from action research by Kim Zeidler-Watters, Director, P–12 Mathematics/Science Outreach. Used with permission.**

EXAMPLE 6 OF A COMPLETE ACTION RESEARCH REPORT

Postsecondary Reading Remediation for High School Graduates

This action research project was initiated because the Council on Postsecondary Education report of students enrolled in reading remediation at the postsecondary level showed that 25% of the graduates of Lancaster County schools take required reading remediation at the postsecondary level. Compared with regional districts with equivalent social economic status (SES) and parental levels of education, our county's profile indicates that our graduates are not achieving predicted levels of competency in postsecondary reading. These graduates are achieving at lower levels in technical reading and in college preparatory reading than students from districts with similar characteristics.

Collection and review of data taken from the Lancaster South High School EPAS reading scores (*Explore* eighth grade, *Plan* 10th grade, and *Act* 11th and 12th grades) assisted in identifying trends and areas of concern leading to postsecondary remediation. Consistent core content test scores in the 80s indicate that the core curriculum is being addressed in classroom instruction. According to Lancaster County School Superintendent, to reach a score of 100 (proficiency) will require instruction focused on critical evaluation. Further analysis of CATS scores and achievement among student subpopulations provided additional understandings necessary for formulating solution options. Failure to reach No Child Left Behind benchmarks for students identified with special needs is a genuine concern. Likewise, the persistent number of novice CATS scores is crucial to understanding the depth of this problem. In addition, as Lancaster South High School is beginning year 3 as a participant in the Striving Reader's Grant, we have shown marked improvement in literacy analysis but are consistently failing to meet proficiency in technical reading. Data from this project were collected to determine which literacy strategies are being integrated into classroom instructional practices, as well as the breadth of implementation. This action research project utilized the analysis of school, district, and regional data to articulate viable solutions for addressing the problem of our school's technical reading deficiencies.

Research Question

The primary research question for this project is stated as follows: What literacy strategies can be used to prepare Lancaster County graduates to achieve at higher levels in technical reading and in college preparatory reading?

Subarea Guiding Questions for Research

Several subquestions guided inquiry for the primary research question for this study:

1. What can the high school leadership teams do to assure greater postsecondary reading proficiency of our high school graduates?

2. Which, and to what breadth of implementation, are literacy strategies being integrated into high school classroom instructional practices?

3. Which high school courses currently use technical reading?

4. What research-based reading strategies and programs improve technical reading at the secondary level?

Example 6 of a Complete Action Research Report   **191**

5. What professional development is needed to increase technical reading achievement in our school?

6. Where can we acquire good models for technical reading assignments for the core curriculum?

Review of Literature

A review of literature concerning instructional strategies for improving reading proficiency for secondary students indicates a trend in intervention programs focusing on word recognition, comprehension, fluency, and self-esteem. These strategies are intended to be embedded into the core classes of social studies, language arts, and science. Secondary students are often unable to read the textbooks in core classes, which attributes to the cyclical effect of failure, low self-esteem, and avoidance of any reading materials. The review of literature indicates that when teachers in the core content teach and use reading strategies on a regular basis, student achievement rises (Bryant, Linan-Thompson, Ugel, Hamff, & Haugen, 2001).

Word Recognition

Research emphasizes the importance of word recognition to vocabulary attainment (Stanovich, 1996). High school students with limited word recognition find the reading of technical textbook passages too overwhelming. It is an exhaustive effort for students to use all of their working memory capacity to decode information. Inability to recognize words results in a lack of comprehension and in the loss of meaning at the expense of decoding (Glavach, 2007). Furthermore, research concludes that older students acquire about 3,000 new words each year, and that over half of these words are learned through reading (Stahl, 2000).

In addition to decoding, phonemic awareness is crucial to high levels of word recognition. The development of phonemic awareness is a sound predictor of how well children will learn to read during the first 2 years of instruction. In the same respect, the levels of middle and high school student phonemic awareness can predict the ability of the measured students to read quickly and accurately (Shaywitz, 2003).

Instructional strategies targeting secondary students with word recognition reading deficiencies include a variety of interactive strategies. Such strategies include word mapping, multisyllabic recognition, prefix and suffix awareness, Word Wall, and Frayer Model.

Comprehension

The overall goal of reading is for the reader to comprehend what has been read. For the secondary student, the concept of comprehension is the critical key to success in many core classes. Research supports the premise that to ensure comprehension, the reader must read critically by using strategies that help the reader to relate content to prior knowledge, to practice mental imagery, and to locate the main idea (Sousa, 2005). Effective strategies that encourage readers to relate the reading to what they already know include journaling to connect with their own lives, double-entry organizers, KWL (a graphic organizer for learning that represents what I *Know*, what I *Want* to know, and what I *Learned*), and ordered sharing activities.

Mental imagery is a strategy that encourages the reader to form a visual image of what he or she is reading (Sousa, 2005). This mental picture of a character, a setting, or a scene enables the reader to remember and understand what is being read. To locate the main idea in reading, instructional strategies such as paraphrasing and reading aloud enable students to grasp the meaning of complex texts (Fisk & Hurst, 2003). Effective instructional strategies such as a detail map and structured note taking can be helpful as students develop the understanding of the main idea.

Fluency

The ability to read orally with accuracy, proper expression, and speed is referred to as *fluency*. Fluency bridges the gap between word recognition and comprehension (Sousa, 2005). Fluent readers do not have to spend all of their efforts on decoding and trying to recognize words. They can focus their attention on the meaning and expression of the text. Strategies for teaching fluency include guided, repeated oral reading; literature circles; and independent silent reading. Sousa suggests that to teach fluency, it is important to have students read aloud and to provide feedback for improvement.

Self-Esteem

Young children are motivated to learn. Even after encountering frustration and failure, they show remarkable resilience. This motivation and optimism begin to fade by upper elementary (Hock, Schumaker, & Deshler, 2003). In middle school, readers are learning new vocabulary, organizing, summarizing, and interpreting information (Readance, Bean, & Baldwin, 1998). Struggling readers find themselves in high school unprepared for the academic expectations of core textbooks and reading assignments. At this point, the motivation necessary for reading success is gone and the reader's lack of self-esteem discourages any attempts at reading. To reach students with these issues, action must be taken to gain the students' recommitment to learning and refocus their attention back to instruction that encourages success and improvement (Hock, Schumaker, & Deshler, 2003).

Strategies that help students learn how to adapt to a high school classroom and the world of an adult learner can be beneficial in lifting self-esteem. SLANT: A Starter Strategy for Class Participation, designed by Edwin Ellis of the University of Alabama, is one such strategy (Ellis, 1991). SLANT is a five-step process that empowers the students to become productive members of the classroom by S = sitting up, L = leaning forward, A = activating thinking, N = naming key information, and T = tracking the talker.

Summary

Effective instructional strategies for improving reading proficiency for secondary students focus on word recognition, comprehension, fluency, and self-esteem. Literature review supports the premise that these strategies must be embedded into the core classes of social studies, language arts, and science in order for proficiency to be reached.

Methodology and Research Procedures

This research was accomplished through collaborative efforts of the school principal, district curriculum specialist, and building-level literacy coach to study effective technical reading instructional strategies to ensure greater postsecondary reading proficiency. The initial step was to conduct a literature review of research and academic opinions relevant to effective secondary reading strategies. The review of literature established a foundation of information and knowledge, reference data, and potential instructional strategies for recommendations.

The collaborative team included educators who have expertise in and understanding of numerous literacy initiatives, experience in action research, and thorough knowledge of the Federal Striving Readers Grant. The comprehensive knowledge of the team brought professionally sound and balanced analysis of the research findings.

A variety of data was collected for analysis: (a) demographic data for students performing at novice, apprentice, and proficiency in reading; (b) reading student achievement data from EPAS, ACT, and KCCT; (c) qualitative perception data from focus groups and surveys; and (d) quantitative data from walk-through evaluations. Demographic data came from the Lancaster South High School student data tool provided by the state department of education. All confidentiality requirements were maintained throughout the study by assigning numbers to students in lieu of recording given names.

Example 6 of a Complete Action Research Report   **193**

Following the review of literature, the study identified students performing at novice, apprentice, and proficient levels from the 2006, 2007, and 2008 EPAS, ACT, and KCCT scores from the Lancaster County South High School state performance report for reading. These data were then disaggregated into student performance data in the reading subdomain areas of interpreting text and critical stance. The disaggregated subdomain data were then used to create graphic representations of the reading scores in these areas.

Teacher surveys were conducted with all 9–12 core content teachers to provide data concerning which—and to what breadth of implementation—literacy strategies were being integrated into classroom instructional practices. The survey also included professional-development needs for increasing proficiency in technical reading. Student focus groups were held to provide data regarding classes that were incorporating technical reading into student instruction.

Finally, walk-through observation data were used to provide quantitative data of the frequency, breadth, and types of literacy strategies being used in core content classes. These walk-throughs also provided perceptions of the effectiveness of currently used core content literacy strategies.

The members of the research team met with the researcher individually and as a group to review research and study data. On the basis of the findings, the team recommended the implementation of literacy strategies focused on word recognition, comprehension, fluency, and self-esteem for the following semester in core content classes of language arts, social studies, and science. The team recommended that this plan be added to the SIP (School Improvement Plan) to ensure the buy-in of all stakeholders, clear delineation of responsible participants, and a formal process for evaluation.

Problem Analysis

Upon completion of student focus group responses, classroom walk-throughs, and teacher surveys about the usage of content literacy strategies and reading materials in core content classes, a number of pertinent findings have been revealed. Student focus groups of classes that incorporate technical reading into instruction revealed a tendency for increased usage of technical reading in 11th and 12th grade core classes. Nine of the sixteen students participating in the focus group responded that technical materials are being used in their classes (Figure 1). Five of the sixteen students rated the amount of technical reading to be appropriate to the core content standards for the course in question.

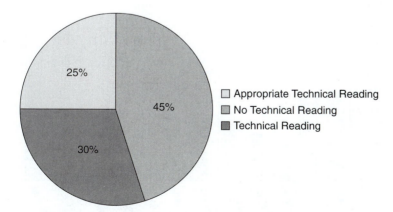

Figure 1. **Technical reading in core classes from student focus groups (*N* = 16).**

From the framework of the Striving Readers Grant, 12 literacy strategies were chosen on the basis of their relevance to increased proficiency in technical reading. These strategies include the Frayer Model, Word Wall, Anticipatory Guide, Double Entry Journal, Main Idea/Detail Frame, Text Coding, Parallel Reading, Read Aloud, Choral Reading, Readers Theater, Café Conversation, and Think/Pair/Share.

The researcher's walk-through observation data reflected a few common literacy strategies being applied in most of the 16 core content classes. Table 1, a log of observations conducted, highlights the walk-through data that specifically showed that all but one of the classrooms observed use two common strategies: (a) Café Conversation, and (b) Think/Pair/Share. Both strategies are appropriate for cross-curricular application and encourage content dialog among learners, promoting greater participation and engagement. Conversely, the data confirmed that the strategies of Text Coding and Reader's Theater were not observed in the walk-throughs.

Table 1
Teacher Utilization of Literacy Strategies (n = 16)

Reading Strategy	Used in Current Lesson	Evidence From Prior Walk-Through
Frayer Model	4	8
Word Wall	2	7
Anticipatory Guide	0	3
Double Entry Journal	1	5
Main Idea/Detail Frame	3	5
Text Coding	0	0
Parallel Reading	0	3
Read Aloud	7	16
Choral Reading	1	7
Reader's Theater	0	0
Café Conversation	5	10
Think/Pair/Share	7	8

Nineteen core content teachers completed online surveys to evaluate their utilization of literacy strategies. To establish a standard of comparison, sufficient application of a strategy was defined as three or more times a semester. The data indicated that 100% of the teachers participating in the survey sufficiently utilized the Read Aloud strategy, whereas only 16% of the teachers surveyed applied the strategies of Text Coding and Reader's Theater (Figure 2).

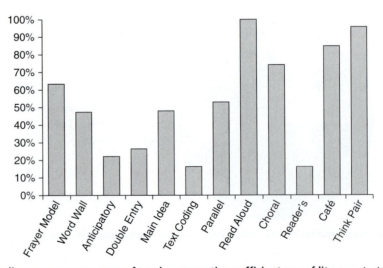

Figure 2. **Online survey percentage of teachers reporting sufficient use of literacy strategies.**

As shown in Figure 3, over 50% of those teachers participating in the online survey requested that Text Coding and Reader's Theater strategies be covered in professional-development opportunities offered in the future. However, none of those surveyed requested

Example 6 of a Complete Action Research Report **195**

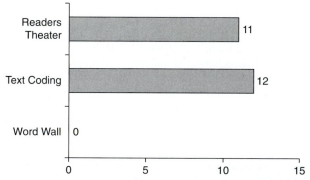

Figure 3. Number of teachers, from the online survey, who requested professional development (*n* = 19).

future professional-development opportunities for Word Wall. Review of the 2008–2009 professional-development logs for Lancaster South High School confirmed that the most recent mandatory Striving Readers training targeted the Word Wall literacy strategy.

Conclusions and Recommendations

Data analysis from classroom observations and the teacher online survey confirmed teacher usage of at least three strategies to improve literacy proficiency: Read Aloud, Café Conversation, and Think/Pair/Share. Text Coding and Reader's Theater were the least-used strategies, and over half of the teachers responding to the online survey requested professional development on these two strategies.

The following recommendations are designed to achieve proficiency in the comprehension, fluency, and critical evaluation of technical reading in core content classes at Lancaster South High School:

1. Secondary students are often unable to read the textbooks in core classes. This inability contributes to the cyclical effect of failure, low self-esteem, and avoidance of any reading materials. When teachers in the core content teach and use reading strategies on a regular basis, student achievement rises (Bryant, Linan-Thompson, Ugel, Hamff, & Haugen, 2001). Therefore, additional resources and instructional support are needed for literacy strategies that target proficiency in technical reading.

2. For the secondary student, the concept of comprehension is the critical key to success in core instruction. To promote proficiency in reading comprehension, instruction will include strategies of Think/Pair/Share, Café Conversation, Double Entry Journal, and Main Idea/Detail Frame to help the reader relate content to prior knowledge, to practice mental imagery, and to locate the main idea (Souse, 2005).

3. Fluency bridges the gap between word recognition and comprehension (Sousa, 2005). To promote proficiency in fluency, instruction will include strategies of Parallel Reading, Reader's Theater, Read Aloud, and Choral Reading to focus the readers' attention on the meaning and expression of the text.

4. Critical evaluation of technical reading material requires the use of instructional strategies such as paraphrasing and reading aloud to enable students to grasp the meaning of complex texts (Fisk & Hurst, 2003). To promote proficiency in critical evaluation, instruction will include strategies of Anticipatory Guide, Word Wall, Text Coding, and Frayer Model.

5. To meet the requests for content literacy strategy professional development, the Lancaster South High School Professional Development committee will request that 3 hours of required professional development be included in the Professional Development plan for the Lancaster South High School teachers for the 2009–2010 school year.

References

Bryant, D. P., Linan-Thompson, S., Ugel, N., Hamff, A., & Hougen, M. (2001). The effects of professional development for middle school general and special education teachers on implementation of reading strategies in inclusive content area classes. *Learning Disabilities Quarterly, 24,* 251–264.

Burley, H. W., & Butner, B. K. (2002). Should student affairs offer remedial education? *Community College Journal of Research and Practice, 24*(3), 193.

Cunningham, P. M. (1998). The multisyllabic word dilemma: Helping students build meaning, spell, and read "big" words. *Reading and Writing Quarterly: Overcoming Learning Difficulties, 14,* 189–218.

Ellis, E. (1991). *Slant: A starter strategy for class participation.* Lawrence, KS: Edge Enterprises.

Fisk, C., & Hurst, B. (2003). Paraphrasing for comprehension. *The Reading Teacher, 57,* 182–185.

Glavach, M. J. (2007). Closing the gap: A new model for adolescent reading intervention. *Academic Leadership,* 3.

Grego, R., & Thompson, N. (1996). Repositioning remediation: Renegotiating composition's work in the academy. *College Composition and Communication, 47*(1), 62–84.

Hock, M. F., Schumaker, J. B., & Deshler, D. D. (2003). *Possible selves: Nurturing student motivation.* Lawrence, KS: Edge Enterprises.

Readance, J. E., Bean, T. W., & Baldwin, R. S. (1998). *Content area literacy: An integrated approach* (6th ed.). Dubuque, IA: Kendall/Hunt.

Shaywitz, S. E. (2003). *Overcoming dyslexia: A new and complete science-based program for reading problems at any level.* New York: Knopf.

Shefelbine, J., & Calhoun, J. (1991). Variability in approaches to identifying polysyllabic words: A descriptive study of sixth graders with highly, moderately, and poorly developed syllabication strategies. In J. Zutell & S. McCormick (Eds.), *Learning factors/teacher factors: Issues in literacy instruction* (pp. 169–177). Chicago: National Reading Conference.

Sousa, D. A. (2005). How the brain learns to read. Thousand Oaks, CA: Corwin.

Stahl, S. A. (2000). *Promoting vocabulary development.* Austin, TX: Texas Education Agency.

Stanovich, K. E. (1980). Toward an interactive compensatory model of individual differences in the development of reading fluency. *Reading Research Quarterly, 16,* 32–71.

Note. **Adapted from action research by Janet Sivis-O'Connell, CEO Coordinator and Social Studies High School Teacher. Used with permission.**

EXAMPLE 7 OF A COMPLETE ACTION RESEARCH REPORT

A Comparative Review of High School Schedules

Marfax County secondary schools currently use a 5-period/block day in the two full service high school buildings and the Career and Technical Center (CTC). CTC offers a variety of mostly elective courses related to career education and serves both high schools, as well as the alternative school. The issue has come up that the 5-period day may not be the most efficient schedule for the county. Some have wondered whether or not this schedule currently meets the needs of the students. The charge is to look into other schedule types to determine whether another method of structuring the day would be more effective. This is a countywide issue because of the use of the CTC building by both schools; changing the schedule at one school could affect how CTC offers services to both schools.

Research Questions

The primary research question to be addressed for our county school system is as follows: What is the most effective method of structuring the school day? Data collection to address this question will be driven by the following research guiding questions:

1. What advantages would be provided to students by a change to a different scheduling model?

2. What does research show about advantages of using one model of scheduling over another and how can a school determine the structure that best meets the needs of the school and district?

3. How does another scheduling model, other than the current 5-period day, provide more opportunities for students to earn credits in interest-driven elective courses?

Study Rationale

Questions have been raised within the district about whether or not we are using our resources effectively or efficiently due to constraints afforded by our current schedule. A task force has been formed to investigate the pros and cons of varying scheduling models and to make a recommendation to the school board. Taking into account the required year-long courses within our system, we note that a student can earn up to 29 credits within the normal school day. By examining other scheduling models, we will be able to determine whether there is enough flexibility within this model to meet the needs of students for proficiency in the state-required curriculum and to sufficiently offer elective options or whether another model affords more options.

Literature Review

A review of the literature of ways in which high schools approach the scheduling process and ultimately decide to set up a schedule revealed a number of trends over the years. Particularly, schools fall into a combination of two of the following categories: traditional or block (with some combining the two), and semester or trimester. Traditional scheduling refers to a 6–7-period day, with periods running 45–55 minutes. Block scheduling is generally a 4- or 5-block day, with periods running 70–90 minutes. Semester schedules are more traditional in the sense that there are two 9-week grading periods in each semester. The trimester schedule uses three 12-week grading periods and is a relatively new trend in high schools.

Comparing Schedules

One of the initial purposes of this project was to review varying scheduling types to decipher whether a more effective use of time was being used or modeled by other schools. Marfax County high schools currently use a 5-block 2-semester schedule. A difficulty arose with the literature review because most of the schedule comparisons related a traditional schedule to a block schedule (Irmsher, 1996; Lawrence & McPherson, 2000). This comparison was usually focused on a 7-period day versus a 4×4 block (2 semesters, each with a 4-block day). This proved problematic for two reasons: (a) Marfax County schools have already transitioned, first from a 7-period day to a 4-block day, and then to the most recent model, a 5-block day, and there is no intention of returning to either schedule. (b) The data gathered and referenced generally support a move to a 5-block day (which Marfax County schools were already using), thereby providing no comparative evidence or data in favor of making a change. Because both high schools bus students to the County Technical Center, neither block, a 6–7-period day, is logical within the current model due to the reduction in class time because of the travel time to the center.

The 5-Block Day

There appears to be plenty support for the current model being employed by Marfax County. A scheduling model using a 5-block day (as compared with traditional schedules) can increase the number of elective classes students can take, lighten homework loads, lighten prep loads for teachers, increase planning time for teachers, reduce the number of class changes, and provide more time for comprehensive instruction and strategies, to name a few advantages (The Principals' Partnership, 2007). Westerburg (2006, p.10) believes that the 5-block day combined with a trimester has more pros than cons, including lots of choices for students, appropriate block time, maximum use of staff, and less time for elective courses than core classes.

Because the advantages of the 5-block day seemed apparent through the review and because of the slim chance that the schools are going to deviate from this model, the focus of the review was shifted to the semester versus trimester model. In Marfax County, each school offers most core classes—English, math, science, and social studies—all year long for 75 minutes a day, and students earn 1 credit by passing each class. All elective courses and some core classes are offered for 75 minutes a semester, and 1 credit is offered for successful completion. Over the course of 4 years in high school, students can earn up to 29 credits through varying combinations of year-long and semester-long courses. A trimester schedule may offer more options to students, but a model to preserve the core subjects would have to be employed to avoid the loss of critical class time to these accountability areas.

Trimesters

One trend did emerge that may provide the possibility to allow students to take more elective courses (which is one of the stated goals of a Marfax County Secondary Task Force that is reviewing this matter), and that was through a trimester schedule (CPSER&CD, 2005). By application of a model similar to the Spring Lake School System, the number of elective courses offered each year would increase, as would the opportunity to earn credits (Westerburg, 2006). If the semester schedule is divided into trimesters and the 5-block day maintained, elective courses could be offered three times in a block for 12 weeks at a time instead of two times per year for 18 weeks at a time. Additionally, by adjusting the social studies curriculum for ninth and 10th grades by distributing the content standards over 4 trimesters rather than the current 6 semesters, an additional 2 blocks would be opened for elective courses. This also creates opportunities for social studies teachers to develop elective courses related to their content area to cover the lost time devoted to a particular social studies course. Using this trimester model, students would have the opportunity to earn at least 31 credits as opposed to the 29 offered by the current model.

The design of the instructional day and how that time is put to use for student learning is of the utmost importance to the teachers and administrators of Marfax County

Example 7 of a Complete Action Research Report   **199**

schools. This literature review was focused on varying methods to best focus the use of the time within the constraints imposed by the school district. Previous changes to the structure of the school day have been made with the agreement that classroom time be held primarily as a sacred time for learning. Before implementation, any further changes to the system will first and foremost have to be filtered through this nonnegotiable agreement.

Methodology

In designing this research project, I worked with the school administrative team—including the school principal, the assistant principal, and the curriculum resource principal—the school counseling team, and a secondary task force convened to review the design of the school day in Marfax County. The task force comprised district administrators, school administrators, and school counselors. The task force met three times over the course of the fall of 2008. The task force reviewed the advantages and disadvantages of the current model and the advantages and disadvantages of altering the structure of the school day and altering the structure of the school year, specifically comparing the semester to the trimester model. At the school level, students were asked to complete a survey that focused on their perceptions of the current model of the school day and their perceptions of the current model of the school year. In addition, students were asked to provide their perceptions of a trimester model structure for the school year. Finally, a data review was completed by the school administration team to determine whether there is a data-supported school-day model to improve student achievement.

The task force had to take a unique approach to the school-day model because implementing this is a decision that is controlled by each school's site-based council for School-Based Decision Making (SBDM). Therefore, although the findings of the committee may show an advantage, ultimately it would be up to the SBDM to make the change. Also, the use of the shared facility, the CTC, had to be taken into account because both schools send students to this facility; and this facility is staffed through full-time [teacher] equivalents (FTE) from both schools. The task force was divided into subcommittees to review articles and information on different models to ascertain whether one model was more conducive to student achievement than another and to find whether one model provided more opportunities for students to enroll in elective courses over the span of their high school careers. CTC offers mainly elective courses, and its survival is dependent upon filling the courses offered and attracting as many students as possible over the course of the year. The task force recommended that the structure of the school day not be changed because of the problems a change would create in the travel of students to and from CTC. It also suggested continued discussion of a trimester model because of the possibility that it may allow students to engage in more elective coursework than the current model does. Discussions within the schools and the district regarding this change are ongoing.

The student surveys elicited student perceptions about a change in the yearly schedule, from the current semester model to a trimester model. The narrow focus is due to the fact that the probability of a change in the school day is unlikely. However, a change to a trimester model is being discussed. Therefore, as part of the discussion, administrators would like to have feedback regarding students' perceptions of this possible change. Specifically, this model would reduce elective classes from an 18-week course to a 12-week course and allow students to pick up one additional credit their 9th and 10th grade years. The trimester model also changes the number of times that student grades are reported throughout the year. A semester model has four official grading terms and four unofficial midterm progress reports. A trimester model could have fewer—three official and three midterm progress reports—or more—three official and six progress reports (every 4 weeks instead of each midterm). The survey gathered information from students about their reaction to midterms versus 4-week progress reports. Surveys were administered to a random sampling of students in grades 9 through 12. It was decided to get feedback from all groups because each offers a different perspective of the high school experience. Seniors were included in the survey, even though any potential changes would not affect them. However, they were included to draw from their experience as students in the system.

The final data piece was a review of the current research data to determine whether one model presents a clear advantage in the area of student achievement. Some of the data reviewed are included in the literature review completed by the researcher, but additional sources provided by other administrators are also included. One of the original research questions pertained to the most effective method of structuring the school day, and this data review was an attempt to address that question.

Because the decision on the best way to structure the school day comes down to the governance of the SBDM, the researcher and the administrative team will discuss findings from this research with the council. The effectiveness of the current model will be reviewed and discussed, as will the possibility of changing to another model.

Data Collection, Analysis, and Conclusions

The primary research question examined the most effective method of structuring the school day. The model in place at the researcher's school was a 2-semester year broken into five 75-minute daily blocks. This model is very popular among the staff and seems to be popular with students as well, but no data had been collected as a measure. Because literature regarding achievement in school systems using a block schedule versus those using a traditional 6–7-period day schedule is inconclusive, it was determined that the agent for change—if there was to be any change—would need to be dissatisfaction with the current model or the possibility of offering more options with another model.

A survey was given to students to determine their level of satisfaction with the current schedule. These students come from a middle school with a more traditional schedule, so they have experience in at least two different models. As shown in Table 1, 59.1% of the students surveyed rated the current model as student friendly. Of particular interest within these data were the 11th grade students because over 64% of them responded that the schedule was student friendly.

Table 1
Student Rating of the 5-Block Day (n = 315)

	Very Student Friendly	Somewhat Student Friendly	No Different From Other Schedules	Somewhat Not Student Friendly	Not Student Friendly
9th Grade	11	25	19	9	2
10th Grade	20	17	17	14	3
11th Grade	24	43	15	14	8
12th Grade	13	33	17	7	4
Total	**68**	**118**	**68**	**44**	**17**
Percents	21.6%	37.5%	21.6%	14.0%	5.4%

The junior class data are of special interest because the junior class was the largest group surveyed, and they tend to be the class that is the most active and vocal advocate for the student body. These results are similar to the findings of Gullatt (2006) that an alternative schedule, differing from a traditional 6–7-period day, had a positive environmental impact on students and teachers.

As seen in Figure 1, students also expressed satisfaction with the model being used to communicate and record grades. This school uses four 9-week and two semester grading

Example 7 of a Complete Action Research Report **201**

periods to post grades. Most of the classes in the core subjects of English, science, math, and social studies run all year long. Final grades for these courses are posted at the end of the year. Official grade reports are sent home after each 9-week period, and progress grading reports are sent home each midterm. When asked about this model, 57.9% of students responding categorized it as a student-friendly model.

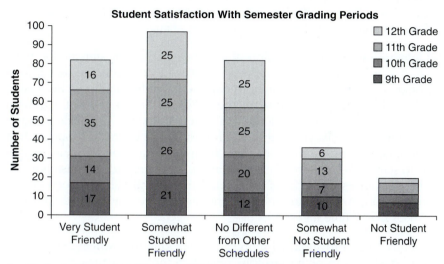

Figure 1. Student ratings of satisfaction with semester grading periods, shown by grade level.

The administrative staff of this school filters decisions about school governance according to what is best for students. With this in mind, we examined the different scheduling models researched to determine what advantages they would provide over the current model and whether another model would offer students more opportunities for learning. One of the models presented to students in the survey, the trimester model, would allow them to enroll in more elective courses over their 4 years in high school. Figure 2 shows that, by an overwhelming margin, students are interested in a schedule that would allow them to explore more areas of personal interest. Students in each grade viewed a schedule with more elective opportunities as very student friendly, by a greater margin than any other item in the survey.

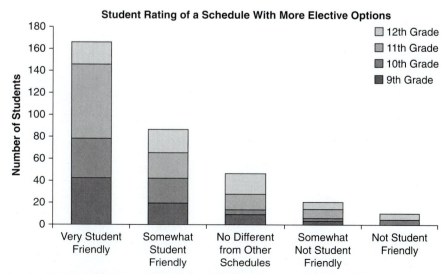

Figure 2. Student ratings by grade level of how student friendly they perceive a schedule to be that offers them the opportunity to take more elective options than are currently offered.

Recommendations

Based on the literature review and the survey data collected, the following are recommended actions:

1. No change is made to the current daily 5-block schedule. Veal and Schreiber (1999) determined that it would be unwise to conclude that one type of schedule (block versus traditional) is generally better than others, independent of other factors within the school. Because this schedule is meeting the needs of the school and the students, the recommendation is made to not change this model.

2. The administration should explore the viability of a trimester model. One of the points that emerged from the survey is that students are interested in a schedule that offers them more opportunity to explore individual interests. Because the current 5-block model is conducive to the year-long organization of a trimester, it is possible that a conversion could be completed. If the key to unlocking learning lies in unlocking time (EIS, 2007), then the trimester may be the best option. Instructors and designers will have to move away from thinking about Carnegie Units (EESU, 2004) to standards-based courses. In doing so, teachers and administrators would be organizing courses on the basis of student learning and a student-focused paradigm, rather than organizing courses on an antiquated time parameter established in the late 1800s that is time focused.

This study brings to light a number of questions that will remain unanswered for now. The study began with questions regarding the advantages of one model over another and regarding whether one model has a greater impact on student achievement than another. Those questions remain. One thing is clear, however: Each system has mixed results, and those results are contingent upon systems in place within the school system (CPSER&CD, 2005). Because each system is unique, it may be that the model which works best is the one that best meets the needs of the students within the system.

Example 7 of a Complete Action Research Report **203**

References

Center for Policy Studies, Education Research, and Community Development (CPSER&CD). (2005). *High school trimester system vs. semester system.* Retrieved from http://icee.isu.edu/policy/policyhome.html.

Education Encyclopedia—State University.com (EESU). (2004). *Scheduling—Historical background of scheduling, selecting a schedule, scheduling models, staff development.* Retrieved from http://education.stateuniversity.com/pages/2385/Scheduling.html.

Education Issues Series (EIS). (2007). *The change process and alternative scheduling.* Retrieved from http://www.weac.org/resource/june96/schedule.htm.

Gullatt, D. (2006). Block scheduling: The effects on curriculum and student productivity. *NASSP Bulletin, 90*(3), 250–66.

Irmsher, K. (1996, March). *Block scheduling.* ERIC Digest104. Retrieved from http://eric.uoregon.edu/publications/digests/digest104.html.

Lawrence, W. W., & McPherson, D. D. (2000). A comparative study of block scheduling and traditional scheduling on academic achievement. *Journal of Instructional Psychology, 44.*

The Principal's Partnership. (2007). *Research brief: Trimester schedule.* Retrieved from http://www.principalpartnership.com.

Veal, W. R., & Schreiber, J. (1999). Block scheduling effects on a state mandated test of basic skills. *Education Policy Analysis Archives, 7*(29), 40–51.

Westerburg, M. (2006). *Creating the trimester school.* Retrieved from http://www.eup.k12.mi.us/608990220112624/lib/608990220112624/TRIMESTERS_AND_BEYOND1.pdf.

Note. **Adapted from action research by Joe K. Matthews, High School Assistant Principal. Used with permission.**

EXAMPLE 8 OF A COMPLETE ACTION RESEARCH REPORT

Middle School Improvement Analysis: Practical Living/Career Studies Test Scores

This action research report addresses eighth grade practical living/career test scores and performances on the state accountability testing system for students at Star Middle School (SMS). There had been a slight increase in test scores until last year when there was a nine-point increase. The state performance report of accountability trends in the subject area evidences the increase. However, analysis of individual student scores for each of the past 3 years shows a significant achievement gap between high and low achievers on the practical living/career studies portion of the test. The main focus of this study was to understand the difference and implement practices to increase proficient and distinguished scores by 3% in 2 years. The primary research question was, "How can SMS decrease the learning gap in practical living/career studies and increase by 3% the number of students achieving proficient or distinguished achievement in this content area by 2006?" Selection of data and research methods came from the following three research guiding questions:

1. What demographic characteristics describe the students at the novice level of the test?

2. What type of curriculum and instructional strategies has been used for students enrolled in grades 6 through 8 in the content area?

3. What programs and/or projects have proved effective in improving scores in the content area?

State goals require all students to reach proficiency by 2014. Therefore, all novice and apprentice students must improve to proficient levels. In addition to the testing demands, students need knowledge in practical living/career studies in order to understand adult and work roles. Students need to understand how to work well in groups, understand professional obligations within the workforce, and provide themselves and family members with healthy lifestyles. In addition, employers are expressing concern about an increasing need for workers to have problem-solving, decision-making, and teamwork skills (Conrad, 1999).

Background of the Problem

Star Middle School is the only middle school within the county school system and serves students in grades 5 through 8 for families who live in the county but not within city limits. The middle school's test scores are above the state scores in all areas except reading. Because SMS serves grades 5 through 8, there are two grades tested in practical living/career studies; however, this project focused on the eighth grade because the fifth grade test is the exit test for elementary school. There were 160 students who completed the eighth grade portion of the test. Table 1 shows the number of students who completed the eighth grade test in practical living/career studies, according to performance levels.

Example 8 of a Complete Action Research Report   **205**

Table 1
2003 Star Middle School Practical Living/Career Studies Performance Levels (N = 160)

Students	Performance Levels				
	Novice	Apprentice	Proficient	Distinguished	Totals
Male	15	41	18	5	79
Female	10	33	18	20	81
Totals	25	74	36	25	160

Table 1 shows 62% of eighth grade students below proficient and indicates the importance of improving achievement in order for these students to reach proficiency.

Literature Review

The literature review included a study of practices that have proven effective for student improvement. The information clearly defines what makes an achievement gap and explains practices that have worked when increasing student knowledge and interest in the areas of practical living/career studies. The review concludes with a discussion of the core content for practical living/career studies in this state. The core competencies designed for schools in this state serve as a guide for classroom teachers when constructing curriculum.

The Achievement Gap

There is a significant gap between high and low achievers with the practical living/career studies portion of the state core content test in Star Middle School. Current instructional practices have not sufficiently reduced this gap. The vision and mission for the educational system in this state express the belief that all children can learn regardless of ethnicity, ability, gender, socio-economic status, native language, or whether they have a disability (Kentucky Department of Education, 2003). The state department of education defines an achievement gap as "a persistent, persuasive, and significant disparity in educational achievement, and attainment among groups of students as determined by a standardized measure" (p. 15).

Current Practices That Work

There are numerous teaching practices, community-oriented activities, and school-wide programs that have proven successful in reducing achievement gaps and raising overall achievement among student populations. Collaboration among teachers helps improve teaching, which in turn can help raise student achievement. The El Paso, Texas, community is a high-poverty area, but student performance increased after monthly meetings for teachers within content areas and work sessions conducted to analyze student assignments (Haycock, 2001).

Community involvement also increases student achievement. It has been estimated that 40–50% of what a child learns occurs in school, and the remaining 50–60% comes from the family and community (Brown, 2002). Teachers, school and district leaders, and community members must work together to design improvement strategies (Southern Regional Education Board [SREB], n.d.). Community involvement focuses on school improvement plans, career awareness programs, and parent and family activities.

There are also schoolwide activities that can reduce the gap in practical living/career studies. Student involvement in career and technical education (CTE) student organizations produces higher test scores. Increased student interest results from involvement in student organizations. For example, a study by Purdue University shows that students involved in organizations are more engaged in learning activities (Brown, 2002).

Schoolwide transition programs are of key importance when raising student achievement in all areas. According to the SREB (n.d.), schools that used improvement frameworks involving transition programs saw at least 85% of students reach achievement goals in reading, math, and sciences. This is not to show a direct connection, but transition programs merit consideration for promoting student learning. Students experience many changes in their school environment associated with transition from elementary to middle schools. Goals in elementary school are mostly task oriented, whereas middle school focuses on performance (Alspaugh, 1998). The changes in expectations can strongly influence student performance.

Practical Living and Career Studies Core Competencies

The state department of education developed core competencies for all areas tested on the state core competency test. The practical living/career studies core content focuses on four sub-domains: health, physical education, consumerism, and job/career (KDE, 2003). Scores from the test are based on multiple-choice responses and open-response questions related to any of these content areas.

Summary

The literature provided suggestions and explanations of successful programs in the areas of practical living/career studies. Recommendations for improvement could be based on the literature for practices such as after-school tutoring sessions, transition programs, and more involvement in student organizations. The research will provide a guide for school improvement.

Methodology and Problem Analysis

After identifying the need to improve learning for students at the novice and apprentice levels, guiding questions were developed to direct the project. The first analysis looked at individual student performances to see how students were performing in practical living/career studies and whether there were achievement gaps within the content. With the definition for an achievement gap as "a persistent, persuasive, and significant disparity in educational achievement, and attainment among groups of students as determined by standardized measure" (Kentucky Department of Education, 2003, p. 15) applied, the greater percentage of practical living/career studies for novice and apprentice showed an apparent gap.

Student Demographics Disaggregation

The first research guiding question posed for demographic characteristics that described the novice-level students on the practical living/career studies. To gather this data, I reviewed the Spring 2003 Kentucky Performance Report, disaggregated by subpopulations of students. The data recognized those populations performing at the lowest levels, which included males with disabilities, students eligible for free or reduced lunch, and Title I participants. Forty-seven percent of students with disabilities performed at the novice level, and 53% performed at the apprentice level. Seventy-four percent of the students eligible for free or reduced lunch performed at the apprentice and below levels, and 70% of Title I students performed at apprentice or below. Figure 1 shows performances based on these student populations.

Once I identified those students performing at the lowest levels, I then interviewed teachers within the practical living/career studies department to discuss current teaching strategies and curriculum guides being used to instruct students. Interview questions were open-ended, with question content based on the practical living/career curriculum guides and instructional practices. Member checking of the interview transcript by these

Example 8 of a Complete Action Research Report   **207**

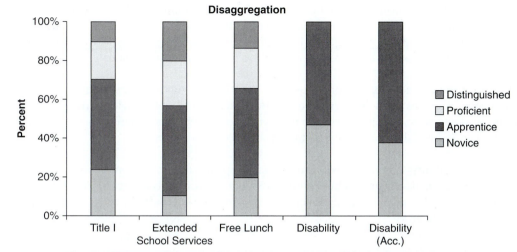

Figure 1. **The greatest percentage of students scoring below proficiency in practical living/career studies had some type of disability. Students who participated in extended school services had the greatest number achieving proficient and distinguished.**

teachers and multiple data triangulation were strategies that strengthened integrity of qualitative data interpretation.

Current Teaching Strategies and Practices

There are currently three teachers who focus on the practical living/career studies curriculum. These are the industrial technology teacher, the family and consumer sciences teacher, and the physical education instructor. Students have each class for a semester. Industrial technology and physical education are taught during the seventh grade, and family and consumer sciences is taught to eighth grade students.

The family and consumer sciences teacher focuses on the consumerism, health, and job/career subdomains of the test, and the physical education teacher focuses strictly on physical education. The industrial education teacher reinforces the job/career portion. Figure 2 breaks down the performance of students within each subdomain of the open-response portion of the core content test. Figure 2 shows an obvious weakness on the part of students when answering open-response questions, signifying a need for more experience in answering open-response questions. The lowest percentage achieving proficient or above is in physical education (22 %). Health, consumerism, and job/career have a similar percentage of proficient or above (range from 35% to 40%).

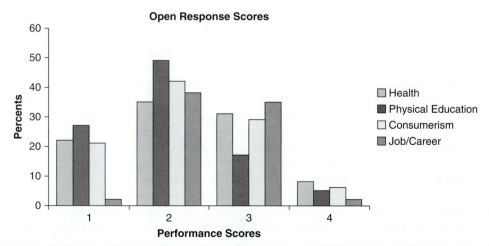

Figure 2. **Performance levels are shown for eighth grade practical living/career studies for subdomain content areas from the state core content test. 1 = Novice level of performance, 2 = Apprentice, 3 = Proficient, and 4 = Distinguished.**

Interview questions for teachers asked about unit plans and development of lessons. All teachers develop lessons around the Kentucky Core Content. Unit plans are also developed around the core content. I questioned teachers regarding instructional practices focused on group work, the use of textbooks, and writing activities.

All three teachers implement group and hands-on activities, averaging two per unit. The textbooks were used as learning tools, but teachers did not feel dependent upon the texts. Students were required to write responses for at least one open-response question per unit in industrial technology and family and consumer sciences.

The weakness within the department was appropriate assessment tools and teacher and student reflection. The teachers all expressed a concern about how to properly assess student knowledge at the highest levels. Table 2 recognizes the type of assessment tools used by the teachers.

Table 2
Types of Assessment Measures Used Each Semester by Practical Living/Career Studies

Assessment Types	Industrial Technology	Family and Consumer Sciences	Physical Education
Performance assessment	10	12	15
Multiple-choice tests	6	8	3
Open-response activities	6	15	5
Total assessments	22	35	23

Teachers said that they allow little time for student reflection within lessons. However, effective learning is balanced with opportunities for reflection (Zemelman, Daniels, et. al, 1993). The teachers also mentioned that there is little time for collaboration and curriculum planning. Department meetings usually focus on analyzing data but do not focus on assessment and evaluation of student performance. After interviewing the three teachers, I then focused on past and current practices that have improved student performance in the areas of practical living/career studies.

Discussion and Conclusions

A review of quantitative data on characteristics of students scoring less than proficiency in practical living/career studies showed more than half of the students scoring less than proficient on the state core content tests. This is a problem of concern, achievement less than expectations, and an area addressed by this action research study for improvement.

Identifying characteristics of the students scoring at novice and apprentice were compared according to the total numbers and percentages for all students scoring novice or apprentice. It was found that 70% of males versus 53% of females were below proficiency in core content for practical living/career studies. Thus, strategies to improve scores to proficient should give particular attention to males and students with disabilities because these two groups have the highest percentage below proficiency.

Qualitative teacher interview data triangulated with information from the literature review, quantitative data on open-response assessment for the four subdomain content areas, and types of assessment measures used for those content areas led to several conclusions. Lack of teacher collaboration and types of assessment were two areas of concern revealed from the teacher survey. The literature showed the importance of teacher collaboration as a strategy for improvement of student learning and closing achievement gaps (Haycock, 2001). Quantitative review of the types of assessments used per semester and the performance levels in each subdomain indicate that attention on more practice on open-response questions in all content areas, and especially in physical education, is important. Frequency of student practice in performance assessment is to be commended

Example 8 of a Complete Action Research Report **209**

in all subdomains, but open-response needs additional practice in industrial technology and physical education.

Comparing effective instructional strategies and programs to raise achievement with the two student characteristics for those with the greatest need for improved achievement suggested some strategies from literature for consideration. Community involvement and participation in community-based activities such as career shadowing and career and technical student organizations (Brown, 2002) most likely would appeal especially to males. Collaboration with special education personnel to identify teaching and learning strategies especially helpful for students with disabilities could be of great benefit for all subdomain areas.

Finally, students need to be exposed to transitional programs and after-school activities that focus on the practical living/career studies core content. According to the SREB (n.d.), schools that used improvement frameworks involving transition programs had at least 85% of students reach achievement goals in reading, math, and sciences. Students experience many changes in their school environment associated with transition from elementary to middle school. Goals in elementary school are mostly task oriented, whereas middle school focuses on performance (Alspaugh, 1998). The changes in expectations can strongly influence student performance.

Stakeholder Input for the Analysis

I worked closely with the Star Middle School administration to identify an area for improvement. Upon identifying the problem, we then developed guiding questions to further address the issue. I also relied on the building principal and guidance counselor to help me understand the data and to supply me with the appropriate data for the research project. Following the data analysis, I shared recommendations with the administration. I also discussed the areas for improvement with members of the practical living/career studies department at Star Middle School.

Recommendations

With knowledge based on data interpretations and conclusions and input from stakeholders, the following recommendations are made to improve student performance on the practical living/career studies portion of the core content test. It is even more important to bring all students to proficiency in practical living/career studies. Improving student learning in these subdomains can improve their proficiency for their life and careers.

1. Develop a designated time for teacher collaboration (Haycock, 2001) within the practical living/career studies department. During this time, teachers will assess student work, develop common tools for evaluation of work, discuss good instructional practices, and openly reflect on past lessons. Also, plan collaborative sessions with special education to identify teaching and learning strategies most effective for students with disabilities.

2. Develop community-oriented activities (Brown, 2002). SMS needs to develop job shadowing and school-to-work programs that reinforce the job/career portion of the core content.

3. Encourage participation in student organizations (Brown, 2002). Involve all eighth grade students in organizational activities associated with industrial technology and family and consumer sciences education.

4. Provide after-school tutoring sessions for those students struggling in the area of practical living/career studies. The programs could provide assistance in understanding the curriculum and offer strategies to improve test-taking skills. Disaggregated demographic data support this recommendation by showing that the highest percentage of students in extended school programs attain proficient or distinguished levels.

References

Alspaugh, J. W. (1998). Achievement loss associated with the transition to middle and high school. *Journal of Educational Research, 7,* 20–25.

Brown, B. (1996). *Community involvement in K–12 career education.* (Report number 177). Washington, DC: U.S. Department of Education. (ERIC Document Reproduction Service No. ED402473).

Brown, B. (2002). *CTE student organizations.* ERIC Clearinghouse (ERIC). Retrieved from http://eric.ed.gov.

Conrad, C. A. (1999). *The American workforce in the new millennium.* Washington, DC: Joint Center's Corporate Council.

Haycock, K. (2001). Closing the achievement gap: Helping all students achieve. *Educational Leadership, 58,* 21–25.

Kentucky Department of Education. *Closing the achievement gap.* Retrieved from http://www.kentuckyschools.net.

Kentucky Department of Education. (2002). *Spring CATS performance report.* (KDE website). Retrieved from http://www.kde.state.ky.us.

Ruhland, S., & Brewer, J. (2001). Implementing an assessment plan to document student learning in a two-year technical college. *Journal of Vocational Education Research, 26,* 141–171.

Southern Regional Education Board. *Making the middle grades work: Raising the academic achievement of all middle grades students.* Retrieved from http://www.sreb.org/programs/MiddleGrades/publications/Middle_Grades_Work.pdf.

Zemelman, S., Daniels, H., & Hyde, A. (1998). *Best practice: New standards for teaching and learning in America schools.* Portsmouth, NH: Heinemann.

Note. **This example report was adapted from action research by Laura Arnold, Technology Center Principal. Used with permission.**

GLOSSARY OF RESEARCH-RELATED TERMS

Definitions in this glossary explain the meaning of terms in the context of their use in this text.

Action research: A systematic process for learning and problem solving in the context of practice. Action research clearly identifies learning and action needs to reach a major goal. This process includes stating the primary research question and guiding research questions that focus on a primary goal and its related learning needs and sources. After stating the research questions and developing a statement of the problem, the research begins with studying the identified, relevant, current knowledge; collecting and analyzing additional data also on the basis of the guiding questions; and developing conclusions and recommendations to make decisions for improvement. Implementation and evaluation of the resulting change complete the research study.

Action research report: A report for communicating research results with a constituency of peers and stakeholders. The report can take a variety of forms but generally is less detailed than a theoretical research report. It introduces the need for the research and states specific research questions, summarizes relevant literature specific to the research questions, describes the process steps and methodology adequately to verify credibility of the outcomes, presents results from data analysis, and states conclusions and recommendations for action based on the analysis of findings. A complete list of references is added at the end of the report. Supplementary data may be added as appendices, if needed.

Applied research: Systematic study to gain knowledge or understanding necessary to determine the means by which a recognized and specific need may be met (as defined by Federal Financial Accounting Standards and National Science Foundation Survey of Funds for Research and Development).

Basic research: Systematic study directed toward fuller knowledge or understanding of the fundamental aspects of phenomena and of observable facts, without specific applications toward processes or products in mind (as defined by Federal Financial Accounting Standards and National Science Foundation Survey of Funds for Research and Development).

Bias control: Recognizing, recording, and reviewing potential personal bias and/or influence on research results in order to reduce or eliminate such influence.

Cloud computing: Off-site digital memory storage purchased from digital storage vendors. The storage data site allows you and others whom you designate to access the stored data from computers in different locations.

Collaborative inquiry or research: Research for new learning or problem solving completed jointly with colleagues who share mutual interests.

Collaborative school structures: Teams or groups of school faculty or staff involved in specific leadership responsibilities. These types of organizational structures give the groups a voice in decisions and plans for continuous school improvement. They may be ongoing structures such as communities of learning, leadership teams, or distributed leadership with specified individuals responsible for certain school functions. Faculty meetings or electronic communication can be effective collaborative structures if plans and issues are well defined for efficient use of time that includes a process for reaching or refining decisions. Because technology in schools is available for efficient communication, the use of meetings solely to distribute information is usually an inefficient use of time.

Computer spreadsheet: A worksheet in a computer software spreadsheet program. A spreadsheet consists of rows and columns for inserting data and uses formulas to calculate numerical data entered into the spreadsheet cell locations (data-entry block within each row or column).

Concept map or diagram: A visual illustration of the linking of elements within major concepts to show relationships of elements.

Council of Chief State School Officers (CCSSO): A nonpartisan, nationwide, nonprofit organization of public officials who head departments of elementary and secondary education in the states, the District of Columbia, the Department of Defense Education Activity, and five U.S. extra-state jurisdictions. CCSSO provides leadership, advocacy, and technical assistance on major educational issues. The Council seeks member consensus on major educational issues and expresses its views to civic and professional organizations, federal agencies, the U.S. Congress, and the public.

Data interpretation: The search for meaning that supports or refutes conclusions related to research questions through grouping data in different ways, performing calculations, comparing and contrasting data for similarities and differences, and reflecting on the pros and cons for each interpretation.

Data sources: The resources that and people who can provide the necessary data. Sources of data may come from records and reports and persons knowledgeable about the research problem and may be gathered by such methods as observations, surveys, focus groups, student work, interviews, questionnaires, field notes, content matrices, and audio or video recordings.

Data triangulation: Collecting and comparing data from multiple data types, sources, and/or data collection methods to verify conclusions relevant to each research question.

Data: Facts, statistics, or items of information.

Debriefing: The sharing of interpretations of data by the researcher with knowledgeable colleagues during data analysis in order to test understanding and accuracy before finalizing conclusions and recommendations.

Demographic data: Statistical characteristics of populations and population subgroups identified by such factors as participation in certain programs or services or having common gender, ethnicity, education level, interest, or achievement.

Descriptive statistics: Calculations that show totals or percentages, and mean, mode, median, or standard deviation, in describing numerical data.

Document coding: A research-analysis process for marking concepts that become evident in studying and interpreting qualitative data. This process involves studying text documents and identifying major patterns and trends that are meaningful for the research question and that re-occur among different information sources and multiple data instruments. The purpose of marking and observing terms or actions that repeatedly show up in the data is to confirm or disconfirm interpretive understandings of responses and conclusions for the research question(s).

Figures: Terminology used by the APA style manual to refer to all illustrations other than tables in a report. APA figures may include graphs or other charts, diagrams, drawings, or pictures. Other style manuals, such as that of the MLA (Modern Language Association) or *The Chicago Manual of Style* may identify and format figures in slightly different ways. Some include three categories for these types of report materials—tables, figures, and illustrations—or may label all visual depictions as figures.

Focus groups: A data-gathering process similar to an interview but that involves questioning a group of from about 4 to 12 participants to gain insight about their shared understandings and insights. The main purpose is to document attitudes, feelings, beliefs, experiences, and reactions revealed by listening to participants' everyday language as they interact.

Format: Consistent placement, font size and style (bold, italics, capitalization, indention, or spacing) of similar parts of a document. These parts include such items as headings and subheadings; in-text reference and reference lists; tables and figures or other illustrations included in reports and other published documents.

Guiding research questions: About three to five questions aimed at collecting relevant data to inform the primary research question. Guiding research questions identify the subtopics or sources of data expected to help formulate positive actions for improvement. They may refer to possible causes, possible solutions, and topics that have likelihood for helping to answer the primary research question. They are formulated on the basis of professional literature describing previous related research, along with previous related knowledge and experience of researcher-practitioners. Guiding questions convey the information and sources necessary to help answer the primary research question and focus the study on the need-to-know areas rather than on the broader general scope of an issue.

Historical records: Records, reports, and other documented information.

Interstate New Teacher Assessment and Support Consortium (INTASC) Standards: Standards developed by the Council of Chief State School Officers and member states to serve as a model for essential knowledge, performances, and critical dispositions that are important for all instruction regardless of area of study. Complete copies of these standards may be downloaded from the Council's website at http://www.ccsso.org.

Interstate School Leaders Licensure Consortium (ISLLC) Standards: Standards developed for school leaders by the Council of Chief State School Officers and member states. Copies may be downloaded from the Council's website at www.ccsso.org.

Interviews: Direct verbal interaction between an interviewer and persons interviewed to gain perceptual or factual information based on specific responses to interviewer questions or open responses to topics posed by the interviewer. Questions may solicit facts related to an issue, opinions about events, insights about occurrences, or corroborating or disconfirming evidence about summaries or conclusions from data. They may also seek other sources of relevant information.

Literature online databases: Collections of online resources usually accessed from library subscriptions such as Academic Search Premier, Education Resources Information Center (ERIC), and Psychological and Behavioral Sciences or a collection of journals or similar education resources.

Literature review: The acts of collecting, reviewing, and analyzing various professional-media publications from reliable and knowledgeable sources (journals, books, blogs, websites, and conference presentations) relevant to the research primary and guiding questions and preparing a summary and analysis of information that has potential for studying and improving the research problem.

Member checks: Providing members of a study population with an opportunity to review a draft transcript or summary of information that they provided in order to validate its accuracy.

Mobile technology: Electronic devices with the size and connectivity capability for use when the user is traveling in different localities. Examples are cell phones, smart phones, electronic tablets, and other portable computer technology.

Observations: The observing of people or processes as they occur for teaching, learning, or other school functions. Observation notes, checklists, audio or video recordings, interaction charts, or other types of charts may be used to record what is observed.

Open-response question: A question posed on a survey or other data-collection method that does not list specific choices as the answer. Each response is individual to the responder's perception or knowledge of the topic.

Peer-reviewed resources: Publications that include content such as research or perceptual articles or chapters that have been reviewed by peers (colleagues) who are knowledgeable of the field related to the topic discussed. For publication peer review, the editor or editorial board of a publication selects persons as reviewers who are recognized as knowledgeable about the topic and bases decisions about publication of the material based on reviewer comments. The comments from reviewers rate and describe items such as the level of quality of the submitted article or other material and its readiness (or lack thereof) for publication.

Practitioner-researchers: Individuals who conduct systematic research on problems or issues in their work setting in order to improve their understanding and practice in that work context.

Primary research data: Data pertinent to understanding the research problem that is original data not previously available and that is to be collected as part of this research study.

Primary research question: A question that forms the goal to be attained for improving an issue or problem (What?, When?, Where?, and/or How?). It names the specific aspect of problems to be studied, as well as the specific desired outcome.

Problem solving: Making decisions about problems or issues by identifying the issue, gathering information, framing possible choices that intend improvement, implementing action(s) most likely to bring the best result, and evaluating results.

Problem statement: A description of reasons that the problem is of concern and its importance to student achievement. A problem statement may begin with a broad statement about the problem's importance in a wider context and then add a comparison of that context with the research setting. For internal action research, the only necessary context description relates to evidence or events that document the issue as a researchable problem and the importance of the problem in accomplishing organizational goals. (For schools, the primary focus is student achievement.) The problem-statement section in a report may incorporate the research questions, or they may be added as a separate section.

Professional development: A purposeful activity focused on increasing knowledge or skill and that results in improvement of an individual's professional practice and performance, as well as advanced skills for career progression in the professional field of work. Professional development may be completed through a variety and combination of formats such as individual study, community learning groups, individual or collaborative research, observations, discussion seminars, conferences, workshops, advanced coursework (for credit or otherwise), webinars, shadowing a skilled practitioner, and other job related skill development. Also, professional development may be completed through online technology, face-to-face meetings, or a combination of delivery modes. Reimbursement for professional development usually requires a proposed plan consistent with approvable activities and outcomes established by the employing agency.

Prolonged engagement: Researcher persistence in observation of and interaction with the research setting over a time sufficient to ensure understanding of the context for data interpretation.

Qualitative data: Information gained from perceptual knowledge of individuals, based on their background, experience, knowledge, and interpretation of a situation, issue, or problem.

Qualitative research: Interpretive research that seeks understanding of a problem or issue and gathers and analyzes multiple types of data from relevant sources, including perceptual data, demographic data, process data, and progress data. Although qualitative analysis is heavily dependent on descriptive words and word patterns, data collection may include numerical data. However, rather than relying on statistical tests for numeric analysis, numeric qualitative data interpretation involves descriptive statistics that are based on meaningful data arrangements and on contrasts and comparisons with interpretations of word descriptions from multiple sources.

Quantitative data: Numerical measurements and statistics.

Quantitative research: Theoretical research that applies statistical formulas to test theories about the problem as well as data variables and their relationships.

Reflection: A part of a learning process that requires thoughtful, deliberative consideration of issues, events, or actions that analyzes "what was, what is, and what should be" (Schön from Chapter 6 References).

Reflective learners: Individuals in a learning process who can clearly articulate and identify knowledge or skill for learning, define evidence in their work that reflects specific learning, and sets future learning goals. Reflection takes place before, during, and after learning.

Reflective practitioners: Individuals who use reflection as part of improving practice applicable in the work that they do and who have "the ability to assess situations and make thoughtful, rational decisions" (Bainer & Cantrell, 1991, from Chapter 6 References).

Research integrity: Credibility of the accuracy and reliability of the systematic research process and its results.

Research leadership teams: Interested and knowledgeable individuals who agree to work together to complete specific research tasks or to guide the overall inquiry process by making decisions and accomplishing tasks for completion of a collaborative research study.

Research participants: Researcher-practitioners responsible for study tasks and/or others providing source data for the study.

Research population: Research participants, including all people to whom the research question applies or a smaller sample population with characteristics representative of the total population.

Research recommendations: Critical decisions about actions to be taken as a result of new, logical evidence-informed perspectives gained through interpretation of what was learned from inquiry and research, along with previous knowledge.

Research reliability: The inference that repetition of the same measurement of research data in a similar context would yield the same or similar results.

Research validity: The inference that research data are supported by objective truth and that the research data accurately measure what is purported to be measured.

Research: A systematic study directed toward fuller scientific knowledge or understanding of the subject studied. Research is classified as either basic or applied, depending on the objectives of the sponsoring agency (as defined by the Federal Financial Accounting Standards and National Science Foundation Survey of Funds for Research and Development).

Research: Diligent and systematic inquiry into a subject in order to discover and analyze data that contribute to understanding of the subject for the purpose of revising a theory or improving practice.

Research conclusions: Statements describing meanings derived from the research data through analysis and synthesis.

Research methodology: Description of the systematic processes and steps involved in completing a specific research study. These steps should be explained clearly enough for replication in other studies.

Researchable school problems: Issues of school practice that deviate from a standard or expectation, have an unknown cause, and create concern over time. These are issues because they recur over time or require intensive study due to the magnitude or complexity of the problem.

School-improvement planning: Collaboratively developed plans by each school and school district that ensure conformance to standards, planning criteria, and appropriate involvement; review of student performance measures, school progress, and history of program improvements; needs assessment based on district and school information and collected data analysis; and key research findings, goal setting, and evaluation criteria.

School action plan: Improvement plans for initiatives or programs within a specific school. The action plan generally includes specific plans for core content programs and targeted programs. The components of a school action plan may include goals and objectives; component managers; priorities and contributing causes or factors; research-based interventions or effective practices with measurable objectives; reflection on progress; community and family involvement; safe learning environment; staff development activities; student activities; evaluation processes; and plans for periodic review, evaluation, and revision.

School process data: Organizational and operational procedures, activities, and policies such as financial allocations, curricula content and implementation, facilities, staffing, instructional practices, support services, parental and community involvement, environment and climate, cultural values, mission and goals, scheduling, faculty and staff preparation, and professional development.

Schoolwide research: Research study focused on topics or problems of general concern because they affect school learning or school processes, to some degree, for students and/or staff throughout the school.

Scientific research: Systematic study or inquiry of facts, statistics, or items of information gained through observation or experimentation which collects, arranges, and analyzes information that contributes to knowledge of the material world or improvement of practice or a product.

Secondary research data: Data already available that have been previously described and recorded for records and reports or other purposes and that are pertinent to understanding the research problem.

Source note: A note placed under a table or figure that identifies the source for the data displayed.

Spirit or culture of inquiry: A characteristic of an ongoing learning process evidenced by individuals who continue to seek new learning that adds to knowledge in areas of practice or of interest.

Standard deviation: Data calculations that help interpret the spread of individual scores from the mean by comparison to an expected normal distribution of scores. The normal distribution refers to the approximate shape of a bell curve if all scores were plotted on a linear scale with zero at the center of the scale. The model bell curve used to measure distribution variability of a set of scores from the mean would show an evenly divided distribution of scores from the center, with approximately 50% of the scores falling to the right and approximately 50% to the left of the mean. If you compare the variability of 2 sample populations, the sample with the larger standard deviation has the greatest variability from the mean. To interpret variability of 1 set of scores, McClave and Dietrich (1986) suggest asking these questions: How many measurements fall within 1 standard deviation of the mean? Fall within 2 standard deviations? Scores that form an approximately symmetric histogram cluster around the midpoint of the distribution, with the mean, median, and mode all about the same. This symmetry falls away rapidly for scores farther from the mean. According to McClave and Dietrich (p. 44), an empirical rule (rule of thumb) for the variability of a set of scores that fall within a normally expected range of variability for mound-shaped scores would be within 2 standard deviations from the mean. Variability of three standard deviations departs rapidly from the expected normal distribution. The rule of thumb for understanding variability of 1 set of measurements states that one standard deviation will have 68% of the scores falling below (to the left of the mean) and 68 percent above (to the right of the mean). About 95% of all measurements fall within two standard deviations above or below the mean. Essentially all will fall within 3 standard deviations.*

Student achievement: Evidences of student progress in academic and personal growth and progress toward achieving knowledge, skills, and attributes required to function successfully as a mature and contributing citizen in a local, state, national, or international economy.

Student learning data: Information that includes standardized test data and proficiency levels based on predetermined criterion measures but also may include perceptual evidences of growth and development.

Style manual: A published or predetermined guide that establishes one way to present different parts of a manuscript and provides specific technical formatting guidelines such as those for capitalization, punctuation, format, and spacing for the purpose of consistency throughout a document. The goal is for the user to present a work product that gives a professional appearance and makes a positive impression. The style rules to be followed for research reports apply particularly to headings, subheadings, text source citations, reference lists, tables, and figures (charts, graphs, or other illustrations). Style manual rules covered in this resource come from the *Publication Manual of the American Psychological Association* (APA) and are widely used for educational leadership publications.

Surveys: Questionnaires used to gather standardized information from all subjects in a population or representative sample population for particular research questions. Surveys can efficiently gather information from large groups of people. They may require responses to yes or no, true–false, or numeric ratings type questions, and may include open-ended questions that require thoughtful, unique responses by respondents.

---

*McClave, J. T., & Dietrich, F. H., II. (1986). *A first course in statistics* (2nd ed.). San Francisco: Dellen Publishing Company, a division of McMillan, Inc.

Synthesis: An interpretive thought process that gleans and describes holistic meaning from review and study of information such as research data and specifics by such methods as categorization, comparison, contrast, establishment of themes, and recognition of patterns or descriptive categories to interpret meanings from multiple sources.

Systematic research process: Research that seeks understanding as a result of the researcher following specific steps and protocol to learn about a clearly defined problem. It applies research procedures aimed toward eliminating bias, protecting confidentiality of information linked to an individual informant, and uniformly applying defined research procedures without partiality.

Tables: Visuals that arrange words and/or numbers in rows and columns for display and interpretation.

Title case: A term that indicates the capitalization format of titles or headings wherein major words begin with an uppercase letter and prepositions or articles of four or fewer letters begin with lowercase.

Traditional research: Research based on a stated theoretical assumption that applies quantitative statistical tests and quantitative data to test validity and relationships of relevant characteristics.

Trend data: Comparison and contrast of similar data elements over time, usually a period of at least 3 time intervals such as years, weeks, or months.

URL: Uniform Resource Locator that identifies online sources and websites. Keying the specific URL on the Internet browser following http:// or clicking on a URL embedded in an online document or Internet web page usually will bring the particular resource document to the screen. For example, http://www.aasa.org locates the home web page for the organization of the American Association of School Administrators.

Walk-throughs: Frequent, short observations for a particular purpose. School leaders often do walk-throughs over time in multiple classrooms to complete an easily marked checklist used to gather data for purposes such as measuring the degree of implementation of a schoolwide practice related to a goal previously set and jointly discussed with the faculty or to establish frequent administrator–teacher informal dialogue about instruction.

Word tables: Visual displays of word relationships that simplify communication of lengthy or complex concepts. Arranging words in rows and columns may convey such concepts for a better understanding in a more meaningful way than would be true of lengthy text explanations in narrative form.

INDEX

A

Accountability
  achievement, 27, 34
  in "we are in this together," 106
Action plans
  component sample, 112–113
  components composite, 108, 110
Action report examples. *See also* reports
  Comparative Review of High School
    Schedules, 197–203
  Content Reading Instruction at Roger Vale
    Elementary, 146–158
  Mathematics Performance of Jewell High
    School Students, 182–189
  Middle School Improvement Analysis:
    Practical Living/Career Studies Test
    Scores, 204–210
  Postsecondary Reading Remediation for High
    School Graduates, 190–196
  Reading Skills of Struggling Reading Students
    at Melody Lane Elementary, 159–171
  School Improvement Analysis: Writing
    Achievement of Hispanic Students,
    136–145
  Sophomore Coaching Initiative,
    172–181
Action research. *See also* Reports
  change in practice and, 106–107
  characteristics, 5, 6
  as collaborative inquiry, 12
  comprehensive planning and, 107–108
  definitions, 5
  dissemination of, 93
  integration of, 110, 114, 115
  knowledge base in, 15–29
  leadership for, 12–13
  literature review, 15–23
  presentations of, 93–99
  problem solving comparison, 4
  in professional practice, 103–118
  reflection on, 93
  school problems of practice for, 6–12
  in school settings, 3–14
  teams, 3
  what it is not, 6
Advanced organizers, 149
Alexander, P. A., 16
Alspaugh, J. W., 206, 209
Alternative assessment, 139–140
Anderson, G. L., 53
Anderson, S., 3, 105
Anderson, T. H., 148
Appendices, 90–92
Applied research, 6
Armbruster, B. B., 148
Arthaud, T. J., 160, 162
Assessment
  formative, 163
  integration of, 110
  multiple types of, 122–123
  standards as guide, 121–131
Audiences, presentation, 93, 97

B

Bainer, D., 87
Baldwin, R. S., 192
Bar graphs, 63, 64
Barton, P., 113, 174
Beagrie, S., 75
Bean, T. W., 192
Beaulieu, L. M., 175
Beck, I., 148
Beech, D. M., 107
Bello, T., 138, 139
Berman, B. T., 84, 184, 186
Bernhardt, V. L., 35, 172
Bias control, 54
Bibliography, 92
Black, P., 164
Boog, B., 90
Borg, W. R., 42, 44, 46, 53
Borkowski, J., 119
Bower, B., 84, 186
Brainstorming, 149
Brophy, J. E., 44
Brown, B., 205, 209
Brownell, M. T., 161
Bryant, D. P., 191, 195

C

Camburn, E., 123, 124
Cantrell, D., 87
Career and Technical Education (CTE) survey, 58
Carr, M., 119
Carson, C., 173
CCSSO. *See* Council of Chief State School
    Officers
Cells, 63
Circle graphs, 63, 65
Clarke, S., 164, 169
Classroom observations, 44–46, 47
Code sheets, 71, 72
Collaboration
  communication, 17
  cooperation and, 107
  literature review, 27
Collaborative reflection, 86–87
Collaborative school structures, 106
Collaborative-writing strategies, 27
Collier, P., 139, 143
Column graphs, 63, 65
Comparative Review of High School Schedules
  action report, 197–202
  conclusions, 200–201
  data analysis, 200–201
  data collection, 200–201
  5-block day, 198
  literature review, 197–199
  methodology, 199–200
  overview, 197–202
  recommendations, 202
  research questions, 197
  schedule comparison, 198
  study rationale, 197
  trimesters, 198–199

Component action plans
  beginning sections, 109
  composite, 110
  description and summary, 108
  sample, 112–113
Comprehensive School Improvement Plan
    (CSIP), 172
Comprehensive Test of Basic Skills (CTBS),
    34, 152
Concept diagrams, 72, 73
Concept mapping, 72, 73
Conclusions
  Comparative Review of High School
    Schedules, 200–201
  Content Reading Instruction at Roger Vale
    Elementary, 155–156
  development of, 79
  emphasis, 79–80
  illustrated examples, 83, 84
  leading to recommendations, 83
  Middle School Improvement Analysis:
    Practical Living/Career Studies Test Scores,
    208–209
  Postsecondary Reading Remediation for High
    School Graduates, 195
  Reading Skills of Struggling Reading Students
    at Melody Lane Elementary, 166–169
  School Improvement Analysis: Writing
    Achievement of Hispanic Students, 143
  statements, funneling through primary
    questions, 82–83
  stating, 79, 82
  as synthesis, 81–82
  terms to avoid, 82
Confirmation validity, 54
Confirming/disconfirming data, 54
Conrad, C. A., 204
Content reading, 147–148
Content Reading Instruction at Roger
Vale Elementary
  action research report, 146–158
  data analysis, 152–155
  index disaggregated reading data, 154
  literature review, 147–151
  methodology, 151–152
  overview, 146
  rationale for study, 146–147
  recommendations, 156
  research questions, 146
  results and conclusions, 155–156
  state performance report, 153
  struggling readers versus proficient readers,
    148–151
  surveys, 154–155, 157
Convenience sample population, 42
Copeland, M. A., 3
Corey, S. M., 5
Council of Chief State School Officers (CCSSO)
  career continuum, 124
  defined, 121
  InTASC Model of Core Teaching Standards,
    124, 129–131

"Transforming Education: Delivering on Our Promise to Every Child," 122
"Transforming Teaching and Leading: A Vision for a High-Quality Educator Development System, 124
working papers, 121–122, 123
Cover sheets, 96
Cowan, G., 37, 38, 46, 56, 73, 88
Craig, J., 113, 174
Credits, 26–27
Cross-checking data, 55

D

Daniels, H., 208
Data
    confirming/disconfirming, 54
    cross-checking, 55
    demographic, 36–37
    identification and selection of, 33–37
    perceptual, 37
    primary, 40–41
    recording, 37, 58
    research types of, 34–37
    school, 34, 35
    school processes, 36
    secondary, 40–41
    sources, 37–38
    staff, 37
    storage, 57–61
    student learning, 37
    types of, 37–38
    visual display, 41
Data analysis. *See also* Qualitative analysis
    Comparative Review of High School Schedules, 200–201
    Content Reading Instruction at Roger Vale Elementary, 152–155
    defined, 74
    School Improvement Analysis: Writing Achievement of Hispanic Students, 141–143
    section illustration, 75–78
    statements/terms to avoid, 74
Data collection
    Comparative Review of High School Schedules, 200–201
    Content Reading Instruction at Roger Vale Elementary, 152–155
    field tests, 52
    focus groups, 46–50
    interviews, 46–50
    Mathematics Performance of Jewell High School Students, 183–187
    methods, 40–41
    observations, 44–46
    questionnaires, 44
    research population, 42–43
    review of, 41
    Sophomore Coaching Initiative, 175–180
    surveys, 44
Data organization
    data storage and summaries, 57–61
    descriptive statistics, 56–57
    quantitative tables and graphs, 61–65
Data reduction, 70
Data triangulation, 35
    defined, 55
    description for research, 55

document coding, 72–74
    process, 72–73
Data-informed decision making
    data identification and selection, 33–37
    data-collection instruments and research populations, 41–50
    data-collection methods, instruments, and protocol, 40–41
    defined, 1, 33
    research participant involvement, 38–40
    review of information needs, data types, and data sources, 37–38
Day, R. S., 16
Debriefing, 54
Demographic data, 36–37
Denbo, S. J., 112, 174, 175
Descriptive statistics
    defined, 56
    formatting, 58
    mean, 56
    median, 56
    mode, 56
    standard deviation, 56–57
    statistical formulas, 57
Deshler, D. D., 192
Diamond, J., 123
Dietz, S., 33
Distributive leadership, 123
Document coding
    code sheets, 71, 72
    concept mapping, 72
    data triangulation, 72–74
    defined, 70
    diagrams, 72
    patterns, 71
    themes, 71
    word tables, 72
Downey, C. J., 46
Ducker, M., 143

E

EBSCOhost, 18
Editing, literature review, 27
Education journals
    peer-reviewed, 19
    resources for improving student achievement, 21
ERIC (Education Resource Information Center), 18

F

Ferrance, E., 104, 106
Figures. *See* Graphs
Fisk, C., 191, 195
Flash cards, 150
Focus groups
    defined, 49
    purpose of, 49–50
Formative assessment, 163
Formatting
    graphs, 63–65
    literature review, 25–27
    report, 90, 95–96
    tables, 62–63
    topical plan for, 26
Frederick, T., 121

Fried, M. D., 156
Furner, J. M., 84, 184, 186

G

Gall, M. D., 42, 44, 53
Galvan, J. L., 27
Gardner, D., 113, 174, 175
Garner, R., 119
Gellar, J., 112, 174, 175
Gibbs, A., 49, 50
Gilmore, T., 79
Glavach, M. J., 191
Goracke, T., 160, 162
Government educational resources, for improving student achievement, 20
Graphic organizers, 149–150, 151
Graphs
    bar, 64
    bar,, 63
    cells, 63
    circle, 63, 65
    column, 63, 65
    description and purposes, 63
    formatting, 63–65
    legend, 64
    line, 63
    planning, 63
    preparing, 63–65
    quantitative, 61–65
    reports, 74
    saving, 65
    types of, 63
Grissmer, D., 173, 174
Grossnickle, F., 188
Guba, E. G., 35, 53, 54
Guiding questions
    defined, 8
    examples of, 9–10, 11
    in literature review, 16, 17
    making list of, 38
    Postsecondary Reading Remediation for High School Graduates, 190–191
Gullatt, D., 200
Gutierrez, M. B., 139

H

Hager, J. M., 147
Haller, E. J., 23
Halverson, R., 123
Hamayan, E. V., 139, 143
Hamff, A., 191, 195
Hanushek, E. A., 3, 107, 174
Harris, A., 123
Hougen, M., 191, 195
Haycock, K., 205, 208, 209
Headings, literature review, 24–25
Hedges, L. V., 3
Hendricks, C., 90
Herr, K., 53
Hettinger, H. R., 160
Historical resources, 53
Hmelo, C. E., 16
Hobson, E. H., 161, 169
Hock, M. F., 192
Hopkins, D., 5

Horn, S. P., 3
Huberman, A. M., 55, 69, 70, 71, 82
Hunter, M., 16
Hurst, B., 191, 195

I

*Improving Student Achievement in
    Mathematics*, 84, 184, 188
Information needs
    for multiple research questions, 38
    in planning chart, 39
    specifying, 37–38
InTASC Model of Core Teaching Standards.
    See also Standards
    content, 124–125
    defined, 129
    self-assessment, 130–131
Integration
    importance of, 110
    knowledge, 104
    outcome, 114
    schedule, 116
    three-phase transition, 114, 115
Integrity
    elements of, 53
    research techniques for, 54–55
Interstate School Leaders Licensure Consortium
    (ISLLC) Standards. *See also* Standards
    comparison, 126–128
    defined, 121
    functions and, 126–128
    review and reflection, 125
Interviews
    elements of, 46–48
    protocol example, 49
    questions, 48–49
    questions example, 49
    setting for, 49
    summary of, 49
Irmsher, K., 198

J

Jackson, S. E., 3
Jaekyung, L., 140
Johnson, A. P., 23, 90
Johnson, E., 27
Johnson, P., 160, 162, 170
Johnston, R. C., 119
Jordan, H., 105
Journal writing, 151
Journey as destination, 111–116
JSTOR, 18
Judy, J. F., 16

K

Kain, J. F., 3
Karasek, K., 3
Kincheloe, J., 35, 53
Kleine, P. F., 23
Knapp, M. S., 3
Knapp, N. F., 160
Knoeppel, R., 120
Knowledge base, 15–32
Kober, N., 186
Koedinger, K. R., 84, 185
Konstantopoulos, S., 3
Krantz, J., 79

L

Lambert, L., 3
Lawrence, W. W., 198
Leadership
    for action research, 12–13
    distributive, 123
    styles, 123–124
    teacher role, 107
Learning Forward, 12–13
Leedy, P. D., 56, 79
Leithwood, K., 3, 105
Library websites, 18
Linan-Thompson, S., 191, 195
Lincoln, Y. S., 35, 53, 54
Lindsey, C., 138
Line graphs, 63
Ling Pan, M., 24
Liston, D. P., 86
Literature review
    action research, 15–23
    collaborating on, 27
    communication system, 17
    Comparative Review of High School
        Schedules, 197–199
    Content Reading Instruction at Roger Vale
        Elementary, 147–151
    development, 23–27
    editing, 27
    elements of, 15
    format example, 26
    formatting, 25–27
    guiding questions in, 16, 17
    headings, 24–25
    as important action research step, 105
    introductory content, 24
    main body of, 24
    Middle School Improvement Analysis:
        Practical Living/Career Studies Test Scores,
        205–206
    Postsecondary Reading Remediation for High
        School Graduates, 191–192
    potential topics, 16
    Reading Skills of Struggling Reading Students
        at Melody Lane Elementary, 160–164
    referencing, 25–27
    resource recording and identification, 22–23
    School Improvement Analysis: Writing
        Achievement of Hispanic Students, 138–140
    Sophomore Coaching Initiative, 174–175
    source selection, 17–21
    statistics and, 28
    subheadings, 24–25
    technology in, 16–17
    topics organization, 24
    writing, 27
Livingston, J. A., 120
Logan, J. P., 120
Lynch, M., 174

M

Maslach, C., 3
Mathematics Performance of Jewell High School
    Students
    action report, 182–189
    data collection, 183–187
    entry-level courses, 185
    indices, 183
    mathematics strands, 186–187
    overview, 182
    problem analysis, 183–188
    problem background, 182–183
    recommendations, 188
    research procedures, 183–188
    stakeholder input for data analysis, 188
    students' perceptions, 186
    trends and subgroups, 184
Maxwell, J. A., 56
McKeown, M. G., 148
McPherson, D. D., 198
Mean, 56
Median, 56
Mellard, D., 83
Member checking, 54
Member-checking process, 70
Mendro, R., 38, 105
Metacognition, 120
Metacognitive knowledge, 120
Methodology
    Comparative Review of High School
        Schedules, 199–200
    Content Reading Instruction at Roger Vale
        Elementary, 151–152
    illustrated examples, 80–81
    Middle School Improvement Analysis:
        Practical Living/Career Studies Test Scores,
        206–208
    outline, 78
    Postsecondary Reading Remediation for High
        School Graduates, 192–193
    Reading Skills of Struggling Reading Students
        at Melody Lane Elementary, 164–166
    School Improvement Analysis: Writing
        Achievement of Hispanic Students, 140–141
    Sophomore Coaching Initiative, 175–180
    writing, 78–79
Middle School Improvement Analysis: Practical
    Living/Career Studies Test Scores
    achievement gap, 204
    action report, 204–210
    core competencies, 206
    current practices that work, 205–206
    current teaching strategies and practices,
        207–208
    discussion and conclusions, 208–209
    literature review, 205–206
    methodology, 206–208
    overview, 204
    problem analysis, 206–208
    problem background, 204–205
    recommendations, 209
    stakeholder input for data analysis, 209
    student demographics disaggregation,
        206–207
Miles, M. B., 55, 69, 70, 71, 82
Mills, G. E., 5, 23, 90
Mirror image, 86
Mode, 56
Moss, B., 147, 148, 156
Moustafa, B., 148
Multiple bar graphs, 64, 65
Munby, S., 106
Murphy, J., 105

N

Nagarajan, A., 16
Nathan, M. J., 84, 185
National Assessment of Educational Progress
    (NAEP), 34

Nihlen, A. S., 53
No Child Left Behind (NCLB) Act, 173
Notes
    choosing for written review, 23
    paraphrasing, 23
    recording, 22–23
    source, 62
Nye, B., 3

O

O'Brien, R., 79
Observations. *See also* Data collection
    classroom, 44–46
    instruction chart example, 47
    responses, 59
    sample chart, 60
Online databases, 18
Open-response questions, 59, 60
Ormrod, J. E., 56
Ostertag, J., 148

P

Participants
    faculty, 38–40
    focus group, 50
    involvement of, 38–40
Participatory validity, 54
Partnering, 12
Patterns, 71
Perceptual data, 37
Perry, L., 188
Planning
    chart, 39
    comprehensive, 107–108
    graphs and tables, 63
    integration of, 110, 114
    integration schedule, 116
    principal/superintendent in, 12
    school-improvement, 108–110
Populations
    categories of people, 42
    convenience sample, 42
    representative, 54
    research, 42–43
    sample, 42
Postsecondary Reading Remediation for High
        School Graduates
    action report, 190–196
    comprehension, 191
    conclusions, 195
    fluency, 192
    guiding questions, 190–191
    literature review, 191–192
    methodology, 192–193
    overview, 190
    problem analysis, 193–195
    recommendations, 195
    research procedures, 192–193
    research question, 190
    self-esteem, 192
    teacher utilization, 194, 195
    word recognition, 191
Practice
    action research and change in, 106–107
    research contributions to, 104–105
    teacher, improving, 107
Pragmatic validity, 55
Predicting, 150

Preece, J., 90
Presentations
    audience, 95–96
    development of, 92–97
    visual display, 96–97
Pressley, M., 119
Primary data, 40–41
*Principal and Standards for School
        Mathematics*, 188
Principals, active involvement, 115
Printy, S., 106
Problem analysis
    Mathematics Performance of Jewell High
        School Students, 183–188
    Middle School Improvement Analysis:
        Practical Living/Career Studies Test Scores,
        206–208
    Postsecondary Reading Remediation for High
        School Graduates, 193–195
    Reading Skills of Struggling Reading Students
        at Melody Lane Elementary, 166
Problem solving, 4
Problem statements
    defined, 8–10
    example, 11
    Reading Skills of Struggling Reading Students
        at Melody Lane Elementary, 159
    statistics and, 28
Problems
    defined, 7
    examples of, 9–10
    guiding questions, 8
    identification, 7–8
    knowledge on, 17
    researchable, 8
Process writing, 138–139
Professional development
    as learning applied to practice, 17
    standards as assessment guide, 121–131
    survey responses on, 73
Professional organizations, with student
        achievement resources, 19
Prolonged engagement, 54
PsycINFO, 18
*Publication Manual of the American
        Psychological Association (APA)*, 11, 15, 25
Putnam, D, 75

Q

Qualitative analysis
    document coding and, 70–74
    predetermined boundaries and, 70
    purpose of, 70
    results, 74–78
    systematic interpretation, 69
Qualitative data-collection methods, 69
Qualitative perceptual information, 34
Quantitative numerical measurements, 34
Quantitative tables and graphs, 61–65
Questionnaires
    coding, 43
    questions, 44
    using, 44
Questions. *See also* Guiding questions
    Comparative Review of High School
        Schedules, 197
    Content Reading Instruction at Roger Vale
        Elementary, 146
    interview, 48–49

open-response, 59, 60
Postsecondary Reading Remediation for High
        School Graduates, 190
    questionnaire, 44
    Reading Skills of Struggling Reading Students
        at Melody Lane Elementary, 159
    School Improvement Analysis: Writing
        Achievement of Hispanic Students, 137–138
    Sophomore Coaching Initiative, 172
    survey, 44

R

Ramirez, R., 79
Random sample selection, 42
Readance, J. E., 192
Reading
    content, 147–148
    first, 22–23
    organization strategies, 150–151
    strategies, 162–163
    student strategies, 149–150
    teacher strategies, 150
Reading Skills of Struggling Reading Students at
        Melody Lane Elementary
    action report, 159–170
    formative assessment and stated learning
        objectives, 163–164
    instructional consistency and intentionality,
        161–163
    language-saturated classroom, 160
    literature review, 160–164
    methodology, 164–166
    outcomes, 167
    overview, 159
    problem analysis, 166
    reading instructional strategies, 168–169
    recommendations, 169–170
    research procedures, 164–166
    research questions, 159
    research results and conclusions, 166–169
    statement of problem, 159
    student feedback, 161–162
    student work, 167
    teacher feedback, 168
Reckzeh, J., 188
Recommendations
    Comparative Review of High School
        Schedules, 202
    Content Reading Instruction at Roger Vale
        Elementary, 156
    as critical decisions, 87
    illustrated examples, 88–89
    interpretation, 88
    as last report section, 89
    Mathematics Performance of Jewell High
        School Students, 188
    Middle School Improvement Analysis:
        Practical Living/Career Studies Test Scores,
        209
    Postsecondary Reading Remediation for High
        School Graduates, 195
    Reading Skills of Struggling Reading Students
        at Melody Lane Elementary, 169–170
    reflection for determining, 86–87
    research, 87–90
    School Improvement Analysis: Writing
        Achievement of Hispanic Students, 143
    Sophomore Coaching Initiative, 180
    stating, 88

Record and report data, 37
Reference lists, 22
References, 92
Reflection
    action research, 92
    benefit, 87
    collaborative, 86–87
    for determining recommendations, 86–87
    guide, 96
Reflective learners, 121
Reflective practitioners
    defined, 87, 119
    living as, 119–121
    term beginnings, 86
Reinhartz, J., 107
Reitzug, U. C., 3
Reliability, 53
Rentner, D. S., 33
Repetition, 53
Reports. *See also* Action report examples
    appendices, 90–93
    components of, 90–93
    content, 74
    cover sheet, 96
    data analysis, 74–78
    drafts, 10–11
    example illustration, 91
    example pattern, 6
    format deviation, 12
    format example, 95–96
    formatting, 25, 90
    literature review, 15–23
    methodology, 78–79, 80–81
    recommendations, 87–90
    references, 92
    research conclusions, 79–84
    research studies, 89–90
    results, 74–78
    rubric, 93, 94
    style, 11–12
Research data types
    demographic, 36–37
    multiple, using, 35
    perceptual, 37
    qualitative perceptual information, 34
    quantitative numerical measurements, 34
    record and report, 37
    school process, 36
    student learning, 35
Research integrity, verification methods, 53
Research knowledge integration, 104
Research methodology. *See* Methodology
Research population, 42–43
Research procedures
    Mathematics Performance of Jewell High
        School Students, 183–188
    Postsecondary Reading Remediation for High
        School Graduates, 192–193
    Reading Skills of Struggling Reading Students
        at Melody Lane Elementary, 164–166
    Sophomore Coaching Initiative, 175–180
Research recommendations. *See* Recommendations
Research results
    Content Reading Instruction at Roger Vale
        Elementary, 155–156
    data analysis and, 74–78
    Reading Skills of Struggling Reading Students
        at Melody Lane Elementary, 166–169
    Sophomore Coaching Initiative, 178–180

Research studies, 89–90
Resources
    credits to, 26–27
    education journal, 19, 21
    first reading, 22–23
    government education, 20
    historical, 53
    leads to, 19–20
    professional organization, 19
    recording and identifying, 22–23
Response to Intervention (RTI), 89
Responses, confidentiality, 43
Riddlemoser, N., 139, 143
Rivers, J. C., 105
Rivkin, S. G., 3
Ross, D., 17
Ross, S. M., 107
Rowan, B., 123
Rubric, 93, 94

S

Salend, S. J., 139
Sample populations, 42
Sanders, W. L., 3, 105, 107
Scheerens, J., 44
Schön, D., 86
School data
    detailed examples of, 35
    processes, 36
    sources, 34
    types of, 35
School improvement
    component action plans, 108–110
    composite of components, 109–110
    planning, 108–110
    processes and components, 108
    research for, 105–106
    two-year cycle for, 116
School Improvement Analysis: Writing
        Achievement of Hispanic Students. *See also*
        Action report examples
    alternative assessment, 139–140
    conclusions and recommendations, 143
    data analysis, 141–143
    difficult writing skills, 140
    instruction in two languages, 139
    literature review, 138–140
    overview, 136–137
    process writing, 138–139
    research findings, 141–143
    research methodology, 140–141
    research questions, 137–138
    review of processes, 140
    stakeholder input for data analysis, 141
    student characteristics, 140
School practice, research contributions to, 104–105
School problems
    for action research, 6–12
    identification, 7–8
    problem statement, 8–12
    researchable, 8
School reform, 3
Schreiber, J., 202
Schumaker, J. B., 192
Scientific research, 104
Seashore-Louis, K., 3, 105
Secondary data, 40–41
Self-assessment, InTASC Model of Core
        Teaching Standards, 130–131

Sharing learning intentions, 163–164
Sharing sessions, 115
Shaywitz, S. E., 191
Sheakoski, M., 150
Shulman, L. S., 8
Single bar graphs, 64, 65
Slagter, M., 90
Smith, M. K., 86
Sophomore Coaching Initiative
    action report, 172–181
    coach survey results, 179
    core content test data, 176
    data collection, 175–180
    literature and, 175
    literature review, 174–175
    MAP data, 176–177
    methodology, 175–180
    overview, 172
    qualitative data, 178–180
    quantitative data, 175–177
    rationale, 173
    recommendations, 180
    research procedures, 175–180
    research questions, 172
    student survey results, 178
    teacher survey results, 179–180
Sousa, D. A., 191, 192, 195
Spillane, J. P., 123
Staff data, 37
Stahl, S. A., 191
Standard deviation, 56–57
Standards
    as guide, 121–131
    InTASC Model of Core Teaching Standards,
        129–131
    ISLLC, 121, 123, 125
    ISLLC comparison, 126–128
    professional growth, 124–125
Stanovich, K. E., 191
Statistical formulas, 57
Statistics
    descriptive, 56–58
    in problem statement, 28
Streifer, P. A., 33
Stiggins, R. J., 164
Stoner, J. A., 3
Stratified random samples, 42
Stringer, E. T., 5, 54, 55
Student achievement
    accountability, 27, 34
    education journal resources for improving, 21
    elements of, 6
    government educational resources for
        improving, 20
    professional organizations with resources, 19
    types of, 35
Student learning data, 35
Studies, research, 89–90
Study guides, 150
Subheadings, literature review, 24–25
Summarization, 151
Surveys. *See also* Data collection
    Content Reading Instruction at Roger Vale
        Elementary, 154–155, 157
    CTE graduates, 58
    example, 45
    as instrument of choice, 42
    open-response questions, 59
    questions, 44

responses, 59
sample data, 61
using, 44
Systematic procedures, 54
Systematic research, 6

T
Tables
formatting, 62–63
planning, 63
preparing, 62–63
quantitative, 61–65
report, 74
rows and columns, 62
word, 63, 72
Tacit knowledge, 82
Talbert, J. E., 3
Tam, K. Y., 162
Tannenbaum, J., 139, 143
Taylor, J., 123
Teachers
beliefs and attitudes, 173
effectiveness, 3
leadership role, 107
Teams
literature review, 38
organization, 16
problem knowledge, 12
research leadership, 38
Technology

in literature review, 16–17
security, 17
Themes, 71
Theorell, T., 3
Thomas, W., 139, 143
Thompson, S., 149, 150, 151
Three-phase transition, 114, 115
Topics, literature review, 24
Transcription, 69
Triangulation, data, 35, 55, 72–74

U
Ugel, N., 191, 195

V
Vacca, R., 147
Validity
confirmation, 54
defined, 53
participatory, 54
pragmatic, 55
Veal, W. R., 202
Vescio, V., 17
Visual presentations. *See also* Presentations
example, 98
orientation to, 97
preparation for, 97

W
Wahlstrom, K., 3, 105

Walker, B. J., 162
Walk-through checklist, 48
Walk-through URLs, 48
Walther-Thomas, C., 161
Wankel, C., 3
Webbing, 150
Weerasinghe, D., 105
Werner, M., 175
Westerburg, M., 198
Whittaker, C. R., 139
Wilhoit, G., 136, 138
Wiliam, D., 164
Wolcott, H. E., 53
Wood, M., 161
Word sleuthing, 150
Word splash, 150
Wright, S. P., 3
Writing
journal, 151
literature review, 27
methodology, 78–79
process, 138–139

Y
Yin, R. K., 48, 49

Z
Zeelen, J., 90
Zeichner, K. M., 86
Zemelman, S., 208
Zirkel, P., 75